To Ridgewa

with hopes +

successful cooperation

13.07. 15.

Petr Aven is a Russian banker and economist who served as Minister of Foreign Economic Relations for the Russian Federation (1991–2). He holds a PhD in Economics from Moscow State University and is now Chairman of the Board of Directors of Alfa Bank, Russia's largest commercial bank. He is a trustee of the Centre for Economic Policy Research and a member of the Board of Directors of the New Economic School in Moscow.

Alfred Kokh is a writer and economist who was a Deputy Prime Minister of the Russian Federation in the 1990s and a chief architect of Russia's privatization. He holds a PhD in Economics from the St Petersburg Mathematics and Economics Institute of the Russian Academy of Sciences and is the author of *A Crate of Vodka: An Insider View on the 20 Years That Shaped Modern Russia* and *The Selling of the Soviet Empire: Politics and Economics of Russia's Privatization*.

"Aven and Kokh provide a fascinating history of the second Russian revolution of 1989–92, as told by participants to participants, and focusing on the central role of Yegor Gaidar. Even the most imaginative novelist could not match the drama and clash of personalities as vividly as these interviews."
William Nordhaus, Sterling Professor of Economics, Yale University

"In 1990–3 Russia was transformed from a centrally planned to a market economy (with Russian characteristics) – a period of economic and political turbulence for all involved. This fascinating book records, through interviews two decades later, the recollections, reflections, and re-evaluations of key leaders in that dramatic transformation. A remarkable collection."
Richard N. Cooper, Professor of Economics, Harvard University

"This fascinating book records the recollections and ideas of the key participants in Russia's attempts at market reforms, with a special focus on the central role of the brilliant and cunning Yegor Gaidar. For anyone who lived through these reforms without the benefit of hindsight, or who has studied what went right and what did not, the key players and events jump off the page with action and insight. No one ever knows all of history. This oral history allows us to know far more than we have to date."
David Lipton, First Deputy Managing Director, International Monetary Fund (IMF)

GAIDAR'S REVOLUTION

The Inside Account of the Economic Transformation of Russia

Petr Aven & Alfred Kokh

I.B. TAURIS
LONDON · NEW YORK

New edition published in 2015 by
I.B.Tauris & Co. Ltd
London • New York
www.ibtauris.com

First Published in the United States in 2013 by The Gaidar Foundation

ISBN: 978 1 78453 122 5
eISBN: 978 0 85773 958 2

A full CIP record for this book is available from the British Library
A full CIP record is available from the Library of Congress

Library of Congress Catalog Card Number: available

Typeset in Adobe Garamond Pro by A. & D. Worthington, Newmarket, Suffolk
Printed and bound by CPI Group (UK) Ltd, Croydon, CR0 4YY

CONTENTS

ILLUSTRATIONS

12. Boris Fyodorov, Anatoly Chubais, Alexander Shokhin, and Vladimir Shumeiko at the IX Extraordinary Congress of People's Deputies of Russia, 1993. (© Alexander Sentsov / ITAR–TASS)

13. "Burbulis was the founding father of the Government Reform," 1992. (© Alexander Chumichev / ITAR–TASS)

14. "We all came from science," Alexander Shokhin, the Academician Stanislav Shatalin, Gennady Burbulis, and Yegor Gaidar, 1992. (© Photo from the personal archive of Alexander Shokhin)

15. Alexander Shokhin, Edward Dnieper, Tatiana Shokhin, and Mikhail Poltoranin at Alexander's dacha in Arkhangelskoye. (© Photo from the personal archive of Alexander Shokhin)

16. Yegor Gaidar, Petr Aven, and Alexander Shokhin at his dacha in Arkhangelskoye, 1992. (© Photo from the personal archive of Petr Aven)

17. Negotiations on external debt. Horst Koehler (Deputy Minister of Finance, 1992, and President of Germany, 2004–10), Petr Aven, Alexander Shokhin, and Boris Yeltsin, 1992. (© Photo from the personal archive of Petr Aven)

18. Minister of Foreign Economic Relations Petr Aven, 1992. (© Yuri Abramochkin / RIA Novosti)

19. Press conference of First Deputy Prime Minister Yegor Gaidar, 1992. (© Alexander Chumichev / ITAR–TASS)

20. Yegor Gaidar and Andrei Nechayev, December 1, 1992. (© Alexander Makarov / RIA Novosti)

21. First Deputy Minister of Economy and Finance Minister Andrei Nechayev, 1991. (© Valentin Cheredintsev / ITAR–TASS)

22. Chairman of the Russian State Committee for State Property Management, Anatoly Chubais, during a press conference at the White House regarding privatization. (© Sergey Nikolaev / Kommersant)

23. Minister of Foreign Economic Relations Petr Aven and Deputy Prime Minister Anatoly Chubais (left). (© Valery Khristophorov / ITAR–TASS)

24. Deputy Prime Minister Anatoly Chubais, September 18, 1992. (© Boris Kaufman / RIA Novosti)

25. Petr Aven, presidential representative for relations with industrialized countries (G7), Boris Yeltsin, and George Bush, Munich, 1992. (© Photo from the personal archive of Petr Aven)

26. Petr Aven and Boris Yeltsin in negotiations, 1992. (© Photo from the personal archive of Petr Aven)

27. Yegor Gaidar and Gennady Burbulis at the Congress of People's Deputies, April 18, 1992. (© Alexander Sentsov / ITAR–TASS)

FOREWORD

I HAVE READ THIS BOOK WITH THE GREATEST INTEREST and—sometimes—
deep emotions. It deals with one of the most important developments in
modern history, described and analyzed by people who were not mere
observers of this crucial process but its participants. And they—the reformers, the Gaidar team—were on the side of individual freedom, especially
economic liberty, which is the key to prosperity. Therefore, they were on the
right side of history and on the side of basic human rights. I perceive it to be
a great injustice that they are still so often blamed for results of actions that
were not theirs or were beyond their control.

The book contains a lot of interesting information and insights presented
by key players in Russia's early transformation. For example, conversations between the reformers help to clarify how their economic views and
programs developed in the 1980s.

The book shows how the Soviet Union during 1990–1 was moving
toward collapse without the full knowledge and intent of the key political
players. This reminds us of the law of unintended consequences in history.
The conversations in the book depict a striking contrast between the understanding of and support for reforms in the USSR, and then Russia, presented
by the Bush-Baker team in the 1980s and early 1990s, and the neglect and
ignorance on this issue displayed by Clinton and his administration after
the 1992 US elections.

From the historical perspective, including the fairly recent civil war in
Yugoslavia, the amazingly peaceful dissolution of the Soviet Union was a

miracle. How this was achieved, how the danger of a potential catastrophe was prevented, is one of the topics of this fascinating book. It was a historic achievement by key political actors such as Gorbachev, Yeltsin, Gaidar, Kozyrev, and Grachev. The book also sheds light on one tragic exception— the war in Chechnya—and suggests that it could have been avoided if not for the miscalculations and blunders of some people around Yeltsin, and Yeltsin himself.

The authors do not shy away from asking some difficult questions. One of the key questions is whether the liberal-democratic camp (the early reformers) could have fared better politically if it had pursued a different political strategy: that of building its own political party much earlier and distancing itself from Yeltsin when his path clearly diverged from the views and program of the reformers. This is a dilemma best discussed by the insiders; an outsider like me can only offer some comparative remarks.

First, whether and when a person engages in electoral politics depends on his or her personality and preferences. I perceived myself as a technocrat entrusted in early September 1989 with a historic mission: to stabilize Poland's economy, which was in the grip of hyperinflation, and transform it into dynamic capitalism. It was for me a sufficiently large mission to which to dedicate 100 percent of my time and energy. I think Gaidar's attitude was similar; in the Czech Republic, Václav Klaus's views and preferences were different. My first period in government ended in December 1991, and only in early 1995 did I decide to enter electoral politics by becoming leader of the free-market party Freedom Union. After the elections in autumn 1997, we created a governmental coalition with a political bloc organized around Solidarność, and together we pushed some important reforms—first of all major privatizations, fundamental pension reform, and local government reform.

Second, the inherited economic situation in the former Czechoslovakia was much less dramatic than Poland's in 1989, not to mention Russia's in late 1991 and earlier. The leader of the economic team in Czechoslovakia simply had more time to dedicate to non-economic issues than the leaders in Poland and Russia.

Third, the reformers' party, headed by Gaidar, achieved quite a success in the elections in late 1993, becoming the largest party in the Duma. The same happened with the reformist party in Poland in 1991 and 1993. Neither in Poland nor in Russia had the reform parties achieved a majority in the parliament. And the electoral success of the Choice of Russia party in 1993 appears to be all the greater, given the economic dislocations suffered by the population, not so much because of the reforms but rather owing to the inherited economic situation. The demise of the reformist party in Russia during elections in 1996 should therefore be explained by the developments of 1993–6. One of these had probably been the perceived association of the party with Yeltsin's unpopular policies during this period. But what would have been the alternative scenario? Would the communists have won the elections if the party had distanced itself from Yeltsin? And, if so, would Russia have followed the Lukashenko path? This danger could not have been dismissed out of hand, and certainly it must have existed in the minds of reformers in Russia. The reformers in the Czech Republic, Poland, and other Central European countries did not face such dramatic choices.

Finally, the political success of an early economic reformer does not guarantee in every case great success for economic reforms. Much depends again on personality and preferences. The extent of market reforms in Klaus's Czech Republic is not larger than in other Central and East European (CEE) countries, and the growth record of that country is worse than Slovakia's, for example. And sometimes the reverse is true: people perceived as non-reformers pursue reforms, forced by circumstances or because their previous opposition stance resulted from insufficient information or political posturing. According to the book, this seems to have been the case for Viktor Chernomyrdin while he was prime minister of Russia. One should, therefore, differentiate between the political success of the reformers and the success of the reforms. When in 1998 I proposed a flat tax in Poland, it was blocked in parliament, but a couple of years later it was reintroduced largely by the parties that previously had opposed it. I regard this as one of my greatest triumphs.

One of the issues discussed in this book (on a much larger scale) is the kind of economic system that emerged in Russia in 1990, and the rather disappointing economic performance of Russia from 1991 onward. Inflation remained very high for a long time, and gross domestic product (GDP) started to grow only during the second half of 1999, after a substantial decline. How to explain these developments? First, I would note that the statistical decline in GDP in Russia overstates the decline in welfare—to a much larger extent than in the CEE countries—because the share of military production was much larger in Russia. Therefore, the shrinkage of the military sector was much more pronounced in Russia than in the CEE, and this substantially reduced GDP but not overall welfare in Russia. Building fewer tanks does not lower the general standard of living. However, even with this correction, the question of Russia's rather disappointing economic performance largely remains.

This fact cannot be blamed on the defective economic knowledge of the Gaidar team. My own personal impressions as well as those of other people strongly suggest that they were in this respect certainly on par with their Polish colleagues.[1] However, the Russian team acted under much more difficult and constraining circumstances. First, they inherited some time-bombs that we in Poland did not have. The main one appears to have been the authority granted to the Central Bank as early as 1991 to increase the ruble money supply. And the ruble zone was supported by the International Monetary Fund (IMF)! The uncoordinated emissions of the ruble were sufficient to prevent a successful early stabilization.

Second, the Gaidar team had much less time for reforms, and during this short time faced much stronger political constraints than the Polish team. We in Poland had more than two years (from early September 1989 to December 1991) for a decisive reform push, facing first a friendly parliament, and later at least a non-hostile one. It allowed us to launch widespread liberalization, to dismantle monopolies, to reorganize parts of public administration, to start a decisive macroeconomic stabilization, and to begin the privatization of state-owned enterprises (though, even under these rather favorable political circumstances, privatization was delayed relative to my plans). Gaidar and his team, as I have already stressed, had much less time and faced much stronger political constraints. And Gaidar had to deal with issues I did not have to—for example, preventing conflicts in some parts of Russia. This more limited room for maneuver most likely explains the more limited economic liberalization in Russia, with less de-monopolization of the economy than in Poland—features that unfavorably affected the later evolution of the Russian political and economic system and, as a result, its performance. The Russian reformers dealing with privatization faced uncomfortable trade-offs that did not exist in the CEE countries, such as whether to permit loans-for-shares programs. On the one hand, it was not difficult to foresee that this scheme was likely to strengthen the oligarchic groups, resulting in negative political consequences. On the other hand, one could not dismiss as a mere fantasy the danger that, in the absence of such programs, there could be a pro-communist shift in Russia.

In view of the time-bombs the Russian reformers had inherited—the short time they were in government, the political constraints they were exposed to, the special dilemmas they had to face—it is a fundamental intellectual error (or intellectual dishonesty), and a great injustice, to blame them for the evolution of the Russian politico-economic system and for the related rather disappointing performance of the Russian economy. Given

---

1.   For example, Marek Dabrowski, "The World Bank and the Russian Transition, 1999–2000," mimeo, 2001.

these circumstances, it is very hard to see what more or what else they could have done. They were rather brave kamikazes (to borrow an expression used in this book) battling against prevailing odds, and in the service of a mission of truly historic proportions. They deserve deep respect, and especially deep gratitude.

And this is particularly true of Yegor Gaidar. The conversations in the book strengthen my personal impression that he was an exceptional individual. He combined very high moral standards, intellectual rigor, vast knowledge, decisiveness, and mild manners. What a rare combination!

I am sure he was a hero of contemporary history in Russia—and the world. It is very important that this great book helps to restore his rightful place in public opinion. And we should continue our efforts in this respect.

Leszek Balcerowicz
Warsaw, October 2012

FROM THE AUTHORS

THIS BOOK IS A COLLECTION OF OUR CONVERSATIONS with members of Russia's first post-communist government, which took office in November 1991 (as well as with James Baker, then US secretary of state). This government is usually named after Yegor Gaidar, the leader of its economic segment. In fact, we initially wanted to talk about Gaidar, as we wished to protect his memory from stupid myths, dismayingly unfair accusations, and diverse lies. But the very first meetings with our interlocutors exceeded the boundaries of "conversations about Yegor" to embrace a much broader range of issues: the situation in the USSR before the Yeltsin-Gaidar reforms, possible alternative scenarios, the reformers' mistakes and compromises, reasons for successes and failures, and so on.

Being economists, we realized that an important factor in the success of any undertaking is the comparative advantages of the players. We had two. The first was our participation in the events under discussion. Second, we had close and trusting relations with each of our interlocutors. We think these advantages enabled us to harvest unexpected and new information from the protagonists of this book, and to learn and understand something new to us and our prospective readers.

The Gaidar government was in office when the Soviet Union broke apart, the sociopolitical system changed in every former Soviet republic, and the foreign-policy direction of the country shifted, among other things. We were amazed at how different the recollection of the same events by different participants could be, and how differently they interpreted the facts.

As it turns out, everyone has "a truth of their own" (even if people belong to the same political forces, the same "team"). This does not mean, though, that recollections are pointless or that it is impossible to learn "the real truth." On the contrary, honest evidence from the participants in those events—especially as they were sincerely prepared not only to defend what they had done but also to speak about their mistakes or hesitations—gave us a maximally clear idea of "what really had happened," and helped us to draw necessary conclusions for the future.

Most of our conversations were published on the website of the Russian edition of *Forbes* in 2010–12 (and in the print magazine in abridged versions). We would like to express our profound gratitude to Vladimir Fedorin, who supervised the project at the magazine and later on became the editor of the book. We are especially grateful to the founding father of Polish economic reforms, Leszek Balcerowicz, who kindly agreed to write the foreword, and to Carl Bildt, who wrote the afterword—and of course to all of our interlocutors.

Petr Aven, Alfred Kokh

A BOOK WRITTEN UNDER DURESS

Do not give what is holy to dogs; and do not throw your pearls before swine, or they will trample them under foot and turn and maul you.

MATTHEW 7:6

I DO NOT WANT TO WRITE THIS MATERIAL. It comes out clumsy, heavy, spiteful, and I do not want to. And I understand why: I simply do not want to harp on the same tune for the thousandth time. That is, that Gaidar saved the country from famine and war and gave a chance for freedom and other things our opponents call rubbish.

I read the online comments on his death. There was some (and I think it was an abundance) of our good old Russian meanness that would not have occurred to either my associates or myself if any of our brave critics had died. For example, Doctor of Workers' Sciences Vasily Shandybin died shortly after Yegor, but did any of us make such comments as "a cur's death for a cur" or "may this never stop"? No. Yet Vasily Ivanovich never spared us. He made false allegations sometimes, and, to be frank, told lies.

But they let Yegor have it. Not just one or two. They were enthusiastically jeering. What can I say—fine Christians. No match for those attenuated Czechs or Portuguese. Gavriil Popov and Yuri Luzhkov were surprisingly creative, saying that Gaidar made people starve to death.[1] They claimed they were telling the truth. They called a lie—blunt, deliberate, and cynical—the truth.

---

1. Luzhkov Yu., Popov G., "One more word about Gaidar," *Mosckovskiy Komsomolets*, January 22, 2010.

xxi

Neither fasting nor prayer can rid me of the blind disgust and hatred for these "kind people." I have no Christian meekness. That makes my words come out clumsy and heavy. Anger smothers me and grudge grips my chest. It would not have mattered if it had been all about me. Honest! I let those dear Russians have it often. As they did me. We're even in that sense. But Yegor ... he loved them all. I know that for sure. He stoically endured the abusive words. I thought his enemies would finally shut up after his death. They should be glad, they outlived him! But no! They still kick him although he is dead—they dance on his coffin, and they sneer and try to outdo one another in their attacks. And they lie, lie, lie.

I was being buffeted by my thoughts when Petr Aven called me and said: "Listen, I think there has been so much absurdity around Yegor and our whole government that we cannot keep silent any longer. I reject the apologetics to which some of our friends are given and the cheap tales spun by Luzhkov and Popov. If you are ready for a calm and maximally objective dialogue, I would like us to write about Yegor, our government, and those times."

"Am I ready for an objective and impartial dialogue? Hell, yes! I am a model of impartiality and don't-give-a-shit-ism. Let's do it. I've been wanting to do it for a long time. In the best traditions of objectiveness and impartiality. It's just the right time to do it, given my elegiac and mellow mood. Quiet and lyrical, melancholy and conciliatory. Isn't that the right mood for creating an objective and impartial text?"

"Terrific! I will come over tomorrow and we will have a talk."

The next day Petr was punctual, elegant, ironic, and erudite. His speech was brisk and clear. He spoke in rapid, clipped phrases. I could tell he had thought about everything.

Alfred Kokh, February 2010

PETR AVEN: I think we must speak about Gaidar. The latest article by Popov and Luzhkov is highly telling. And the reaction to it is even more so. I think it is very important to tell the truth. Naturally, everyone has their own truth, but if everyone tries to be objective, we will get a more or less correct impression of him and his role in the history of our country.

ALFRED KOKH: I am very glad you had this idea. I am itching to talk about Yegor with you, because there are few people who can discuss him without being pompous or resorting to liberal or great-power slogans.

AVEN: It is very important not to fall into extremes. On the one hand, some say that Gaidar is responsible for everything that is going on in Russia—the disintegration of the Soviet Union, the destruction of the defense industry, economic ruin, and lots of other things. On the other hand, frankly, I am equally irritated by pompous speeches declaring that Gaidar and his team, to which I am honored to have belonged, saved Russia and that if not for us then Russia would have been hungry and cold.

KOKH: Petr, let's analyze the main myths created around Yegor and that government.

AVEN: I am ready. And the first myth I propose to analyze is that no one wanted to join the government at the end of 1991—this is widespread. They claim that only the Gaidar team dared to do what nobody else wanted to do. I think this is not true. Plenty of people other than Gaidar were seeking power, and many of them wanted to head the government. The name Yuri Vladimirovich Skokov was mentioned most often. The day before the decision was made, everyone was wondering who Yeltsin would prefer—Gaidar or Skokov?

KOKH: It is hard for me to judge what alternatives he had then. I was still working in St Petersburg. Nevertheless, Yeltsin chose Gaidar. Why was that? Who played the decisive role? Golovkov? Burbulis? Gaidar himself?

AVEN: I think we will come back to this issue. And now I would like to speak about one more thing—a topic of recent debates—that the Gaidar team saved Russia from hunger, cold, and a civil war. Being a liberal economist, I think that neither starvation nor cold happens if the government does not meddle in the lives of people. Although in 1991 shops were empty, and it was impossible to buy anything without having to stand in line, I did not see a single dead horse being cut into chunks in the middle of Tverskaya Street in Moscow, the way it was in 1918.

I also remember that restaurants were open in Moscow in 1991, and no one actually died of hunger; and although there were panicky rumors of cold, there was no terrible cold, actually. In my opinion, excessive praise provokes excessive criticism.

KOKH: I have nothing to say about restaurants operating in Moscow and St Petersburg at that time. I know nothing about it because I had no money to go to a restaurant. I was the chairman of the Sestroretsk district executive committee. It may seem to us now that it was a fun job, but life did not look so easy to me back then. I remember a truck bringing chicken to a shop once. The shop was about to close, and people elected an organizing committee to guard that chicken through the night so that "the shop staff did not give it to their preferred customers." I had to assign a policeman to guard the truck because people refused to go home otherwise.

There were countless deputy commissions formed at the district council to distribute humanitarian aid: Bundeswehr food rations, sneakers, ragged clothes. There was Chinese canned meat, some foreign-made by-products, and it was very humiliating—alms, handouts. But it was highly welcome. The West was simply saving us from hunger. So it would be rather naive to say that everything was fine because restaurants were open and people did not eat dead cats, dogs, or rats.

Luzhkov and Popov went too far in claiming "thirty-six cases of death by starvation" in Zelenograd. They lost their sense of proportion. I don't doubt that there may have been some who starved to death, but there are some today as well.

Just recently [February 4, 2010] I saw this on the internet: "RIA Novosti reports a dual tragedy on Zelenogradskaya Street: a father and a daughter died, the father died of a heart attack, and the neglected daughter died of starvation. The Moscow police are verifying circumstances of the death of a 40-year-old man and his three-year-old daughter. According to preliminary forensic reports, the man and the baby girl died about 30 days ago. Forensic experts presume that the father and the daughter died during the New Year holidays. *Life News* said that the man, 40, died of cardiac arrest, while the three-year-old baby girl with disabilities he was raising alone died of starvation. The bodies were taken to a morgue. A criminal case is pending. There was a similar incident in October 2009. A man and his son were found dead in an apartment house in Moscow's Khoroshevsky district. The man was 32 years old, and his son was 18 months old."

So what? Naturally, that is tragic, but it does not occur to anyone to blame Luzhkov for those deaths. And one more thing: assuming the incidents really happened, it is quite characteristic that Luzhkov and Popov, who speak about these tragedies, do not feel their culpability. And they were in charge of the Moscow authorities (Zelenograd included) at that time. Obviously, if these deaths happened for real, they are much more responsible for them than Gaidar! These gerontocrats have totally lost their capacity for self-criticism.

AVEN: Concerning the hunger deaths in Zelenograd, I fully agree with you.

I am not an apologist of the Soviet regime, as you understand. My wife spent four hours a day buying food because she had to go to every nearby shop to find anything.

KOKH: Was that after you came back from Vienna?

AVEN: That was both before we went to Vienna and after our return. About Vienna: when colleagues and friends came to visit me there, I took them to butchers' shops. It was a shock for them.

KOKH: Yes, I took a picture of myself in front of a butcher's shop in Helsinki in the same period.

AVEN: True, things were very bad in Moscow and the whole country back then. It was impossible to buy anything—life was miserable. When they claim now that the Soviet Union was heaven on earth, they lie. But we must understand there was no great famine, either. People bought chicken somehow. But it might have come to famine if liberalization of prices had been delayed further.

KOKH: Exactly! I realized then we were very close to that. And, by the way, I told Yegor (although it is bad to say that) that we should have waited for famine to begin. God forbid—naturally that is an exaggeration. But if it had really happened and people had experienced it briefly, then our actions would have been appreciated. But hunger was stopped by our efforts five minutes before it started knocking on the door, and now people can say whatever they want.

AVEN: That is correct. However, if Gaidar had come to power a year earlier, probably he could have implemented reforms instead of urgently saving the country. That is a big problem for reformers: they start passing reforms just when the country needs salvation, and that frequently contradicts the reforms.

KOKH: Absolutely. I spoke a lot about that with Yegor, and he agreed. What he did was not market reforms or liberal reforms or shock therapy. For the first five months he was doing what he had to do, and he had no choice whatsoever. He did whatever any responsible government would have done in his place.

AVEN: Not quite, but that's almost the case. That is what I am talking about: such situations are inherently a mix of reformism and salvation.

KOKH: "Salvation" sounds pompous to me. There is another way of looking at it. Do you remember what they taught us at school: the principle of rational egoism? If you want to keep your position, you have to do that; otherwise they will wipe you out. Besides, the situation required either rapid action or no action at all.

AVEN: Judging by what you say, any person in Gaidar's place would have done the same.

KOKH: Yes, if he is a responsible person who is about doing the job and not just stealing money.

AVEN: That is correct.

KOKH: And now the question is whether the previous government, of Silayev, was irresponsible. That is, Silayev seemed to be a very responsible person. But his government did nothing but the most necessary things, and failed to prevent the exacerbation of problems, which made the Gaidar government policy so painful.

The Harvest 90 was a pure scam.[2] And the agreement with Noga, which deprived Russia of its sovereignty—who did all that?[3] Silayev and Kulik? Yes! The damage, both material and reputational, is impossible to evaluate. It was huge. As our national leader likes to say: Who went to prison? They wrote about some impossible reforms, the 500 Days program. Absolute daydreaming. The Silayev government, which ruled the country for 18 months, was totally inadequate to the situation!

AVEN: But aren't you forgetting that the Soviet Union and, naturally, the Soviet government existed practically throughout the term of Silayev's

2.   "Harvest 90" — a scheme for the purchase of foodstuffs from farmers at state (low) prices, giving an opportunity for the sellers to purchase scarce goods like cars, household appliances, etc., in the future.

3.   Noga — In spring 1991, the Council of Ministers of the RSFSR concluded a 420 million ruble loan contract with Swiss company Noga for the purchase of foodstuffs. Russia waived state immunity under this contract. The debt had to be repaid through oil supplies. In 1993, the government of Russia cancelled the contract. Noga seized Russian property in foreign countries several times until 2007 when the Swiss Supreme Court ruled in favor of Russia.

office? Although Russia's sovereignty was proclaimed on June 12, 1990, it was formal and inoperative to a large extent. That government had no powers to implement extensive reforms.

KOKH: Maybe I'm going too far here, but that stagnation for two or three years made the natural and simple steps Gaidar took, such as price liberalization, so brutal and shocking, so painful, and so politically colored.

There is no politics in price liberalization, just as there is no politics in appendicitis surgery. If it is not removed, the patient dies—that's it. Why all those discussions? When to act, to what extent, and in which sequence—all this idle talk is bullshit. It had to be removed yesterday, immediately and drastically. Partial removal would be more painful and in the end have the same result.

AVEN: Obviously, if everything had started simultaneously with the events in Poland, the Czech Republic, and Hungary—that is, in 1989—lots of things could have been done more easily and with lower costs, both monetary and political.

KOKH: As you remember, the year 1991 did not start with the appointment of Gaidar! Gaidar took office on November 7 (which is symbolic, by the way). The government got down to business only in January. You spent two months laying down the normative framework for the reforms. Actually, operational control of the economy only started on January 1.

AVEN: Not quite. Even before the New Year we had to obtain and distribute hard currency, buy drugs, distribute rubles, run industries. Operational control started on the very first day.

KOKH: But the government started doing its real work on January 1.

AVEN: It would be more correct to say: the government started to operate within its normative framework on January 1.

KOKH: Correct. And actually, the first act that showed us we had a new regime was price liberalization. That was supposed to be the main thing.

AVEN: That actually *was* the main thing.

KOKH: But, before that, many things happened in the year 1991. For instance, the April monetary reform done by the Soviet government of Valentin Pavlov. I am amazed they do not speak about that at all. It was Pavlov's reform, not Gaidar's, that nullified people's savings! As the district executive committee chairman, I remember that reform perfectly. I was the local official who executed that reform! I remember that all deposits bigger than 5,000 rubles were frozen for five years.

AVEN: No one remembers that at all anymore.

KOKH: By the moment Gaidar and his team took the governmental office, those deposits were long gone from the USSR Sberbank. All the deposits were withdrawn by the Soviet government and covered the Soviet budget deficit. So Gaidar could not simply nullify people's savings (or, as some say, steal them). There was nothing to nullify. Remember the film *Operation Y*, where a character said, "There is nothing to steal, everything was stolen before us"?

AVEN: Absolutely. There was no money at all for the last six months. That was the first big lie about Gaidar—that he was the person who destroyed people's savings. There were no savings by then; there were records, but they meant nothing. Gaidar simply acknowledged that fact, without being evasive or inventing excuses.

KOKH: According to the accusers' logic, Gaidar set off inflation, and thus depreciated the deposits.

AVEN: There were no deposits by then, so that was totally absurd. There can be no inflation when there are no rubles. What I really think should be discussed is the neglect of social security. First and foremost, I mean pensioners. They could have come up with special ways to support pensioners in 1992, even purely symbolic ones—for instance, a privileged issue of vouchers to elderly people, or giving them more land for allotments or orchards or private homes.

KOKH: That would not have helped much at the time.

AVEN: There would probably have been no fundamental change, but at least some attempts could have been made to ease pensioners' lives with what the government had, such as land. The issue should probably have been given more thought, and the fact it was neglected is a shortcoming, in my opinion. People would have seen that the government was at least trying to do something for them.

KOKH: That would have been more a PR campaign than real assistance.

AVEN: Not quite. And, by the way, PR campaigns were another of the most important things we overlooked. There was no contact with the people at all. That was fundamental. No one remembers now that it was Pavlov's reform that nullified savings, not Gaidar's. And a major reason they don't remember is because we didn't tell them, and still don't. A failure to approach them was a major and critical shortcoming.

KOKH: My role here is rather odd: I have to find excuses for the government in which you worked, while you attack it. Actually, it suits me!

I have many questions, which I posed to Yegor. Everyone keeps saying "the Gaidar government, the Gaidar government—Gaidar took the power." And I think that Gaidar had no power whatsoever!

AVEN: This is one more rebuke of mine to our government—and the key one.

KOKH: First, he had no real influence on monetary policy because he did not control the Central Bank.

AVEN: That was just part of the problem. He more or less controlled the Central Bank. At least the Central Bank coordinated its policy with us to an extent. That was not what we wanted, but that was at least something. Viktor Gerashchenko was Gaidar's choice.

KOKH: And what about the *siloviki*, the power structures? And the propaganda machinery? And the Foreign Ministry?

AVEN: Absolutely true. Mikhail Poltoranin—who was not our ally, to put it mildly—was in control of propaganda. He was an opponent. The *siloviki* were a separate concern. Just as Luzhkov and Popov now accuse Gaidar of essentially being a US agent, the *siloviki* accused us of spying for all intelligence services then. They sent absurd weekly reports to Yeltsin.

In short, my main rebuke to our own team is that we were not the authorities. We were close to power—and reforms implemented by those who are not those with the power always end like they ended here, for the whole country and the reformers. And, certainly, for Yegor.

KOKH: We have mentioned that Skokov was considered a candidate to lead the reforms alongside Gaidar. There must have been many candidates considered, weren't there?

AVEN: We have said before that not many people would have declined that offer. I don't think that Luzhkov would have, nor Yavlinsky, nor Lobov. So it's a lie to say that Gaidar was the only one while all the others opted out. Yeltsin chose Gaidar. Why did he choose him? We really thought that Skokov was the main candidate.

KOKH: And what about Yavlinsky?

AVEN: I think Yavlinsky would not have declined the offer, either. He might have bargained a bit, like he always did, and asked for special powers or something else; but in fact he would have accepted the offer. Why did Yeltsin choose Gaidar? I think there are two reasons. The main reason—and that was Yeltsin's greatness (I am not scared of this word!)—was that he realized at a certain moment that we needed a drastic change. All those people from old teams—Lobov, Popov, Luzhkov, Skokov, any one of them—they all proposed standard Gosplan[4] measures, and those measures did not work.

KOKH: A backwoods variant of Hungarian socialism?

AVEN: Yes—a sort of socialism with market elements. But we needed an absolutely radical change. All the old methods, the defunct socialist recipes, did not work. I have just read the memoirs of Chernyayev, who was probably Gorbachev's smartest advisor. And I recalled Gaidar telling me in the 1980s about the previous generation of Gorbachev's reformers: about Chernyayev, Shakhnazarov, Bovin. We were boys, and deemed them to be big thinkers. Gaidar was the first to describe them without piety; he had no illusions. Yegor knew his own value well, and could easily show his true measure to an interlocutor. He realized very well how other people measured up. And he said that the Gorbachev team was extremely weak—they were totally incapable, but self-important: not very smart, not quite educated. Marxist reformers, in short. Gaidar gave them a very sober evaluation very early on. When I read his memoirs now I can see how right he was.

Back to Yeltsin and his choice. I can say that Lobov, Skokov, and all the

---

4.   The state planning committee.

rest were intellectually rooted in the Soviets, and that was not what was needed. Yeltsin understood the need for something completely new, and Gaidar was that new thing.

That is the first and, I think, the most important thing. Second, Yeltsin found Gaidar's way of communicating a culture shock. Naturally, Gaidar won him over with his education and economic knowledge—and, what was no less important, with his determination. In fact, Gaidar was much less determined than he could seem when he wanted to. I think Yeltsin was positive that these were guys who feared nothing: he may have thought they would move heaven and earth, were not linked with Soviet influence groups, had no sentiment about any people in high places, and would grab power. That was another reason for Yeltsin's decision, in my opinion.

I am confident Yeltsin felt Gaidar really wanted to do it. You see, when you hire a person who is so eager, his energy and determination have an effect on your decision. When a person is so eager, he will try harder. Gaidar was very eager! I think Yeltsin chose Gaidar although he understood that many would have accepted the job. Yavlinsky would have accepted. But Gaidar really wanted it—that is a great difference. I think Yeltsin felt that, too.

KOKH: But what you say now contradicts what you said earlier: that Gaidar lost because he did not fight for power. Please, clear up this contradiction.

AVEN: Both are true. Gaidar longed for power because he was a reformer, but he was not prepared for political struggle. You could say he was an "ideal" reformer, to a degree.

KOKH: In that case, he had rather idealistic notions about political struggle. He did not suspect that political struggle simply has no rules.

AVEN: Absolutely. He was eager, but he did not know how to act. Yet his desire was obvious.

KOKH: Maybe—that fits my impression of Yeltsin. I am positive that Yegor underwent a certain transformation because he did not want power in the last period of his life. I think his story was the following: he wanted power at first; then he learned what must be done to take it; and then he did not want it anymore. Because he did not want to do the things he had to do to get power.

AVEN: Certainly he was not what you'd call a political fighter. He could not hog the blanket brazenly and aggressively. But I think he was very eager when he spoke to Yeltsin in fall 1991.

KOKH: It seemed to him the ground was clear, and a big positive result could be achieved with a tiny quantity of inevitable nastiness.

AVEN: Yes, and the shit hit the fan when the young reformers bumped into the first complications, concerning not only behind-the-scenes but also public political struggle. Complications, nastiness. Being a rather experienced man, Gaidar endured that at first. But passions flared as time passed following the end of the stagnation; and if Gaidar had adequate ideas about political struggle, they were good for the 1980s, but not for the 1990s.

KOKH: I am not going to settle a political score now, but I want to remind you that 1991 did not start in November. Something was happening in the country before Gaidar took office. You may have more information than me. What really happened, and why didn't Yavlinsky implement his program? The Russian Congress of People's Deputies gave him carte blanche, and the only thing he failed to achieve was getting the consent of the Union parliament. But he did not really need it after August.

AVEN: This is strange. I have been reading about 1991, and I have an impression that no one actually had power. Before that, power always belonged to somebody. And then came complete anarchy—it was impossible either to make a decision or to cancel it.

KOKH: Still, some decisions were made, weren't they?

AVEN: They did make decisions, but it was no use. Petty lobbying. Such as the Harvest 90 program, or the benevolence of the Union authorities— "Come on, fellows, let's be friends!" No—no one had real power. And reforms required a rather authoritarian style.

KOKH: And Yeltsin suddenly gained power in a fairytale way in November 1991?

AVEN: That seems to be the case. By then Yeltsin had amassed sufficient power for a huge number of reasons, and it became easier to make the necessary decisions. He was legitimate enough, enjoying the support of the people and the Russian parliament, and the Union authorities were gradually losing power because of the separatism of the republics, because many took Yeltsin's side. And, most importantly, the Union authorities lost people's support after August, after the GKChP[5] putsch.

KOKH: There was an inter-republican committee led by Silayev, and Yavlinsky was his first deputy.

AVEN: By the way, that is the answer to your question about Yavlinsky—I think he bet on the Union government and lost. That's probably why he could never forgive Yeltsin, and Yeltsin could not forgive him.

KOKH: I think you are right about anarchy. And here is my liberal assessment: we had had practically no government since August or, to be frank, since January 1991. And nothing happened. So I presume we do not need a government at all!

There is one more idea I like. What do the opponents of the Yeltsin period, which we had in the notorious "Wild 1990s," say? They keep saying that Yeltsin brought to ruin the army, the navy, and the economy, and that we were weak, and so on. But now allegedly Putin has strengthened all that—he has strengthened sovereignty, and no one is going to attack or rob us now. The question is, if the threat of attack or our treasure being stolen has been a permanent threat through the entire history of Russia, why did no one attack us or occupy us in those ten years when we were weak and everything lay in ruins?

AVEN: Because no one wants us.

KOKH: Yes, but here's a natural conclusion: if no one wants us, no one attacks us, and no one is going to do that, why strengthen our army and navy? Why do we waste our money on that?

AVEN: Remember Professor Preobrazhensky saying in *Heart of a Dog*, "Do you want to open a discussion right now?" That is, if you want to discuss the army and the navy, that would be quite a different subject.

KOKH: All right, let's talk about the foreign debt. This is another strand of criticism addressed to Gaidar and your government—and to you personally, as the one in charge. Why did you take on the entire Union debt?

---

5.   State Committee on the State of Emergency.

AVEN: What was the foreign debt situation? First of all, it took the West a long time to decide who to speak to: us or to the Union authorities. Actually, they had de facto ceased to exist by that time, but Western bureaucrats refused to understand and acknowledge that.

KOKH: Was the West against the disintegration of the Soviet Union?

AVEN: The Western bureaucrats, strictly speaking. The West and Western bureaucrats are two different things. Western bureaucrats in charge of collecting the foreign debt certainly had objections.

KOKH: Do Western bureaucracies follow political logic and political authorities more than the Russian bureaucracy does?

AVEN: They have the same criteria as any bureaucracy—security and stability. When I was in charge of the foreign debt, their first reaction was horror. Who should they negotiate with about collecting the foreign debt, and how? That was not clear to anyone. They refused to speak to us for a long time and to recognize the obvious—that the USSR was gone, and so were the rules to which they were accustomed at the negotiations. At first we wanted to share the debt proportionately between all the former Soviet republics, but Western bureaucrats bluntly refused to hear that: they wanted to negotiate with just one, not with a group of sovereign republics of dubious sanity.

We understood that, if we did not settle the debt problem with the West, there would be no loans, investments, or credits from the IMF, governments, or companies. That is, we would be unable to enter the global capital market—and that was critical to us. Hence, under the influence of our Western colleagues, we elaborated the position of joint and several liability. They said, "You've scattered, but you are all responsible for the foreign debt. It does not matter to us how you divide it among yourselves, but the responsibility would be yours."

It soon became clear that that formula did not work, either, because a number of the republics could not pay a cent—for instance, Tajikistan and Moldova, and even Georgia. And, as you know, the principle of joint and several liability implies that if even one country fails to pay, everyone else is accountable.

Besides, even with joint liability, the debt had to be divided among the former republics. The West was very scared of that, because it was apparent that the question of how to divide it would drag on for years, even decades. Everyone had arguments. For instance, the Baltic republics refused even to start such negotiations; and that was not the most difficult part of the problem. So we decided it would be reasonable to take on responsibility for the entire debt, considering the circumstances.

Kokh: Why?

Aven: First of all, because we needed access to the capital market. It was impossible to overcome the destructive recession without that. We needed direct investments, as well as IMF loans and the like, for financial stabilization. We received IMF payments largely, if not exclusively, because we settled the debt problem.

Besides, more than 61 percent of the debt fell on us. If we had divided the debt, the Russian chunk would still have been large—whether by GDP or on a per capita basis, or by anything else. So our additional commitments were relatively small. Second, we thought that, while the USSR certainly had large debts, it was owed no less. Total liabilities to the Soviet Union stood at approximately $150 billion. Plus, if we were the only legal successor to the USSR, then all of its property located abroad was to be made Russian, which meant billions of dollars. We also expected a good rescheduling of our debts. Besides, the decision generally complied with the logic of the legal succession of the USSR, which gave Russia a place at the UN Security Council and the status of a nuclear power.

Thanks to our position, we received IMF consent to grant financial assistance by January 1992, when the process started. That is why Luzhkov and Popov said that Gaidar won billions of dollars in financial assistance. We got it—$1 billion—in summer 1992. Certainly that was very little, but it was critically important aid. They gave $3 billion more to Chernomyrdin in 1993.

Kokh: Yes, I remember that we got a ridiculously pitiful amount in the 1990s. So the logic was the following: we had not only debts, but also assets in the form of debts to us, assets abroad, and a political solution—membership of the UN Security Council, and so on. Am I right that one of the arguments you have just listed proved erroneous: we hoped for a good rescheduling, but that did not happen?

Aven: Wrong. It happened. The agreement with the Paris Club was wonderful. Its terms were not inferior to those of the deal with the Poles and the other countries of Eastern Europe. Really. The conditions we negotiated in 1992 and signed in 1993 were very advantageous. And Russia became a recognized country, and relations with the West normalized.

KOKH: And what happened to the debts owed to us?

AVEN: We had both ups and downs. For instance, payments from India were significant. India alone owed us $10 billion.

KOKH: Did it pay?

AVEN: It did, mostly—starting in 1994. The general situation with the hard-currency debt was the following. The USSR owed $97 billion in 1997, when I started working for the government, including $48 billion to the Paris Club and the rest to companies and its own citizens. The debts to us were $150 billion, including $70 billion from Comecon countries. Those debts were hard to collect. Certainly there were bad debts and, like other creditor countries, we had to write off the lion's share of that. There were the sub-Saharan African nations, and similar countries.

KOKH: Correct. No one could have given you a real evaluation of the debt, so I think the outstanding experts of the Soviet government never viewed those debts in terms of collection.

AVEN: That was the ideology of the USSR—these were, so to speak, purely political decisions.

KOKH: And what can you say about assistance from the West?

AVEN: Assistance from the West was very meager. We asked the IMF for $6 billion in 1992, and we were given $1 billion. Luzhkov and Popov claim Gaidar received mythical billions of Western money.

I want to shatter one more myth now. Gaidar did not follow instructions from the West, and the West did not help him carry out the reforms. In some cases, such as the settlement of the Soviet debt, the West had a destructive position, especially at the start. The same can be said of financial backing for the reforms—it was miserable.

KOKH: Can we say that the Western position—such as insisting we pay about $6 billion in Soviet debts in 1992 and get only $1 billion in financial assistance—was the cause of hyperinflation, which created a social background hostile to the reforms?

AVEN: Yes and no. I would say it was one of the reasons but not the only one.

First, inflation was predetermined by the colossal money supply the population had in the late 1980s and the early 1990s, due to the absolutely irresponsible monetary policy of the Union authorities. The careless increase in salaries for all categories of workers and specialists, the payment of pensions to working pensioners and many other things were the stubborn continuation of the Stalin-Brezhnev price-regulation norms but also made inevitable a hike in inflation, leading to uncontrolled prices. That is what actually happened—prices really grew. Wholesale prices grew by three or four times, while salaries only doubled or tripled. The question of who was to blame for later inflation is a truly interesting one.

KOKH: Do you mean the disbursement for covering the budget deficit? Or the disbursement initiated by the Central Bank directly for enterprises in what they called "the replenishment of circulating assets"?

AVEN: Both. The thing is that, of the disbursement, 40 percent went to cover the budget deficit and 60 percent went to enterprises. It's an open question whose fault it was that the Central Bank's disbursement policy was not quite coordinated with the government.

We had three types of budget policy in 1992. In the first few months, the policy was rather firm. Then, by summer, Gaidar had made concessions to industrialists and politicians and significantly relaxed the budget policy. But in fall we started bringing it back onto the required course. As a result, the budget deficit in 1992 was half the size of the deficit in 1991: it was 20 percent of GDP in 1991 and only 10 percent of GDP in 1992.

Of course, that was a big deficit—practically lethal. But halving the budget deficit within a year—I would not call that a heroic achievement, but there was *something* heroic about it! I suppose we could have been even firmer, but then our opponents would have a logical disconnect: on the one hand they criticize the "shock therapy," and on the other they oppose inflation; but "shock therapy" was the only possible way to fight inflation, at least at that moment.

KOKH: The advantage our opponents have over us is that they are not constrained by logic.

AVEN: That is for sure. Now let us go into details. Direct funding of enterprises by the Central Bank was an absolutely irresponsible step. I don't know how much that was coordinated with Gaidar, yet 60 percent of the Central Bank disbursement went directly to enterprises. Anyone would tell you now that it was insanity; back then our deputies called that policy quite reasonable.

Kokh: I recall a meeting at the St Petersburg administration when the head of the St Petersburg branch of the Central Bank gathered representatives of enterprises in a big hall and explained to them in detail how to open accounts at the Central Bank, and how those accounts would be supplied with money.

Aven: Nevertheless, I don't think that 60 percent of inflation could be attributable to the policy of the Central Bank alone. I think that Gaidar must have taken part in Central Bank decisions, because it is impossible for the Central Bank to be fully independent from the government under our circumstances, which means the government bears a certain degree of responsibility.

Finally, the halving of the budget deficit within a year testifies to a reasonable budget policy considering the scale of economic and social transformations. For instance, Andrei Illarionov still writes that Gaidar was not a firm financier but a populist politician—but that is not fair.

Kokh: Still, you are too demanding of Gaidar and your government as a whole. Don't forget that the Central Bank chairman was appointed by Khasbulatov's Supreme Council, which was already in firm opposition to Yeltsin and his policy. Just remember when Rutskoi claimed to have "briefcases full of compromising material" about Yeltsin? Under those circumstances the Central Bank policy could be not just uncoordinated with government policy, but even absolutely opposite to it. That is not Gaidar's fault.

It's another matter that Gaidar's efforts were not enough to win support from the majority of deputies and officials. Probably he would have achieved more if he had used intrigues, deception, bribes, and betrayal, and if he had established relationships with the scum and rogues. But he did not. As far as I know, he didn't know how to do that. I don't know anyone worse equipped than Yegor for that sort of activity. You may argue that this means Gaidar was professionally inadequate as a politician (and therefore as premier), because any genuine Russian politician must be brilliant at being low-down. I have no retort, because Yegor called himself a mediocre politician, a C grade.

Aven: I'm glad you brought that up. We must speak more about Gaidar as a personality. Gaidar was a very brave man. You said once that he was a very Russian man—I do not think so. Alas, in my opinion, the modern Russian man is highly capable of compromises with himself. I think that in Russia, the Revolution of 1917, the destruction of churches by those who had been believers, and the subordination to Stalinism for decades happened because there was a huge class of people—primarily peasants—who lacked firm moral principles.

But there were also Russian officers with very firm principles. In my eyes, Gaidar is precisely a Russian officer: he grew up in a military family. He may be the most upright person I know. He was very principled, and had very firm ideas of honor and dignity. For instance, Gaidar could not be rude at all—he was not rude, ever. Yegor told me he had a fight in his kindergarten years when he saw that a girl was being hurt: a girl should not be beaten under any circumstances—that is what he thought till the last days of his life. I have absolutely no doubt that Gaidar would immediately have started a fight if anyone had been rude to a woman in his presence. Although he didn't know how to fight at all, still he would have defended her. He was absolutely principled about that.

He was not a geek. He was totally aware of the world. He knew the power structure well, and he had a perfect sense of hierarchy.

He was very brave. He could be easily imagined as the commander of a sinking ship. He had no fear—he would never run scared, and he behaved very decently. He was a man of honor. That is a wonderful quality. And his moral principles were very firm. We keep discussing the rich and the poor. But how could one discuss bribes and corruption with him?

KOKH: And he was a man of very modest means.

AVEN: Precisely. The subject was totally unacceptable for him. He could never be involved in this type of discussion. Nemtsov tells the story of how he brought him caviar, and Yegor kicked him out. That is absolutely true. He was a man of honor, and that is a very rare quality.

On the other hand, we also must say that he was an introvert. Communication with strangers was hard for him. He was actually at a loss—he simply couldn't speak with miners who came to demand a pay rise. It was very hard for him to resist the pressure of people—real, live people. And that quality showed in his relations with Yeltsin. He never had enough nerve to tell him what he didn't want to hear while looking him straight in the eye. Yeltsin was a very strong man—especially in the early 1990s.

Gaidar was a complicated man. But in my opinion his principles were his most distinctive feature. I must say that not a single person on the team was even close to him in principles and high moral qualities—no one. Many tried to emulate him, but they simply could not. That pretty much determined why he was our leader.

KOKH: Maybe that is why some of our comrades are still afloat? Because of the flexibility of their morals?

AVEN: Certainly. Interestingly, Gaidar didn't like to speak about morals.

KOKH: I think he thought it would be vulgar to speak about morals seriously. However, morals, in the broad sense, are an inevitable part of any polemical discussion. If you are a part of it, you must be able to speak about it. And Gaidar tried to avoid polemics!

AVEN: Yes. Here is my analogy: Zinaida Shakhovskaya, who loved Nabokov all her life and therefore thought about him a lot, wrote that Nabokov kept speaking about the former wealth of his family—you remember, the Rolls-Royce, and so on. The frequency of his recollections makes it clear that he was never that rich. When Felix Yusupov, bankrupt, moved to Paris, he would order dinner without thinking that he did not have a single franc in his pocket. After he finished eating, he would say, "I thought money would turn up somehow." He had always lived in a situation where there was money—there was never a shortage, and he didn't have to think about it. Money did not exist for Yusupov as a substance, a subject of thought. But it existed for Nabokov. The same for Gaidar: he never spoke about principles because they were invariable and non-debatable for him, and he didn't have to think about them.

KOKH: There is one more nuance. If we take, for instance, the biography of an average Soviet person and the Gaidar biography, we may say that Gaidar actually grew up in a gilded cage. As a man who had grown up in such an environment, he had a rather idealistic idea about the God-fearing Russian people. So when he started getting to know the people better, after he headed the government and later on, I think it was a revelation to him.

AVEN: I think you're right. And one more important detail: I think that both he and Chubais treated Yeltsin with too much reverence.

KOKH: That's true—although Gaidar was much more sober about Yeltsin at the end of his life.

AVEN: When we first took office, that reverence was a serious obstacle to having our own policy, rather than being an adjunct of Yeltsin. It was necessary to remember always that Yeltsin was nearby, but he was not us.

KOKH: Speaking of Yegor in the last years of his life, I can say that he made a very big impression on me with the stoicism and courage with which he bore his cross.

Actually, there are many more defeats than victories in one's life. That is normal. People should not fear defeats—that is the only way they will become real men.

If you view business as a model of life, when one out of ten projects you start proves viable, that's a good record. Nine are slag. I used to think this was Darwinism, or a universal law of nature, or just human nature. And then I saw an Animal Planet film about predators—it appears they secrete the hormone of happiness very rarely, because they have only one success per ten hunts. So they were angry all the time, and in a lousy mood. But you always take a predator seriously—it's no good joking around with him.

AVEN: I really think he grew a lot.

KOKH: There is one more feature of Yegor that must be noted. He never could break with power. He was attracted to power. He was a statesman.

AVEN: He was absolutely a statesman. He was undoubtedly a great-power nationalist, in every sense of that word. And he was absolutely not a democratic dissident, any more than the rest of us. We, the Gaidar team, were quite prepared to make a career in the USSR—a normal career of economists, scientists, and advisors. In our young years Yegor saw himself as the head of a group of consultants at the Soviet Communist Party Central Committee: "reforms within the possible framework." We were somewhere in the middle between the Soviet party *nomenklatura* and the "democratic psycho public"—the same as most of the academic and creative intellectuals—and that was the democratic public that supported us initially in 1992.

KOKH: Oh yes. But the democratic public rapidly sided with Yavlinsky. It's not that you created a perfect life for them, is it?

AVEN: That's because we weren't them at all. We were not dissidents.

KOKH: Whenever they ask why Yegor kept providing consultations and cooperating with the incumbent anti-democratic regime of KGB colonels, his adherence to great power is the answer. It would be impossible to explain his conduct without that.

Yegor confessed to me a couple of years ago that the beginning of Putin's rule was the happiest period of his time in power. He was a co-leader of the faction of the Union of Right Forces in the State Duma and a deputy chair of the budget committee. He drafted the law on the flat income tax scale, and worked on budget legislation and land laws, and so on. He said that practically all of his initiatives were warmly welcomed and quickly approved: "I was received everywhere, they listened to me, and that was all I had dreamed about my whole life." So, he meant that the work of an advisor suited his temperament and outlook better than the work of a reform organizer and public politician.

AVEN: Now, that is complicated. I think he would have accepted the premier's job if he had been offered it, even now: he was a great-power nationalist and wanted to serve his country. I remember well the year 1993 and his second appointment to a government position. I had intended to discourage him, since they wouldn't let him do anything and it would be bad for his reputation. But when I met him I realized that he badly wanted to return. And he was waiting for my approval—which I gave him, faintheartedly, succumbing to his wish.

KOKH: Maybe. But his chance of return after 1994 was zero—because of his personal qualities, I think. Even the much more pragmatic Mikhail Kasyanov couldn't find a niche for himself in this regime.

AVEN: Yes, intellect, adherence to principles, and an introverted nature were probably his most distinctive features. His personal qualities could make him a leader, but his introverted nature was an impediment. He actually understood people and human relationships, and could build relationships. He could stir enthusiasm in those around him. But that was not enough. A leader must be capable of working with a large number of people, and it was a serious problem for Gaidar that he didn't feel comfortable among strangers. He couldn't be a public politician.

KOKH: Everyone is uncomfortable among strangers.

AVEN: Allow me to disagree. I think Yeltsin felt comfortable in any crowd. I think that a true leader frequently becomes everyone's friend; he forms friendships. Yegor did not have that trait. That was very hard for him. He had to be personally interested in someone to be able to win them over. And he could take an interest only in people of a certain intellectual level. He couldn't be enthusiastic without that interest, and couldn't stir enthusiasm in others; he had no desire to be liked.

That was largely why there were so few of us. We didn't enjoy broad support—that was a weak point of our government.

KOKH: Then I don't understand what you consider a good leader. Give me an example of a good leader. I don't really get Yeltsin's management style.

AVEN: It's not about management style—it's about political style. I think, for instance, that Putin is a natural politician. He has a profound understanding of people, he has no illusions about people, and he has managed to make lots of people his allies. The only question is which goals he sets, what he believes to be good for the country; but in terms of his personal qualities he is an undoubtedly brilliant public politician. His ideals are far from the ideals of the Gaidar team, but Putin is a true leader. He can stretch the truth if necessary—he can speak not only to intellectuals, he can speak to people, he can charm. These are elementary qualities of a political leader. Yegor had no such qualities.

KOKH: There is plenty more to be said about Yegor. Shall we continue sometime later?

AVEN: Gladly. But let's bring in some of our former government members and hold three-way conversations.

KOKH: Terrific. Let's do it.

GENNADY BURBULIS

"Yeltsin Served Us!"

GENNADY BURBULIS WAS THE FOUNDING FATHER of the Gaidar government. He was the link between Yeltsin and Gaidar, the one who made it happen.

Gena is an unemotional, reserved, reasonable, and very sober man. Yet there is concealed passion in him. It manifests itself when he plays soccer. I then played with him, and I can tell you that his manner of playing—powerful, forceful and brisk—reveals a remarkably powerful temperament.

But Gena is a master of his emotions, and it was really difficult to interview him. Petr and I continually provoked him, but he stuck to his guns in his strident voice, and all of our aggressive questioning and our attempts to subvert his demeanor were as ineffectual as mosquito bites.

Petr and I had a good cop–bad cop routine. I was mean, pushy, and played a little dumb. And Petr was rational, sensible, and more even-tempered. We were role playing. But still there was no other way to stir up Gena.

Alfred Kokh

ALFRED KOKH: I have already told you that we are writing a book about Yegor. So we want to speak to members of his government. We shall start with you because you were the founding father of that government.

PETR AVEN: You were somewhere in between Yeltsin and the Gaidar team. You frequently organized our brainstorming meetings. Back then I did not quite understand Yeltsin's attitude toward us and what ours should be toward him. You were much older and knew Yeltsin much better. Let us start with August 1991—our rise to power came as a consequence of the putsch.

So let us begin with Yeltsin and Gaidar.

YELTSIN: TOGETHER AND NEARBY

KOKH: Tell me, did you have any illusions or were your eyes always wide open to Yeltsin?

BURBULIS: I recall the State Duma election in December 1993. In fact, it was the real culmination of our relations. We had to convince Yeltsin to support the Choice of Russia party without any ambiguities. As I already had no possibility of confidential contact or any other influence on Yeltsin, Yegor was supposed to convince him of the need for this support. We had very long and serious discussions and concluded there could be no murkiness. The president must support us, period.

KOKH: Then Yeltsin's ideologists suggested a proposal that the president was the president of all Russians, not just one party. That gave Yeltsin an illusion that he could be above the fray. You considered that a mistake. And did you try to convince him to support you?

BURBULIS: Yes. I said the situation was so important for what we did that we could not have an ambiguous position in the election. On the one hand, we supported the president, and on the other hand, the president turned either his side or his back on us. In short, Yegor met with Yeltsin but achieved nothing.

KOKH: Did he at least say what happened?

BURBULIS: Yegor used a banal cliché: "I have no other president, he is who he is, and there is no other way." Something like that ... My idea was the following: if we jeopardized ourselves with our adherence to these ideas, to Yeltsin, and he did not share that stand or at least give no public support, we should make a different choice. We should participate in the election but without associating ourselves with the ambiguous and, actually, risky position. You all know the results. In my opinion, 1994 was the year of the collapse of Yeltsin as a historic personality.

KOKH: Gena, when did you start working with Yeltsin?

BURBULIS: We met in the election of Soviet people's deputies in 1989. We organized a movement for democratic elections in Sverdlovsk and nominated Yeltsin as a candidate in one of our districts. We came to Moscow to make arrangements, and there already was a group, which set the target: District No. 1, the national district, that is, all of Moscow. It was where he won in the end.

Nevertheless, we started our networking, printed his leaflets, and brought them from Sverdlovsk. We were holding the election campaign in the technological and organizational sense. Our meetings with Yeltsin began ahead of the congress in March and April, and it was when we became personally acquainted. Many did not know Yeltsin when we started forming what soon came to be called the Interregional Group (IG) of deputies. Yeltsin was always rather reserved and did not speak much at heated sessions of the IG, the very complex and heated discussions over forming a collective position, an appeal, or a draft law. As I see it, that was a period of intense learning under totally different circumstances, in a new environment, a period of the radical renovation of Yeltsin's outlook.

At this point I think it is important to mention that Yegor had rather an elevated idea about Yeltsin until the end of 1993. When his regard for Yeltsin ran out, he left. In January 1994.

AVEN: Odd. He did not know Yeltsin in 1989 or in 1990.

KOKH: But from what Gena says about Yeltsin's behavior in 1989, there could be no basis for any kind of regard, or even apologia. There was a man sitting silent and reserved, and so on. When did the regard or rationalizations start?

BURBULIS: Actually, I have never particularly analyzed the causes of this exaltation of Yeltsin by Gaidar. I think Yegor felt that way about Yeltsin for a very long time. Was it first normal human sensitivity? I think Yegor felt extreme respect for Yeltsin's trust in him. It was gratitude for being given the job, appreciation of the trust given to the Gaidar team and the reformist government. In other words, he always was aware of what Yeltsin had done for him.

AVEN: Certainly! He and every one of us were grateful for the chance to realize our ideas, for doing what we believed in.

BURBULIS: And that high respect for Yeltsin was much stronger than even the powerful rational mind that displayed in other situations. Generally, his mind was merciless. Truth and reality were the most important factors for him. At the same time, Yegor was quite unabashed in his self-evaluation. Obviously, he knew his own value. And by any objective standard it was high. He was unique: a combination of good and profound knowledge of a certain system of ideas on the one hand and a willingness to show daring and boldness in their executions, unusual and surprising for a thinking and intellectual person. That is courage.

KOKH: Were you equally charmed by Yeltsin, as overwhelmed by him as Gaidar was?

AVEN: You tell us that Gaidar stuck to Yeltsin, although it was probably politically expedient to act independently in the State Duma election in December 1993. And Yeltsin refused to support the Choice of Russia. Did that change your feelings about him?

BURBULIS: Yeltsin had an animal instinct for power. But I am confident that he constantly needed a moral and intellectual feed, which he could get only from Yegor at that moment. When he lost that source, the cause was lost. But I think it would be an exaggeration to say that Yeltsin made use of us at every turn and that he relied only on those who were essential to him and who displayed stronger skills. Yeltsin was a person of multiple merits, and one of them was his phenomenal, peculiar memory and his very particular frame of mind.

AVEN: When he dismissed you, were you surprised?

BURBULIS: No. We had been working in an environment since the beginning of 1991; the need to sacrifice someone to the cause could occur at any moment.

AVEN: Did you discuss that with Yeltsin?

BURBULIS: Certainly. We called it "political decisions."

AVEN: And how was that formulated?

BURBULIS: Well, I had a "special relationship" with Yeltsin at that time. That was a separate matter.

AVEN: That is why I am asking.

BURBULIS: When we started the presidential election campaign—that was in spring 1991—where we had a firm agreement that Yeltsin would be the president and I, Burbulis, would be the vice president. Everyone who had the slightest knowledge of the situation was aware of that. Then the last day comes for the presidential candidate to name his vice president to the electoral commission, and Yeltsin called for me in the evening. I entered the room and he said, "Gennady Eduardovich, here is the situation. I have come to a conclusion, I have been thinking for a long time. There is a risk. Since you are a good man—"

AVEN: What risk? He had a 90 percent rating!

BURBULIS: No, no. "There is a risk, so I have fears."

AVEN: He gained over 64 percent. What risk? He could have gained slightly less, 54 percent for instance. What is the difference? And Rutskoi hardly brought him 10 percent.

BURBULIS: I said, "Well, you may be right, but who will take my place?" Yeltsin said, "I want Rutskoi." Certainly I felt terrible. I told him, "We will try to win the election, I will do my best. But you are making a mistake and we will be paying for it for a long time and with much difficulty." A risk of defeat? There was no such risk.

KOKH: Yeltsin was a shrewd politician! I give him credit: "Why make him the vice president if he works for me just the same?" If you had said that you felt free to move away and would stop working for him, he would have made you the vice president. He saw through us all. And Gaidar too.

AVEN: You were in shock. You were much older than us, you were 46. Was it a surprise and an unexpected thing to you? People did not do that in the circle you used to deal with!

BURBULIS: Perhaps. After all we had been through and had done. But you presume that to serve Yeltsin was more important for Yegor, for me, for many of us than maintaining a set of views, convictions and ideas. In fact it was the other way around: it was not us, it was Yeltsin who served as an irreplaceable, inspired mechanism toward an ideal. It was not service to Yeltsin. In the end, he was serving us.

AVEN: I would say it appeared in the end that we served him.

BURBULIS: No!

AVEN: Yes. And he abandoned us. He actually did that twice to you, Gena. He let you down again! There was a moment. After you were shoved away from the vice presidency, you worked for less than a year and then he tricked you again, that time with the position of state secretary.

BURBULIS: In the profound and complex fight between the old and the new, which is rooted in centuries of Russian history, how can one take the position personally? There was no possibility of doing anything without Yeltsin.

KOKH: Gena, we are deliberately provoking you. It may seem that we feel negative about Yeltsin, but we value and love him. He gave us a chance for self-realization. But I am interested in your motives. You say you were implementing a certain concept of the salvation and liberation of Russia, its modernization. An idea.

BURBULIS: To live normally.

KOKH: And Yeltsin looked like the only route to achieving this goal. Why did not you not consider another route: the building of a political party, the winning of a majority in elections, and the nomination of your own president? And you staked it all on a man born in the village of Butka in 1931 who had a successful career as an apparatchik and who was more comfortable with Rutskoi than with you. You were not close to him. You did not speak the same language! Yes, both of you thought you were making use of the other. But it appeared that Yeltsin used you, and you did not use him.

BURBULIS: I think you are wrong. We managed to do a lot. That the events could have taken another turn is another matter. As for your just reproach, actually I think that our lack of understanding and will for creating a new political structure was the most serious mistake of 1991–3. The most serious mistake. And I discussed that many times with Yeltsin. It is clear to me now that we should have continued without him in 1993, as soon as he isolated himself from us. We could have been with him in 1991, when our government got going. But not after it.

AVEN: How could you have gone on without Yeltsin in 1993 if his government still had Chubais, Gaidar, Shokhin, Boris Fyodorov? You had to go on without Chubais and Gaidar. That is the point.

KOKH: And that was impossible. It appeared that Gaidar's return to the government in the fall of 1993 guaranteed Yeltsin that Gaidar would not participate independently in the election in December 1993. And when the danger disappeared after the election, he calmly and bureaucratically forced him out of the government in January.

AVEN: I have the impression that Yeltsin was very cynical and calculating about us. In fact, that is only natural for a true political leader. And, actually, what you have portrayed here, Gena, is a typical relationship between a weak intellectual, with his ideas on relations, decency and fatherland, and a totally cynical fighter for power. He was doing that all his life.

BURBULIS: No, Yeltsin was more complex than that. His personality, his nature, his conduct, his particular actions.

AVEN: He always took the side that was advantageous personally to him or, the way he understood it, was beneficial for the cause. As Yumashev recounted in his memoirs, Yeltsin cried, "I was tormented, worried." But he fired anyone as soon as he deemed that expedient! You were his right-hand man. The main assistant at the most difficult moments of his accession to power. He bumped you first out of the vice presidency, although you had an agreement, formal and discussed many times, and then in spring 1992 he ousted you from power completely.

KOKH: Gena says now that Yeltsin was different after 1993. As if it was not obvious when he was dumping you.

AVEN: I started to understand something in spring 1992 when that discussion of whom to give up and whom not to give up began. Gaidar brought some lists from Yeltsin. He told us nothing; it was Golovkov who told us who the president wanted out. That came as a shock to me. I thought we were one team, us and Yeltsin. And it appeared that Yeltsin and we were two totally different worlds. Did you come to realize that earlier than me? You were older. And you learned about him earlier than us. And he had already thrown you out by the time you were helping him to form our government. That happened just a few months earlier.

KOKH: Yeltsin threw away Gorbachev like a dog. Even without a pension. And it was Gorbachev who brought him from Yekaterinburg and actually made him the master of Moscow. He did not destroy him completely—he gave him a job at Gosstroy.[1]

AVEN: I do not condemn Yeltsin. A true leader cannot be sentimental. He has to think about the country, rather than about the feelings of his employees. What surprises and disappoints me is that we had no clear understanding of that at the time. But why was Gaidar so sentimental about Yeltsin?

KOKH: He threw out Chubais twice! But Chubais loved him even more. He was in heaven when he was called back. And he gave long and confused explanations and said it was all right when he was thrown out.

BURBULIS: I will tell you two stories now. Don't think I am so sentimental, but they mean a lot for my understanding of Yeltsin. These stories are unique. One had no witnesses, and the other was witnessed by Mikhail Sergeyevich Gorbachev. The first happened in summer 1991, before his speech at the Twenty-Eighth (the last) Congress of the Soviet Communist Party, where Yeltsin planned to announce his withdrawal from the party. He was already the president. It was around midnight; there were just two of us. And he needed to think it over again and to decide what he would say and how he would do it. He was not just tormented over his coming speech. He was very perturbed by what he was about to do. He was confused, he was at a loss. And he said, without concealing anything, "But it raised me!" He meant the party. He was breast-fed by the party, like a baby is breast-fed by his mother. And it was a torture to see him really suffering.

KOKH: And here is a different interpretation. He might well have been suffering, but he was also well aware that his future political career was possible only outside of the party. What is more, the party was finished, that was why he had to quit. He was suffering, he took it hard, the party looked after him but he washed his hands of them like he did to other people and other parties later on.

A truly suffering man, being aware that the party was finished, would nevertheless have made the decision not to quit, because he would have wanted to help the party revive as a democratic organization.

BURBULIS: I will finish my story about the situation and the experience I

---

1. State Committee for Construction.

shared with him. I saw a man capable of very deep emotions, an extremely sincere man in that situation. There was no need to pretend in front of me, but the degree and scale of what he was planning were easily read on his face. He was not suffering publicly, although he could play any role, tragedy or comedy, perfectly in public. This particular dilemma—his decision to leave the party—something deep inside him. That was impossible to miss if you saw Yeltsin at such moments.

KOKH: Certainly I believe that he was suffering. But he was guided by reason, not by sincere feeling. All that suffering is worthless if it comes from simple calculation of benefit.

BURBULIS: Here is the second story. The attempted coup in August 1991 was over; Gorbachev was brought back and taken to a rally and, on the next day, to a meeting of the Supreme Soviet. You may remember that Gorbachev came to the Supreme Soviet meeting and Yeltsin humiliated him in front of the whole world by forcing him to sign a decree on the disbanding of the Soviet Communist Party. That was a cruel and malevolent act. The whole of Yeltsin's predatory nature was there, his wolfhound instincts. The Supreme Soviet meeting ends.

AVEN: And did you discuss it beforehand, his conduct?

BURBULIS: We did discuss the need to disband the Soviet Communist Party, but we did not discuss the way he did it. After the Supreme Soviet meeting we went to Yeltsin's office—Gorbachev and I with our wives. I was stunned at what then happened. Yeltsin started in a roundabout way, "Gorbachev! We have been through a lot, such events, and such shocks! You had a hard time in Foros and we did not know how that putsch would end, and our family and Raisa Maximovna, we all worried so much." And then he said, "Let us have a family dinner!" Yeltsin says that to Gorbachev! "Naina Iosifovna, Raisa Maximovna." Yeltsin offered a family dinner to Gorbachev. After the shock of the unbelievable trial they had been through.

AVEN: What did Gorbachev say?

BURBULIS: Gorbachev gave him such a look. And I realized that it was a simply unthinkable proposal. Yeltsin had just humiliated him, and then there was such openness, such friendliness and warmth. Gorbachev said, "No, we cannot do that now. We should not." And Yeltsin immediately froze, and then he got it! He must have forgotten what he had done in public just a few minutes ago. And here he was, full of gentleness and even some humbleness.

"No, we cannot do that, we should not." Gorbachev must have understood that his wife, Raisa Maximovna, would never agree to a dinner with the Yeltsins. But here was Yeltsin—entirely gentle and cordial. I saw that rush of emotion as almost childish, almost naive.

KOKH: Or maybe he wanted to keep torturing him while sharing a cup of tea at home? Or, probably, he felt nothing, but that it was all a comedy played out for the deputies, the cameras, and you and Gorbachev?

I was always amazed by Nemtsov. We met at live televised programs several times and had hard clashes with our opponents, among them Rogozin.[2] We cursed on TV, and Rogozin demanded we be imprisoned and executed. I was very emotional and it took me a very long time to calm down. But Nemtsov and Rogozin would chitchat and drink coffee as soon as the program ended and we were back to the makeup room. I was always amazed with that. It was all theater. And it was unclear where the theater was: when he drank coffee with you or when he called for killing you. And Yeltsin just dipped the man in shit and then said, "And let us come to my place, spend some time together, eat cucumbers and mushrooms and drink some vodka."

AVEN: "And we will execute you tomorrow. But it will be fine, it won't hurt. In a comradely way, yes? Just like we communists do."

BURBULIS: Let me explain once again. I did not work for Yeltsin. I followed the program of my life, my strategy, and my own viewpoint.

AVEN: I disagree. If it happened the way you describe it now, and you speak very reasonably, very correctly and courageously, then you would have had your own political party. But you worked for Yeltsin.

BURBULIS: You will not find the truth if you hold to events and facts and fail to understand the tissue of human life, human relationships, and feelings of every person. Gaidar, Yeltsin, Burbulis.

---

2.   Dmitry Olegovich Rogozin, diplomat and politician, became deputy prime minister in charge of the defense industry.

The Appearance of Gaidar

AVEN: How did Gaidar show up? Why was he Yeltsin's choice? We have our own theories. I can tell you what they are so that we can decide whether to stick to them or not.

First, I think that Yeltsin needed something completely new. He did not need the old Gosplan traditional reformers: Skokov, Popov, Abalkin. He was a grand man and he realized that those times were gone. There were two new personalities, Yavlinsky and Gaidar. I think that he chose Gaidar because—No, I won't tell you. You tell me. Why did he choose Gaidar?

BURBULIS: Something new? It just happened that something new was chosen. And by the process of Yeltsin's choice, the process of his grasp of the situation and its evaluation, it was certainly not the choice between the old and the young but between the essence and the exterior.

AVEN: Correct. I did not mean age when I said new! It was the question of new ideas rather than the age of their carriers. If the new ideas were borne by a 60-year-old academician, he would have picked him, no problem. Is that correct?

BURBULIS: Here is the situation. There is the reproach of Yeltsin (and me) repeated for the hundredth time that Yeltsin in September 1991, after the GKChP, went to Sochi. He should have stayed in Moscow, dismissed the Supreme Soviet, liquidated local councils, and created a new political system based on the then strong support of the people.

In fact, the situation was extreme because our heritage was monstrous. And Yeltsin understood that well. In spite of his sybaritic habits, he had the knack of a party manager. He knew better and more precisely than anyone else how much milk a region produced, how much a loaf of bread cost in another region, what the average salary was in a third region, and how many available homes there were in a fourth region. He knew the dynamics also, and was a master of the details too. With his grasp of detail he could easily demonstrate his special erudition to professionals.

The country was on its way to collapse. It appeared that we had the power but not the resources to solve everyday problems—how to feed people, how to heat their homes, and how to save the country. The Union government broke down, and the Russian government was partially transformed into a quasi-Union government named the Interrepublican Committee, led by Silayev and Yavlinsky. And that committee was not capable, either, no matter what Yavlinsky might say now, post factum. In fact, and we must be clear about this, the country had no government. Neither republican nor Union.

The situation was also aggravated by the fact that the Russian Federation never had a government. Russia was the only Union republic without its own economic authorities. Only 7 percent of economic relations were the area of the RSFSR[3] government, and the rest belonged to the Union. And that situation of power without power, responsibility without resources, could not last for ever. We had to form a capable government rapidly. And, in the middle of all this, Yeltsin goes to Sochi. True, we agreed before he left that we would be considering some radical proposals. And then Gaidar began his work.

KOKH: And why not Yavlinsky?

BURBULIS: Yavlinsky was Silayev's vice premier in 1990. That was when we were pushing his 500 Days program through Union structures and signed the Gorbachev–Yeltsin declaration; in short, it was before our—Yeltsin's—presidency. I was holding endless negotiations with Nikolai Ivanovich Ryzhkov, that was before Valentin Pavlov. But by September 1991, Yavlinsky had moved to Gorbachev's set-up and his actions were no longer relevant.

So, we begin. We met with Yegor for the first time in August; Ilyushin had told me several times there was a group that could be of interest. … We started to formulate tasks. When a more or less lucid document came to Dacha 15, where the Gaidar team was housed, we discussed it at the State Council and brought it to Yeltsin in Sochi.

AVEN: Were there any alternative documents?

BURBULIS: No, there were not. I did spot you there but I am told now that did not happen. Back then they said that he was nominated by Yeltsin. But that is not so. I am perfectly aware of Yeltin's attitude toward Yavlinsky. He would not have even considered his candidacy.

AVEN: Didn't you nominate Yavlinsky?

BURBULIS: No. I went there to nominate Gaidar!

AVEN: And Yavlinsky told *Forbes* that you offered him the job before Gaidar. And you do not remember that; how is that possible? He asked you two

---

3.   Russian Soviet Federative Socialist Republic.

questions: "Will that be Russia or the Union?" You said there would be no Union. There would be just Russia. And there was also one more thing that did not suit him.

BURBULIS: I could not have offered Yavlinsky that job because that job was different. Yavlinsky was incapable of it. I knew from the start he could not do it. But now back to Gaidar. So, I went to Sochi. I took Yeltsin the drafts from Dacha 15. Everyone was waiting to see what would happen, counting the hours, not days. Gorbachev even published a sort of memorandum, "Burbulis went to deliver documents suggesting how to break up the Soviet Union," as if the Soviet Union still existed. It was gone after the August events, after the putsch attempt. One should not tell stories about breaking up the country, which was already nonexistent 20 years after.

BURBULIS: So, our search was not "to be or not to be the Soviet Union" but what to do and what not to do in the situation in which we found ourselves. Then came events seen and heard by no one. There were three of us. There was also Korzhakov, who brought us food and proposed entertainment from time to time.

AVEN: What kind of entertainment?

BURBULIS: Like tennis, steam baths. And then I saw another Yeltsin, one no one else had ever seen in such a state. "What do you propose?" "Here it is. We have no other way out but to undertake the entire responsibility for the Russian Federation, but that responsibility implies concentration of the entire capabilities of the Russian Federation. What shall we do about the republics? We will cooperate mildly, we have no food or drink for them. The configuration is entirely different."

What was good was that Gaidar's papers backed up ideas with particular steps and instruments. A law—a decree, a decree—a law, a resolution. And it was all clear what was proposed and how it could be done. We went through it for the first time. Yeltsin, said, "I can't do that. How is that possible? Is that the only way?" "That is the only way." "Is there any other possibility?" "No." And day after day, as we squandered our time in endless discussions, these other possibilities were vanishing into thin air. But finally Yeltsin said, "If there is no other way, let us do it."

AVEN: And did you decide from the beginning there was no alternative?

BURBULIS: That is my impression; I think it is precise and substantial. There are situations in which one does not choose from a spectrum of possibilities but decides when the choice is so limited that it is actually the question of what cannot be done. I mean, you could either do it or not do it; we did not have a choice. We had to!

AVEN: That is what we were talking about. That at first a reformer has to do things that are strictly determined and are not a part of the original concept.

BURBULIS: Yavlinsky was completely unable to understand that: he always said he would do only what he wanted instead of what was necessary. So, the critical situation was clearly defined by the Yegor team and it coincided with Yeltsin's rational thinking. A precise, clear, and dynamic task and its solution. But there was no decision concerning Yegor personally at that time. It all happened later on, when Yegor met him.

AVEN: So you left Sochi without a decision about Gaidar?

BURBULIS: Certainly, without a decision. I told Yeltsin, "When you come to Moscow, you will meet him."

AVEN: And who, apart from Yegor, was a possible candidate for the reform leader—Yevgeny Fyodorovich Saburov?

BURBULIS: No, no. Saburov was no longer an option.

AVEN: Then who? Yavlinsky? Or did you not discuss personalities at all?

BURBULIS: There are different stories around now. Some speak about Yuri Vladimirovich Skokov, some about Oleg Ivanovich Lobov, and some about Yavlinsky. I don't rule out that Yeltsin might have discussed someone or other with somebody else. But not with me. Because I had only one candidate, Gaidar, and that for me ruled out any other names. I brought his reform plan and told Yeltsin that he should meet with Gaidar and speak to the team and its leader. There was no doubt that Gaidar was the leader of that team.

AVEN: And Alexander Nikolayevich Shokhin says you asked him to lead the economic bloc. Isn't that so?

BURBULIS: Well, maybe, in the Silayev government, after Yavlinsky was gone. I cannot remember now.

But here is a lyrical and historical question. Why did Yeltsin choose Gaidar? I think that the final stimulus, the motive for his decision, was Yeltsin's personal meeting with Gaidar. Yeltsin, a man with a certain psychology, grace, and inner strength, meets a man who was not inferior to him by his own standards. That came as a psychological blow for Yeltsin.

He saw a young talent who presented his views calmly and very clearly, in contrast with the variety of unintelligible ignoramuses loading him with self-serving chatter over the past 18 months. He was now hearing from Gaidar convincing answers to the most difficult questions, and, above all, a list of measures to be taken.

So, the first explanation for choosing Gaidar was content. The second, and no less important one, was that Yeltsin had an eye for what I'd call social depth. He looked inside a person. And thirdly, they had a common memory: "our Sverdlovsk roots": that was a rare case of bonding. They were from the same land, from one volcanic rock, from one root. Besides, Yegor was romantic. All that utopianism, myths of Bolshevik boldness, and service to the same idea, they were all in that boy. The historical-cultural and socio-romantic codes pressed into a single whole. And Yeltsin might have imagined—we had a bit of discussion later on—how wonderful the combination of substance and passion would sound to the people and how welcome that would be.

KOKH: And did Yeltsin frequently meet with educated and smart people capable of clearly expressing their ideas? Yegor had a fresh style of oratory, colorful and graphic. Bureaucrats did not talk like that. Was that a cultural shock for Yeltsin, who mostly communicated with apparatchiks?

BURBULIS: I don't know about shock, but he was charmed. And then there was the trust and bond that came with mentoring. He felt a closeness to Yegor.

When problems did arise and decisions needed to be made quickly, he often told Yegor to act and distanced himself from the decision. That too was a way of expressing confidence. As soon as Yegor came onto the scene, Yeltsin claimed often that he was tired and didn't stay tuned in to the essence of a problem for long. That was surprising for me, but I was even more surprised that Yegor accepted this situation very quickly. He had no experience then. We planned, we would consider tasks, formulate instruments for their achievement, hold detailed discussions and make decisions together with Yeltsin. But before long he would simply tell us, "Come on, get on with it." There were instances in which we needed his input badly but got nothing except silence in reply to our pleas. And, I repeat, Yegor accepted this position very quickly.

AVEN: Yeltsin probably felt that he would be meddling with Gaider's decisions. And thought it would be better this way?

KOKH: He simply realized quickly that there would be big minuses in addition to big pluses, in particular, in terms of popularity. So he quickly distanced himself. He could then easily get rid of the team with the snap of a finger and save himself. After all, Yeltsin was a great politician.

BURBULIS: I must say that Yeltsin really worked full steam when he grasped tasks that required enormous mental concentration. But he got tired very quickly. And his weariness with detail revealed itself very quickly. He would draw a line between "bookworms" and "enforcers." "Bookworm" was not a pejorative term, it meant an intellectual, a person not given to simplifying. Enforcers did not necessarily have military rank; they were people with mobilizational skills, people who favored a command system to get things done. At a certain point during his presidency, when we were seeking answers to the questions of how to hold power and how to handle power and how to fulfill our popular mandate, he would increasingly rely on enforcers. That was when dangerous sinecures started. They had the joy of power without the burden of duties. Your friend Nemtsov contributed to this climate of enforcer power in a shameful way. "Tsar Boris" this, "Tsar Boris" that. This became Nemtsov's vocabulary, which he used like a lackey, hoping to be the successor.

DÉMARCHES AND RESIGNATIONS

AVEN: Let us recall our démarche of government resignation in April 1992. I have already said that we were young and had little experience when we took office, and we regarded Yeltsin as our father and patron. We thought the same about Burbulis. I also think that Yegor had more complex feelings about Gena.

This may seem odd today, but it came as a shock to us when we learned about the attack on the government, and Yeltsin's basic consent, under pressure from the Supreme Soviet and the directors, to fire some of Gaidar's ministers. Fuel and Energy Minister Lopukhin, Health Minister Vorobyov, me, and somebody else were on that list.

The position of the directors of large state plants was expressed by Arkady Ivanovich Volsky, the head of his Union of Industrialists and Entrepreneurs. Back then he was a media favorite, and was treated like sort of a guru who openly claimed to know how to lead the country out of the crisis.

Actually, the shock passed rather quickly, but I was in a foul mood. Now I realize that my idea of Yeltsin was totally inadequate; I thought he was the patriarch who would fight for us until his own resignation. I understand now that we were totally unprepared for being used as a bargaining chip so easily: "I will fire this man and you do this in exchange, and now I fire that man and you won't raise that question."

In that period I met Gaidar daily, and I can say that he was very upset. Then, at a certain moment when we understood that we were being given up, we abruptly tendered our resignations. I have my own theory about when and how we decided to do that. But the most important point was that we did not warn Burbulis, who was practically our boss and father of the Gaidar team. I think that was a big surprise for Yeltsin.

But I think he might have liked our surprise for its boldness. We didn't feel that we shouldn't do it because he might not like it. We were right; his reaction was not harsh, although he fired Lopukhin rather quickly after that.

That was the only case when we were so decisive. But Yeltsin's readiness to fire us under pressure opened the first crack in our relationship. We realized that we were not united. That was a very important lesson for me. Gena, could you tell us your story, your experience of that situation?

BURBULIS: We are talking about the April 7 congress of RSFSR people's deputies. They were having a loud and heated discussion of the first results of our work. I must say that, in the corridors, Yegor explained rather actively and convincingly the problems we had, what we were doing, what decisions were possible, and what urgent measures were necessary. Hence it was obvious that all the serious questions would not start a grand discussion: no one could offer a serious alternative to our course. There were emotions, shouts, and pleas. We realized that those circumstances created a big problem for Yeltsin—what to do at the congress: there was nothing to discuss, but the congress needed outward signs of obedience, certain public concessions.

But things solved themselves. There was a famous episode: Ruslan Khasbulatov said something like, "Why are they so upset? The kids are afraid we will scold them, let us be lenient ..." It was a classic insult.

AVEN: You stood up, and we followed suit.

BURBULIS: Yes. And we left the congress.

KOKH: "Lost their heads." That was what he actually said: "Lost their heads."

BURBULIS: Correct. And the government tendered its resignation on April 13. I like that episode very much, although it also made me shudder, because the decision was made and the position was declared in my absence. I think now that was an interesting, daring, and finally correct move, considering the stakes.

AVEN: What was the effect?

BURBULIS: The effect was the compromise stand of the congress. It led to the decision to add the so-called practitioners to the government—Shumeiko, Khizha, and Chernomyrdin. And it was confirmed, by the way, by Yeltsin that we would carry on the policy of reforms, and that Gaidar would pursue it; and in July, before visiting the US, Yeltsin signed a decree appointing Gaidar as acting premier.

But let us go back to the so-called government surrender. I remember our bargaining with Khasbulatov about Yeltsin's concessions that would make the congress tolerant of us. When we agreed that economic executives would come and Lopukhin would go, the name of Chernomyrdin was already pulsating in Yeltsin's head. It came from the corridors in the Soviet Communist Party Central Committee.

And my resignation happened this way. One evening Yeltsin and I—

AVEN: Did you feel some coolness, or did it come unexpectedly—just like that?

BURBULIS: What coolness? They had a chat with Khasbulatov. Yeltsin came out approximately an hour later. That was an odd situation for our kind of relationship. He came out and said, "Gennady Eduardovich, speak to Ruslan Imranovich, he has something to tell you." I came in and Khasbulatov told me, "See, we have agreed with Yeltsin that you need to resign. That will help our future work. At least the government will have more options."

KOKH: Classic Yeltsin. Letting Khasbulatov do the explanations.

BURBULIS: When we left the congress, Yeltsin was angry with me that evening: "What did you do that for?" I told him, "First of all, that was an impromptu act, it would have been hard to plan that. Second, that was the reaction to the stress accumulated over many months."

AVEN: And why was he so eager to come to terms with them? I just don't get it. What could they do? He had popular support. Even a year after, when the reform consequences pulled down his rating, he easily defeated them in the referendum. He could dismiss them easily. The reforms had just started—everyone still loved him. Why did he react that way? Why did he calmly watch us leave? Why did he give up his closest advisor—you? And why did he have those endless conversations with Khasbulatov?

KOKH: That was very strange but also very characteristic of Yeltsin. Do you remember his long fight for Khasbulatov as Supreme Soviet chairman?

BURBULIS: First of all, I never had problems with Yeltsin. We discussed the possibility of my resignation many times—if it was necessary for our cause.

AVEN: That's demagoguery. "If, then." Don't tell us that now! What was there to discuss? Certainly you would leave if that were necessary. That was clear by default. So, you were still working after the congress. And then Yeltsin fired you in May or June. And what actually was the last pretext for the resignation?

BURBULIS: That I personified radical anti-communism.

KOKH: Personified the liberated woman of the highlands—

BURBULIS: Alfred! Cut it out! So on April 13, two days after our demonstrative departure from the congress, Gaidar announced that the government would resign. The deputies appeared to be unprepared for that. They realized that there was actually no alternative to what the government was doing. They simply did not like personalities. They didn't fit the apparatchik's idea of a government. But they had no apparatchik replacement for those "laboratory heads" adequate to the task. Still, deputies didn't want to look like supporters of "predatory reforms" in the eyes of the population. They wanted to be re-elected—and that, in their opinion, required an image of opponents of the "anti-people" government.

AVEN: Yegor did not want to go. He said we should hang on until the congress banished us, and make the reforms irreversible in the meantime.

Yegor did not want that resignation—it was not his idea.

KOKH: Whose was it?

AVEN: As far as I remember, it was Shokhin's and mine. Then I spoke to Chubais, and Chubais met with Gaidar and convinced him. After that Gaidar gathered everyone but Gena and said there was this idea.

BURBULIS: Certainly, Yeltsin's reaction was very nervous. He could not understand what he should do.

AVEN: There was a compromise with the deputies. Gaidar relaxed the monetary policy, which was extremely harmful but was wanted by the directors and deputies, and the government got a deferral, a break. Yeltsin didn't expect that, but we stayed to work, except for Lopukhin and Burbulis.

I think that our resignation démarche contributed to the firing of Gennady. Yeltsin realized finally that, in spite of the influence and the important role of Gena, Gaidar, not he, was the natural leader of the team. And that resignation made Gaidar stronger.

KOKH: Then why did he relax the monetary policy, if he was stronger?

AVEN: Those were parallel processes. No matter how strange it may sound, the compromises made Yegor stronger. He retracted no fundamentals—convertible ruble, free-market pricing, private property, and "grand" privatization—although the pressure was very strong. And he really matured over that summer. But, certainly, the relaxation of the monetary policy was a rotten compromise. It cost the country a lot.

So let us go back to Gena's resignation. I repeat: I am confident that the strengthening of Gaidar was a result of that resignation. Gena, am I right?

BURBULIS: Right, right. What's more, I think Yeltsin established a dialogue with Yegor, and I realized that my firing would not be fatal for the team. It came as a relief for me, because my role was to provide political and ideological communication between Yeltsin and the government. To a large extent, I also personally assumed responsibility for certain actions and steps to spare professional ministers the daily strain we lived under.

AVEN: Here is the explanation of the relaxation of monetary policy. Gena was a shield protecting us from attacks, to an extent. And then he was gone.

KOKH: Do you mean Gaidar overestimated his ability to resist the pressure of Yeltsin and the Supreme Soviet? That Gena was firmer?

AVEN: Certainly.

KOKH: When he came face-to-face with that pressure, Yegor gave in. True, he tightened the policy again by fall. Or was it the pressure that had weakened?

AVEN: No, it is just that everyone realized hyperinflation was better than money deficit.

BURBULIS: I think the maneuvering to relax monetary policy was rather justified. We could not have permitted the collapse of the congress and the government!

KOKH: Or, probably, we should have forced the conflict to a head right away, instead of doing our best to delay it until October 1993, when it developed into an armed confrontation. Gena, you said that the congress should have been dismissed after the GKChP, and new elections should have been held!

BURBULIS: No, I said there were such considerations ...

KOKH: And what do you think: Should that have been done or not?

BURBULIS: I was thinking: How can we dismiss them if they supported us against the GKChP? We all stuck together! Deputies, Khasbulatov, Rutskoi, Yeltsin ...

KOKH: And you opposed that idea?

BURBULIS: I never discussed it seriously. We were blamed for that later ...
AVEN: It seems to me now that the inevitability of the head-to-head confrontation must have been clear already in spring 1992. And we should have known how it would end up in October 1993.

KOKH: Certainly. We should have built up tension constantly, like our demonstrative resignation did; and instead we gave them 18 months to organize themselves, to form their structures and combat units, and to appoint their leaders ...

AVEN: That was true, but we also gained 18 months for reforms, and that was important. Though Gaidar resigned at the end of 1992—and, soon after that, some other ministers, including me.

BURBULIS: For a long time, Yeltsin did not react emotionally to a situation—and then came the explosion, and he would spring into reflex action and start seeking graphic and brutal solutions. The resignations helped him reach the compromises he wanted, and that he expected would stabilize the situation. I think he thought the guys would keep working away, that we would replace some of them with industrialists, practitioners, amend the fiscal policy a bit, and that passions would calm down. But it was not that easy …

KOKH: The road to hell is paved with good intentions. Alas, that is a cliché. There are all kinds of compromises. But how can one differentiate?

THE DISINTEGRATION OF THE USSR

KOKH: Okay, let's change the subject. Gena, tell us about Belovezh and its global and historical significance.

AVEN: Right, Gena. Remember the eve of your trip to Belovezh, just the day before, there were negotiations with Antall, the Hungarian prime minister. We were sitting side by side, and you were drawing charts of the new community. One chart presented practically a single state—the union of Russia, Ukraine, and Belarus, and probably Kazakhstan. The other chart presented a softer structure including everyone else (with the exception of the Baltic republics, of course). Then, a few days later, we saw there was no chart at all. How did that happen? How unexpected was that? The main legend in the public mind is that Kravchuk stood firm—no deals—and it ended the way it did. Is that true or not?

BURBULIS: This is not a legend. This is a "humano-historical" truth. Actually, the realization ripened slowly that there was a need for a serious and substantive meeting to answer the main question of the legal form of sovereignty of the former republics of the Soviet Union.

    A key point was the swamp of the Novo-Ogaryovo process.[4] It seemed

---

4.   The ill-fated "Nine-Plus-One" treaty or "Treaty of the Union of Sovereign States" was a draft treaty that would have replaced the Soviet Union with a new entity named the Union of Sovereign States. The preparation of this treaty was

to me sometimes that Gorbachev's agreement in Novo-Ogaryovo resembled the putsch of August 1991. I was the Russian coordinator of that process, and we took the outcome very seriously. Our seriousness was demonstrated in our securing the preconditions for bilateral relationships, starting from November 1990.

KOKH: Was that the year before Gaidar?

BURBULIS: Yes, and by the end of 1991 we already had bilateral agreements with Ukraine, Kazakhstan, Belarus.

KOKH: In short, you had some collateral documents to preserve a certain fabric of cooperation in case the Union broke down?

BURBULIS: Not even that. I would say they were more technological. We told Gorbachev, "We are drafting an agreement on the renewed Union. Treat this as a useful and very important process: the republics have started talking to one another: bilateral obligations, bilateral interest, and bilateral responsibility. We should rely on that!"

AVEN: That was how you sweet-talked him? He must have realized that bilateral relations between republics essentially excluded the role of the federal center. That was obvious.

BURBULIS: What sweet talk? Everything was more or less clear. We adhered to the concept "nine and that is it" in Novo-Ogaryovo. And he wanted "nine plus one," which means in this scheme the Union center remained as an important factor of the new agreement.

AVEN: So you wanted to liquidate the Union center from the start?

BURBULIS: Yes! Yes!

KOKH: This means it was a myth that you came to Belovezh without a plan to break up the Soviet Union, and that the idea to denounce the Union agreement popped up at the negotiations and did not come from the Russian

---

known as the Novo-Ogaryovo process, named after Novo-Ogaryovo, a governmental estate where the work on the document was carried out and where Gorbachev talked with leaders of Union republics.

delegation? From what you say, you set the objective of Union disintegration at least a year before it was actually liquidated?

AVEN: Another interesting point is mentioned by Gorbachev's assistant Chernyayev in his memoirs. Yeltsin maintained his consent to the presence of the center until fall 1991. He said the center would exist, and the only question was what it would do. The idea of the full liquidation of Gorbachev and the center as a class was never expressed publicly. That was a cunning move: to support with words and to break up with deeds.

KOKH: Gorbachev told me that just yesterday. He thinks they simply pulled him around by the nose.

BURBULIS: Just a minute. I want us to differentiate between two things. First, the formation of the concept of the renewed Union agreement. That is what the Novo-Ogaryovo process was.

AVEN: There was no agreement in the end.

KOKH: Petr, don't you understand? That is simple: there was the Novo-Ogaryovo process. And it had nothing to do with Belovezh.

BURBULIS: That is not true! There was a direct link!

KOKH: Then why was there no Gorbachev in Belovezh?

AVEN: Because they understood their union as an association without a center. In those days, Russia spoke about a confederation.

KOKH: But that was not the Novo-Ogaryovo process. The Novo-Ogaryovo process had a center!

BURBULIS: Let me explain once again. We should not forget about the main motive of GKChP members. They rejected the Novo-Ogaryovo agreement that had been prepared for signing. That is, the Novo-Ogaryovo process was doomed; the center itself did not support it—with the sole exception of Gorbachev.

KOKH: Gorbachev gave me details. He certainly blamed the GKChP for the disintegration of the Soviet Union. If not for the putsch, the Novo-Ogaryovo agreement would have been signed on August 20. And then he would have tightened his grip, and everything would have been all right. But what you are saying changes my idea of the world very seriously. Because, in my opinion, the course toward the dismantling of the Soviet Union was taken by the presidents of all republics, among them Yeltsin, after the GKChP. And it appeared that you started doing that in November 1991, when the Soviet Union was quite capable, and even pursued monetary reform in April 1991, which was impossible to do without power.

AVEN: Gena! Just be straight with us. Why did you decide you did not need Gorbachev? Just be honest. You and Shakhrai must have made the decision before Yeltsin did. You were younger; it was easier for you to sever that bond. You can be frank now—it all happened 20 years ago. Mind, we are not judging you. That was probably a good decision.

BURBULIS: When we saw within the course of a year that the Congress of Soviet People's Deputies was inadequate to the tasks we were facing, and preparations began for elections to the RSFRS congress in 1990, then we had to adopt a new strategy. We had to do that because the congress did not support the ideas of the Interregional Group of deputies, and Gorbachev continued his dangerous maneuvering between wishes and practical steps. And since the aggressively obedient majority of the congress maintained the illusion of its might while the country was sliding into a total crisis, we made it our strategy to concentrate on the Russian Federation. Yeltsin was elected as RSFRS head, the Supreme Soviet chairman, in May 1990. That was the culmination of the new strategy we were discussing and implementing in the complex trench-fighting inside Russia.

I emphasize that we realized in November 1990 that the Union no longer had the serious capability for timely and adequate reactions to the gravest problems in every republic, and the whole country. It was necessary to feel our way to a new legal and administrative reality, with bilateral agreements. Nobody rushed to say the Union was doomed. We realized that we would need a new Union agreement. No one made specific proposals about its form—a federation, a confederation, or an association.

Here is an important detail: our group organized the presentation of Andrei Dmitriyevich Sakharov's draft constitution at the Union congress. I say that so you do not jump to the conclusion that we were strategists with the original idea of dismantling the USSR.

AVEN: No one is condemning you. Everything is clear. And how would you sign the Union agreement in Gorbachev's version? It preserved the Union authority and the position of the Union president?

BURBULIS: The agreement made that position purely ornamental. And Gorbachev was perfectly aware of that.

KOKH: Gena! Do you understand what I mean? I condemn absolutely no one. I simply want to understand the chronology of events. It is one thing when Yeltsin, Burbulis, Shakhrai, and company come to Belovezh and believe, even earlier, while holding negotiations with the Novo-Ogaryovo process, that there was no alternative to the Union center—no matter what: ornamental, critical—but it must exist: there must be one country, one subject of international law, one army, one currency.

Or they come with the idea that the center is sort of an intermediate phase—it is needed so far, but they already have an alternative in their back pocket that they have been developing since fall 1990. That is a completely different setup, especially given the psychology of Yeltsin, who hated the idea that Gorbachev was and would be his boss. Any scenario in which Gorbachev was not the boss had much greater appeal from the outset, subconsciously.

AVEN: And what orders did we, members of the Russian government appointed in fall 1991, receive from Burbulis and Yeltsin? We were ordered not to cooperate in any form with the Union government. We were told: "Formally, we politically support the Novo-Ogaryovo process, but actually we adhere to the absolute sovereignty of Russia." That was the idea from the very first day I joined the government.

BURBULIS: Petr, do you remember the first meeting on November 15, when you were still working for the Foreign Ministry and we discussed the so-called economic agreement? It presupposed that mystification—that there was an economic field ...

AVEN: For us to plant the crops ...

BURBULIS: So you are right: we had no illusions about the Union.

KOKH: I have read the memoirs of Pavlov, may he rest in peace. He thought that the point of no return was passed when Gorbachev gave Union republics the right to issue rubles. He decentralized the money disbursement function. In Pavlov's opinion, the Union was doomed from that moment.

AVEN: Did that happen in spring 1991?

KOKH: That was right after the monetary reform, in May or June. Nothing could be stopped after that: once they gained a real and powerful tool of authority, the heads of the Union republics would have never abandoned it. They would have delegated certain secondary powers to the new Union, but the country would have disintegrated financially just the same. Because the existence of several disbursement centers within one currency zone implies that each should have its own currency or money disbursement, and everything would fall to pieces.

You were not the only ones who wanted to break up the Soviet Union. Everyone wanted to do that. That's a totally different picture from that of you coming to Belovezh full of bright hopes, but faced with Kravchuk's obstructive position, having to bow to the inevitable and denouncing the Union agreement.

BURBULIS: There was no mission to break up the Soviet Union at first. The idea was to find possibilities and resources for governing the Russian Federation under capable authorities. That is a different emphasis! Not to break up the Soviet Union, but to find methods, techniques, legal and material opportunities to bear responsibility for one's country, republic, 145 million people …

After the August putsch, the second most important impetus to the Belovezh events was December 1, 1991: the referendum and elections in Ukraine. Kravchuk won the presidential election, and the Ukrainians voted for full sovereignty of their republic at the referendum.

We started writing and calling, trying to reach that free Ukraine, and soon realized that we needed an urgent meeting because the main question was how to deal with the euphoric Ukraine. There was no stretching of the truth: what we needed to decide in Belovezh was what form of interaction with Ukraine we could have.

AVEN: So you are saying that there was no goal to break up the Union, and you did not go there to dismantle it but to reach some agreement among yourselves—which, actually, did not happen.

KOKH: As a result, a mountain gave birth to a mouse. We got the CIS, an ornamental organ, a new excuse for presidents to drink and party.

BURBULIS: As for partying and drinking, that is too much. A literary exaggeration.

KOKH: I am a writer! I have artistic license.

BURBULIS: The first task of Belovezh was to understand in what form the country could be preserved, and whether that was possible at all. Actually, Kravchuk was the most insistent and stubborn in his denial of the Union. It was very hard to convince him of the need for at least minimal integration. Although he was a reasonable man, his hands were tied by the referendum. And Kravchuk explained to us for the hundredth time that the Union agreement problem did not exist for Ukraine—it simply did not exist, and no integration was possible. The renewal of any union, with or without the center, was ruled out.

And we kept telling him: "What about economic relations, technological issues, nuclear armaments, basic necessities, and the ruble? How to govern the territory you have proclaimed to be a sovereign state?" We said, "Let us all think about it. Do you have any ideas? We have none so far."

And since you, Petr, are right—we hadn't only just thought about it; we had some serious rough drafts for that case, so I started working with each president separately—the issue was not easy, but delicate. I insist: our delegation did not intend to realize our rough drafts. We went there to solve completely different questions—to make a decision on practical aspects of cooperation with Ukraine. But, in the end, the conversation turned out differently, and it was not our fault.

When we understood Kravchuk's position, we decided that it was impossible to make any attempts to return to the idea of the Union, either renewed or updated, or anything else. Kravchuk even proposed to ban the very word—he said it must be struck from our vocabulary, our conscience, our feelings. As there was no Union, there was no Union agreement. Then we started thinking about the achievement of certain results under those circumstances. Certainly we had some rough drafts—we realized the preconditions.

Here is one more nuance—I do not know whether Gorbachev commented on that for you: in fact, it was planned that four delegations would meet in Minsk. We were also expecting Nazarbayev.

KOKH: Gorbachev said he forced Nazarbayev's stopover in Moscow. He was already on his way to you.

BURBULIS: What's more, while we spent the day looking for the slightest chance to keep Ukraine within the common space, we were in contact with Nazarbayev and his assistants practically every two hours, and they told us, "We are refueling ... We will depart in two hours ... We are refueling." But we knew that he was with Gorbachev in Moscow. We trusted him for the first few hours and waited for him, but then we grasped that there was a rationale for the situation. When we realized there would be no new union, we had a perfect historical and legal opportunity. The countries that had formed the Union in 1922 had every right in 1991, from the perspective of the international legal culture, to draw some historical conclusions and give a legal shape to the status quo. The agreement preamble actually said that the three republics that had established the Union of Soviet Socialist Republics in 1922 declared that the USSR, as the subject of international law and geopolitical reality, ceased to exist. And then ...

KOKH: Who authored that phrase, you or Shakhrai? "Geopolitical reality"—that is your style!

BURBULIS: It had so many authors, it would be improper to claim ...

KOKH: There are fewer now. It was taken as a victory then, but now it is devalued.

BURBULIS: We met in Moscow a few years later, and Shushkevich and Kravchuk joined us. Shushkevich said, "Here is the way it all happened ..." And he said that Burbulis authored all that. Kravchuk stopped him and said, "Wait, Burbulis is a good guy, he is smart, but I came up with all that!" And then something else came up ... That was a normal process of collective creation, and I lay claim to nothing.

KOKH: All right. Was Gaidar in Belovezh?

BURBULIS: Yes. Our delegation included Shakhrai, Kozyrev, Gaidar, and a small expert team. We were working in two modules. There was the sextet—the three presidents and the three premiers. I acted as the premier. When it became clear on the evening of December 7 that we were drafting an essentially new document, not a Union agreement, the substantial work was done by Gaidar, Shakhrai, and Kozyrev, who shaped its text, concept, content, and articles.

What's more, Yegor wrote down formulas they had agreed upon, as he was a man with a taste for editing and familiar with the work, and personally brought the text to the typists.

KOKH: Characteristically, only about ten people in the then Russian Supreme Soviet voted down the ratification of these agreements. All the others voted for it, including the huge number of present-day accusers who claim it was the biggest crime of the century.

BURBULIS: Alfred! The ratification was done on December 12. Actually, several hours after we submitted the agreements. That certainly mirrored the existing mainstream.

AVEN: The same people accused us of breaking up the Soviet Union, trampling upon ideals, and so on.

KOKH: A similar thing happened to Germany in World War I. When the war ended in 1918, no one in Germany wanted to fight; the whole army deserted, just like in Russia. But a decade passed, and suddenly the story was that everyone wanted to fight that war but the country, the army, the people, and so on had been stabbed in the back by mythical plotters.

BURBULIS: That is a good analogy, and why I'm skeptical of *allegedly* objective recollections.

KOKH: How did Yeltsin behave at that moment? Was he enthusiastic about Kravchuk's position? Did it lift the weight from his shoulders? I think Yeltsin breathed a sigh of relief, because he went there to take that position, but it was easier for him that it was taken by Kravchuk and that he was not the one who buried the USSR.

Gorbachev told me that Yeltsin hated him very much for God knows what; it was Gorbachev who had brought him from Sverdlovsk to Moscow, to the national level. And Yeltsin was very much burdened with the feeling that Gorbachev was his boss. Gorbachev explained that he was in charge of an agrarian district committee, and Yeltsin was in charge of an industrial district committee. And the unpublished table of ranks in the Central Committee always placed heads of industrial district committees higher than heads of agrarian ones. So Yeltsin was highly distressed about being Gorbachev's subordinate.

BURBULIS: And did Gorbachev explain his reasons for giving Yeltsin a job at Gosstroy?

KOKH: He said it was a humane act. After all those events at the plenary meeting, the Central Committee Secretariat was ready to send him to the middle of nowhere, expel him from the party, and not give him a job. And he felt sorry; he said, "How could we do that? He was an experienced man, a builder. Let us send him to Gosstroy, let him work; we should not throw people away." Gorbachev said he opposed the Central Committee majority. They wanted to destroy Yeltsin. When he spoke at the plenary meeting, 24 Central Committee members, without prearrangement, strongly criticized Yeltsin.

BURBULIS: That is a very important admission by Gorbachev.

KOKH: No one could imagine when he was dismissed that Yeltsin would make a big career as a democrat. Because, by the logic of party functionaries, what happened to him meant political death.

BURBULIS: I would like you to think about the following. The personification of political history is a characteristic feature of Russia. But, obviously, without the concrete policies of Comrade Yeltsin, his arrival in Moscow, his fall, resurrection, and so on, there would have been other names, because the country had to face that crossroads.

KOKH: Trust me, I was on Yeltsin's side on the question of the disintegration of the Soviet Union. I had absolutely no doubts about that. So you are preaching to the choir. I am absolutely confident that the disintegration of the Soviet Union, like the disintegration of any other similar conglomerate that today is called an empire, was a natural process. Certainly there would have been somebody else if not Yeltsin, and it would have happened the next year if not in that year. It would have happened just the same, because the basic motivation of all the politicians was that it was better to live separately than together—that was what Ukraine was thinking, that was what the Caucasian republics were thinking, that was what the Central Asian republics were thinking, that definitely was what the Baltic republics were thinking. So if not Yeltsin, there would have been somebody else, and the process would have taken place just the same.

I have the next question for you, Gena. The nuclear arms situation. How were you engaged in that?

BURBULIS: We signed a quadripartite agreement on nuclear arms between Russia, Ukraine, Belarus, and Kazakhstan in Almaty on December 21. It said that only Russia would have nuclear armaments, and they would all be moved to its territory.

KOKH: Who was doing that? You, Kozyrev, or Gaidar?

BURBULIS: All of us were doing that. Gaidar was handling the economic aspects, because they were very difficult. I can say that Yegor did not just find a formula but also created such attractive and binding possibilities for our partners that they would not be tempted even for one second to keep even one warhead.

KOKH: Did they part with nuclear arms easily?

BURBULIS: Rather easily, because what to do with them was a much more difficult question than how to live without them—although there were more difficulties with Ukraine, because we had the Black Sea Fleet and strategic aviation on their territory. You could say they were more interested in bargaining than others.

These delicate, detailed discussions were always a strong point of Yegor's. He did that perfectly. I believe that the way we managed the nuclear arsenal showed that the CIS idea was correct and unchallengeable.

AVEN: Or it simply proved the wisdom of Nazarbayev, Kravchuk, and Shushkevich.

Still, Gaidar was actually handling all kinds of matters, and Yeltsin trusted him very much. Although this did not prevent him from firing Gaidar's ministers.

KOKH: And then firing Gaidar himself. By the way, how did Viktor Stepanovich Chernomyrdin happen to be handy then?

BURBULIS: Chernomyrdin was first made the vice premier for fuel and energy, and Lopukhin was dismissed. The ministerial position was vacant for seven months, until the appointment of Shafranik. The firing of Lopukhin was Yeltsin's personal decision.

AVEN: When Lopukhin was dismissed in the end of April, you, Gena, had already gone. You had gone immediately after the congress. Maybe

Khasbulatov could not forgive you for the shame of us standing up and leaving at your order, and making him look very silly. When Yeltsin dismissed you, our reaction was weak. There was much talk about it, and it didn't come as news to us. But I remember well the dismissal of Lopukhin.

There was an oil sector conference. The oil workers had lots of complaints, so there was a special conference on the fuel and energy sector; the entire government and the fuel and energy generals were invited to attend. It was not a government meeting but the whole government was there—at least the economic bloc.

We were seated at a big table, and industry representatives sat by our side. Lopukhin was to make a report. And here we were: Gaidar, Lopukhin, Chubais, and me. Yeltsin appeared after a three-to-four-minute delay (which happened very rarely), opened his file, and said (without any hellos): "I will sign an order dismissing the minister." Everyone froze. "Which minister?" He said, "Lopukhin. And I appoint Chernomyrdin as the minister and vice premier for fuel and energy." I think Chernomyrdin entered the hall behind Yeltsin.

Some old apparatchiks from the Union cabinet were present. One of them (I think it was Churilov) even started to applaud. Yeltsin closed the file and gave it to Ilyushin. Gaidar's face went crimson, and Lopukhin was deathly pale. Everyone was still; there was an impression that he would keep tearing the government into bits. Lopukhin was supposed to make a report. Yeltsin whispered something to him and then told Gaidar, "Yegor, you make the report." And, without saying a word, Yegor took Lopukhin's report and went to the stand to read it.

Lopukhin was totally dumbfounded; I thought he would die. Then Chernomyrdin took the floor. Then we went out, congratulated Chernomyrdin, talked a bit, and went to our offices. We came to Lopukhin's dacha in the evening. I am not sure whether I told Yegor that night, but I definitely told him later, "Giving up a close associate without any objections is a mistake." Whenever your subordinate is fired without your knowledge, it shows that you are no longer the boss. Yegor gave a pragmatic answer: "We have reached a crucial point, and what shall we do—resign?" He meant we had to sacrifice somebody; a bad situation, but we had to work as long as we had the slightest chance.

KOKH: And why do you think it was a landmark decision?

AVEN: Because Yeltsin fired one of our team without notifying Gaidar in advance.

KOKH: And why don't you think that the dismissal of Gena was a bigger landmark? It was the first, and done in the same manner.

AVEN: Gena was not dismissed over Gaidar's head. Gena was directly subordinated to Yeltsin. But firing Gaidar's subordinate without even speaking to Gaidar was a demonstrative step that showed Yegor his true place in the hierarchy. That was unexpected for Gaidar. Probably Yeltsin discussed that decision with Gaidar as a possibility, but not as something definite.

KOKH: Or could Yegor be a good actor?

AVEN: I am confident that it was unexpected for Yegor. And for our government it was a landmark move because Yeltsin realized there would be no resistance—that our sudden resignation démarche that surprised him so much was an exception, not the rule. If it had been the rule, he would have treated us differently, more seriously, or maybe even cautiously. But he saw that the guys would swallow anything. And after that, no harsh personnel change was ever coordinated with us, at least not that I remember.

KOKH: Were there any before that? You told us that none of you, unfortunately, ever questioned anything. Then why be so dramatic? That was what amazed me about Yeltsin: Why all that drama?

BURBULIS: Well, it was sometimes tacky, sometimes rude, sometimes vulgar, but sometimes it was appropriate.

KOKH: When was it appropriate?

BURBULIS: Here is an example. We moved from Arkhangelskoye to the White House[5] on August 19, 1991. Korzhakov arrived at about 11:00 a.m., and said we were being surrounded by tanks. Yeltsin roused himself: "What? What are they doing?" "Some tank drivers climbed out to speak to people." And he said, "Really? That is interesting—I will go there." And I said, "Exactly where is 'there'?"

KOKH: What do you mean, where? Climb the tank!

BURBULIS: "We have no idea what is going on there, what their plans are." "No, I will go." I said, "You cannot do that, that is impermissible, because

---

5.   The seat of the Russian parliament.

it could be an act of sabotage." He said, "Okay, let's go look at the street from the balcony." He went to a balcony and saw some movement on the street. "No, I will go there. Give me our written appeal, I will go there." I tell him again, "Look at all those roofs and windows—there could be a provocation any moment—shooters, snipers, whatever." Still, we go. Yeltsin climbs a tank and reads out the appeal. And ten minutes later the whole world watched TV and saw the complete picture of what was happening in our country.

KOKH: I absolutely agree that reading a declaration from a tank is appropriate and right, and the fact that Yeltsin understood that meant he was a brilliant politician. I'm talking about his decisions on personnel, which he sometimes made spontaneously and publicly—why did he do that?

ABOUT GAIDAR

AVEN: Listen, leave Yeltsin alone. Let's talk about Gaidar. Gena, what haven't we asked you about Yegor that you think is important to say? Everything that people do not understand, do not know, and do not feel. I don't believe that time will put everything in its place. I think we should start putting everything in its place ourselves.

BURBULIS: There's no question of "place." I think Yegor had a number of astonishing qualities, which in combination really distinguish a remarkable man worthy of personifying the Russian reforms of the early 1990s. When Yegor passed away, he was often compared with Speransky, Witte, and Stolypin—which, by the way, was quite appropriate. And it is quite obvious to me now that the history of new Russia has a proper name: Yegor Timurovich Gaidar. As for his personal qualities and activity, I believe it is important to understand the following. Yegor's work was his mission and passion. It was cognitive work. He had a merciless, thorough, and inquisitive mind. And the truth was his lover 24 hours a day. But surprisingly—and oddly, given his earlier biography—before our cooperation began, he had a rare quality, which I define as a "capacity for practical logic." There aren't many thinking people, but there are enough of them. The number of people capable of generating programs and concepts is even smaller, but they still exist. But there are very few people who have the will and ability to implement them. In that sense, Yegor, in my opinion, was an exceptional person for that time—the one and only person.

KOKH: On Gaidar's birthday, March 19, the NTV channel showed a film about him, and it included a very interesting interview with Khasbulatov. He said he had not expected Yegor to be so firm. That was very interesting. It looked like Khasbulatov simply underestimated Yegor; he was confident he was dealing with a geek, and Gaidar proved to be a man capable of firm decisions.

AVEN: People associated Gaidar with violence and all the misfortunes of the early 1990s. So he was the focal point of hatred—and he endured that in a very courageous and dignified way.

BURBULIS: Gaidar is the type of man described by Gramsci's formula, which was very close to Schweitzer and Gandhi: "Pessimism of the intellect capable of grasping the tragedy of human nature and the futility of trying to live by the rules, and optimism of the will." At probably the most important moments, Yegor certainly had optimism of the will. And there was something inside him that ruled out compromise, procrastination, or the shirking of responsibility.

KOKH: Especially when I was watching Yegor in the last years of his life, I can say that I have a better understanding of the source of his boldness and courage. I realize that Yegor must have inherited that trait. He did not care about his health. He was sort of relativist: let it be. He loved life in all of its manifestations, but he didn't value it very much. They may be related, actually. In this context, I completely understand Yegor's distribution of submachine guns, first in Ossetia and then near the Moscow City Council. He might have easily gone into the firing line with that submachine gun.

BURBULIS: That is an interesting example, because on the afternoon of October 3, 1993, I drove up to the silent, paralyzed Kremlin, the symbol of Russian power. When Yegor arrived and called for arming our supporters and bringing them out onto the street, I believed we could not do that. We could not do that because our first responsibility was to the people.

KOKH: In that sense, Yegor definitely had no complexes.

BURBULIS: But people really stood up and went onto the street, and it appeared that Gaidar was absolutely right.

KOKH: I'm telling you, Khasbulatov was shocked! He did not expect such a strong and well-judged reaction. He thought his side had already won. But it was Gaidar's victory. Tanks shooting on the White House came later, but first there were people armed by Gaidar near the Moscow City Council.

2

ANATOLY CHUBAIS

"We Destroyed the People's Idea of Justice with Voucher Privatization"

GRIGORY GLAZKOV ONCE SAID, "Chubais is an institution." His capacity to supervise a dozen projects simultaneously has become a cliché. Even when he is tired and relaxed he radiates extraordinary energy. He is built to fight like a gladiator, immune to sentiment and impervious to pain. The world around him may explode and go to ruin, but Chubais seeks out his goal like the Terminator, regardless of the price. Sometimes I am scared of him. He reminds me of a remark about Lenin: "… or he could have slashed you …" It is a terrible feeling, like being close to a ticking bomb.

Like Petr, I have known him for over 20 years—long enough for a person to become a part of you. I am not myself without him. He taught me a lot. Or, rather, he himself was a lesson to me. That was one of the main lessons of my life: never complain. Endure, don't whine.

He has been with me for so long, inside of me, that I don't even know if I like him or not. Sometimes it seems to me that I adore him, despite all his nonsense, like "I never change a decision I make." Sometimes I want to kill him—especially when he, like an idiot, does not change a decision he has made.

Chubais is one of the most extraordinary people I have ever met, perhaps the most unusual person in my life. He is one of the smartest and best educated, and one of the dumbest and most ignorant.

He is extremely methodical, and everything is well organized in his head; he is total chaos, his head is a muddle. He is a stubborn fool; he is an inspired genius. He is kind and charitable, like Mother Teresa; he is cold and indifferent to people, like a coffin maker. He is disgustingly honest; he lies all the time …

It is impossible to stop. Someday I will write a long book about him. But not now. Now read our interview, and draw your conclusions.

Alfred Kokh

PETR AVEN: Let me start, Tolya. We are writing a book of recollections about 1992. Or, maybe, a longer period—the end of the 1980s and early 1990s. It is about our government, about Gaidar. We do not want to touch on the more recent past; it is more topical and thus everyone will be more cautious talking about it. You told me once that an interview was an act of political struggle. So let's speak only about the rather distant past, about the period around 1992.

ANATOLY CHUBAIS: Yes, lots of interesting things happened in 1992. I started reading your interview with Burbulis—a very interesting text. For instance, I did not know that Yavlinsky's candidacy was not offered seriously to Yeltsin.

AVEN: You had a special relationship with Yeltsin, which …

CHUBAIS: I had no relationship with Yeltsin at all in 1992.

ALFRED KOKH: Gaidar told me that Yeltsin did not really like you and felt cautious about you in 1992. Yegor said that Yeltsin felt at ease drinking and talking with him, but was cautious about Chubais.

CHUBAIS: This is a well-known fact.

AVEN: But the political game you and Yegor were playing, in particular in the political discussions with the Supreme Council, did you take part in it at your own risk or did you coordinate with Yeltsin? I was far from that, but you were in the epicenter, for instance, when bargaining with the Supreme Council about the co-optation of "old-timer manufacturers" in the government. You even brought Georgy Khizha from St Petersburg.

KOKH: Come on, even a genius makes mistakes sometimes!

AVEN: In both congresses you were in demand for political discussion and more.

CHUBAIS: My involvement in political discussion was quite extensive. But did I have any personal contact with Yeltsin in doing that? No, not at all.

AVEN: I think Gaidar saw you as a political figure more than anyone else.

CHUBAIS: I was really involved not only in the drafting of speeches but also in the elaboration of the political strategy, which was just appearing, at the congresses; that is true. But I did not discuss that with Yeltsin. April was one congress, I remember that; and then there was the December congress. There were two or three rather large political intrigues at the April congress. We organized them—I was directly involved in them and even designed them myself.

AVEN: There was one intrigue that you did not design, but you made it happen. It was when we resigned. I tried to convince Gaidar to join us, but failed. Then I incited you to resign, and you persuaded Gaidar.

CHUBAIS: I remember that. Pressure on us grew from the very start, and for six or seven days. It got worse each day.

I remember lists of candidates for the new government, the list of resignations demanded by deputies; the Civil Union, Volsky, Rutskoi, some others, their meetings with Yeltsin, ultimatums and lists. And the congress was tougher and tougher. Our work was presented as riddled with mistakes at first, then with major mistakes—then as criminal, and then as the breaking up of the fatherland. Demands were made to bring us to justice, and then appeals to arrest us right in the congress hall. We tried to get in touch with Yeltsin at that moment but we couldn't reach him. That was a tense moment, really heated; and then one of us proposed going on the offensive instead of playing defense: "Since they want to wipe us out but have not done that, we should present them with a black-and-white picture and then they'll have to beg us, not the other way around." The logic was to make a preemptive resignation statement accompanied by a draft resolution of no confidence. That required, first, the consent of Gaidar; second, a draft resolution; third, a press release. And I was getting all that done with Yegor, while he remained unable to speak to Yeltsin.

AVEN: He did not speak with Gena, either.

CHUBAIS: Why was Gena sidelined on this?

AVEN: Gaidar told me that this was very risky and wrong, but that he then spoke to you and you convinced him. He gave you carte blanche and you sprang into action.

CHUBAIS: So, we made a resignation statement and a no-confidence motion. There was a vote, and then the congress cooled down. There were not enough votes for no confidence, so we had confidence by default. The congress was over. While that action was taking place, I wrote the statement and our demands. There was then a press conference—we arranged chairs and tables in the Kremlin ourselves, as there was no one and no time to organize it. Then we went out on Red Square, where crazy old ladies attacked us, shouting, "Democrats!"

MUSCOVITES AND ST PETERSBURGIANS

AVEN: I have the impression that I first met Gaidar and you simultaneously, at Gaidar's place.

CHUBAIS: I am not sure my memory is correct about the time of the event called "my first meeting with Gaidar." Before that happened we sent a special agent on a mission. We sent Grigory Glazkov to Moscow not to work on his thesis or do other silly things, but to look for normal people. Then came Glazkov's canonical story about attending a Moscow seminar and seeing one decent face, Oleg Ananyin's, among a variety of—how can I put it gently?—not very attractive faces. Glazkov took a seat next to him. After they got acquainted, he asked the question that was the purpose of his visit: "Are there any decent people here?" And it was he who said Gaidar.

AVEN: Glazkov went to the institute where Gaidar was working, and they got acquainted. After that Yegor invited you, Vasilyev, Glazkov, Ananyin, and me to his place; that was our second meeting at most, or maybe even the first.

CHUBAIS: Masha baked pies, I remember that well. She and Yegor were newlyweds. That must have been 1984. And we established a good relationship. Actually, we differed from one another a lot. Practically all the Muscovites were from elite families, and we of St Petersburg were ordinary, average people.

KOKH: Some of us here, like me, can be associated only partially with St Petersburg.

CHUBAIS: See, I did not stress that, but expressed myself more delicately.

AVEN: Tolya, how did you feel and understand what was happening to the country? I recently read a wonderful piece by Slava Shironin—he is a clever man—and he explains precisely why Gaidar was the leader of the movement. Because Gaidar was meant to be just that. Everyone had a different interest beyond government, personal life, or something else. But Gaidar was the only one who from his youth had been thinking about ways to reform the country.

CHUBAIS: I would disagree in one respect. I do think he was actually meant to do that; that is absolutely true—but I also was meant to do it. But Gaidar became the leader.

KOKH: Now we have only two personalities to discuss, Chubais and Gaidar. Why did Gaidar become the leader while Chubais did not?

CHUBAIS: That is an easy question. Obviously, Yegor was a much more cultured man, with incomparably greater academic knowledge and a stronger intellect.

AVEN: What was your expectation of events in the country? Gaidar was already anticipating changes, and preparing himself for that. That is why he became the leader. Probably his sense of time was keener than ours. He certainly prepared for changes, and even felt they might start soon. I, for instance, had no such feeling at that moment.

CHUBAIS: First, I would like to speak about my impression of Gaidar and your whole team. You cannot even imagine how big the shock was for us. We lived in the isolated world of St Petersburg, which was, let's say, ideologically sterile. And you had lectures by Aganbegian, Shatalin, and Yasin! That was something!

Glazkov returned from the seminar and said, "Hey, listen, you know Moscow was really awesome. Do you know how they feel about market economy advocates?" I asked, "How?" St Petersburg banned the word "market," because it sounded anti-Soviet. And Moscow treated them like the West treats homosexuals. A market-economy advocate speaks, and someone asks, "Who's that?" The answer is, "Not one of us." That's all! No persecution, no party inquiry, nothing. That really stunned me. The atmosphere was completely different in St Petersburg.

So we were in an absolute vacuum, in spite of the intellectual and personality background of 1984 and the five-year practice of the submission of work plans—written reports with a bibliography of about 70 authors in several languages. How can you describe your feeling when you learn that people in Moscow discuss our problems and share our language, our understanding of the essence of the situation and our expectation of the pending catastrophe? And yet they discuss it calmly, like something absolutely natural rather than strictly forbidden—practically an armed revolt against Soviet power. That was one of the strongest experiences in the years before 1991. That is a part of the answer to your question.

The other part is about my sense of the country. I felt that official economic scholars were absolutely impotent in the face of the imminent economic disaster. The house was on fire, but they were discussing changing the paint color.

THE INEVITABILITY OF CHANGE

AVEN: And when, in the course of all your Leningrad economic get-togethers, did you realize that paint was not the answer, and that it was necessary to rebuild the walls and foundations?

CHUBAIS: I think it occurred by the end of the 1970s.

KOKH: No.

CHUBAIS: Are you telling me about me?

KOKH: Yes, I am telling you. I remember the way it was.

CHUBAIS: You were a fifth-grade schoolboy—how can you remember?

KOKH: First of all, I was a sophomore in the late 1970s. Second, I remember you were all enthusiastic until the mid-1980s about János Kornai and Hungarian socialism the way it was presented by the journal *Acta Oeconomica*, and thought that Kadar's "goulash" socialism was the limit of your wildest dreams.

AVEN: No, no, Tolya. Alfred is right. It was not the end of the 1970s!

CHUBAIS: Alfred, may I tell you about my discussion with Grigory Yuryevich Glazkov and Yuri Vladimirovich Yarmagayev in September 1979?

KOKH: Please do.

CHUBAIS: The discussion was the following. Do you remember the resolution of the Central Committee and the Council of Ministers No. 695 of 1979, on "the upgrading of the economic mechanism"? It introduced standard products.

KOKH: How can I forget? It was drummed into us at industrial economics seminars.

CHUBAIS: We had six hours of discussions of that resolution, with shouting and screaming, and we nearly came to blows. My position was that the resolution was a step in the right direction. Glazkov said it was totally unfeasible, and that that direction should not be taken. That was 1979, Alfred.

KOKH: Just a second. Let us separate these three ideas. First of all, I quite believe you could have had that position; it actually disproves your theory that everyone in the group understood by the end of the 1970s that Soviet socialism had exhausted itself, and that a sticking plaster would change nothing. Second, I quite believe that Glazkov could have called it absolutely absurd for the simple reason that Glazkov says that about everything. As for Yuri Yarmagayev, his position is clear, too. He was a bright and unusual person, and he could take that position. But it was not the group consensus. If Grisha Glazkov had been offered a market economy as an alternative, he would have called it a total absurdity and its author an idiot.

CHUBAIS: Alfred, you present the question in terms of psychological peculiarities.

KOKH: No, I do not. It is just that your story does not prove that everyone thought by the end of the 1970s that it was necessary to build a genuine market economy, with attributes such as uncontrolled prices, private property, a stock market, capital movement.

No, I think the awareness came later. I was watching the evolution of Mishka Dmitryev; I was watching the evolution of Mishka Manevich. I did not yet know Glazkov and you, but I already knew them and Seryozha Vasilyev. There is no doubt they were advanced guys, but there was no conviction that the Soviets were doomed in the late 1970s—that is for certain.

CHUBAIS: I disagree, and I will tell you why. The realization of the need for and inevitability of change is a very important subject. I remember that our first discussion was about the rate of transformation. By 1982 we had a consensus about the need for radical transformation, and Sergei Vasilyev and I described that fully in an article published that year. We disagreed only on the speed. Our article presented two scenarios of transformation in the USSR, one evolutionary and the other radical but more systemic, without any breaking of public institutions and totally nonviolent. I proved in that article why the first scenario was no good and the second one was necessary.

KOKH: So profound! I never would have guessed. Listen, I have no objections—you were great, and who can dispute that? I simply think that your radicalism did not go beyond the so-called cooperative socialism of the time.

CHUBAIS: Maybe. I really have the impression of my radicalism only because back then Hungarian, and especially Yugoslav, varieties of socialism were beyond our reality. I even recall Yegor's opinion: "Self-sufficiency is right, and self-financing is premature." But, on the other hand, there were bona fide advocates of market economics among us, arguing that "the bared teeth of capitalism" represented our bright tomorrow. One of them was Yuri Yarmagayev. I held a more moderate position on transformation in our intellectual community. I actually represented the less revolutionary, rather conservative wing.

KOKH: I agree. Misha Dmitriyev brought me once, in the early 1980s, to a seminar where Yarmagayev was speaking. They spoke about the Indian philosophy of Jainism, some kind of extremely complex mathematics, economics, and social reforms. He reminded me of a crazed professor so engrossed in his inner world that he had trouble communicating with others. He was a very colorful guy, but at the time he seemed autistic to me.

CHUBAIS: He was a genius: the man in our group who discovered financial stabilization and the meaning of money. He actually discovered the essence of macroeconomics. He made the discovery without reading anything in the Western literature (he was not good at languages), in a homegrown way, just the way Grisha discovered cost criteria and revenue.

KOKH: I am just sharing my personal impressions of those people. It seemed there were both radicals and conservatives in the group, but even the most radical did not go beyond Hungarian socialism in the late 1970s. And that was not a radical change of the system.

CHUBAIS: That is not true. Radicals went further than the cautious types, like me.

KOKH: And Gaidar?

CHUBAIS: Gaidar was closer to me than to Yarmagayev, for instance.

AVEN: That is, those who called for a capitalist revolution were marginal personalities and did not express the opinion of your group?

CHUBAIS: No, they were just a part of the group.

AVEN: Around 1984 Shatalin formulated a task: find a relatively successful example (a country) and write a program of reforms for the Soviet Union based on that example. We thought for a while, and then chose Hungary and Yugoslavia as the examples. I asked Yegor: "Why are we writing about them? Let's take Sweden!" Yegor said, "Let's talk about what is realistic."

CHUBAIS: Yegor actually wanted to avoid utopia. He avoided premature discussions of "capitalism is better than socialism." I remember being very angry in 1987 when Larisa Piyasheva wrote an article, "Where Pies Are Puffier," in *Novy Mir*. This was the first introduction of this subject into the public discourse: "The existing system is temporary, and sustainable development under Soviet-type socialism is impossible."

KOKH: And why were you angry with her?

CHUBAIS: Because we thought she was revealing things that specialists already understood perfectly, but she presented them in a sociopolitical light and started a public discussion. And that worked against us at the time, because a public discussion of the sacrifice of the sacred cow could trigger a reaction from the authorities—it was fraught with the possibility of restricting glasnost and postponing genuine reforms for a few more years. That is what we thought then.

AVEN: Gaidar and you are really alike in your political realism. You two were the keenest on practical reforms. How did your relationship develop?

CHUBAIS: It seemed to me then, and I still think now, that our relationship formed at once. We asked Yegor to speak at our seminar in 1985. That was a shock for young scientists of the Leningrad Engineering and Economics Institute. We had invited Ananyin first, and he was interesting, but was not a revelation; and then we called Yegor. In short, Yegor shocked the Leningrad community. The community thought there were individual Glazkovs, Chubaises, who were trying to invent something, but that it was obviously semi-legal and had nothing to do with official life. And here came a legal and serious academician from Moscow! And he spoke the same language and had the same intellectual outlook. That was very important.

WITH YELTSIN OR WITHOUT

KOKH: I will ask the question we may simply forget to ask and will feel sorry later for having forgotten. Gena Burbulis said that after the shooting at the White House in November 1993 there was an election campaign, and Gena, although he was already banished from heaven, remained a major functionary of the Choice of Russia. So Gena tried to convince Yegor that he must force Yeltsin to give clear support to the Choice of Russia, and then we would win the election. If Yeltsin started waffling in his usual manner and telling us he was the president of all Russians, then we should go ahead without him, and offer criticism. In short, we should act as an independent political force without a backward glance at Yeltsin, or checking only when it suited our interests. Gaidar agreed and went to see Yeltsin, and Yeltsin did the customary thing.

AVEN: Treated him kindly?

KOKH: He was kind, but he gave no support. Yet Yegor still did not separate himself from Yeltsin in the election campaign, and we got what we got: second place to Zhirinovsky and the slow degradation of the democratic movement. Do you agree with what Burbulis said, and if so, why didn't you do that?

CHUBAIS: I don't quite remember that crossroads. But the thing is that one's own position is always important in such situations. Petr won't be offended if I say that neither he nor Burbulis was a leader of the Choice of Russia, but Gaidar and I were. And we were still members of the Yeltsin government. I think the position of Gennady Eduardovich was slightly modified by his status then.

KOKH: So he was prepared to go radical as regards Yeltsin and you were not—is that it?

CHUBAIS: Certainly he was in a less responsible position from the inner, psychological point of view. Actually, he was cut off. If we had taken that path, we would have stayed with Burbulis but without everyone else. Because the organization, Democratic Choice of Russia, had a political mission, and Burbulis's share in it was 10 percent, and the share of others was 90 percent, in terms of the internal party situation. As for the external conditions, I would say that, at that historical stage of the country's development, in late 1993, only 18 months after the democrats had come to power, an attempt to attack Yeltsin would have caused a loss of electoral support rather than winning voters. Support in this particular field and denial of support in another would have had many more negative consequences than positive. By the way, the same confrontational situation, but in a much more acute form, appeared later. The year 1996 witnessed the Chubais–Gaidar situation, rather than the Burbulis–Gaidar one.

KOKH: Yes, I remember that. We had another dilemma: to support Yeltsin or not to support him. Gaidar was nursing the idea of Nemtsov for president. And in the beginning of 1996 (or the end of 1995) the Democratic Choice of Russia congress decided to withdraw support from Yeltsin in the presidential election, because of the war in Chechnya. That was a decision of the party congress, which was led by Gaidar.

CHUBAIS: And then I had a complicated discussion about the issue with Yegor, and there was another congress of the DCR. Finally, during an open and frank discussion the congress decided to support Yeltsin.

AVEN: Alfred, you keep formulating essentially the same question: how possible and realistic was it to see ourselves without Yeltsin? When we tendered our resignation in April 1992, Yeltsin was expecting it, as was Gena. Yeltsin realized that Gena did not control us. An indirect and unexpected consequence of that move was the rapid resignation of Burbulis.

CHUBAIS: Or perhaps, with historical inevitability, Yeltsin was distancing himself from the most radical solutions, and those personifying them?

KOKH: All this talk, it's in the nature of "we're all going to die anyway." Today he doesn't distance himself, tomorrow he does. How many times did Yeltsin do that to you?

CHUBAIS: Once. In January 1996.

KOKH: And remind me who was fired in 1998?

CHUBAIS: Shall I remind you that, six months before that, I sent my insistent letter to Yeltsin requesting his permission to quit the government?

KOKH: Bullshit! You were forced to write that statement, in the middle of our writers' scandal.[1] If a man does not want to work, no one can force him to do it. He simply resigns, and that's it. It does not require anyone's consent. Just like you did in the notorious month of April 1992.

Come on, Tolya. Even if that book scandal had not happened, all of us would have been fired just the same because Berezovsky demanded it. You are perfectly aware of that. They would have found another excuse.

CHUBAIS: That's really superficial. What did Berezovsky have to do with it?

KOKH: Superficial? You, on the contrary, are overcomplicating things. I remember very well how it was.

AVEN: You're at it again! Let's get back to our discussion. Tolya! Remember, Leszek Balcerowicz visited us and said we needed to fight for power. I now think that it was one of our fundamental mistakes. He told us, "If you don't fight for power, you won't be anybody." I knew him well from my time in Vienna. And Yegor had profound respect for him. He also said, "If you don't counterpoise yourselves to Yeltsin, you'll never become a political force of your own." Václav Klaus told us the same. But we almost never did that. Our resignation in 1992 was the only time. So, the question is: could we oppose ourselves to Yeltsin in 1992? Could we try to form our own political force without him, and do the same in 1996–8? Am I right in saying that our attachment to Yeltsin was a fundamental weakness of our team?

CHUBAIS: As you understand, I have a slightly different point of view.

---

1.   In Autumn 1997, the NTV channel, which was owned by Vladimir Gusinsky, accused five reformers, including Kokh and Chubais, of taking bribes from Vladimir Potanin in the form of payment for an as yet unwritten book. As a result of the scandal, Chubais was removed from the office of finance minister. The book, *Privatization. Russian-Style*, was published in 1999 by the Vagrius publishing house.

KOKH: Here comes the famed Chubais "special opinion."

CHUBAIS: First of all, I think that personal life had a clear impact on that position.

AVEN: And how can it be separated?

CHUBAIS: It is absolutely necessary to separate it out. Certainly, Petr, you bear a grudge for your dismissal. But that was nothing.

AVEN: Okay. Maybe, to an extent. Go on.

CHUBAIS: I believe that in this issue there is only one legitimate perspective. Everything must be seen from the point of view of the country.

KOKH: Spare us your emotion, will you? But if we do speak in terms of the country, how could we have left an ailing president alone to face that pack of Berezovsky, Gusinsky, and the rest in 1998 without giving him the backup of Chubais, Nemtsov, and so on—without going into personal considerations of whether one wants to work in the government or not?

CHUBAIS: I left him to face them only because I believed that my resignation would not change the government situation at that moment. If I had refused to join the administration in August 1996, there would have been no other efficient personnel solutions. And events would have taken a negative turn, in my opinion—if we are talking about the country, pardon the expression. So I went to work in the administration. The situation was completely different in 1998—such developments were ruled out.

KOKH: Oh, yes. I forgot. You think the correct decision was made in 1999?

CHUBAIS: Yes, I think the correct decision was made in 1999, although I opposed it. By the way, you also thought then that the decision was correct. Otherwise you would not have agreed to fight Gusinsky.

KOKH: I did help Putin to deal with Gusinsky. I gladly helped him with that. And I never regretted that for even a second. But I still do not think the correct decision was made in 1999.

AVEN: You're at it again! Let's start with 1992. Tolya, answer my question about Balcerowicz.

CHUBAIS: I must admit I haven't thought about this seriously for the past 12 years. Besides, my opinion, like yours, is naturally influenced by my experience, considering I was a government member. I think we should evaluate the political weights—our aggregate weight and that of Yeltsin. In late 1991, and you may agree, I think the relationship was approximately 0 to 100. At its maximum, in the third or sixth month of our government, it might have been 5 to 95. Compared with us, Yeltsin was Russia. It would have been senseless to follow Balcerowicz's advice under those circumstances.

Balcerowicz must have been correct in the Polish context, where the relative weight of the people and the authorities was completely different, where there was no profound difference between intellectuals and people, and where the entire scale was totally different.

As I see it, there is another categorically and radically important relationship between "the leader, the tsar, the secretary general, the president" and the subject named "the parliament." If we had followed Balcerowicz's advice, we would have had to answer the fundamental question first: who is your presidential candidate? Gaidar? Hardly. One may say that we should have sought a candidate and nurtured him, but there was no one but Yeltsin who fitted that role at that moment.

KOKH: There was no need to find a president—it was the parliamentary election. Why are you discussing a different subject?

CHUBAIS: It is not different! The question is why we did not form our own political force independent of the president?

AVEN: I was asking about the political party. I am much more practical. A party Yeltsin would have had to reckon with, which he would have listened to.

CHUBAIS: Yavlinsky took that path and became a professional presidential candidate. He has been a presidential candidate his entire life. Because he formed an independent, unaffiliated political party with one tiny shortcoming: it could nominate a presidential candidate, but did not have the slightest chance of electing a president.

AVEN: Yes, he failed.

CHUBAIS: Yavlinsky could never be the president in his whole life, under any circumstances, at any moment, or in any election. And I will tell you why:

he could galvanize no one and nothing around his candidacy.

AVEN: But Havel, who was not the common type, became the president in the Czech Republic, and then there was Klaus.

CHUBAIS: And Kazakhstan elected Nazarbayev. And he's still there. Why do you keep looking to the West? Trust me, this is not a political position. I think this is a misunderstanding of what the country named Russia is.

AVEN: And which of us understands it better?

CHUBAIS: I think our understandings are simply different. Who knows better? I do not know. We should not accuse each other of misunderstanding.

KOKH: So you think that Russia is somewhere inbetween Kazakhstan and the Czech Republic? That the shortage of democracy is its characteristic feature?

CHUBAIS: I think there is no genuine demand for democracy in Russia now. You may say that the demand cannot form by itself, that it should be encouraged.

KOKH: Was there demand for democracy in 1993?

CHUBAIS: Yes, there was, until October 3. And after that it weakened significantly. Just look at the result of the December 1993 election and the triumph of Zhirinovsky.

KOKH: I think those results are rooted in the position of Yeltsin, who did not support anyone. So they elected what they elected.
     When we spoke with Gena (and we did not plan that in advance, but the idea appeared in my conversation with Gena), a suggestion was made that Yeltsin possibly appointed Gaidar to the government before October because …

AVEN: Because he wanted to disband the Supreme Council together with Yegor, and because he wanted Gaidar to be alone in the elections, without having any commitments to Yeltsin. And as soon as Gaidar stopped being dangerous (after the elections), stopped being needed, he allowed

Chernomyrdin to use his careful apparatchik methods to force him out of the government.

KOKH: And did not protect him. Yegor told me how he was being forced out.

CHUBAIS: Just think for a second: if you remember, Gaidar joined the government in August. The early elections were held in December. Neither Yegor nor Yeltsin could have imagined that there would be elections in December in which they would have to take part, and they could not have imagined the bloody battle of October 3. Following your logic, Yeltsin must have thought, "I will hire Gaidar, then I will open tank fire on the White House, then I will arrest Khasbulatov and Rutskoi, then I will take part in the elections, and if Gaidar decides to take part in the elections, I will not allow him to." Come on, Petr, control that creative imagination.

KOKH: He knew all of that and anticipated it. He appointed Yegor on September 18, and on September 21 (only three days later) he signed Decree No. 1400 disbanding the Supreme Council. Or do you mean to say that Yeltsin did not know three days earlier, at least in general terms, that he would fight Khasbulatov and Rutskoi?

Okay, I can put it a different way. Yeltsin was largely an intuitive man. He felt that Gaidar was on his own, he had some political weight, and that if he left him for long off the leash, as they say, he might develop into an independent political force. Why would he need that? Irrespective of potential conflict or friendship with that force.

CHUBAIS: Are you saying that about a man who staked his entire life on his fight with Khasbulatov for the future of the country?

KOKH: That was why he consolidated forces, summoned the cavalry.

CHUBAIS: Alfred says that Yeltsin brought Yegor into the government with the sole purpose of depriving him of room for maneuver at the next stage, in the Duma election.

KOKH: Guys, that is just to say the same thing in different words. Consolidation means binding.

CHUBAIS: That is totally absurd.

AVEN: It is the same.

CHUBAIS: Oh, no! The first is the truth, and the second is lies.

AVEN: Let us finally talk about the results: unconditional support for Yeltsin without any right to opposition was a mistake. Such close relations with Yeltsin, in which our hands were tied and he was free to do whatever he wanted, were a fundamental mistake. What is more, there is an opinion that the conformism of the liberals, and the constant desire of their leaders to be close to power, were the main reasons why liberal ideology was discredited in Russia. They forgave everything: the war in Chechnya, the deviation from real economic reforms, corruption.

CHUBAIS: That is another essential difference between us. In the episode we are discussing, a civil war was prevented.

AVEN: There was no threat.

CHUBAIS: I read your interview, and I absolutely disagree with you.

KOKH: Petr, I also disagree. The threat was quite real. I saw those people in Smolenskaya Square and near the mayor's office. That was the beginning of war. They moved on and killed policemen. They crossed the Rubicon and there was no way back for them.

AVEN: I think that today's situation derives from conformism, including our own.

KOKH: We could have supported Yeltsin while being independent.

AVEN: That is also correct.

CHUBAIS: Elections are a very crude process, in delicate statements such as "I articulate my support but register some reservations," or "I am organizationally independent but not in opposition" make no sense. Things are routinely either black or white. You must have learned that when you supervised the campaign office of the Union of Right Forces. None of those "tricky" structures survive parliamentary elections.

The wish to "figure out moves" frequently appears in analysis after the fact, but it is totally useless in real politics.

AVEN: I repeat, I'm certain that our constant conformism not only led to the absence of political results, but also discredited the democratic movement. Our bows and curtseys to Yeltsin brought some tactical results but obviously caused strategic losses.

CHUBAIS: I disagree with both of you. The correct answer is that Russia is not Poland.

AVEN: That is an absolutely flawed position—absolutely! And it is totally unfair. The main problem of Russia is that its elite believes that to be true. And that is why it connives with every whim of the authorities. The thinking is, "Well, we're barbarians, what can you do about that?" That is a very comfortable position. Certainly Russia is not Poland. But that does not mean it is genetically unprepared for democracy and capitalism.

CHUBAIS: In my opinion, the correct formula is this: Russia and Poland and Russia and Kazakhstan. One more reason for the lack of understanding among us is that, in contrast to you, I worked my ass off for 15 years doing exactly what you are now urging me to do—that is, organize the democratic movement in Russia. That had nothing to do with my direct professional duties and, as a rule, impeded their execution. No matter what I did, there were always strict judges saying: "Why doesn't Chubais consolidate the democratic movement?" I have taken so much shit! If you know how to do that correctly, you are welcome to it! Alfred here did that a bit. He had enough for the rest of his life, I am sure.

KOKH: I had enough, that is true. Okay, let's drop this subject. Since you do not want to either remember or suggest why Yeltsin did not support us in 1993, I will tell you why.

CHUBAIS: And why was that? He will say something else nasty now.

KOKH: Yes. But it is a nasty thing about us, not about Yeltsin. Yeltsin was an outstanding politician. He did not support us because he knew we would stand by him whether or not he did. If there had been some incident or public conflict ripening, he would have supported us. That is it. Why support those who were already in his pocket? Why narrow the space for his political maneuvering to support people who were not going anywhere?

CHUBAIS: Then give the full answer, now that you have taken this position.

You say that if he had supported us he would have lost a substantial measure of political maneuverability. That's a position that can be discussed. You present the sweet half and forget about the other.

KOKH: No, I haven't forgotten. I can say that if he had supported us, we would have been a self-sufficient political force. Probably we could have formed a Duma majority. In the end, that would have been beneficial for Yeltsin.

CHUBAIS: Even with 12 percent?

KOKH: No! First of all, without Yeltsin's support we got slightly more than 15 percent, plus many winners in single-mandate districts.

CHUBAIS: And we could have had 17 percent!

KOKH: Much more. We would have used administrative resources, even without special orders. Governors would have felt the trend. Stop pretending—you know exactly how it all works. He didn't do it either in 1993 or in 1995. The democratic political party, which did not affiliate itself to Yeltsin, Yavlinsky's Yabloko, won the State Duma election in 1995, and Gaidar did not. We can argue endlessly, but I think it was a mistake.

AVEN: Tolya, really, why did Yavlinsky win in 1995 while we and Gaidar did not? Was that because Yavlinsky could criticize Yeltsin and Gaidar could not? And why couldn't Gaidar criticize Yeltsin? Maybe it was you who convinced him not to do that? If the DCR had had good results in the Duma election in 1995, there would have been a completely different background to the presidential election in 1996.

CHUBAIS: Everyone is judging Chubais.

AVEN: I am not judging Chubais; I urge him not to take our discussion as a reproof.

KOKH: Yeltsin's achievements in Russia were not market reforms and freedom—we received them from Gorbachev, not Yeltsin. His main contribution was the constitution of 1993, which established the federative republic.

CHUBAIS: If you think that the constitution was the main achievement of Yeltsin, with which I fully agree, then you have to agree that the election (held simultaneously with the constitution referendum) in December 1993 had two goals. One was to bar the communists, and the other was to endorse the constitution. Yeltsin was personally behind both tasks, and his resources were limited. The question is, on which should he have focused—to get our party an election rating of 20 percent instead of 12 percent, or to get the constitution approved? He chose the second.

AVEN: We had a team of ten to 15 people. We were strong and young. We could have become a serious political force. And I think our later attempts to create an independent force were much more complicated, if not doomed. As you, Tolya, justly said, the demand for democracy was gone. And we had lost administrative tools. There was no alternative to us, and we fully controlled the economy until fall 1992. But we had no electoral leader. Gaidar could have become ours, but for various reasons he did not.

We were too childish about power, and I think that was a flawed attitude. Our entire positioning in that political space was erroneous. I think Grisha Yavlinsky was much more productive. Although you, Tolya, are right, and he could not have seriously aspired to power.

CHUBAIS: A short time ago I read Comrade Trotsky, who was loved and respected by everyone for almost a hundred years.

KOKH: The title is *My Life*. A wonderful book!

CHUBAIS: This is not just an interesting book—it is absolutely fantastic! Beautiful language—and I found answers to many of my questions. It has several layers, and one of them is about the question we are debating. What amazed me is that, in the late nineteenth century, Trotsky came from a village to a plant in Mykolaiv. He met a worker; they started to discuss Marxism, and formed an organization. They gathered 20 people at first, then 40, then 100, and then 200—and then they had a demonstration. Then there was the first strike.

I have two thoughts to explain my position in the dispute with you. It's an absolutely fantastic, totally incomprehensible response of people to a set of ideas. Some boy, 17 years old, comes to a plant. He was not appointed; he had neither position nor money—he had nothing. But then he suddenly organized everyone, and they followed him. They responded to what he said.

And the second layer was no less important—the depth of his integration with the people. It makes clear the essence of Bolshevism: they all had folk origins. Meanwhile, we (probably excluding Alfred, because of his exile roots) never had folk origins. We come from Moscow or St Petersburg, and that is not Russia. In this sense, I view folk origins as a fundamental thing—you either have it or not.

We failed to become a genuine political force based on that, rather than on poor administrative resources or lack of support from Yeltsin.

KOKH: But we had Borya Nemtsov—the only one potentially capable of that.

CHUBAIS: Borya Nemtsov was potentially capable of that, but, if you remember, Borya was not with us until 1995. Let us speak frankly about our strength. We had Burbulis, but was he a people's orator?

AVEN: We didn't set ourselves that goal, Tolya.

CHUBAIS: We could not have set that goal because we had a radical lack of understanding of the country and the people, due to our urban origins and lives. We did have a commanding understanding of the subject called "economic reforms"—the best in Russia.

I think that the question "folk or not folk" is absolutely historic. It just so happened, for a number of reasons, that people shifted to liberalism in the late 1980s.

AVEN: That sounds mystical! A regular electrician from a Polish shipyard could incite half of the country to action, and we are talking about a crisis of leadership!

CHUBAIS: Now you're speaking about Poland again. Kazakhstan and Belarus are around us, Petr, not Poland.

A COMPLICATED CHOICE

AVEN: Tolya! Did you have serious disagreements with Gaidar?

CHUBAIS: Yes.

AVEN: What?

CHUBAIS: I have gone over our biggest conflict. In 1995.

AVEN: And you persuaded him?

CHUBAIS: Frankly, that's not quite so. The technology was a bit different. Yegor was a party leader at that moment, not a government member. Then there was the Chechen war, and I found myself in an awful position, being a government member together with Soskovets, Korzhakov, and others.

I asked Yegor's advice on whether I should quit or not. After Black Tuesday,[2] monthly inflation in January 1995 was 18 percent, if I am not mistaken. And we had currency reserves sufficient for only a few days of trade. I was the first vice premier in charge of those affairs. Our common decision was that I could not quit. It is no exaggeration to say that financial stabilization meant the country's survival. Then there was an odd conversation with Sergei Adamovich Kovalyov, which we had arranged with Yegor. It was strange because, as far as I understood, Kovalyov clearly said "don't quit," but in his memoirs he remembered it slightly differently.

I was surrounded by enemies in the government. I was the only one left by early 1995. Who was next to me? There was no Yegor and no Borya Fyodorov. Chernomyrdin had a big problem himself: his personal doctor was killed. Yegor was the leader of a party seeking election to the Duma, running against the war. But once we decided that I should stay, I kept my opinion on the Chechen war to myself, while Yegor naturally could not do that, and had to bring that issue to the parliamentary elections of 1995.

In short, I was working on financial stabilization throughout 1995, and Yegor was organizing anti-war rallies and making speeches. The results of that year: monthly inflation fell to 4 percent by December, and Yegor was leading the party, which opposed the Chechen war and, naturally, Yeltsin. We entered 1996 with the presidential election. Until then, each of us did what he had to do, but then we had to move on into tomorrow and make a decision about the presidential election. My position was that Yeltsin represented the only real chance to save the country from communist revenge. The Democratic Choice position was that Yeltsin could not be supported after he had started a war in Chechnya. At that moment, in January 1996, I was actually (only that one time!) fired from the government; but that naturally did not end my support for Yeltsin. As a private citizen, I went to Davos, where we came to an agreement with the oligarchs, and I joined the campaign. Yegor also started campaigning, but under the "against Yeltsin"

---

2.   "Black Tuesday"—the plunge of the ruble in October 1994.

banner. We met several times to discuss what we should do. Yegor understood what was coming, and I understood how the current situation had developed. Paradoxically, we had practically the same opinions in spite of the serious difference in our political positions. The essence of Yegor's position was: "This is a question of the country's future, not of particular personalities. But," he said, "you must understand that I cannot tell the country that I've changed my mind and will support Yeltsin. So we have a plan—you will organize the congress and prepare the ground for us, and I will go there and try to develop the situation." That is what we did.

AVEN: I am interested in Yegor's reasons for supporting you. Did he think that the congress should convene and review its decision but simply not want to do so himself?

CHUBAIS: He organized the congress himself.

KOKH: Did Gaidar realize that the nomination of the second candidate alongside Yeltsin would mean the failure of both?

CHUBAIS: Certainly.

KOKH: And that there was no chance to convince Yeltsin that he should not take part in elections?

CHUBAIS: Yes.

KOKH: Is that why he gave his support? That is, it was simple math? Did he support Yeltsin as the lesser evil, and not because he wanted to support Yeltsin?

CHUBAIS: Bullshit! The question of sincerity is one to ask a psychiatrist or a lover, not a man responsible for the country's future. Gaidar sincerely wanted to stop the communists, and he did everything necessary to do that.

AVEN: Do you mean Yegor really tried to find another candidate at first?

CHUBAIS: Yes. He was trying to convince Borya Nemtsov at first.

KOKH: What is more, he managed to convince Borya. He visited him in Nizhny. And Borya told me he had agreed. Allegedly he went to Yeltsin and told him, "Your rating is 3 percent," and Yeltsin responded, "Russia's enemies told you that. My rating is 50 percent." That was the end of their conversation. There was no chance of convincing Yeltsin in January 1996 that he did not have 50 percent. Borya said, "I was trying to explain, but to no avail." They did not show the real rating to Yeltsin. Korzhakov and Soskovets were telling lies to Yeltsin. They showed him fake ratings by FAPSI,[3] while they were preparing to disband the Duma by April and declare a state of emergency.

CHUBAIS: Borya is right—that's how it happened. But, in my opinion, no one had persuaded Nemtsov, and he refused to take part in the elections.

KOKH: This means Yegor really tried to consider every option. But when Yegor realized there was no chance to make Yeltsin withdraw, that he would stand just the same and split the democrats, he made the decision to support him. So, even though you call it bullshit, this bullshit is very important for me psychologically.

REFORMS AND THE COLLAPSE OF THE USSR

AVEN: Did Yegor ever tell you his opinion of the loans-for-shares auctions?

CHUBAIS: If it had been something extremely negative, I would have remembered that—which it means it was more or less okay.

AVEN: Well, he told me that was an outrage.

CHUBAIS: He never said anything like that to me.

KOKH: Yegor spoke about that with me probably in 2004. He did not like the loans-for-shares auctions in 1995, and thought they were harmful. But six years later he saw it had been the right decision. He said he had analyzed statistics—the performance of enterprises, what had happened to them, what debts they had—and understood that it had been impossible to carry out privatization in a different way in 1995, and that if it had not been done, all the enterprises would have been dead by 1996.

CHUBAIS: I knew nothing about that logic. In that sense my position was completely non-economic. I still think that the loans-for-shares auctions laid

---

3.   Federal Agency for Government Communications and Information.

down a political foundation for the irreversible defeat of the communists in the election of 1996. Those were the real "commanding heights," the largest enterprises of the country led by "red directors." That alone was enough to call the auctions a positive phenomenon.

AVEN: You bought support.

CHUBAIS: It is a question of who bought whom! It is not clear if we bought their support or caught them on our fishhook! After all, the pawned shares could be bought only after the election, and privatization was out of the question if Zyuganov had won the election. That would have meant their money was wasted. And you have to agree that the election results were achieved mostly thanks to the loans-for-shares auctions.

AVEN: I agree. If we say that the end justifies the means, then the loans-for-shares auctions helped. Would you hold them in a similar situation now?

CHUBAIS: Certainly.

AVEN: Incredible! It's bad enough that you sold the enterprises cheap—your actions crushed the idea of justice! That was the real trouble.

CHUBAIS: So tragic: we crushed the idea of justice that lived in Aven's head. I can live with that. The people's idea of justice was crushed already by voucher privatization. Alfred, tell him.

KOKH: Parting with the Soviet cult of justice, Petr, was the price paid for market reforms. Including privatization.

CHUBAIS: Yes, it could not be saved.

KOKH: Petr keeps publicly distancing himself from the loans-for-shares auctions, as if he were accused of organizing them. And I always have a counter-accusation to bring against him!

CHUBAIS: Don't tell me you are going to blame him for ruble convertibility?

KOKH: What objections can possibly be made to the convertible ruble? I blame Petr for the recognition of the Soviet debts.

AVEN: I have already answered that question in my interview.

KOKH: Sure you did. Just as Chubais answered your question about the loans-for-shares auctions. But that does not mean I agree with the answers. You say, "We exchanged that for a seat at the UN Security Council." To hell with the seat at the Security Council! Ukraine has still not dropped its claims to Soviet property abroad.

AVEN: We would not have opened markets or received IMF loans without that.

KOKH: What could they have done? Or were our negotiators that bad?

CHUBAIS: Alfred, let me tell you this. What I did I remember well, but I did not delve into the details of what Petr was doing.

AVEN: And I did not interfere in what you were doing.

CHUBAIS: We fully trusted each other. I knew for certain that Petr showed up for work at 9:00 a.m. and left at 11:00 p.m., and that everything he was doing was right.

KOKH: And did you have disagreements with Gaidar for the first time in 1996?

CHUBAIS: Yes. It was the first time that we had essentially different political positions. He was against the election of Yeltsin and I was for it. But I never quarreled with Yegor in my life; we were still friends in 1996.

KOKH: Let's talk about 1992. Unfortunately, the two of you stopped my journalistic spree, because I wanted to make fun of people who decided to replenish the circulating assets of enterprises in summer 1992, which led to hyperinflation. Tolya, do you think Gaidar had the ability to resist that?

CHUBAIS: He was resisting the best he could—I remember that. But he did not have enough power, because Yeltsin had the support of banks and enterprises for that action.

KOKH: Gaidar appointed Gerashchenko—was it his choice?

AVEN: Yes, his. Fully, absolutely. They were choosing between Matyukhin, Fyodorov, and Gerashchenko. Gaidar told me that Gerashchenko was an amazingly competent man. He was what we needed.

CHUBAIS: One of the mysteries of my life is what role Gerashchenko played in 1995. I have already talked about January 1995, when hard currency reserves were practically zero, the ruble was falling, monthly inflation was insane—18 percent—and so on. Tatiana Vladimirovna Paramonova was the acting chairperson of the Central Bank. Actually, she and I were responsible for everything that happened in 1995—the ruble, the dollar, the exchange rate, the inflation, the budget deficit, and Central Bank revenue. She was a student and faithful supporter of Gerashchenko. The entire set of decisions, which prevented a macroeconomic catastrophe, was absolutely market-based, extremely liberal, and extremely firm. And at the same time, professionally she was amazingly positive. I could not have ensured a single decision without her, and she was coordinating everything with him. How could he have fully supported the merciless measures in 1995?

AVEN: Gerashchenko was a man of conviction; he believed that economic growth was a function of the Central Bank. I asked him about the unlimited emission of 1992 once (we always had a good relationship), and he said, "Petr, we have a great country and developed industries, and it is a function of the Central Bank to support it."

KOKH: Then why did he change his position in 1995? Do you think he learned the lesson of 1992?

CHUBAIS: Yes. Besides, there was Black Tuesday. Those were good lessons for him. In spite of his age, he was capable of learning, and his position on [the oil company] Yukos is further proof of that for me.

AVEN: Tolya, a fundamental question is about the disintegration of the Soviet Union. We wrote all kinds of different papers, but I don't think we had any real part in that decision.

KOKH: Apart from what Yegor wrote in Belovezh—playing, as Burbulis put it, the role of editor—because among us he was professionally the best suited to it. Unfortunately, we cannot ask Gaidar if he was for or against it.

CHUBAIS: He was not an ideologist of the Union's breakup. And he was not the driver of the negotiations. But he realized fully (a) that it was inevitable and (b) that this formula was the best way to minimize catastrophic consequences. He saw that clearly.

KOKH: And Gorbachev told me in the May interview that even he sees that inevitability now.

CHUBAIS: The idea of the inevitability of the disintegration of the USSR was a shock to me when I first heard it articulated. I remember that, probably in 1987, either Borya Lvin or Vitaly Naishul formulated the three inevitable barriers we had to cross: from authoritarianism to democracy, from planned economy to market, and from empire to post-imperial structure. No one had posed the question that way before—and, by the way, they said that the transition to a market economy would be easier than the transitions to democracy and from empire. That was an intellectual breakthrough! At least for me personally.

KOKH: Back in the 1960s, Andrei Amalrik wrote a rather convincing book titled *Will the Soviet Union Last Until 1984?* And let's give credit to Borya Lvin, who understood that well. He said in 1988 that the USSR would be gone in three years.

CHUBAIS: I am telling you about my own feelings. I did not read Pasternak or Amalrik at that time. We had no access to such books in St Petersburg. I remember Petr telling me later that you guys were total idiots who did not understand what Uzbekistan was. It was a different world, a different planet with different oxygen. You did not have the slightest idea of what it was, and you were trying to introduce self-sufficiency and self-financing there. They had a totally different life. I remember that well.

AVEN: That was in September 1991 in Alpbach, when we adopted the famed declaration. We firmly decided then that we had to move on our own.

CHUBAIS: We understood that the breakup of the USSR was inevitable, and put our understanding in writing (the text of the Alpbach declaration is well known). In essence, that meant reforms would have to be enacted in Russia, not in the USSR. Second, what did that mean to us? That meant the rethinking of large blocks of our ideas, from the petty issue of macroeconomic stabilization (with one central bank or with 15 central banks) to customs, and so on. The inevitability of the USSR's breakup created the necessity of revising the reform program, rather than the reform program leading to the breakup of the USSR. That is a very important nuance, actually.

OCTOBER 1993

KOKH: One more question. There was a referendum in April 1993, which now is called the "Yes-Yes-No-Yes," and you took an active part in it, judging by what Arkady Yevstafyev told me. I think you would agree that, although there were no serious legal grounds, the referendum gave Yeltsin more lawful rights to dismiss the Supreme Council and the congress than he had six months later, in October.

CHUBAIS: I agree.

KOKH: Then why did he not do that? Or did no one raise that question?

CHUBAIS: Let me start from the end. I think it was wrong that he did not dismiss the Supreme Council at that time: there would have been less chance of bloodshed. True, that is what I think now, but I am not sure I thought the same back then. Second, we must admit that the action would have been as illegal as Decree No. 1400 of September 21, 1993, "On Phased Constitutional Reform"—or, simply, on the disbanding of the congress and the Supreme Council.

Here is the question: who were his political advisors at that moment? If I am right, that was the period when Gena was already gone and our intellectuals—Livshits, Baturin, Satarov, and others—were yet to arrive. Yeltsin's political and intellectual backup was Korzhakov, Ilyushin, and the like. Yet such decisions require a circle in which they can be discussed and developed.

KOKH: Wait a second—did the circle change drastically in October 1993? Were there any people demanding the bombardment of the White House?

CHUBAIS: What you call "the bombardment of the White House," I call the suppression of the armed revolt of communists supported by fascists and bandits—a slightly longer name, but I think it is more to the point. That was demanded by the logic of the political process, not by his advisors.

KOKH: Who wrote Decree No. 1400?

CHUBAIS: I think it was Sergei Shakhrai.

KOKH: And was Shakhrai not there in April? In fact, he was. He was also in Belovezh, and moved his pen over the agreement. There was no difference between the April and September teams, with one exception: Yegor was the only man who was added to the team in September.

CHUBAIS: No. My position is absolutely clear. I think that Yeltsin had a sort of shift in August, and rethought the situation. He understood that he must move on, not stopping but bringing things to a close. I do not think he was preparing some special tasks. He simply did two things: (a) he hired Gaidar, (b) he issued the decree. Both resulted from his inner decision.

KOKH: But before hiring him he had to meet him?

CHUBAIS: So he did.

KOKH: And told him, "I want to invite you back into the government." And Yegor replied, "On the condition you disband the Supreme Council. That is the question on which I am ready to go to the end with you."

CHUBAIS: Come on, that is nonsense. How was Yegor involved in all that? As I understand it, Yeltsin let him know that dramatic events were pending when he took him on.

KOKH: I remember that Yegor's first trip in his new capacity was to Khabarovsk and Komsomolsk-on-Amur, and I traveled with him. He had been working for only a few days. I can tell you that when Yegor and I returned from Khabarovsk, I went to my hotel in Plotnikov Lane, and then took a walk to Smolenskaya and saw those guys headed toward the mayor's office. The next day they burned down the mayor's office and started killing policemen. That was on October 2. That was actually Gaidar's first trip outside of Moscow. On the way back to Moscow we made a stopover in Omsk to pick up Kazannik, who soon became the prosecutor-general.

CHUBAIS: What do you mean? Do you mean that Gaidar convinced Yeltsin to sign that decree?

KOKH: I don't know. That is not important. But it was a decision made jointly with Gaidar. I am sure of that. It fitted Yegor's nature well—you know, he was a bold man.

We Never Fought in Thirty Years

AVEN: Sure, Gaidar was brave, but your opinion, Alfred, is disputable. Tolya, let us conclude our conversation with some personal words about Gaidar. How did you see him as a person, and what did he mean to you?

CHUBAIS: Let's start from my personal opinion of his place on our team. I think he was an absolutely fantastic phenomenon. I mean, he was a leader of such scale that he gave a new quality to the others due to (a) his profound intellect, (b) his moral and ethical standards, and (c) his background.

He was our senior by the position he held before joining the government, and that was also important—by Soviet standards he was on the level of a Union minister. This meant he was prepared for the job in all senses, and his class changed the quality of the entire team and the entire reform. That is the objective estimation.

As for the personal side, that was a truly amazing story. We never quarreled in 30 years of friendship; I always knew he would stand by me in the most dramatic situations—and he did, by the way, even when circumstances were the hardest. It is well known that the truth comes out when interests come into conflict rather than when they coincide. Whom do you love more, Papa or Mama? That is the correct, fundamental, and historical question. Whenever a choice has to be made, the true face of a person shows. For me the situation I was in—deep, over my head actually; and Yegor did not have to take care of me, but he did help me—was totally essential to me.

Certainly the depth of Yegor's understanding of the subject called "national economy" was always a head taller than mine. I remember in 1989 (when I was fostering the work of engineers, and Yegor was working for the journal *Kommunist*) I went to his place and we talked. We were doing the so-called Leningrad experiment. Yegor asked me to write an article about our work for *Kommunist*. I wrote it and took it to him. Yegor tore it to shreds. I realized then what a professional analysis meant, irrespective of close friendship. I realized how much I fell short of his requirements. I also saw his fantastic depth and integral view of the economy. Yegor had that quality more than any of us. Amazingly, he was practical, which is a rare combination. He combined it all.

Grisha Glazkov recently called Yegor "an aristocrat." Aristocrat in the full sense of that word, meaning that there are democrats and there are aristocrats. Aristocrats are a class bearing responsibility for the future of the country, fully aware of their place as regards other classes, and they do not even try to play the usual democratic game. I may be conveying this idea rather badly—but this is an interesting thought.

Kokh: Obviously Gaidar was a very brave man. When we spoke with Gena, we found out that Gaidar's bravery, if not wholly then partially, was explained by his lack of interest in life. Can you say something about that?

Chubais: I know Yegor's family story, which started with his father. That was a mysterious story, described with the formula "lack of the fear gene." Yegor thought he had passed that gene to his daughter Masha. Remember Masha hanging under the bridge demonstrating?

Kokh: We do.

Chubais: That was how Yegor explained her actions: there is no fear, it does not exist. He never said that about himself, but he said it about Masha. He described their genealogical line to me.

Kokh: You see, bravery is the ability to defeat one's fear. But is it bravery when you simply do not value life?

Chubais: Might that be practically the same thing—no fear of death and placing no value on life?

Kokh: These are different things. You are brave when you overcome your fear; but when you have none, you do not value life.

Chubais: You're probably right.

Kokh: His death is a proof of how little he cared about his life.

Chubais: I do not know. I remember Yegor near the Moscow City Council in 1993.

Kokh: I imagine very well how he would have taken up a submachine gun. He would have missed; he didn't know how to use one.

Chubais: In the Ossetian–Ingush conflict, when Yegor met with one of the sides for negotiations, they strewed the porch with corpses with the backbones hacked open for some reason—I don't know why. Probably they wanted to scare him. And Yegor came out of the negotiating room and just kept on walking. I remember him on the night of October 3, 1993, when his life was practically hanging by a hair. Absolute intellectual concentration, intensive thinking. Very firm and, at the same time, efficient actions—both his own actions and the commands he gave to others. And not even a millimeter of fear.

KOKH: But Petr expressed the very interesting idea that Yegor personified violence in the eyes of most people. Those two submachine-gun episodes create a similar impression.

CHUBAIS: With all his seeming softness, he was quite firm. But you can't try to govern Russia without this firmness.

KOKH: It seems to me he did not value life, and was certain that people just pretended to value it.

CHUBAIS: No, he rather thought like an aristocrat. He had a mission, and he acted. The country needed that, so he had to act. The visit to the Moscow City Council was one of the main events of that night, which prevented a massacre in Russia. And he was the first to arrive there!

KOKH: In Sheremet's film, which was screened to mark Yegor's birthday, I liked the interview with Khasbulatov, who repeated the same phrase several times. He said he did not know that Gaidar was such a cruel man.

AVEN: We were all half children back then.

CHUBAIS: Well, we stopped being children by 1993, but we still did not know the country.

KOKH: No one knows it now. You can't know it even if you want to.

CHUBAIS: All right, then. Thank you.

3

ALEXANDER SHOKHIN

"We Took as Much Power as We Could"

ALEXANDER NIKOLAYEVICH SHOKHIN is the oldest member of the Gaidar team. He looks like a geek, primarily because of his thick glasses (one eye is −18 diopters, and the other is even worse). But his appearance is very deceiving. Among us, Shokhin has always been the most down-to-earth, sober-minded, and shrewd—in the good sense of that word. It may be due to his origins; we all come from families of intellectuals (living in Moscow and St Petersburg), but Sasha spent his early childhood in a village in the Arkhangelsk region, and then moved to a barracks in Kapotnya, near Moscow, with his mother, a teacher who raised him, and his brother.

He had a fantastic career in the USSR. He was under 40 years old when he became a doctor, an advisor to a Politburo member (!), and practically the director of an academic institute. It is hard to explain the significance of these achievements to those who have no memories of that life.

The reason was not only his extraordinary acumen. In contrast to some of our colleagues, Shokhin was a really big economic scientist. He was thoughtful, and his texts were original. He was capable of unexpected and paradoxical conclusions.

He was also a remarkable bureaucrat—thorough to the point of boredom, very hardworking and responsible, loyal to his superiors irrespective of his opinion of them. (Unlike Chubais, for example, Shokhin never idealized his bosses.) That was the main reason for his long life in high places.

In spite of his excessive (in the opinion of ill-wishers) conformism, Shokhin has always had firm principles and stamina. His sudden withdrawals from the governments of Viktor Stepanovich Chernomyrdin in 1994 and Yevgeny Primakov in 1998 are illustrative of this.

I also think that Shokhin has a remarkable combination of big ambitions, self-confidence, excessive caution, and insufficient (in my subjective opinion) readiness to take a risk. That might be a consequence of his background or an acute protectiveness toward his family. I think his extremely bad eyesight might be a reason: any internal problem reduces the strength one needs to deal with external ones, and leads to the unconscious wish to save one's energy (elderly people narrow their circle to save strength this way). At least twice, Sasha did not take a risk when he could have. It happened for the first time in 1991, when he did not even try to fight for the position of economic leader, even though he had as much reason as Gaidar to do so. The second time happened in the early 1990s, when he rejected my urgings to leave government work for business.

Excessive caution also explains Shokhin's keen attention to people, their behavior, and their conversations. He views history not as a struggle of social forces or "a change of socioeconomic formations" (although he is extremely knowledgeable about that, too), but as people and their wishes, deeds, relationships, betrayals, and rare heroic feats. This makes his interview extremely interesting for those who personally know the individuals he mentions and much less interesting for the general public. Still, I am positive it will be of interest to historians: no matter what historical materialism might claim, the personal qualities of participants in those events and their relationships were not the least important factor in the historical process.

It is easy to interview Shokhin. He is self-confident, and therefore frank; he is not afraid to make mistakes or give offense. He told us plenty of interesting and unexpected things. True, he also omitted a lot. In short, Shokhin is a grand man. Very wise. And it is a pleasure to speak with him.

Petr Aven

PETR AVEN: There are people who believe you could have taken charge of the economic team. You were the eldest. You were the only one holding an important state position. You were an advisor to the foreign minister.

ALEXANDER SHOKHIN: What does being an advisor have to do with it? I had already been a minister in the Silayev government!

AVEN: Even more so.

SHOKHIN: I agreed to join the Russian government on August 19. Before that I was offered a place in the Silayev cabinet as a representative of the Russian Social Democratic Party if I joined that party. I did not want that, and I did not want the position of labor minister in the "secondary" republican government, either. I reaffirmed the idea of Grisha Yavlinsky—back then the real work was only in the Union government.

AVEN: I guess Sasha would be the best expert on Yavlinsky of that period.

SHOKHIN: Yavlinsky asked me to join the Russian government a year earlier, as the labor minister. And I declined the offer for that very reason: I didn't quite understand what one could do in the RSFSR government when the main decisions were made on the Union level. Options appeared only after the putsch, when the Dacha 15 team was formed.

The search for an alternative team was, naturally, initiated by Gennady Burbulis as the state secretary. First of all, he wanted to have his vision of reforms and his team, and he had no economic team of his own to oppose such heavyweights as Skokov and Lobov. Second, he wanted a no less reformist vision than the Yavlinsky team did. Hence he readily accepted candidates proposed by Alexey Golovkov, who actually formed that team and led Gaidar by the hand. Unlike me, Gaidar was a free actor. I was a government member and operated inside the system in August 1991, while Gaidar remained an independent expert and, as the director of the Economic Policy Institute of the Academy of the Economy, was an ideal candidate to write an alternative reform program. It was also important that he rapidly formed an efficient team of his colleagues and friends.

ALFRED KOKH: Alternative to what? I want to understand.

HOW MANY PROGRAMS WERE THERE?

SHOKHIN: Actually, there were two more programs.

KOKH: But was Yavlinsky's writing on his own initiative?

SHOKHIN: I think so. Besides, Yavlinsky never wanted to link himself with the Russian Federation. He wanted to be the "economic tsar" of the Soviet Union. Therefore, he needed a program.

KOKH: So that was why Burbulis did not rely on Yavlinsky—it was actually

Yavlinsky who did not want Burbulis to rely on him!

SHOKHIN: In Yavlinsky's eyes, the republic level strongly limited his idea of his role in history. He thought Gorbachev could preserve the Union.

KOKH: Do you mean the thesis that, before he "made an offer that cannot be refused" to Gaidar, Burbulis made the same offer to Yavlinsky, is impossible because it never could have happened? Gena strongly denies making some proposals to Yavlinsky.

SHOKHIN: There could have been such a conversation, but I think Yavlinsky might have rudely snubbed the republic-level nonsense.

AVEN: Even if there was, it must have been pro forma, mostly to clear the conscience.

SHOKHIN: First, to clear the conscience; and, second, Burbulis had to explain to Yeltsin why he had brought in a team Yeltsin did not know. That was a good explanation: Yavlinsky didn't care about the Russian Federation and was building his system for the Union government. Another reason that was a good explanation is that it was true.

After the August putsch many well-known people returned to Gorbachev. For instance, Shevardnadze returned to the position of foreign minister in mid-November 1991. Vladislavlev became his first deputy for foreign economic policy at the ministerial level. We used the same formula later on: Petr Aven initially headed the foreign economic committee at the united Foreign Ministry.

KOKH: Do you think that Yavlinsky believed in the inviolability of Union institutions because he was not Russian? He was born in Ukraine, and so on. Could that be why he didn't see himself as the leader of a government seated in Moscow?

SHOKHIN: I also had an impression that he saw himself as the leader of the Union government because of his complex life story. He was born in Lvov and studied there, but he made his career as an economist and a politician in Moscow.

KOKH: I learned about Yavlinsky from TV when he was appointed Silayev's vice premier for economics and reforms at the Russian Congress of People's

Deputies in 1990. But I was still in Leningrad, and you were working in Moscow. Was Yavlinsky known as a scholar in the young academic circle—economists, sociologists, and others—to which we belonged in the second half of the 1980s?

SHOKHIN: Grisha wrote a rather revolutionary report when he was working for the Labor Research Institute, where I met him.

AVEN: When was it?

SHOKHIN: In 1980 or 1981. He proved that resolutions "on new upgrading measures" were insufficient. And he presented rather serious arguments that a crucial restructuring of the economic management system was needed. Grisha even thinks that his forcible hospitalization started at that very moment, and they found a diagnosis that was not mental, as was usually done in those days, but purely physiological. They said he had a lung problem and needed intensive care, or even an operation.

KOKH: The doctors told him that?

SHOKHIN: In such cases our doctors were closely linked with the Lubyanka. It was not hard to make the "correct" diagnosis, especially when there was no diagnosis at all. When Abalkin became the main reformer of the Union government, he offered Yavlinsky a position as a department head at the Economic Reforms Commission. Other department heads were Yasin and Melikian. Shcherbakov was the commission's deputy head. I also spoke to Abalkin, and he offered me a job.

KOKH: In what capacity did Abalkin want you?

SHOKHIN: As a department head, just like Yavlinsky, Yasin, and Melikian. I think that was 1988. I asked him, "What powers do we have, and what are we expected to do?" And he told me if we wrote a good program we would urge our government colleagues to implement it. Then they might start doing what was necessary. The scenario did not look convincing to me: actually, there was no order for a reform from the political administration, but there was a vice premier writing a program jointly with knowledgeable experts, without a purpose. It was when Grisha started his rise. The Abalkin commission played a key role in writing the program. Grisha was a notable and brilliant elaborator, in particular of the 500 Days program. Yasin was very happy with him.

AVEN: Yes, Yasin adored him.

SHOKHIN: Yavlinsky and I went our separate ways for the first time when he became a Russian vice premier and I refused to join his team as the labor minister. In my opinion, Grisha is not a politician, because politics always means a fight for power, and Grisha was not an active fighter for power. He built some ideal structure in his head and expected it to work: he wanted to promote his ideas, disregarding practical reality and the crude truth about techniques to access power. That was why he had never won it.

KOKH: That was not the reason. I think he actually did not want power.

SHOKHIN: You're wrong—he wanted power. But he wanted to get that power by showing: "See what a beautiful program I have! Won't you give me power?" And later on, when he started fighting for power and even when he could have been nominated as the common candidate of the opposition, he refused to make blocs with other political factions and people, even if he liked them personally, because he did not want to ruin the "purity" of his structure. I discussed electoral scenarios with him in detail in the presidential election in 1996. I told him, "Grisha, you can rank third by electoral support. But you will have to unite with others to achieve that. You need the support of all liberal and democratic forces. Your task is to be number three, as you cannot aspire to more. If Zyuganov gets second place, you may get 15 percent, which actually exists in that electoral sector. That result will enable you to aspire to the premiership. But to do that, you will have to urge your voters to support Yeltsin in the second round." He refused. He thought any compromises would undercut the chances of implementing his own program.

RECOLLECTIONS ABOUT THE CANDIDATES

SHOKHIN: All right, we've digressed. Let's get back to the teams. There was also the team of Zhenya Saburov, which included many well-known people, such as Materov and Lopukhin. Saburov joined the Silayev government on the same day as I did. I was appointed labor minister in August 1991, and he shifted from the position of deputy education minister to economic minister. They started writing a program for the Silayev government. But as Silayev was appointed to the Union Committee for Operative Control of the People's Economy (later known as IEC), their client sort of started vanishing. It was like having a client and not having one. Around

September Yeltsin took offense at Silayev (probably for sitting on the fence), and made that committee his permanent job, while Lobov was made the acting premier.

It was a fairytale job in that government. The meetings were chaired either by Silayev, by an experienced manager from the "red directors," or by Lobov, and they focused on operative tasks of the kind.

KOKH: Where is Lobov now? He was a founding father of the First Chechen War. As far as I remember, he was the Russian Security Council secretary in 1994.

SHOKHIN: He has some international organization, which used to have headquarters on Petrovka, in the building opposite the Marriott Aurora. The prosecutor general's office is there now.

AVEN: He doesn't care, he is a pensioner.

SHOKHIN: But then, in fall 1991, he had strong aspirations for premiership because he was the acting premier, and the second candidate was Skokov. Burbulis had to find a team not so much to write a good program but to override the premiership ambitions of Skokov and Lobov. He needed the program to be written by people who could join the government. Formally, I was the only government member related to Gaidar's program. Not just formally—I had a real relation to it. I was the only one who was a minister. I dropped by Dacha 15 in Arkhangelskoye in the morning, and then in the evening after work.

KOKH: Is that where you met Burbulis?

SHOKHIN: Burbulis hired me as labor minister together with Silayev. I got acquainted with him after the presidential election of June 12, 1991. Nearly a week after the election I was in his office, and he took me to Silayev's office. Silayev asked me, "So, you're not a member of the Social Democratic Party and you want to be labor minister?" I said, "Not particularly; but they want me."

Formally, I was the only government member in the Gaidar team. And the idea of my heading the government's economic bloc was suggested first by Poltoranin, who visited Dacha 15. He was wondering what was going on there. He asked me who those people were. His dacha was nearby. He asked if Gaidar was good enough to be finance minister. And I told him he was even better.

AVEN: Were there any candidates? It seemed at the time that Burbulis was pulling ministerial candidates out of his sleeve.

SHOKHIN: The thing is, there were no candidates. Poltoranin told me: "I have a proposal. Let's divide the government into two parts. You will control the economic bloc, and I will control the political. We will be two first vice premiers." And I asked, who would be the premier? He said we would decide that later. He started listing candidates: Gaidar could be the finance minister. Were there any other worthy candidates? I said, "A lot!" He told me to nominate anyone I wanted for positions in the economic bloc, but on one condition: there must be no Burbulis at all.

AVEN: All of Yeltsin's men disliked Burbulis a lot!

SHOKHIN: He said he would be in charge of the political bloc and, if I agreed, I would control the economic bloc, and he suggested I start organizing. I decided that it was a provocative idea to an extent: it might discredit me in the eyes of the Dacha 15 team, and isolate Gennady. So I decided to have no aspirations—otherwise I could have been involved in some murky political intrigue.

In the end, even though Yeltsin appointed Yegor to that bloc, the Poltoranin structure of the government came into existence one way or another. The government was still divided into two parts. We had no access to the media, not to mention more serious political issues.

By the way, that was when another "genius" idea was implemented to override Lobov, Skokov, and all sorts of Poltoranins: to convince Yeltsin to be the acting premier for a while, which was allowed by the constitution. That was our proposal. He could not grasp for a long time why we needed that, and he had a gut feeling that it was wrong: there was a government that could be blamed for everything, and as president and premier at the same time, he would bear full responsibility!

We gave him the following argument: as the Fifth Congress entrusted him with special powers for a year to issue decrees with the power of law in economic matters, it would be logical to issue those decrees as government resolutions in order to avoid a schism between him and the government. That, by the way, led to rehearsals for government meetings, held on Tuesdays, when we would fight each other and seek solutions. The idea was that, since the official government meetings were held on Thursdays, we would have our coordinated positions ready to present to Yeltsin without having to wash our dirty laundry in front of him.

KOKH: With whom did you have the biggest conflicts, and why? There were no conflicts inside the team, as far as I understand.

SHOKHIN: The first decrees of November 15 concerned the economy: uncontrolled foreign trade and liberalization in general. That was a definite impulse that formed the government ideology.

KOKH: Did you cause a lot of controversy?

SHOKHIN: There was no controversy, with the exception of one item. Gaidar spoke about economic matters in front of the cameras, and I spoke about social matters, and then Yeltsin said, looking into the camera, "Do the cabinet members have any additions or proposals to make?" And Gaidar was prepared. "We would like to make a statement. Reforms are a period of ordeal, so we, members of the government you have appointed, wish to refuse our privileges—our apartments, dachas, and special stores—until the life of our citizens improves." Yeltsin looked around and said, "Look what heroes we have here." And suddenly Andrei Kozyrev asked, "Yeltsin, may I ask you a question?" "Yes, you may," he said, expecting even more emotion. "You know we are planning to live together with my mother, and we are exchanging a three-room apartment and a two-room apartment for a five-room apartment. Can we do that? It won't disagree with Gaidar's statement, will it?" he asked. Yeltsin practically choked. "You may, you may!" he said, making it clear that declarations were one thing, but business was business. Kozyrev ruined the emotional moment.

AVEN: He was not a member of our team. He had been a minister—one of the first.

SHOKHIN: The way the cabinet was formed fit the team technology. The government "organizing committee" consisted of Yeltsin as chairman, Burbulis as deputy chairman, and three organizing committee members: Gaidar, Shokhin, and Shakhrai. We met at Yeltsin's office in the Kremlin and discussed the most important draft decrees; he asked questions and often got extremely simple answers, and he signed degrees appointing government members with no particular delay.

We had lots of decrees drafted at Dacha 15. Yeltsin said, "Before you present our drafts, I would like to discuss one personnel issue. There is a wonderful man, Gavriil Kharitonovich Popov. He would like to be the RSFSR foreign minister"—basically the Shevardnadze scheme plus

overseeing foreign economic policy. "What do you think?" Gaidar and I
said, all together, "You know, Yeltsin, Gavriil Kharitonovich was our professor, our teacher, our dean. But he is not a member of our team. If you want
to spend half your time analyzing the opinions of different parts of your
team, we have no objections. This is your right." Yeltsin said, "Actually, I do
not insist on Popov; that was just an idea, I wanted to know your opinion."
It was then that we realized we were lucky. We could reject Popov so quickly
(Yeltsin said he was just testing our opinion), and that meant he was paying
attention to our opinion. What's more, Burbulis must have persuaded him
that the team that wrote the program should implement it.

After that the formation of the cabinet was purely technical. We needed
candidates to fit ministerial positions by their professionalism, do managerial work, and publicly defend their positions, primarily at the Supreme
Council.

KOKH: Did the team aspire to power from the beginning?

SHOKHIN: I remember well the approach we used to seize commanding
positions. We decided, for instance, there would be no separate ministries of
finance and economy. Why? Because Gaidar could become finance minister, while the position of economy minister might have been given to a "red
director," which would have made a confrontation inevitable. Hence, we
combined the ministries of economy and finance, and minimized possible
conflicts.

Another example: I was labor minister, but there was also the State Labor
Committee. We merged the Labor Ministry and the State Committee and
formed the Labor Committee at the ministry. This was administrative
reform, in effect, to exclude competing structures that could express different opinions on the same themes.

Alexey Golovkov and I spent much time implementing that structural
reform. We wanted to make the government smaller and more compact,
bearing in mind that we had a limited number of candidates for key positions. First, state committees and other entities were absorbed by ministries
and became ministerial committees, and their heads became deputy ministers. Second, we hired "bourgeois," or rather Soviet, specialists, so that they
would side with us when they came into our employ (such as Anisimov
from Gossnab). That made the government understandable to the Supreme
Council: by appointing to secondary positions people who already held
them or were first deputies, we demonstrated our loyalty to the system.

So I cannot say that we were not fighting for power. We took as much power as we could at that moment. To take all the power was unrealistic then. As a result, we were able to assume responsibility for socioeconomic policy (as much as we could), largely thanks to the administrative reform—I think it was the best of all subsequent administrative reforms.

AVEN: You're talking about tactics, while the general inclination was to take control of economic levers only.

SHOKHIN: Yes, at least economic levers.

KOKH: So there were no plans to gain control over the media, or political departments?

SHOKHIN: No, that was unrealistic. We did not even think about political aspirations.

THE KAMIKAZE GOVERNMENT

AVEN: Why were we so modest, do you think? Or were we not modest? Did we not give enough attention to power matters?

SHOKHIN: I think a reason was the mood of that government. We convinced not only ourselves but also Burbulis and Yeltsin that our mission was to clean the Augean stables and do unpopular dirty work. No one could do that work for us, because no one would be patted on the head for doing it, and we would be kicked out of the government in a year at best, or maybe by spring.

AVEN: Judging by your political career or Chubais's, that's what happened.

SHOKHIN: We were actually called a kamikaze government. We believed that Grisha Yavlinsky and Zhenya Saburov would never agree to do dirty work, such as price liberalization, and then quit.

KOKH: To public hooting and booing.

SHOKHIN: Yes. That was the way we were. We wanted to do the job and did not need political positions. "You, Shokhin, are in charge of the social bloc, and you'll probably be the first to go." The social consequences would be immediate.

AVEN: "Yes, I'll be the first to go," Shokhin responded.

SHOKHIN: No way. I am cunning.

KOKH: An ordinary person is unlikely to enjoy being a messiah because of the cross, in the end.

AVEN: Alfred, I really don't think we were prepared to carry the cross to Golgotha. A mature judgment would say that was a technique, a means of taking power: "We are temporary, guys, don't you fret! You will be back, we will just clean the stables a bit and you will return wearing white, and will either put us in the hold or throw us overboard." And many actually believed that!

SHOKHIN: Including the team members.

AVEN: The team members were the first to believe it. Some, not all.

SHOKHIN: Come on, you're so smart now. As if you were as experienced and cynical 20 years ago. Maybe deep down none of us believed in the messianic role. But politics was new to us—there was no sense of the need to engage in politics seriously and for long. It looked like we could get involved and then quit. That is what happened to many.

AVEN: Craftiness.

SHOKHIN: The brief involvement in politics?

AVEN: I mean being kamikaze.

SHOKHIN: I can say for sure that the situation changed when we presented our resignation to the congress in spring 1992, when Khasbulatov insulted us.

AVEN: Let's get into that episode.

SHOKHIN: Look back to the episode chronology, when Burbulis gave the order and everyone stood up and left. If you watch it in slow motion, you will see that I started packing my briefcase immediately after Khasbulatov's words. I had lots of papers. Then Gena gave the order. I was packed by then.

AVEN: You just started to pack your briefcase; it had nothing to do with Khasbulatov's rudeness.

SHOKHIN: But it did. I thought, "I'm not going to let a boor give us a tongue-lashing!" So I'm saying that when we resigned in spring 1992, the situation was different. In November 1991 we were certain that we were the kamikaze government. And no one really wanted to quit in April 1992, when we announced our resignation. The only man who took all that seriously was the late Titkin: "Come on, guys, I am not going to resign!" But no one wanted to resign! That was a mechanism of political pressure on the congress, and he was the only one who got scared.

AVEN: When I wrote the statement at the end of 1992.

KOKH: I remember you telling me how you all agreed to go home and write statements of resignation. And when you wrote the statement, you turned out to be the only one.

AVEN: No one wanted to write one. What's more, I was persuading Sasha to go into business with me.

SHOKHIN: I was a fool, certainly.

AVEN: I wrote the statement not because we had an agreement, I just thought I had had enough. Besides, Chernomyrdin would have fired me all the same.

SHOKHIN: I still dream of going into business and making money. But I want to say that only one person believed our intentions were serious when we tendered our resignation in spring 1992.

KOKH: And was frightened.

SHOKHIN: And was frightened. The others thought it was a cunning move, a powerful mechanism of pressure, and the deputies would have no way out.

AVEN: That is what actually happened.

SHOKHIN: In fact, we gained levers of control, and not only of the economy. That was first of all.

AVEN: And understood how that really worked.

SHOKHIN: Yes. Second, Yeltsin still had special powers; he had the right for the next six months to issue decrees with the force of law. It would have been silly not to take advantage of that and not to go further while that was still possible.

KOKH: Burbulis said he was surprised by your ability to take such a bold step as the collective resignation. Yeltsin was also surprised—he was even somewhat at a loss.

SHOKHIN: The move surprised him, but he also liked it. I had an impression that he realized the guys shared his mentality, they were not four-eyed scholars, but were capable of serious political actions.

AVEN: Of an act.

SHOKHIN: Right. They were capable of reaching agreements, and they displayed that ability. I think Yeltsin liked that at first. His position was shaky at the congress. As far as I remember, he nearly started repenting and begging for pardon. He was very uncomfortable, and our move allowed him to restore balance and to mobilize himself. He always needed something to spur him, and our resignation mobilized him, and he was practically the winner at the end of the congress.

I remember my meeting with Yeltsin. I told him, "The congress had 400 votes for my resignation. The reforms are good but their consequences are bad, so the social vice premier must resign. I won't explain the cause and the consequence, but I recommend that you don't give me up for nothing. Whenever you dismiss a team member, you need to arrange it as a gain, not as a concession." So we talked, and then I left and Burbulis visited him. Burbulis told me about that later. Yeltsin was frowning. "Shokhin came to me and said, 'I would not recommend that you give me up.' What does that mean?" In the end he dismissed me from the position of vice premier and labor minister, and made me vice premier for CIS affairs and foreign economic policy. The way he understood it, I was taking care of myself. But I actually gave him the advice that he should not sacrifice a team member without gaining something in exchange.

I can imagine how shocked he was when I came and actually gave him an ultimatum: "Don't you give me up or you will face the consequences." He was stunned by my trick, and decided not just to let me be but also to give me a less vulnerable position.

AVEN: Could we have built on the success of the collective resignation? Tried to gain more powers from Yeltsin or from the congress?

SHOKHIN: Here things become more complex. I will remind you of your initial question: Should we tell the truth or stay loyal to each other? We chose the first. We had a rather clear, black-and-white picture of the world before April, and nuances popped up in late April.

AVEN: In May, with the surrender of Lopukhin.

SHOKHIN: The way Lopukhin was surrendered! I remember the Kremlin meeting on fuel and energy. Everyone was seated, and Lopukhin was expected to make a report. Yeltsin entered, followed by Chernomyrdin, and took a seat. Yeltsin said, "I have signed a decree. Gaidar, you make the report." And it was clear what decree he had signed.

AVEN: He said, "I signed a decree to dismiss a minister." Then he went silent. And then he added, "Lopukhin."

SHOKHIN: Yegor delivered the report that Lopukhin managed to hand him. Actually, that was done under the powerful pressure of oil and energy industry executives who were mad at the appointment of this minister.

KOKH: What was the essence of their claims? Was he a big impediment?

SHOKHIN: I don't think he was an impediment at all, but the fuel and energy lobby was the strongest and they wanted their own man.

KOKH: Their own, but to do what? To reduce duties?

SHOKHIN: Someone who spoke their language, rather than Lopukhin. Our government was a group of technocrats-slash-academicians. Whenever we gave them arguments that were industrial on the one hand and theoretical on the other, it naturally irritated the oil generals. I think Lopukhin's manners infuriated them, too.

Actually, there were several irritating people. Lopukhin was irritating, Aven was irritating, I was irritating. Lopukhin irritated them with his mentoring manner. He showed them from the very start that he had a profound knowledge of the oil business, the energy industry.

KOKH: He was a typical honor student, a geek.

SHOKHIN: He was an honor student, plus he came from an elite Moscow family. His father was the director of the GKNT institute dealing with industrial espionage. He knew academicians from his childhood. His uncle gave Lenin's body embalming boosters—he was the head of the laboratory that preserved the body. And the genius boy from a good family became a minister, and started lecturing people. As I understand, the generals wanted him gone not because they disagreed with his opinions but because they disliked his manner.

I can tell you about Petr. He always talked very fast; Yeltsin didn't always grasp the meaning or manage to keep up. And when Petr asked me, "Why doesn't Yeltsin like me?" I told him, "It is just that you work at different speeds. He just can't keep up with you." He did not like me for wearing thick glasses—they were so thick because of outdated technology. They kept him from understanding what was on my mind. So there were plenty of psychological factors.

AVEN: I know what you mean. I accompanied him on the trips. Everyone drank heavily, and I didn't drink a lot in those days. He didn't feel comfortable boozing when I was around. He liked traveling with Gaidar more. That was natural. There are some of my bank guys I want at the table and some I don't. Age matters, common values matter, the attitude to drinking matters.

SHOKHIN: The same with Lopukhin. But I don't think the surrender of Lopukhin was the turning point. No matter how strange it may sound, the turning point was the lowercasing of Gena Burbulis's title: he was the State Secretary and then he became the state secretary. That happened before Lopukhin's dismissal, in May.

KOKH: Who suggested that?

SHOKHIN: Khasbulatov. He said there was no constitutional post of State Secretary, and proposed to de-capitalize it. That showed that Yeltsin was already making concessions. First you invent the State Secretary title for your associate; then do not let anyone harm him. He should have abolished the position and made Gena an ordinary vice premier. Afterward it snowballed, and particularly in May. There were some counterbalancing steps in June. Gaidar became the acting premier.

I must say that the appointment of Gaidar as a first vice premier (that is, the second first) in March, before the congress, was a certain deviation from the original principles. Because of that, Burbulis stopped being the only first vice premier and actual head of the government. The original idea of a compact government was for a first vice premier and two vice premiers. New vice premiers appeared later on—Poltoranin, Shakhrai, Shumeiko, Makharadze, and Khizha. There were lots of people. Shumeiko became the third first vice premier.

KOKH: How did Gena react when he stopped being the only first vice premier?

SHOKHIN: In my opinion, his reaction was very calm. He is strictly a team player. He makes something of a person, and if this person can go up higher, that is also his success. That is his moral principle.

When Gaidar became acting premier, he changed a lot. He stopped being the "economic tsar" and became a politician. He also had a goal, which was quite justified, in my opinion: if a reformer can become the premier, why not? Concessions, swaps, coalitions, and so on—all that became possible. By the way, the appointment of Gerashchenko as the Central Bank chairman was fully Yegor's initiative.

KOKH: I didn't know Yegor proposed that. I thought he simply didn't object to that appointment—and now you tell me that was his initiative!

SHOKHIN: That was his choice. It was clear that the Supreme Council had staked a lot on Gerashchenko. Yeltsin had objections. I attended at least two meetings where the subject was discussed. At Vnukovo, Yeltsin was flying off somewhere—he was in a "jolly" mood. And then Gaidar presented a draft letter nominating Gerashchenko for the Central Bank chairmanship. Yeltsin said, "Are you nuts? I have two volumes of compromising material about him, and you propose to nominate him as the Central Bank head!" Then there was a meeting of vice premiers, vice speakers of the Supreme Council, Gaidar, and Khasbulatov with the president, I think, in Novo-Ogaryovo. Gaidar felt somewhat uncomfortable nominating Gerashchenko again. So he approached Khizha, who had just been appointed. "Georgy Stepanovich, do you agree?" I heard Gaidar asking Khizha. Georgy Stepanovich said, "Yeltsin, the government has discussed it once again, and we ask you to think about the appointment of Gerashchenko." Yeltsin, "We discussed that." The moment was chosen correctly, because Khasbulatov and the vice speakers were there. They all raised a racket: "Say, that's a good alternative.

The government made a good proposal." Gaidar was sitting to one side, but it was he who orchestrated that. He needed support from the parliament leaders. He was preparing for the congress that was due to approve the premier.[1]

THE ELECTION OF THE PREMIER

KOKH: That's why it was necessary to swap the Central Bank chairman for the premier?

SHOKHIN: I think Yegor acted on that premise. But he was not a politician at the time. He thought he was doing a favor, which would be appreciated. But when the congress started, the deputies had already digested it. They had forgotten about it. Yeltsin was also preparing for the congress, which was supposed to approve the premier. Gena was removed from the government, and Yeltsin was already playing his own game.

KOKH: Was Yeltsin playing against Gaidar?

SHOKHIN: No, but he had a different game already. He wanted to gain approval of his premier at any cost. When we discussed that among the team members, we decided there were two options. The first one was to sacrifice the team and to nominate Yegor for premier, and then to decide what to do next: a mass surrender in exchange for the premiership. The second option was to hire a technical premier and not to give up the team. Yegor chose the second option. Yegor was told, "Choose any candidate." We went to Toliatti and took a look at Vladimir Kadannikov. I went to Paris to speak to Ryzhov, who was the ambassador to France. I told him, "Yuri Alexeyevich, we need you. We need a premier to give us a political shield, even if he knows nothing about the economy. I beg your pardon for my frankness, but that is you." "No, thank you, I'm fine here in Paris." "Too bad."

KOKH: In the end Yegor decided on Kadannikov?

AVEN: That wasn't sincere.

SHOKHIN: It was not.

---

1.   The Seventh Congress of People's Deputies held in December 1992.

AVEN: He wanted to keep the post himself.

SHOKHIN: I didn't like Kadannikov. Why appoint a "red director"—even if he wasn't all that "red"? I liked the candidacy of Ryzhov much better, as a political figure.

KOKH: We didn't need a pragmatist—we needed a politician, a democrat, a liberal. And Kadannikov was certainly pragmatic.

SHOKHIN: Various factions started to nominate candidates in November. The candidate list turned out to include Gaidar, Chernomyrdin, Shumeiko, Skokov, and Kadannikov. Gaidar gathered the nominated vice premiers, Shumeiko, and Chernomyrdin. The congress was already on. He told them, "Look, if they don't appoint me"—this is what Chernomyrdin told me—"you must withdraw, too. We are one team." He argued, "If we are one team, why would we decline the appointment? On the contrary, we should take the candidate who got the most votes in the first round and pool our votes."

Yegor didn't like the idea, especially as Chernomyrdin had a better chance of winning as a candidate. Kadannikov would have been better for Yegor, because the plan was to hire him (apparently no one had told him that, and he realized it only when he stood on the rostrum). In the end, Yegor's plan was inflexible: Yeltsin had to understand that his only candidate was Gaidar. If they did not elect Gaidar, then the Supreme Council and the congress had to be kicked out. However, I personally—and I'm confident I wasn't the only one on our team—was not eager to start a confrontation; a different scenario was possible. Then came the next stage of this story. When Yegor was denied approval, Yeltsin was prepared to dismiss the congress.

KOKH: The dismissal might have prevented 1993, to some extent.

SHOKHIN: October 1993—because the same events would have taken place in December 1992.

KOKH: Back then deputies were not prepared for an armed confrontation. Most likely there would have been no casualties, or they would have been much fewer.

SHOKHIN: One way or another, Chernomyrdin was approved as prime minister, and everyone reconciled themselves to it. The question was how and for how long. As it turned out, not for long.

Certainly Chernomyrdin was not Gaidar. He was a man of different ideology and formation. Naturally, there were questions as to whether his reforms would be as rapid as Gaidar's. But that was not Chernomyrdin's problem; it was Yeltsin's. Chernomyrdin was ready to adapt and to carry on the reforms. Of course, there were pauses, in October 1993 with the election of the first Duma, and in 1994 when the Chechen war started.

BETWEEN GAIDAR AND CHERNOMYRDIN

KOKH: In 1997, when the wars and interruptions were over, Chernomyrdin was absolutely not the one who slowed down the reforms. I thought then that our progress was so rapid because the government included Chubais, Nemtsov, me, Urinson, Sysuyev, and others. But I realize now there would have been no such progress without Chernomyrdin.

SHOKHIN: Chernomyrdin was adamant at first. He told me why: "I would have gotten rid of all of you in the government, but after Gaidar suggested I do just that with the exception of Chubais and Saltykov, I decided to wait a bit on the decision. If Gaidar does not want you, for instance, to be a member of my government, then work for a while and let me see your true worth. I thought that you were a team, but it turns out you have complex relationships."

KOKH: Was your relationship with Gaidar complex by then?

SHOKHIN: Our relations with Gaidar became complex. After that conversation with Chernomyrdin, I met with Gaidar and asked a direct question: "Yegor, is it true that you told him to get rid of me and everyone else but Chubais and Saltykov?" And he said, "Yes." I asked him, "Your reasoning?" "The fewer of us there are left, the sooner they will flop, and we will come back," he said. "Then why keep Chubais and Saltykov?" "Somebody has to keep an eye on what they're doing."

KOKH: So, you had a quarrel with Gaidar.

SHOKHIN: I did, and I told him that he was wrong, to put it mildly. But we should have met, talked, and decided that we would all send our resignations, and make it a political act. But when one is allowed to stay and another is not? Petr wrote his resignation statement and the others were holding off, while Gaidar gave all of them up secretly, without explaining his position. What would you call it?

What did I do? I made Borya Fyodorov the finance minister (worse for me) and Glazyev Aven's successor. The sole principle was to do that urgently, so that we had continuity in the financial policy. When Chernomyrdin asked my advice about a candidate to replace Finance Minister Gaidar, I said that it could be Borya Fyodorov. We had just appointed him as a World Bank director. I called for him and said, "Borya, we must save the country now. Will you be the finance minister?" Borya said, "I've already been the finance minister; that is a dodgy enterprise." And I said, "It is different now—the Union is gone. Now our Finance Ministry is the main actor." He agreed, and we appointed him. Six months later, Borya pissed on me.

KOKH: That's Borya—you should have known. May he rest in peace.

SHOKHIN: Second, it was I who convinced Chernomyrdin to appoint Glazyev, because he was a liberal and was responsible for everything done at Aven's Ministry of Foreign Economic Relations.

AVEN: Aven could rely on him as if on himself.

SHOKHIN: Yes, yes: "If it goes wrong, you, Chernomyrdin, will know it within three months and replace him." He had Davydov in mind, but he could not reach him by phone. I brought Glazyev to meet him only after the appointment. The presidential decree on the formation of a new government had to be promulgated within ten days.

Chernomyrdin met with Glazyev and said, "You, Glazyev, can go, and you, Shokhin, stay. Who is that guy you have brought here?" "Is anything wrong?" I asked in surprise. "Just look at him ... How can I show this vacant-looking guy to Yeltsin?" he asked. "But he is smart!" "Who cares that he is smart!" Later on Seryozha acted improperly—he moved to the Rutskoi team in the "Yes-Yes-No-Yes"[2] referendum and, strangely enough, stayed in office until September 1993.

But you know what question I'd like to go back to? Somehow, not only

---

2.   The historic referendum, approved in spring 1993 by parliament, asked these questions (and the Yeltsin spin machine helpfully suggested replies of "Yes-Yes-No-Yes"): "Do you find President Boris Yeltsin trustworthy?" "Do you approve of Socialist politics, as implemented by the President and government of the Russian Federation?" "Do you think it necessary to hold early elections for the Presidency of the Russian Federation?" "Do you think it necessary to hold early elections for the Congress of People's Deputies of the Russian Federation?" A clear approval for Yeltsin was reported (64 percent of eligible voters participated), but his popularity varied nationwide.

you but Yegor had the idea that I was capable of being in charge of economic matters. I had no such ambition, although I'm not totally unambitious. I simply was not 100 percent sure that we should stick to our plan. That's why I could let the position go even without discussing it. And I think Yegor was jealous. He didn't call me to attend many of the evening sessions, which discussed essential things: "You should not be distracted—you are in charge of social issues. So take care of that, you don't need additional headaches." He started separating me from the teamwork to a certain degree. Why? Frankly, I don't know; our families were on friendly terms, our offices were next to each other when we were still doing academic work. There was an element of duality in our relations—we seemed to be friends, and yet we were not. I felt a change in our relations only when he became the first vice premier. He stopped paying attention. Yet his recommendation that Chernomyrdin should not make any of us members of his government hurt me. I was outraged, and I said all kinds of bad things to him.

KOKH: Did you visit Yegor after your conversation with Chernomyrdin?

SHOKHIN: Our dachas were next door. I saw the lights and knew he was home. So I went over.

On another note, when Gaidar returned to the government as the first vice premier in 1993, there was a question of cabinet reconfiguration. Chernomyrdin leaked to me that Gaidar had proposed removing me from the vice premier post and making me the minister for CIS affairs. In December, after the Choice of Russia failed again in the elections, Gaidar left the government and strongly recommended to Yeltsin again that he downgrade me.

FAREWELL TO GAIDAR

KOKH: I cannot understand why they called it a failure. The result was quite normal. It was the biggest faction at the Duma; they lost to the LDPR[3] only in the party list vote. There was nothing tragic about that—the Choice of Russia together with the single-mandate district winners was still bigger than Zhirinovsky's party.

SHOKHIN: Chernomyrdin, who had been reappointed to the premiership by the State Duma, asked: "So, tell me, will you take the post of minister for CIS affairs? Your associates are forcing you out of the government." I

3.　　Liberal Democratic Party of Russia.

said, "No, I won't." "Now, quit the joking—what do you want?" "To be economy minister or, even better, finance minister." "I will talk that over, but if Yeltsin calls for you, do me a favor: don't argue with him and don't ask him any questions," he said. In the end, I became economy minister and regained the vice premier position in three months. Gaidar got so mad, he bore a grudge for a long time.

KOKH: You were out again by the end of 1994. I think that was before the First Chechen War started.

SHOKHIN: On the eve of the Chechen war, thank God.

KOKH: You were lucky; you left with a clean reputation. Was it Chubais who took your position?

SHOKHIN: Yes, Chubais was appointed as first vice premier.

AVEN: But he did not become economy minister, did he?

SHOKHIN: Yasin became economy minister, and Serov the vice premier for the CIS. And Davydov was vice premier for foreign economic policy. So I covered an area that was later covered by five men. But that is not the point; the point is, it looked strange to me that Yegor continued to bear a grudge against me. Men may have different arguments, even a fistfight. But Yegor took offense.

KOKH: At which conversation?

SHOKHIN: At the conversation we had in December 1992, when he dismissed us all and I told him lots of things in the presence of eyewitnesses.

AVEN: The only eyewitnesses were my wife and I.

SHOKHIN: No, the eyewitnesses were you, Andrei Bugrov (whom I was persuading to shift from the European Bank to Boris Fyodorov's place in Washington), Kostya Kagalovsky (the IMF Russian director), and Masha, Gaidar's wife.

AVEN: Right, Kagalovsky was there.

SHOKHIN: They were visiting us at the dacha, and we were all agitated. I saw Yegor returning home, and I said, "Hey, Gaidar is home, let's go and punch him in the face!"

KOKH: Kostya Kagalovsky was quite a provocateur—he would have incited you.

SHOKHIN: He did. Kostya said, "Come on, let's go." I didn't say anything offensive. I just said, "Yegor, you cannot do that. You have the right to say whatever you want. But I must know about that. If we are members of the same team, why do I not know what you say about me?" Besides, Chernomyrdin said he gave a character sketch of each of us. I asked him, "Why should I believe you?" And he said, "Do you see this notebook? It is all down there. I am an old-school bureaucrat. Shall I read it out for you?"

AVEN: Did he read it?

SHOKHIN: I can't remember now. He might have read out something about somebody else, but not about me. He gave lots of examples—and, really, they were correct.

   Gaidar could have done it differently. He could have gathered us and said, "Here's my request. Let's all quit now. Believe me, we will be back."

AVEN: That is a separate subject: how you, Yegor, and Chubais felt about Yeltsin. I remember one of your descriptions of him as "an average drunken mug."

SHOKHIN: That is your theory, and you keep repeating it. I never described my attitude to him in such words.

AVEN: Okay, let me hear your version.

WINE, YELTSIN, AND THE STILLBORN COALITION

SHOKHIN: Yeltsin sometimes elicited certain feelings in me. I felt terrible several times when I feared that we would become a laughing stock for the whole world. He could fall off a stage, or be an hour late for meetings with presidents and queens because they could not sober him up. He just dropped out of reality, passed out—not just fell asleep.

KOKH: Where did he find the time to get sloshed?

SHOKHIN: He had friends: Korzhakov, Soskovets, Barsukov, Grachev. They kept filling his glass. They had a custom of drinking anything that was available. Say we had a 30-minute break in negotiations—they would haul out a box of vodka.

AVEN: He was the first secretary of the regional party committee for a long time, and he knew his limit. Why get sloshed? Yeltsin gulped down a huge glass at Helmut Kohl's residence in late 1991. They started filling his glass and asked him to say when, and he said, "To the rim, don't you see the rim?"

KOKH: Was it vodka?

AVEN: Wine. Yeltsin raised the glass and drank again. It was his habit to drain the glass.

SHOKHIN: Everyone knew that—so Korzhakov and company could have him sign any documents they wanted. They manipulated him, taking advantage of his weakness and making it even worse. There were odd presidential decrees, and Yeltsin often called me: "Why don't you follow my orders?" Korzhakov and Soskovets disliked me very much; I was obstructing their plans.

KOKH: That group of comrades used Yeltsin to accomplish their tasks—and then they decided to take power.

SHOKHIN: That happened in 1996, from April through July. Chubais played an important role. So did Kulikov. But we should also give credit to Yeltsin, who could be won over by intellect, arguments, firmness, logic, and so on. (Gaidar knew that about him all the time, and Chubais learned later.) That was why he left all those Korzhakovs in the end.

AVEN: Sasha, what do you think? How did we fail to create a powerful political democratic liberal movement?

SHOKHIN: A political movement? What period do you mean?

AVEN: Burbulis thinks we could have done that in fall 1993, immediately after the putsch, before the election by the new constitution.

SHOKHIN: For some reason we keep criticizing Yavlinsky for his unwillingness to unite or yield certain roles. But I will tell you a different story. October 1993. The government seemed to be united. The government was a monolith, excluding Glazyev, who publicly disengaged himself in September and was preparing to become the premier in the Rutskoi and Khasbulatov administration. The Choice of Russia list was being drafted. I was not on that list; Shoigu[4] and Melikian were not there, either, and there was no Kalmykov[5] from the ministers. I asked Yegor, "Are you drafting the list?" "Yes." "Can you tell me why many cabinet members are missing the boat?" He told me, "You are professionals and technocrats—why would you get involved in politics?"

That was approximately October 10. The deadline for the submission of lists was close. Two months were left before the elections. My associates and I gathered: me, Shakhrai, Melikian, Shoigu, and some others. We formed a party, the Party of Russian Unity and Accord (PRUA). We registered that party and held the founding congress in Veliky Novgorod. We gained 6 percent in the election. Not just because Yegor did not want people he didn't particularly like in the new government or the new party. Yet if those people had been invited to the Choice of Russia, it hardly would have been possible to form a new party.

At that moment, Yegor put the question this way: the post-election premier would be Gaidar, the vice premier would be Chubais, and so on, by the Choice of Russia list. I asked him, "Yegor, what about Chernomyrdin? Will you throw him into the dustbin of history?" "We will decide later." "Look, he is the prime minister now, and the way the election will go depends on him a lot. You cannot disregard the question and make a post factum decision. You have to reach an agreement right now, beforehand. If he is not the premier, then who is he? A man needs a position." Yegor waved me away. He was so sure that he would be victorious in the election of 1993—that he would control the State Duma majority and the Choice of Russia would form the majority government. Yet the majority could be formed only jointly with one's supporters. Gaidar said afterward, "The Shakhrai-Shokhin party took 6 percent of votes away from the Choice of Russia." We didn't take them away. We won those votes. They voted for us, not for Gaidar. We took a slightly different position, more evolutionary, in particular because we had to find our own political niche, take part in debates, and win our segment of the electorate. You could not make 6 percent from nothing; no one would have juggled votes for us.

---

4.   Sergei Shoigu, Emergency Situations Minister 1994–2012.
5.   Yuri Kalmykov, Justice Minister 1993–4.

AVEN: Judging by what you say, the party appeared because Gaidar did not want you on the Choice of Russia list.

SHOKHIN: Certainly. Shakhrai had an idea of his own political party, but Shakhrai was very happy that such esteemed people as Shoigu and the first chairman of the Constitutional Court, Tumanov, joined the PRUA. By the way, the Choice of Russia had no candidate for the Constitutional Court chairmanship. And we did.

You say Yavlinsky had bad advisors because they did not counsel him to form coalitions. Did Gaidar have better advisors? They told him, "Let's put only our people on the list, we will take the power into our hands." And what about a broader coalition? Are advisors who do not recommend forming a coalition with people who are ready to be cooperative good advisors? Okay, you had a quarrel with Shokhin a year ago, you fear Shakhrai's ambition—but why would you lose 6 percent of votes because of that?

Certainly the outcome of the elections in 1993 was a cold shower for the Choice of Russia, and that was why Yegor quit the government in January. It was obvious that he wanted to be the leader of the parliamentary majority. But why quit? He was the second man in the government. He could have surrounded Chernomyrdin with his associates. But he quit. I think he wanted to make a triumphant return some time later.

KOKH: I think he wanted to concentrate wholly on the party work, so that he would be prepared for the election in 1995. As a result, the Choice of Russia even failed to pass the 5 percent threshold in 1995 because the new party, Our Home Is Russia, also split the electorate.

SHOKHIN: Yegor was not made to do party organizing work. Although he had a political mentality and vision, he was a truly technocratic premier, and needed powerful political support. He also needed a staff aware of the compostion of the electorate.

GOOD PREMIER

KOKH: I had very positive impressions from the work with Chernomyrdin. I worked for him for four years, and we had our differences, especially with his administration. Now, looking back, I think he was a very good premier.

SHOKHIN: And I wonder why he kept me on for so long. In spite of Yegor's recommendation, I was a member of another team as far as he was concerned.

He realized there were other groups in the government, too—Soskovets and others—to which I did not belong, either. I was an independent player, and I could support him anytime. So when I resigned in November 1994, he gave me hell: "They wanted to fire you more than once—I defended you to the president, and you go and resign!"

KOKH: Did you resign?

SHOKHIN: Yes.

KOKH: And why did you do that?

SHOKHIN: I did not want to resign, actually. I planned to use it as pressure.

KOKH: And Soskovets served you up.

SHOKHIN: Soskovets and Korzhakov gobbled me up, that's right.

AVEN: They could have sent you to prison.

SHOKHIN: Certainly they could have. When I realized the pressure was too great, I thought, "Should I stop trying and step aside?" Then came Black Tuesday in 1994. Gerashchenko was dismissed, Dubinin was dismissed, and I was strongly reprimanded by the Security Council and the Government Presidium for bad coordination of the activity of the Central Bank and the Finance Ministry. I said at that meeting, "I am prepared to accept this reprimand, even have it in my personnel file, but on the condition that I really can coordinate the activity of the Central Bank and the Finance Ministry. Let's write down that Shokhin is responsible for that and that a new finance minister and Central Bank chairman will be appointed only with my consent." That was the decision we made. I walked out, and reporters asked me, "What is your opinion of the new finance minister?" And I asked, "Have they appointed him already?" "Yes, it is Panskov." "Well, if that's the case, I can do nothing but resign."

Chernomyrdin was right when he told me, "You let me down. I kept defending you." I said, "Chernomyrdin! Forgive me, I simply could not control myself." That was it.

KOKH: And what is your opinion of him?

SHOKHIN: Chernomyrdin is a team player. Much of his behavior depended on the guidelines given by Yeltsin and the men who surrounded him. For instance, March 1997, when the "government of young reformers" was formed, showed that Chernomyrdin could head a reform team, too. He was at the crossroads in January 1994, after the October events and the December election. Gaidar was gone, Fyodorov was gone. The probability of shifting to a more conservative course was very high. Partially, that really happened. It simply had to happen, because the share of reformers in the government declined.

But, for the most part, the Chernomyrdin government carried on the Gaidar government's course. We continued cooperation with international financial organizations, which meant we preserved the course toward macroeconomic stabilization, which was vital for cooperation. We needed loans from the IMF and the World Bank to patch up our budget, and Chernomyrdin had to play the role of a liberal premier. I remember him charming IMF managing director Michel Camdessus: he took him hunting in Zavidovo, and tuned the governmental program to monetarist concepts.

So, in my opinion, the pause in the reforms in 1994 was not fatal; the tactic was "two steps forward, one step back," but we basically had progress. In particular, that happened because the government had the right people— not so much me. Sergei Dubinin was acting finance minister. By the way, I never understood why he was not appointed minister after Boris Fyodorov was gone. He was still the acting minister when he was dismissed after Black Tuesday in 1994.

My main conclusion is that the reforms slowed down in 1994 not because that was the wish of Chernomyrdin but because, with the resignation of Gaidar and Fyodorov, the liberal and reformist wing of the authorities became weak. People in the close circle of the president, who originally thought badly of the reforms, had a chance to change the policy. And Chernomyrdin could hardly do much about that. The close circle was push-ing its course, which aimed at the achievement of its own often simple and selfish interests. And that continued practically until 1996.

KOKH: I agree. Chernomyrdin had nothing to do with it. The longest pause of 1994 was in privatization. Although the entire privatization team led by Chubais (and I was his deputy at the time) was safe and sound. When the voucher phase was over, we needed a new program and new policies and procedures, but the communist-controlled Duma blocked their adoption. Until we invented those wretched loans-for-shares auctions, we had no legal grounds to continue privatization.

Also, when the loans-for-shares auctions showed to the Duma that we could move on without it, it became much more conciliatory, and rather rapidly adopted a new privatization program in 1997.

Chernomyrdin did not stop privatization. On the contrary, he tried to bolster it. He kept calling me and asking when the money would come. I remember him being happy with the loans-for-shares auction money and, later on, with the Svyazinvest money.

SHOKHIN: Chernomyrdin was a good premier, and one could work with him. I want to remind you that Andrei Illarionov—one of the most liberal economists in Russia, and not only in Russia—was Chernomyrdin's economic advisor throughout 1993 and most of 1994. Andrei was really educating the premier. Václav Klaus was doing the same. He frequently visited Russia and had multi-hour meetings with Chernomyrdin at the White House and in the countryside. Chernomyrdin became the leader of the reform team, to a large degree. The only reason he did not take on that role fully was that, at key moments, the reformers did not admit him to their team. That happened in December 1992, in fall 1993, and in January 1994. But they should have.

KOKH: I would not overdramatize that. In 1997, when Chubais could have easily replaced Premier Chernomyrdin, he did not do that because he—and all of us— deemed Chernomyrdin one of our team.

SHOKHIN: By then Chubais, who had worked with Chernomyrdin longer than the other reformers, realized that he would be worked with—that it was possible to persuade Chernomyrdin the way one could persuade Yeltsin.

KOKH: In my opinion, it was faster to persuade Chernomyrdin.

SHOKHIN: Faster because Chernomyrdin had fewer influences against that course in his personal circle. And he was less ideologized. Yeltsin had mostly political challenges. By 1994 Yeltsin already couldn't help thinking about the 1996 elections.

KOKH: Sasha, back to Yegor. Tell me, did you ever restore your relationship?

SHOKHIN: Our relationship was restored outwardly: we said hello to each other, asked how things were, and inquired about our families. But, as they say, the bitter aftertaste remained. I regret that now. Anything can happen in life, so why rupture relations over it? I kept thinking we would make up someday. And now it's too late.

4

ANDREI NECHAYEV

"It's Indecent to Blame the Former Regime for Everything"

Andrei Nechayev was the favorite student of Yuri Vasilyevich Yaremenko. For those who do not know, Yaremenko was the last really grand Soviet economist; he sincerely believed in the plan-based economy and the possibility of improving socialism. There was Alexander Ivanovich Anchishkin before him. Stanislav Sergeyevich Shatalin (with whom I was lucky to have long and detailed conversations) had no trust in socialism. I think Nikolai Yakovlevich Petrakov had no such trust, either. We (the Gaidar team) did not take seriously the rest of the economic academicians.

Anchishkin and Yaremenko organized a new institute (on the basis of the Central Economic Mathematics Institute) with a very Soviet name, the Institute of Economics and Scientific and Technological Progress Forecasts. The institute presented the economy as a set of intertwining technological chains, which changed through innovation. I, personally, have always thought that the economy is about people and their preferences rather than about inter-industry balance matrix ratios. But they in the IESTPF believed that plenty of things, if not all, could be predicted and corrected if their estimates were true. Naturally, they needed assistance from the government, which was capable of determining "correct" innovations, putting reasonable emphasis on capital investments, and so on.

Yaremenko uttered the famous phrase: "Development of the Soviet economy would be accompanied by a reduced share of meat in sausage." But they still tried to rescue that economy with valuable advice to the authorities based on their research. They did not rescue it, but the schooling was good.

It is not accidental that the best of the last generation of Yaremenko's and Anchishkin's students are still working for the government.

Nechayev is one of them. He is a statesman (clearly more than Kokh and I), which is why he never went into business. He is specific, precise, and technocratic, extremely responsible and hardworking. In our government of 1992 he did exactly what an employee of the IESTPF was supposed to do—not so much reform as solve particular problems: procurement, support for industries, distribution of budget funds, and relations with regions. Yet it was Nechayev who prepared price liberalization. A brand-new market law on public procurement, the public–private partnership idea, conversion loans, and the new investment policy were his accomplishments, too. He was busy day and night. And he has the best knowledge of the real economic situation of late 1991 and early 1992. In contrast to Shokhin (and to Chubais as well), he is not about "politics and human relationships" but about the economy in its "technological" sense. And about numbers. Which is what we talked about.

Petr Aven

PETR AVEN: Andrei! When did you realize that a fundamental change was coming and it was necessary to prepare for that?

ANDREI NECHAYEV: As you know, I worked with Yaremenko and Anchishkin for my entire academic life. Our cooperation started in 1975, although my formal chief at the Moscow State University graduate school was Shatalin. We were working on the so-called comprehensive program of scientific and technological progress, kind of a long-term plan. So, on the one hand, I knew well the sad condition of the late Soviet Union, but on the other hand, the general idea was that socialism could still be mended.

AVEN: Was that Yaremenko's belief?

NECHAYEV: Yes. As far as I understand, he was a sincere, profound, and quite intellectual adept of the plan-based economy, its real informal ideologist. He gave a brilliant academic description of the administrative command distribution of resources and administrative trading. He thought it was just necessary to tighten certain nuts and it would work perfectly! I must say I shared those illusions until 1990, when we parted. I met Gaidar in late 1990. So my liberal market education was late.

ALFRED KOKH: Speaking of the Gaidar government of 1991–2, how can Andrei be of interest to us? The interest is that despite the fact that he was much less involved in political intrigues than Burbulis or Chubais, he was deeply involved in the economic context.

NECHAYEV: I would say without false modesty that I did a lot of the rough dirty work for Yegor.

KOKH: So tell us about it!

THE STATUS OF THE COUNTRY

AVEN: You were engrossed in the current economic context more deeply than others. We knew well only our own limited sectors. Before I joined the government I worked in Austria, Chubais was a head of the Leningrad City Executive Committee, and Gaidar wrote articles for magazines and journals and was an editor. You dealt with the real economic processes, the full picture, on a daily basis. At Yaremenko's institute you were all crunching numbers and analyzing them.

KOKH: And you did the same thing when you joined the government.

AVEN: So the question is: Did you have many surprises when you became the first deputy economic and finance minister, and soon after that the economic minister? If you did, then what were they?

NECHAYEV: Naturally, that was the hard currency bankruptcy. It appeared that after the financial bacchanalia of the last communist governments, the new government's hard currency reserves stood at $26 million.

AVEN: That was the low point; it was just one day. And for several days the amount stood at approximately $50–60 million.

NECHAYEV: Whether $60 million or $26 million, you must admit that was an insignificant difference. By today's standards, that could be a large trading company or a mediocre bank. As you remember, you and I were deputy chairmen of the governmental currency and economic commission. I chaired meetings of that commission more frequently than you, for some reason. Formally Yegor was the chairman. But he never chaired its meetings. For me, personally, it was a psychological strain when people came to us saying, "What's going on? Where is our money?" And we had to buy insulin and plenty of other vital, absolutely critical things. The so-called critical imports. But we had no money.

I still remember the visit of Academician Semyonov, the director of Energia. The atmosphere was more democratic on Staraya Square (where the government had offices, as you remember), and he brought some kind of unit through security. The commission held its meetings in the hall where the Soviet Communist Party Central Committee Political Bureau used to convene. So he showed me the unit and said, "Here, we invented a food processor in our military conversion project. It's all done, worked out, perfect. But we need electric motors, and this country doesn't know how to build them. They have to be bought from Japan. We have several million dollars in our account. Give it to us so that we can buy the motors." And I told him, "Alas, you have no money." "What do you mean?" he asked. "The money is in our account." And then I explained to him, long and painstakingly, that the money existed nominally but was gone de facto. We had urgent needs. Insulin. Diabetics would die, and so on. And he was looking at me as if I were a complete idiot or an enemy of the people.

KOKH: Tell me, because I consider this a fundamental issue: Was the money gone before you took office or did you spend it?

NECHAYEV: Vneshekonombank[1] was bankrupt, broke.

KOKH: By the time you took office?

NECHAYEV: Yes. Actually, there were plans to declare it bankrupt, but in order not to lose assets abroad and debts to the bank we chose a different path. We did not declare it bankrupt, but we formally froze all its funds. Later on we issued Internal Hard Currency Loan Bonds (the notorious OVVZ).

So Academician Semyonov, who earned his money honestly and had it taken away by the state, looked at me and said, "How can that be?" Then he picked up his unit and left totally confused. We had 20 similar episodes at every meeting, once a week.

KOKH: Were they angry with you or with those who had spent their money?

NECHAYEV: Naturally, the majority were angry with us.

---

1.   Bank of Foreign Economic Affairs of the USSR.

KOKH: That is amazing. Why didn't you tell them the money was gone by the time you took office?

NECHAYEV: That's understandable from a psychological point of view: the one who declares the money gone is the enemy. Each commission meeting had 15 to 20 cases to deal with, or sometimes 30. So I had to keep repeating 30 times, "There is no money, sorry."

KOKH: Even a hundred times. If they accuse you of stealing, you have to explain, even for the millionth time, that you are not the thief.

NECHAYEV: Formally, there was no such decision, but we agreed (and that was Yegor's initiative mostly) that it would be improper to act traditionally and accuse the former regime of all sins, although that was the case in this particular situation.

KOKH: Do you think that was right, or it was stupid?

NECHAYEV: I think it was stupid. To an extent, Gorbachev was the reason. Obviously, by attacking Pavlov, Ryzhkov, and the entire Soviet economic policy of the second half of the 1980s and the early 1990s, we would have actually attacked Gorbachev, and we were actually grateful to him for the democratization of the country. Besides, we had no time to deliver long lectures, as we were working 18 hours a day. In short, we did not elaborate the theme of explaining the legacy we inherited.

KOKH: You actually assumed the responsibility without wanting to.

NECHAYEV: There was another essential moment. Yeltsin told us from the start, and then Burbulis conveyed his idea (although Burbulis might have added something of his own), "You guys are technocrats, and you are doing the economic reform."

KOKH: And the political cover is not your problem?

NECHAYEV: And the political cover, and the information and propaganda support, would be provided by Burbulis, Poltoranin, Shakhrai, "and me, the president of Russia, personally." And sorry for being rude, but they completely screwed up.

AVEN: All right. Besides the hard currency situation, was the rest more or less predictable? Did all the rest more or less meet your expectations?

NECHAYEV: Yes, more or less.

KOKH: Weren't you surprised with the real scale of the defense sector?

NECHAYEV: As I was doing the inter-industry balance and all inter-industry models at Yaremenko's, I had a general idea of the scale—but I agree, it was seriously underrated. Some cases simply amazed me! That was why I cut arms procurements by seven-eighths. With these very hands! But I tried, as much as it was possible, to preserve R&D allocations, which, as you understand, were a down payment for development, the groundwork for the future.

There was an occasion when I, basically a calm person, threatened to shoot everyone with my own hands. I invented a system of conversion loans for the defense sector, and the rates were highly favorable. I came to the Omsk Transmash plant, which was building tanks, and the plant administration strongly refused to start a conversion. The director was firm: we would build tanks, and that was it. He told me, "Andrei Alexeyevich, you would not believe what tanks we make. We make the world's best tanks." I said, "I believe you, but we have the world's worst budget. We have no money for your tanks. We have no money at all." But he kept saying, "Let's take a break and I'll take you to the testing range." We went to the testing range, and it was where he made a big mistake. His tanks were actually jumping, shooting, diving, and flying. This was an amazing sight—I was like a little boy. (By the way, they made the unique Black Eagle tank, which was the only product I agreed to finance. Actually, they built only two of them. These same tanks are still displayed at every military industrial exhibition.) And then I saw something surreal: a clearing in the taiga and there were tanks far and near, rows and rows of tanks covered with snow. How many tanks were there? Thousands, tens of thousands. It was when I lost my temper and shouted, "Scoundrel, you should be tried and executed. There are enough tanks here for three big wars, but you keep begging money from a pauper country to continue making them!" He backed off, and I gave him the money for Black Eagle and we did not order any other tanks. Obviously, that was catastrophic for the plant.

KOKH: My biggest shock when I started in the privatization of the defense industry was that even purely civilian sectors, such as metallurgy, made half their products for war! I simply could not part with money when I saw labor was being squandered when the country needed homes, roads, good cars.

NECHAYEV: That problem was brilliantly described by the late Yuri Vasilyevich Yaremenko. He defined quality and bulk resources. Why did our combine harvesters work for only two weeks before they needed repairs? Besides, they compacted the soil so much that nothing could grow there. That was because of inefficient engineering solutions. If you are denied engineering plastics, aluminum and titanium alloys, because all that was consumed by the defense industry, then what was left for combine harvesters were cast iron, iron forging, bad rubber and paint, and so on. It was a catastrophe—the high-quality resources were mobilized for the defense industry, while civilian machine builders had to be content with leftovers.

Gorbachev understood that. I read the recently published documents of the Politiburo, the Security Council, and others. The problem was raised, actually, but there was no political will to oppose the military-industrial lobby. Yegor gave me the task of maximal reduction of the defense industry budget at the very start.

AVEN: How much was it cut? How much were defense expenditures cut in the first days?

NECHAYEV: By approximately 25 percent.

AVEN: Strange, I thought the cuts were bigger. Didn't you say down to an eighth?

NECHAYEV: We cut arms procurements by seven-eighths. And the defense industry budget was cut by approximately 25 percent. I must say that a slight reduction began two or three years before we took office.

There was one more revelation for me. Gosplan had several defense departments handling arms procurements, current expenditures of forces, and so on. I set them the task of maximal reduction of expenditures. One of the departments was led by Rear Admiral Kandybenko, I remember that. At first he was a captain of the first rank, and then I made him a rear admiral. So Kandybenko came to my office and asked, "Andrei Alexeyevich, how can we do the cuts? We have 2.8 million army servicemen. There are norms for protein, fats, carbohydrates, boots, puttees, soldiers' blouses, and so on. Shall we cut their food rations? Are you prepared to do that?"

KOKH: And how about cutting the army while preserving the norms?

NECHAYEV: That's it. That was when I realized that it was impossible to cut army financing without cutting the army itself. By then our heroic army was already living on humanitarian aid from the Bundeswehr. There was a time when approximately 15 percent of our army's food ration came in the form of humanitarian aid from the German army. How humiliating!

KOKH: They were practically sponsoring the whole Soviet force, the Western Group of Forces, in Germany until 1994, when Yeltsin withdrew it.

NECHAYEV: If only it was just that! Not only the Soviet force in Germany but also military units stationed inside our country. And then I went to Yeltsin and told him that our position was desperate and we simply had to cut the army. He called for Grachev, Shaposhnikov; Kobets and Yegor were there too, of course. They spent an hour and a half accusing me of practically being an agent of American imperialism, but Yeltsin (I must give him his due) eventually sided with me, and we mapped out the reduction of the army, although it took a long time to implement the plan.

KOKH: Was the 2.8 million the entire Red Army or just its Russian share?

NECHAYEV: There were also the so-called united armed forces of the CIS.

KOKH: Financed practically by us alone?

NECHAYEV: Not practically—we were all alone. Time passed before the Ukrainians started to build their own army and Kazakhstan did the same; they divided property and soldiers and started to finance military units stationed on their territories. And back then Russia was the only sponsor of the entire Soviet army. That was a dead end.

Do you know what Gorbachev always did at arms reduction negotiations? As you know, the army has formal and actual strength. The correlation was 100 to 70–80. Really, we had a shortage of men. So he gladly and easily reduced the formal strength. The formal strength was lowered, but not the actual. So we inherited the army, practically unreduced.

KOKH: What were the arguments of your opponents? Did they agree that the country did not need such an army from the economic point of view and that it was an unbearable load, but that retired officers would have to be provided with housing and that could cost more?

NECHAYEV: That was their main argument. But when we made realistic estimates, it appeared that it would not be more expensive. Eventually Yeltsin decided to reduce the army. And the sociopolitical consequences were terrible: you're kicking out onto the street (in difficult times) a half million people who know how to handle weapons.

KOKH: And they marched straight off to the bandits.

NECHAYEV: Not only to bandits! Many of them were in the White House in 1993.

KOKH: Yes, I remember that, Terekhov, the Union of Officers.[2] By the way, that is a serious argument in the current reform of the Interior Ministry. Major reductions are pending, and current officers of the Interior Ministry are more marginal and criminally minded than army officers of the early 1990s.

NECHAYEV: Right. And we had the following situation with procurements. Shaposhnikov's deputy for armaments was the late Colonel Mironov. I wasn't fully installed in my post; we were actually appointed to work in Russia, but I took a seat at the Union Gosplan and operated there without real legal powers; that was a separate funny story. I chaired a meeting on arms procurement, and Mironov's generals said, "We need 45 billion rubles. That would be the minimal arms procurement program for 1992." My informers told me that they would agree to 25 billion rubles. But the budget could not afford that, either. So I said, "I have five. That is our estimate. We have five billion rubles and this is it." No discussion happened. Because bargaining is possible when one says 45 and the other says 40. But whenever one says 45 and the other says five, negotiations end very quickly. There were about 20 3- and 4-star generals there, and they all left. There were just two of us, Mironov and I. I walked him out of my office and he patted me on the shoulder patronizingly and said, "I think we will meet again, young man. I am sure you will change your mind."

The lobbying strength of the army in the Soviet Union was such that they would have crushed even the mighty Gosplan chairman. The kind of decision we made is possible only at revolutionary moments, and when the state is in the process of collapse. Just imagine, 45 and five—that offer could

---

2.   The pro-Soviet group Union of Officers was led by Stanislav Terekhov.

have been accepted only out of despair.

Naturally, I went to Gaidar and said, "Here is the situation; you just remember that they will most probably go to Yeltsin." He talked to the president. Mironov called two days later and said, "Andrei Alexeyevich, give us nine billion, we will call it a deal." "Sorry, just five." We gave them seven and a half billion in the end. That is, he put out feelers and Shaposhnikov ran to Yeltsin.

KOKH: Was Yeltsin fully on your side—actively, not passively?

NECHAYEV: He was then.

AVEN: Yeltsin was a bigger realist than Gorbachev. Gorbachev tried to preserve the status quo till the very end. He took loans and patched holes, thus solving the problem of political opposition to perestroika by the military. That left Yeltsin with absolutely no resources for doing that.

KOKH: But how much did he borrow? For what he saw as such a powerful and huge country as the Soviet Union, he borrowed only $100 billion. Forex reserves of the present-day Central Bank are five times larger. Later the debt appeared to be a very heavy burden. And he thought that was nothing and the debts would be repaid as soon as oil prices went up. How long could the prices go down? For five years, okay; for six, enough already. In fact, they fell for 15 years. Until the early 2000s.

NECHAYEV: Here is the real situation that Gorbachev had to know: hard currency reserves amounted to $25 million, and the foreign debt was $62 billion. And a big part of the debt was short-term.

HUNGER AND COLD

KOKH: The agrarian sector didn't surprise you? Or were you basically aware that it was the pits?

NECHAYEV: I was surprised by its heightened vulnerability: our meat production (mostly poultry and pig farms, large complexes) was based on imported grain. Fully. And imports stopped. Once, in late November or the very first days of December 1991, all of your St Petersburg friends but Sobchak, all those vice mayors, came to the government and said, "We have grain for three days only. Chickens will start dying in three days, and people will follow soon after." They were given loans by the central government to buy US grain, and the loans were frozen. I was chairing that meeting for Gaidar. Then I turned back the ships routed for Murmansk and opened state reserves to save St Petersburg, because I realized that a city that had lived through the siege should not be hungry again.

KOKH: And now Andryusha Illarionov[3] claims that it was all bullshit and there was no hunger threat. Food reserves were sufficient. Everything was fine.

AVEN: I also think there was no real threat of starvation. There was a collapse of the public distribution system. But people had food reserves at home and restaurants and farmer's markets were open. Indeed, everyone survived somehow. There was no threat of total and massive hunger.

NECHAYEV: I remember well the day of my appointment; I dropped into a giant food store next to my home to buy something to eat. That was a truly surreal sight. There was absolutely nothing in the store at all—but someone must have thought it was not good to have the shelves empty, so they filled all the shelves with jars of *adjika* hot sauce. That was it. A huge supermarket, 7:00 or 8:00 p.m. on November 7, 1991. The center of Moscow.

Petr, I don't even want to argue. In the end, the source of hunger does not matter, whether your procurement system does not work or simply that there is no food.

KOKH: Petr, you're presenting your personal impressions as the objective situation. Did the output drop? It did. And I do not have to tell you about the collapse of imports. There were objective facts testifying that the country lacked food. Otherwise, there would have been no humanitarian aid. And that there was a certain number of working restaurants is not an argument: the majority of people could not afford to eat there.

NECHAYEV: A hungry death means great famine. When there is nothing at all.

AVEN: There was no great famine—that's for sure!

NECHAYEV: And whenever I say hunger, I mean the sharp decline in consumption. If you live on a loaf of bread a day, you probably will not die;

---

3.   From 1992, part-time economic adviser to Gaidar.

but you will not be healthy, either, if you keep doing that for any length of time.

AVEN: Anyway, you were saving people, that was true.

KOKH: I remember well when food producers would not allow food to be taken outside of their regions.

NECHAYEV: Producers simply put their goods on hold. They did not supply shops. They were waiting for prices to rise. And then there were just two options: either you liberate prices or you begin to appropriate surplus.

AVEN: But note we're not talking about hunger at that point!

NECHAYEV: We're not? Certainly we are. Alfred is right. Food resources shrank against the backdrop of the catastrophic reduction of imports and the sharp reduction of meat production (because, I repeat, our cattle farms were heavily dependent on imported grain fodder). Probably famine could have been avoided with smart distribution of the available resources, but there was still hunger in the form of reduced consumption.

As for my subjective impressions, I had a dramatic moment at that meeting with the St Petersburg people. The meeting resembled a gathering of party officials and senior economic executives. The hall where the Soviet Communist Party Central Committee Political Bureau held its meetings, the huge table and 25 to 30 people seated at it, everyone was so emotional: "Chickens will start dying tomorrow, and then people will start dying." Then they all stopped talking and looked at me. "You are the boss, you decide." And, actually, I was a scholar accustomed to calm discussions, without yelling or nerves. And here I was to decide!

AVEN: What was needed was the standard decision, which officials of that level make easily.

KOKH: Grab from this and give to that?

NECHAYEV: Right. Only an administrative decision was possible. It was not possible to solve the local task with market methods. But I'm not talking about that now. I thought, "I think I'll just get up, leave the room, close the door behind me, and never come back." It was really very hard to stay there. Especially when you're dealing with urgent matters. Thank God,

Lenya Cheshinsky was there. He said suddenly, "Andrei Alexeyevich, two ships are carrying grain to Murmansk, and things are better in Murmansk. We will send them to St Petersburg instead, on your personal authority." I cheered up immediately. On my personal authority? You're welcome to it! We immediately got in touch with the captains by radio, and then I opened state reserves for a few days (until the arrival of the ships), and then we got some potatoes from Poland in a barter deal. So we made it.

AVEN: Everything changed when prices were set free. Just like that.

NECHAYEV: I went to Yegor after that meeting and said that price liberalization could not be postponed any longer. I remember that the republics dragged their feet implementing the orders. First they planned to do it on December 1, then on December 16, and finally it all happened on January 1.

AVEN: Am I right that you did not chair such meetings and did not make such decisions after price liberalization? If that is so, that shows that procurements were bad and food was available. Price liberation caused a hike in prices and led to a balance between supply and demand. There was no physical absence of food; it is just that prices were too low.

NECHAYEV: No.

AVEN: That was a different situation—it was entirely different. It didn't resemble the situation of 1918, when there was no food physically.

NECHAYEV: No.

KOKH: Actually, it did exist physically in 1918. It was in villages, but they did not want to bring it to the market.

NECHAYEV: Yes and no. Resources really shrank. There were two options for their distribution. You could do it administratively, with appropriation of surplus and ration cards, or with a price hike, which would make food inaccessible for a certain part of the population.

KOKH: Both surplus appropriation and price liberalization have the same objective—

NECHAYEV: But in a different way. Price liberalization is a quick and less brutal solution, while surplus appropriation needs to be organized, some-body needs to be executed, armed units have to be mobilized. Later, Petr, as you recall, we also liberalized imports, economic relations, and trade. Imports resumed as soon as private business appeared, producers opened their warehouses, and food production started to grow.

AVEN: Absolutely. Imports started to grow in spring, which increased physi-cal quantities of food.

CONCERNING MONEY

KOKH: You took office in 1991 and saw that the situation was disastrous. Did anyone explain the reasons to you? You don't need to be a genius to realize that the falling oil prices narrowed revenues and you had to cut expenditures. Yet Gorbachev not only refused to cut expenditures, but even increased them!

AVEN: Starting from 1986 (and Gaidar describes this in detail), Gorbachev was trying to curb expenditures.

NECHAYEV: I have read two interesting books recently: Gorbachev's memoirs, and then his foundation published the Politburo meeting minutes. The records are incomplete, but still. I must tell you, Gorbachev realized that he was running out of money. But his priorities were different. He was nursing that Union agreement; he wanted to preserve the Union.

KOKH: That was 1991, but the collapse started earlier.

AVEN: Gorbachev was trying to list priority expenditures. He shut down "projects of the century," such as changing the course of rivers, and attempted to cut allocations for construction projects.

NECHAYEV: The problem is different. You are right, allocations were cut, but the number of construction projects was not.

AVEN: He could not tackle the lobbyists, who defended every construction project.

NECHAYEV: But he gave them no money, either, and the scale of unfinished projects of the Gorbachev period was unprecedented.

AVEN: He even tried to cut the defense sector and aid to Warsaw Pact countries and other satellites, including Cuba and Angola. He tried, but it seemed he had neither the power nor the strength to resist the lobbying. Here is my next question. Remember the first months of distribution of resources, when Rakhimov was persuading Yeltsin (and then us) to exempt him from paying the crude oil export duty? Actually, who were the lobbyists, and how did the lobbying work? In the end, Gorbachev could not resist them, and the lobbyists were largely responsible for the USSR's breakup.

NECHAYEV: Regions realized very quickly that they should not ask for money, while industries kept doing that. Regions asked for two simple things. First, to keep the taxes they collected. Those were mass requests. The strongest threatened to declare independence—Tatarstan, Bashkortostan, Rossel, Primorye. Those negotiations added to my gray hairs. But we still preserved the federation. Second, they asked for export quotas on crude and similar resources (which had a similar value to money at the moment).

AVEN: They asked for quotas on duty-free crude export.

NECHAYEV: Yes, export quotas were enacted later. If I am not mistaken, that happened around May.

AVEN: Returning to Rakhimov's visit in late summer—he showed us Yeltsin's permission for duty-free export of 15 million tons of crude. We were seated in your office, and he had just met with Yeltsin. We saw that order the day before, and decided that he would hardly have a chance to meet with Yeltsin again for the next few months, because we had the power to keep them away. When he came, you told him, "Do you think we are crazy, or what? Do you think we will really fulfill this order? It would ruin the budget!" And Rakhimov said, "Are you guys crazy? I have the order of the president. It says 15 million tons." We offered him one million, and called three a deal.

NECHAYEV: That was the regular practice. They all had to visit me first (and you, in the case of export duties). After the decree on Tatarstan, they all started drafting decrees on support to particular territories. They had the same arguments: social problems in the case of a region, and a threat of inter-ethnic conflicts in the case of an autonomous republic.

The Komi Republic took the lead. They came to my office and said, "We have a deal with Yeltsin and we are here for you to execute it." "Why are you here if you have a deal with Yeltsin? He signs the decrees, not me. If you are here, then you must have failed to agree to something." And then I acted according to a pattern. I told them to meet with ministry officials, and told every department head cut down, cut down, and cut down. We played good cop/bad cop. They told me, "We have a deal with Fedchenko"—the capital investment department head—"that budgetary investments will be the following." "You must be crazy. That is 10 percent of the country's total resources. I will fire Fedchenko tomorrow and put him on trial." It didn't matter if they had given Fedchenko anything or not, or what it was. They say, "Please, do not do that, he is such a good person. We will go and work with him again." "You go and work; and I am telling you, Fedchenko, straight to your face, that you should not do such silly things again." Fedchenko knew about our performance in advance. They left and they were cut down and cut down again, five times. But psychologically it was unbearable.

SEPARATISM

KOKH: And tell me, while you were in charge of dividing up everything, did Chechnya manifest itself or did it make itself known only in 1993–4?

NECHAYEV: This is the story. A totally idiotic thing was done to Chechnya.

KOKH: When?

NECHAYEV: In 1992, 1993, and you know what happened next.

KOKH: Who did that? That must have been Khasbulatov—who else? It was he who pushed a resolution on the state of emergency in Chechnya at the Supreme Council in November 1991.

NECHAYEV: That was Rutskoi's idea—a resolution on the state of emergency and the deployment of troops.

KOKH: But no one supported that resolution. That is a good example of the degree to which the country was controllable at that time.

NECHAYEV: Yeah. The Supreme Council repealed that resolution later. Rutskoi and Khasbulatov were lobbying for anti-Dudayev steps, and Yeltsin bowed to their wishes. They should have repeated the Tatarstan scenario in Chechnya, 100 percent. I agreed with the Tatars that we would split the crude oil, and that was it. For Chechnya, the main motivation was the oil (in addition to the nationality factor).

KOKH: Besides, Chechnya produced three to four million tons of crude in 1992, and less than one million by late 1994. This means the scale of the conflict should have been smaller than that with the Tatars. Tatarstan produced up to 30 million tons of crude in 1992! That was ten times more than Chechnya.

NECHAYEV: There was one more thing about Chechnya: the Grozny refinery was Russia's sole producer of certain blends of light distillates for aircraft. It made the best blends of aircraft kerosene for the defense industry. When the conflict went too far I started seeking a replacement. In the end, we started production in Volgograd.

KOKH: Was Dudayev the president by then?

NECHAYEV: Dudayev had dismissed the Supreme Council of Checheno-Ingushetia, which was a terrible insult to Khasbulatov, who presented himself as the sole leader of Chechnya and had proclaimed independence and "separated" Chechnya from Russia.

Nevertheless, Chechnya had the economy minister, I cannot remember the name—he was a guy from our Central Economic Mathematical Institute, a postgraduate student. He attended all the meetings that I chaired. They tried to stay in touch. I even think they made some contributions to centralized funds. If we had reached an exemplary agreement on Tatarstan, I think there would have been no further events. We would have told them, "Listen we have an agreement. Here is your money: you divide it and you solve your problems—social or any other." We would have shifted the responsibility onto Dudayev, and it would have not been our business. Dudayev was absolutely—

KOKH: Soviet?

NECHAYEV: Pro-Russian. He had a rather radical circle, but all of his economic departments stayed in touch with us till the end. That guy, the economic minister, disappeared in late 1992 or early 1993, and all the contacts were severed. I remember him being fully supportive of the peaceful, Tatarstan-type scenario. He was lobbying in favor of that, the best he could get.

KOKH: Please, be frank: Who in Moscow, in your opinion, was against the Tatarstan-type scenario? I am looking for the source of confrontation.

NECHAYEV: I think Khasbulatov and Rutskoi first of all.

KOKH: No, that is too high up. Did anyone at your meetings say, "No, that won't do"?

NECHAYEV: No one said that at my meetings because we didn't discuss it. The president didn't entrust me with that.

KOKH: So where was it discussed?

NECHAYEV: Yeltsin was supposed to sign such agreements.

KOKH: Did anyone draft the agreements for him?

NECHAYEV: I don't remember now how I did that; I might have made oral reports to Gaidar and Yeltsin, but there was no order in response to go forth and do it, unfortunately.

KOKH: Why did they okay Tatarstan but not Chechnya?

NECHAYEV: The Tatars proposed it themselves. They tried to make a deal, although they were adamant and even threatened to secede from Russia. They told us, "Now, we want full economic sovereignty. If we are denied that, we will secede from Russia." The negotiations were dramatic, up to the threat to block export pipelines going through Tatarstan. In the end, I found a simple solution. Previously the 28 million tons of crude produced in Tatarstan were divided into five million tons left in Tatarstan and 23 million given to the Union; the new division was 12 and 16. That was the end to their "sovereignty," if we disregard the bowing and demagoguery. Seven million tons of crude (which, by the way, freed us from certain obligations on centralized provision to Tatarstan) preserved the unity of Russia. I think that was a neat solution. They ended up very nearly happy. They even praised me in the local press, although they were hard on me at first.

Chechnya had its own story. Dudayev seized power in a putsch; he dismissed the Supreme Council. Maybe if the Russian authorities hadn't tried to declare a state of emergency in 1991, they might have come to us and offered something similar to the Tatarstan scenario. Now, remember what the Tatarstan scenario meant for Chechnya, with its three to four million tons of crude. The country would not have noticed even if we had let them keep it all.

Working with Gaidar

KOKH: What impression did you have of Gaidar at that moment? By the way, how did you meet him?

NECHAYEV: Yegor worked for our institute for 18 to 24 months; he was with Shatalin. But we just said hello to each other. Then he called me—and Petr says he gave him a hint to do that—and offered me the opportunity to be his deputy in the Economic Policy Institute, given to him by Gorbachev. So I was his deputy at that institute for a year.

AVEN: When we were taking our postgraduate course, Andrei was at the same department as me, but he was older. Andrei was the best postgraduate student of his year. The theme of inter-industry and other balances was very popular back then. Were you dealing with this?

NECHAYEV: I was making inter-country analyses of economic structure and economic growth. I was building certain models based on inter-country estimates to forecast the USSR's development.

AVEN: I was doing similar things. I talked about you with Gaidar—I remember that well.

NECHAYEV: Well, somebody gave him my phone number. It might have been you.

AVEN: I gave him your phone number. He called me. As we were from the same department and your reputation was perfect, I recommended you. And I do not regret that.

NECHAYEV: Thank you. He also had a rather good reputation at the institute. He was quite independent—because Shatalin did not press anyone. We had a complex relationship at the institute. I was Yaremenko's favorite student. But the problem was that Yuri Vasilyevich liked his students to "stay in the hold," as he termed it. Any attempt to attend a conference or to publish an article elicited his sincere protest. "You are being distracted from your work. Why do you want that? You are doing important work. We are saving the country. What conference, Andrei? You will be out for five days. What I am supposed to do without you for these five days?"

AVEN: How, in his opinion, were you saving the country? Did anyone in high places listen to your advice?

NECHAYEV: Both the Central Committee and Gosplan took us very seriously—accepted our comprehensive program. Gosplan was very jealous, by the way. Our work had huge scope. Of course, it was sort of a technocratic improvement of the socialist model. Later on, I read Margaret Thatcher's phrase, which amazed me: socialism is a far-fetched system. But at that moment we were sincerely trying to improve it.

AVEN: How could you be so earnest about that comprehensive program? We were doing similar work at the Certification Institute. But we were not fanatical.

NECHAYEV: We were the lead institute, which meant we drew up the entire balance of all industries. Besides, we contributed our economic estimates.

KOKH: Could we go back to Gaidar? I can see you're revisiting your early youth.

NECHAYEV: Gaidar invited me to be his deputy at the institute, which did not exist at the time—he was just forming it. And I was his deputy for science for a year.

AVEN: That was when you actually got acquainted.

NECHAYEV: Right. Back to your question, Alfred, about Acting Prime Minister Gaidar. I can say that Gaidar intensely disliked doing operational supervision, and that was hard for me, because he shifted a considerable amount of that work onto me.

The conference on saving St Petersburg I have mentioned was supposed to have Yegor as its chair. Yegor must have guessed what the conference would be about, and he asked, "Why don't you chair it for me?" Formally, I was a first deputy economy and finance minister—not even the economy minister! But I chaired meetings on behalf of a key vice premier, and made decisions that were not within my purview, like turning ships back from Murmansk and sending them to St Petersburg.

But the most important thing was Yegor's fantastic ability to persuade Yeltsin—which surprised me a lot, because I thought they were totally different people.

KOKH: Petr, do you remember my theory about October 3, 1993? About the person who started all that?

AVEN: Certainly I do. Alfred thinks that Yegor persuaded Yeltsin to dismiss the Supreme Council and not to be afraid of an armed confrontation.

NECHAYEV: By the way, that was possible.

KOKH: It was not Yeltsin's style, no.

NECHAYEV: Surprisingly, they were very close personally. They could spend hours together, talking, drinking. I also shared drinks with Yeltsin at certain events, but our relationship was a far cry from theirs. I looked up to him, like he was a god. Although he liked me personally and did not quite like Petr for some reason. Probably due to his glasses and rapid talk. It was hard to follow when he was hungover.

KOKH: Why was he cautious about Chubais?

NECHAYEV: I think because of his radicalism.

KOKH: Do you mean Yeltsin was not radical himself?

NECHAYEV: Obviously Yeltsin was a radical person, thank God, but he did not like anyone else to take similar steps.

KOKH: Yeltsin went down in history as a person of radical decisions; but I think he was highly capable of compromise. He made radical decisions only in the cases when inactivity threatened a full catastrophe. And until then he lingered on and searched for compromise.

NECHAYEV: Maybe there were so many of those emergencies that he had to make radical decisions practically every day.

WHEN THINGS SETTLED DOWN

AVEN: Let's go back to the economy. When did you realize that the nightmare, the fear of an approaching catastrophe, was gone? When in 1992 did you feel that things had started working and somehow settled down?

NECHAYEV: I had that feeling several times, probably. The first time that happened was in January. We actually feared the effects of privatization, and even formed a special commission for operational issues, which for some reason was also led by me. Actually, that did not correspond to my status, either. I was appointed as minister on February 19, 1992, like you. And the commission was formed in late December 1991. Nearly all the departments, including the FSB or whatever its name was then, were subordinated to me. I mean, they were supposed to supply me with information.

KOKH: What was the quality of that information? When I was the vice premier and the minister, I received monstrously lousy information, in its reliability and quality of analysis.

NECHAYEV: It was just an assortment of facts. But that is not the point. The point is that I chaired the commission meeting only once. It appeared very quickly that nothing catastrophic had happened—there were no revolts, riots, warehouse pogroms, or hunger deaths.

AVEN: That is what I want to say about hunger and cold. Directors and regions were playing that administrative game: "Give us resources or we will all die." "We will die if you do not give us money." "We will die if you do not resume imports." That is a lie. Actually, people keep on living if no one meddles. People die when their initiative is suppressed. What great famine are you talking about? There was nothing like that.

NECHAYEV: In 1992 we were talking about protests against price hikes, not about hunger riots. Yet the public reaction to that certainly burdensome measure was much calmer than we could have expected.

KOKH: They were prepared gradually. First of all, market economy elements were penetrating into people's minds: there were cooperative societies and kiosks, and the farmers' markets never stopped working. I think uncontrolled prices were unpleasant, but not as shocking as some people try to claim now.

NECHAYEV: I think that the appearance of goods after a total deficit was such a pleasant shock that it significantly compensated for the shock of doubled prices.

There was another interesting thing: I was driving along in sort of a sentimental mood. I looked around and saw public transport working.

What the hell! Trolley buses were here, the metro was open, and girls were walking down the street. Probably life was not so bad after all. That must have been January or February.

Koкн: The big shots from the regions tried to present the situation as something awful.

Aven: Right, they used that resource for bargaining with the center.

Koкн: It's possible that Gorbachev knew how regional leaders operated and took their whining as a sign that all was actually well, and he could relax. The first secretary was making complaints—how could it be otherwise? That formula let him down in the end. In turn, you had no such awareness, so you took them seriously and were overcautious. He was insufficiently cautious, and you were too cautious.

Nechayev: Hell, that might be true. But the sense of imminent collapse was sincere and universal at the end of 1991. Speaking of controllability, when I moved into the Union Gosplan, I started writing instructions for everyone I could find in the Gosplan telephone book if I did not know them personally. They were obedient people, and reported fulfillment of my instructions every day. Then acting Union minister Alexander Nikolayevich Troshin came and asked me, "What is going on? You have no rights here, but you are giving instructions to my employees."

So I told him, "Do you prefer us comparing our strength, or trying to preserve the ministry and its staff and implementing serious economic reforms needed by the country?" Then he issued a unique decree of the Soviet Economy and Forecasting Ministry: "Ministry employees shall fulfill directives of Russian First Deputy Economy and Finance Minister Nechayev Andrei Alexeyevich."

I was euphoric with that complete control at that moment. I wrote my instructions and got their responses. Formally, everything was fine. But when I started reading their responses, I saw that half of them were actually runarounds. It was a swamp, and I could do nothing about it. I became a hostage to my own idea that Gosplan personnel were the country's best, that they were aware of the real situation and of how every particular plant was doing, and that it would be easier to exercise control through these people. But it was a real swamp, actually. Then I had an opposite feeling that I was controlling nothing at all. I was besieged, they told me things every day—but nothing was happening. It took me three or probably four months to become a genuine minister. I persuaded some, fired some others, promoted some, and demoted others. I even gave them market economy lectures at board meetings. And then I became optimistic again and thought we were on the right track. People started doing their work appropriately.

AVEN: Was Yuri Vasilyevich Yaremenko still alive?

NECHAYEV: He died in the middle of the 1990s.

AVEN: What did he think about your work? Interestingly, I recall now that Soviet academicians did not treat us very well. That was strange, as their favorite students had taken office. I don't mean to brag, but we were favorite students of Shatalin, Petrakov, Yaremenko. They should have been happy.

NECHAYEV: Shatalin was more loyal than the others. At least he didn't issue an indiscriminate critique.

AVEN: He was not loyal to Yegor. Yaremenko was not loyal. Lvov was not loyal. Petrakov was not quite loyal, either.

NECHAYEV: I think there is a simple human explanation: it was pure jealousy. Petrakov was Gorbachev's assistant, and Yaremenko was a freelancer but a very influential advisor to Khasbulatov. Abalkin was a Soviet vice premier. Actually, they were close to power.

KOKH: You got their jobs.

NECHAYEV: They were getting close to power, but they were 20 years older than us. That was clear. Men aged 35 to 40 came in, and they were 60 already and realized that everything was over.

KOKH: They trained you to their own detriment.

NECHAYEV: They would never have a chance again. And they understood absolutely nothing about market economics.
AVEN: Certainly we were more educated. Although we didn't quite understand what it was, either—especially under Russian conditions.

NECHAYEV: Let me give you an example. It has nothing to do with academicians, although it may be related to them, too. Do you remember Shilov, whom you lured away from me and made a deputy minister?

AVEN: There was such a man.

NECHAYEV: He was in charge of the foreign economic balance department. I ordered him to draw up a hard currency balance. I never did that myself. But I had a general idea about a hard currency balance and a balance sheet as such. He delivered his balance sheet; I glanced at it and said, "Wait, there is a gap between the debit and the credit. Where is the balance?" He replied, "We will cover the deficit by borrowing." "But you must include that in our balance sheet. There will be liabilities, assets, and so on." There was a long note at the end of the balance sheet, which ran approximately as follows: "We will also sell some gold and borrow some and take some credits against goods, and so on and so forth" "Why is none of this included in the balance sheet?" "Why do that? We will have separate agreements." We had no separate agreements with anyone concerning the balance sheet—we simply had hard currency revenues and expenditures, and I had to explain that to him. The level of professionalism and way of thinking of one of the best Gosplan specialists, who knew how to work numbers and understood the situation, were awful. I don't think that our teachers differed much from Shilov in their knowledge of strictly professional things.

On Mistakes

AVEN: What do you think were the biggest mistakes we made as a team of technocrats hired to implement the reforms? Not political mistakes, but purely technocratic?

NECHAYEV: I don't think we made a lot of purely technocratic mistakes. Well, we probably should not have waited so long before setting free all the prices.

KOKH: Wasn't that done within two weeks?

AVEN: It was several months, actually.

NECHAYEV: Several months? Approximately in December 1992.

KOKH: Did you fix prices?

NECHAYEV: No, we set the threshold of growth.

KOKH: For the domestic market?

NECHAYEV: Not the foreign one. We paid the price they asked for on the foreign market. And the limits were cancelled very soon, for instance, for milk. But we delayed a decision on crude, and on services of natural monopoly entities. That might have been right, but we should have done it sooner.

AVEN: You should have used anti-monopoly regulation, not price regulation.

NECHAYEV: We should have been firmer in general. I think the mistakes we made were mostly political: (a) we explained nothing about the legacy; (b) we didn't get involved in politics; (c) we didn't start early enough to create a public base for our policies.

AVEN: Alfred and I have said similar things.

NECHAYEV: Remember our first attempt with Kadannikov to make some political configuration at AvtoVAZ[4] (that was a desperate attempt and we did not follow it through to the end). We already understood the need for interacting with the congress, the Supreme Council. I remember Yuri Gekht, who was a real bloodsucker—a rare parasite. He had a paper factory in Serpukhov. A total scoundrel. Many years later, I lost money I kept in his bank. But he chaired the faction of industrialists in the Supreme Council, and we spent hours discussing things with him.

KOKH: Did you gain anything?

NECHAYEV: We gained a needed vote, amending the economic policy by their request. For instance, we started indexing depreciation, which they had demanded. They were very grateful to us, and still thank us. But we didn't try to form a pro-government party, so to speak.

KOKH: But you said Yeltsin was supposed to do that in accordance with your distribution of duties.

NECHAYEV: It became obvious at the Sixth Congress, when the government made the resignation statement, that we should get involved in politics, and that we were more or less capable of that.

---

4.   AvtoVAZ is the Russian automobile manufacturer formerly known as VAZ.

KOKH: Why didn't you?

NECHAYEV: On the one hand, we were very busy, and, on the other, Yeltsin was very jealous. He had a father-of-the-nation complex. All those parties, associations, unions—he deemed all that insignificant.

AVEN: We were not prepared mentally. But what would you say about purely technocratic mistakes? I have the impression that we made one big mistake when we practically neglected social security.

NECHAYEV: That is what I can say about social affairs. We had an absolutely correct principle: to cancel universal Soviet benefits and offer targeted security. But Shokhin and Pamfilova actually failed in the mission. It still hasn't been accomplished. It's an extremely hard mission.

KOKH: And what about the monetization of benefits in 2005—is that not the same?

NECHAYEV: It is.

KOKH: So wasn't the mission accomplished after all?

AVEN: But when and how? Very badly!

KOKH: So, do you mean they have not done it yet?

NECHAYEV: Monetization of benefits still isn't complete. They went back on half the measures. The expenditures were enormous.

AVEN: I cannot understand that! The social reform was absolutely clear and spelled out, and a complete failure.

NECHAYEV: You are right about the fulfillment. Social security was the number-one mistake.

BACK TO GAIDAR

KOKH: I'd like your description of Gaidar as a premier and, if you will, a description of Yeltsin.

AVEN: Yes, and about the atmosphere. I have a feeling now (and for the past 20 years) that we had no conflicts at all. Besides the Shokhin–Gaidar quarrel, we had no other big problems. We had a unique, phenomenal atmosphere. How did you feel? And what was Gaidar's role in that atmosphere?

NECHAYEV: Petr, I think that is rather simple to explain. Frankly, Yegor brought us all in. Certainly he did not hire people alien or not pleasant to him, and that was why we had that atmosphere.

KOKH: Then why did he do that to Shokhin?

NECHAYEV: I remember well being at Gaidar's dacha a few days before his resignation and several days after they exchanged sharp words. We must have been drinking, and Yegor suddenly became sentimental. "Listen, Sashka is a phenomenal person—I am so grateful to him," and then he uttered a phrase characteristic of Yegor at that time: "He practically never asked me for money." And for him, people who did not ask him for money and did not make complaints were very valuable; he well understood how difficult it was never to ask for money in that disastrous situation.

I agree that Sasha blew social security to a large extent. But, from Yegor's point of view, he did a big favor to the budget by not straining it.

AVEN: Conflicts started in November 1992. Sasha told us about that. But that doesn't matter now.

NECHAYEV: For what I said I am personally responsible. I had some local conflicts with Chubais when he went completely radical: he demanded, for instance, that we shut down the entire defense sector, the inefficient plants, the senseless institutions and construction sites, as long as people had nothing to eat. I tried to resist: Shouldn't we keep something or someone? And that was when we went to see Yegor.

AVEN: What was the meaning of Gaidar in your life?

NECHAYEV: Gaidar made me the way I am. I do not mean he gave birth to me. Here I thank my parents, the school, upbringing, character, genes.

KOKH: That sounds like an Oscars speech.

AVEN: You should mention several wives, too.

NECHAYEV: Genes, several wives—no, they are all mine. Probably I would have survived without them, too. But without Gaidar I wouldn't have been a member of that team and you wouldn't be interviewing me now. I don't know what I would be. I think I would have hardly remained a scholar, due to my natural mobility. Probably I would have been much more successful in business due to an earlier start. But Gaidar naturally contributed to what I am now.

KOKH: And when did you stop being economy minister?

NECHAYEV: On March 25, 1993. But I must tell you that Gaidar played a very harmful role in my life as a future businessman. I inherited state thinking from both Yaremenko and my genes, because some of my family worked for the defense sector, which meant I was too mindful of state needs. Gaidar also had a state way of thinking. I remember being approached by people (when I was already working for a corporation) with projects suggesting that we would make a lot of money and the national budget might lose some, and I simply showed them out and missed a chance to make big money. And I can also tell you that I was much poorer after my ministerial work than before it.

AVEN: No one believes that; you may discuss it with Kokh. He is so sensitive about that. No one trusts him, either, but that is the truth. And no one believes me, either. In fact, no one is interested in that. There is a certain image, and you can do nothing about it. You simply have to live with it.

NECHAYEV: You know, thank God, I was less affected. No one accused me of being corrupt.

KOKH: Less than we were. That is right.

NECHAYEV: Before I took the ministerial job, I had been delivering lectures in the West and publishing lots of books and articles. I was well paid, and the ministry gave me a salary and nothing else.

KOKH: So you are Gaidar's creation. Was he a good premier? Did he actually have the talent of a top-notch manager, politician, and so on? What were his strong points and weak points?

NECHAYEV: In the end, Yegor was a person of such scale, and those events had such scale, that they probably fit one another 100 percent. Globally, Gaidar fitted his position. To be frank, I cannot think of another person being able to cope with that situation—although Petr thinks it was not so bad. I, personally, had a feeling of the country's ruin in fall 1991.

AVEN: We are arguing about terms. Certainly the situation was serious. No one denies that.

NECHAYEV: No, Petr, I will tell you what: Yegor and I were sitting in his office when the southern military district commander came and said, "Guys, the Ukrainians are seceding. Crimea is a genuinely Russian land. I was thinking I could place nuclear mines along Perekop; they can then try to pass through if they want." Yegor says, "I will execute you, General, and I will do that personally. Personally. I won't even gather a troika [for a court-martial] if you dare to do that." You are laughing now, but I am dead serious: Yegor and I prevented a nuclear war in the center of Europe. There were plenty of such "brave" fellows at that time. The strategic nuclear button was supposed to be in the president's briefcase, but tactical nuclear weapons were everywhere. Whenever I am told there was no threat of a civil war I always remember that general and smile at the claims that everything was fine and all were friends. There is no doubt that Yegor did not fear hard decisions—but he was excessively Bolshevist, and that was what united him with Chubais.

KOKH: Could Bolshevism be the only way to defeat Bolshevism?

NECHAYEV: While you are fighting Bolshevism, yes. But I am not so sure about the construction phase. The firm conviction (even if it is just pretense) that you know exactly what to do is not always useful. What disturbed me about Chubais a bit was his conviction that he knew for sure what must be done to make people happy—even if people didn't know what they needed themselves. If they do not understand that, we will force them into happiness!

AVEN: That is what you say about him. And what about Gaidar?

NECHAYEV: He was less convinced; but Yegor surely had such inclinations. Besides, Yegor was absolutely fanatical about his work. I am surprised he was married several times.

KOKH: What does that have to do with Yegor being fanatical about his work?

NECHAYEV: I am surprised that he managed to marry even once. He was that fanatical about his work.

AVEN: And his work was the reform of the country. Okay. What have we missed out?

PRESENT DAY

NECHAYEV: I think our conversation would have been much livelier if we had been drinking. I told you we should have met in the evening.

AVEN: Still, what have we not asked you?

NECHAYEV: About the present day.

AVEN: Why are so few people interested in this period? What do you think? But briefly, just a couple of words. By 1937, thousands of books had been written about the revolution of 1917, only 20 years after the event. Whites, reds, émigrés. And now 20 years have passed since the disintegration of the USSR, and almost no one remembers anything: neither our government, nor 1991, nor 1993—and worthwhile recollections about Yeltsin were covered by only one or two books.

KOKH: I spoke today to students of the Higher School of Economics, the fourth year, the business journalism department. Their instructor told me it was a good year, lots better than others. I told them about the 1990s, privatization and economic reforms, and how that all started. But they did not seem to care. The only thing that interested them a lot was details of the writers' scandal: how much they were paid, a lot or a little, where the money came from, and how it was spent. They cared about nothing else, either 1991 or 1993.

AVEN: And I still remember names of the delegates to the First Congress of the Council of People's Commissars, and the October revolt chronicle, and lots of other things about the revolution and the Civil War. This knowledge is typical of our generation. And here is the end of Soviet power! You'd think it would be interesting!

NECHAYEV: I would disagree—there is some interest. Certainly I am not Yeltsin, nor Gaidar, but my latest book had a print run of 10,000 copies. That's a lot for economic memoirs, and people are buying the book. Several dozen people who read it wrote in their blogs that it was very interesting. Probably young people do not care because they were born afterwards, and do not understand the dramatic nature of that moment. They do not want to know, Petr, about our differences over hunger. Their only interest is their current life, pleasure, salaries, and career. Probably that is good. I am not sure they read history books at all.

KOKH: The war ended in 1945, 16 years before I was born. When I was more or less able to think over serious things, about seven years old, I took a keen interest in it. My grandfather was a war veteran. I could listen to him for hours. Twenty years have passed since the new era started, and I have students, not seven-year-old children, in front of me, and they care about nothing. Just one question: "Why did they pay you so much? How did you spend that money?"

NECHAYEV: Alas, a substantial part of the population subscribes to a cliché: "They stole and pillaged everything." Then there are nuances, such as "They were American agents or just crooks." Or "They might have done that because they were stupid." Do you know why that is? Because the Soviet economy broke down very quickly, and people actually had had no chance to experience that. As soon as they started feeling the approaching catastrophe, Gaidar and his team showed up. The public got an idea: times were bad, and Gaidar was in office. They linked the breakdown with us, although the breakdown actually started five years earlier. But they associated it with us. That is the peculiarity of historical memory. You can do nothing about it.

Second, we were making absolutely forced decisions, very hard—for instance, in the case of the defense factor. But people didn't care. There was an honest engineer, the father of my secretary; he was in love with aviation, and he designed aircraft. Even though his pay was average, he still loved his job and realized that the country needed it. Now he works for an insurance agency. He has no interest in that at all. But, Alfred, the talented Soviet engineer and his family of five lived in a tiny two-room apartment. That was all the Soviet power gave him. Now he has a dacha and a foreign-made car. But he feels bad. He is not interested, and no one needs him.

KOKH: People like him used to consider themselves members of the elite in the USSR. He was an aircraft engineer, important for the national defense!

And he is an insurance agent now, a regular clerk—although he has money.

NECHAYEV: He had a feeling that the country needed him. And all the others lived in the same apartments—he was lucky to get that apartment, in fact, because not everyone got one. A lot of people lost the feeling of being elite, the chosen ones. And now he has a car. He crashes it and buys another. He has a dacha, but he has no feeling that he is an esteemed person important for his country.

KOKH: And being needed by one's family is, unfortunately, marginal.

NECHAYEV: And there are millions of such people.

KOKH: The logic you are talking about makes sense. And the source of such feelings is also clear. But why are they making up things that never happened? Wild claims are being made that millions of Russian people died in those reforms. They died of hunger, and we are blamed for that. Just read what the internet and newspapers write about Luzhkov and Popov.

NECHAYEV: As you understand, part of that comes from the very top. They want to encourage people's dislike for the 1990s and people associated with that period; and since the old arguments don't work any longer, they are inventing new ones, more dramatic.

KOKH: And why the 1990s? Why not the middle of the 1980s, or the 1970s?

AVEN: There is no doubt this is the ideological tendency. But the main question is why there is no interest. I think Russia wasn't passive in the early twentieth century. There was a discussion after the revolution, and everyone felt that something had happened but lots of things still needed to be changed—it was necessary to fight for something better, for the right things; there was a choice of which way to go. Let's fight for our future. The idea of fighting for the future is gone now. That is why there is no interest in the past.

KOKH: They are fighting for the present.

AVEN: Deflated.

NECHAYEV: You, Petr, identified the main thing: Yegor's passion was at 200 percent.

5

VLADIMIR LOPUKHIN
"That Was the Bone-Breaking Machine"

Vladimir Mikhailovich Lopukhin was in charge of the Russian fuel and energy sector for ten months, three in the Silayev government and seven in the Gaidar government. That was not long, but he did a lot. The highest-profile reforms of the early 1990s—price liberalization, privatization, the altered budget structure, and ruble convertibility—did not involve Lopukhin. But he was in charge at the outset of the restructuring and regulation of the oil sector, which became the driver of economic growth.

Lopukhin had been nursing the idea of vertically integrated oil companies since the 1980s, and he brought his idea to the government. Lopukhin wrote the rough plan of the present-day oil industry landscape.

According to most, he and I least fit the classic image of the Soviet minister. Twenty years later, he still does not look like a minister—he is a typical Moscow economics and mathematics intellectual. Throughout our conversation he kept referring to general subjects, such as morals, the historical path of Russia, and so on. His thoughts were interesting, but we kept forcing him to recall the specifics—the Law on Mineral Development written under his supervision, the founding of companies that were later called Yukos, TNK, and Lukoil, and the discussion of the relatively late liberation of energy prices in 1992. Of course, we also recalled Gaidar.

Petr Aven

PETR AVEN: While you, Alfred, like a punctual German, were running late for this meeting, we listed a number of subjects we would like to discuss. The first subject of my interest is closely related to the present day. There are two sectors, oil and gas, and they are close to one another. Vladimir supervised both at the government. Yet the models of their development are absolutely different.

Several companies were formed in the oil industry: they formed a transport company, sellers, and so on. But on the other hand there was Gazprom,[1] a key achievement of Viktor Stepanovich Chernomyrdin, who, unfortunately, passed away some time ago. Presently this country has only one company producing and transporting gas. Independent companies do not count, especially as they have no pipelines.

The comparison of performance indicators of these two industries for the past 20 years shows, in my opinion, the gas industry has performed less well than the oil industry. Why is that? Who chose two different models?

VLADIMIR LOPUKHIN: I began studying the oil and gas industry in 1976, and my graduation paper was about the Soviet oil industry. I went to Siberia in 1976; Bogomyakov, the first secretary of the Tyumen regional party committee, asked Brezhnev for scientists to analyze the economy and oil-production prospects. That was why I went to Tyumen.

Alik Ryvkin and I wrote an article with a fair analysis of what was going on and what the results would be. As a result, they declared me an enemy and a Trotskyite, and barred me from foreign trips. I was not permitted to be an intern at IIASA, Austria, where Petr went. So I returned to Tyumen; Moscow was suffocating me.

ALFRED KOKH: You smoke too much. That is why you are suffocating.

LOPUKHIN: Whatever. What was important was that when I returned in 1983, I was absolutely in despair, thinking that nothing could be done about the oil industry.

AVEN: Did you live in Tyumen all the time?

LOPUKHIN: Formally, my workplace was in Moscow, at the Academy of Sciences, but I actually kept moving between Moscow and Tyumen. And

---

1.   In August 1989, under the leadership of Chernomyrdin, the Ministry of Gas Industry was reconfigured as State Gas Concern Gazprom, which became the country's first state-corporate enterprise.

not only Tyumen—Vartovsk, Novy Urengoi. I decided to stop it when I was checking my mailbox at home and could not remember if I had just returned or was leaving. I had a bag over my shoulder, and I was totally confused where I was and who I was.

I decided that was it. Actually, the anger was not at my shuttle trips but at my understanding that nothing could be done. All was inefficient, nonproductive. You could not get extreme-cold metal, below −40 degrees centigrade, which was absolutely critical. Ferroconcrete blocks were brought in by transport planes from all the Soviet republics. The whole country was helping Tyumen to build homes. And no one counted the money. You may not know it, but the oil sector had an open ruble account for many years of the Soviet period. There was no limitation of expenditures at all.

AVEN: But why did we end up with what we did? Two different models.

KOKH: The oil industry one way, and the gas industry another?

LOPUKHIN: First of all, the oil industry is much more complicated. How does the gas industry work? You drill a hole, and here comes gas and you do not have to do anything else. Gas stops coming out and you drill another hole. As you know, the oil industry fills a well with water, chemicals, and whatnot. Lots more people, lots more complicated processes—and obviously Moscow lost control of the oil industry back in the 1970s. It was necessary to set up about ten companies simply to regain control and make the situation predictable.

AVEN: Do you mean that there could be just one Gazprom, while a single oil company would have been too complex to run?

LOPUKHIN: Yes. That's one aspect. On the other hand, I opposed Chubais's plans, because Tolya proposed privatization by legal entities. What did I do? I created vertically integrated companies.

KOKH: Did you do that together with Petya Mostovoi in 1992?

LOPUKHIN: Petya was a staunch opponent. The idea for the oil industry was the following: to form large companies with access to the money—that is, to consumers. That required refining and trade, not just production. A full cycle.

KOKH: You could have done privatization by legal entities and then you could have built a vertically integrated company.

LOPUKHIN: They would never have done that. This is not the textile industry, which can stay idle for two months and then go back to work as if nothing has happened. Or it can be idle for half a year. If you don't use an oil well for two months, it's cheaper to just forget about it.

KOKH: But why would an oil well be idle? There are no arguments.

LOPUKHIN: There are arguments.

AVEN: Okay, we have heard your opinion: the oil industry was much more complex than the gas industry, so it had to be divided in order to make it predictable and manageable. That is your argument, I see. But when was the decision made—before you took office or when you were in office? Who formed oil companies, and how?

LOPUKHIN: I introduced that idea, and I reached an agreement with Gaidar.

AVEN: And you decided to let Gazprom be.

LOPUKHIN: Gazprom was a whole different kettle of fish. In my opinion, Gazprom is an element of our superpower statehood. In spite of its monstrous inefficiency and economic senselessness, it was necessary to preserve Gazprom from the geopolitical point of view. That was globally important for the country and its international position—more important than economic efficiency. That's why there is just one Gazprom. That decision was also made when I was in office. "Shall we divide it or not?" The answer was: "We shall not."

KOKH: Who gave the answer?

LOPUKHIN: I gave it myself.

KOKH: You just came and defended that decision.

LOPUKHIN: Yes—for various reasons. It was clear that the absence of gas (as well as gasoline) would present a political risk to the regime. But we had gas, and Gazprom was operating smoothly.

KOKH: I think there is a simpler explanation. By the moment you had to make a decision about privatizing Gazprom—and I can remember that the decision was made a bit later than spring 1992—

LOPUKHIN: Certainly later.

KOKH: —by then Chernomyrdin had become premier, and he would not have allowed it to be restructured.

LOPUKHIN: What do you mean, he would not have allowed it?

KOKH: He would not. Whom would he have allowed?

LOPUKHIN: This is not the point. A decision not to restructure it was made while I still was in office.

KOKH: But listen to me.

LOPUKHIN: I heard Dima Vasilyev screaming that what I was creating was communism, or a return to Soviet times.

AVEN: And did you seriously consider a different structure for Gazprom—for instance, separating off a transport company?

LOPUKHIN: Certainly.

KOKH: In fact, when the Gazprom decree was published, Vladimir was no longer working for the government anymore. That happened when I was in office. And I was appointed in August 1993.

LOPUKHIN: And what happened before that?

KOKH: Before that they simply decided to do nothing, for a while. There was no urgency. That was not the main problem that needed a solution. There was also Chernomyrdin.

LOPUKHIN: Chernomyrdin created an enterprise. That was before us.

KOKH: Yes. That was a legal entity. And there had been no concerns in the oil industry before. There had been just separate oil-producing enterprises.

I remember that well, because it was I who was privatizing the oil industry. I was doing that personally. All those decrees drafted by companies were my work. And yours, Petr, the Tyumen Oil Company, was shaped by me, by adding various refineries and design bureaus. In my opinion, Vladimir is giving us beautiful and complex explanations. But I think there was a government of young reformers who came in and saw: there is an oil industry. It was possible to collect enterprises one way or another—to merge them into a single whole or not to join them at all. As Gaidar put it, "It will glue itself together somehow." And there was Gazprom, already consolidated into a corporation and led by Chernomyrdin, a minister and the vice premier for fuel and energy. He wasn't a vice minister when Lopukhin was there, but he was a big player, and the only one in the country with a huge amount of cash.

AVEN: The oil industry also had cash.

KOKH: But it was not consolidated. The gas guys consolidated their cash right in Moscow. You could jeer, argue, and form vertically integrated companies and a competitive environment all you wanted, but here was the task: you had to fight them to make any change. They didn't care if they went to ruin.

AVEN: Besides, they had hard currency, which was in desperate demand.

KOKH: And you had to pay for the ships carrying wheat to St Petersburg. You were fighting a war in South Ossetia, and you had to buy insulin.

And here is one more important factor we have overlooked: Gazprom has no retail trade, and you are unable to create a competitive environment. Gazprom is everywhere.

LOPUKHIN: There is competition on the gas market in America.

KOKH: I say here. America has it because its pipelines are independent. Here Gazprom is the local monopoly wherever gas is used. Meanwhile, hundreds, thousands, and tens of thousands of gasoline stations are retailers creating a competitive environment.

So, it was much easier to create competition in the oil industry. Plus there was the question of storage. That is also important. It is much easier to build a storage facility for crude than an underground storage site for gas. We had lots of debates about privatization of the electric power industry before we realized that it had to be privatized as a single whole, due to one fundamental problem: the absence of competition. The same monopoly entity was at every place of consumption. And there was a practically unsolvable problem of storage. It is a commodity that cannot be stored—that is why we have been engaged in the complex restructuring process for almost 20 years, and it is still not restructured. The world does not have an ideal formula for the competition-based electric power industry. America has blackout problems, too. And Gazprom is somewhere in the middle, between the electric power and oil industries. It practically has no retail sales, and its storage system is extremely complex. I remember the disputes I was involved in. Petya Mostovoi kept telling me, "Your business is the defense sector. Why are you meddling with my fuel and energy sector?" When Petya was gone, I had to tackle both tasks. We practically came to blows with Chubais. We were arguing which of us was the demiurge to decide what must be done. I told him I was the source of the impulse.

LOPUKHIN: I do not know whether we should publish that, but Vitya Chernomyrdin was a fine psychologist. He learned that Yeltsin could not stand women crying. So he called for an old lady deputy from Novy Urengoi and told her (she was a member of the Constitutional Commission): "I will bury you if you do not start crying at the Constitutional Commission meeting, washing yourself in your tears and wailing, 'What does the constitution have to do with it? My dear Gazprom is dying.'" She performed this number in front of Yeltsin.

KOKH: That was in fall 1993, when the decisions had already been made.

LOPUKHIN: Yeltsin came to the Kremlin and said he would do nothing until the Gazprom decree was signed.

KOKH: Do you understand why that happened? Why was Lopukhin fired first? Why was Yeltsin mad at him more than at anyone else? Vladimir is right in saying that Chernomyrdin was a fine psychologist. He realized the following. He gathered everyone and said, "Okay, guys, either those Moscow assholes restructure us or I have to become the premier."

LOPUKHIN: No matter how strange that may be, my theory is much more primitive than Alfred's. They called us in when the country was in ruins and no one knew what might happen. We survived the winter—the most tragic winter of 1991–2—and it was clear to comrades that people swallowed what we fed them. Then they said, "We must take power back, and we may also shift the blame onto these morons. It is time to return. We were not wiped out or banished, and we also have somebody to blame. That is wonderful."

KOKH: But Chernomyrdin did not know then that he would have trouble, too.

WHY GAIDAR?

AVEN: Vladimir, why did we end up as the morons and not the Zhenya Saburov team, which you were also a member of? You were the only one of us shuttling between dachas. The Saburov team was writing at one dacha in Arkhangelskoye, and the Gaidar team was doing the same at another dacha. I remember you being a deputy energy minister …

LOPUKHIN: No, I was a deputy economy minister.

AVEN: … and supervising the fuel and energy sector.

KOKH: And who was the minister?

LOPUKHIN: Saburov.

AVEN: In the fall, about 45 days before our appointment or even less, I brought to Moscow a group of Americans wishing to invest in oil and gas, and Vladimir met with them in the capacity of deputy minister. Here is the question: Why was our dacha the one chosen from those two?

LOPUKHIN: Zhenya Saburov formed a team of professional economists who tried to understand what was going on before taking some action. They wanted to understand before they could act. And the situation was difficult to grasp. As the Saburov team didn't quite realize what the transitional period was and how to deal with it. And Yegor was great and almighty, sure of the theory, the true value of which everyone present here understands. The theory was very simple: just let it go; you let it go, and it would go by itself. The theory suited the mentality of our administrative *nomenklatura*, but they understood it differently. We understood it from the liberal point of view, while they thought, "We won't be culpable, but we will profit." We increase taxes—that is, broaden the distributive function—but we are not responsible for prices and for production, right? What was privatization?

We are not responsible for your production. And distribution? We could do that. There was a totally new balance of responsibility, and they quite liked it. See what I mean? That was very touching.

Kokh: Didn't Saburov propose to change tariffs or to do something with prices?

Lopukhin: Saburov was trying to find forms of privatization.

Kokh: Wait, privatization is all right, but wasn't he planning price liberalization?

Lopukhin: He was.

Kokh: So what is the difference?

Lopukhin: Gradually.

Kokh: What do you mean, gradually? I don't understand.

Lopukhin: He wanted to do that slowly and cautiously.

Kokh: Slowly would bring on collapse sooner. Gaidar had to liberalize prices because of the shortage of products.

Lopukhin: Naturally.

Kokh: If prices had been liberalized slowly, we would have had no products in March. But Saburov also supported uncontrolled prices.

Lopukhin: The only difference was the tempo.

Aven: In short, Saburov proposed gradualism.

Lopukhin: Yes. Complex formulas. But the most important was—and you're not listening to what I'm saying—that there was no language to explain his complex formulas.

Aven: Everyone knows that if you cannot explain something to a ten-year-old child, then you do not understand it yourself.

LOPUKHIN: Not necessarily.

AVEN: It's true in almost every case—certainly in economics. The greatest economists I have ever known explained the most complex economic phenomena in very simple language.

LOPUKHIN: Well, try to explain Keynes in simple language.

AVEN: It is rather easy to explain the main ideas of Keynes. And judging by what you say, Saburov had neither a program nor a team. Who was there besides you?

LOPUKHIN: Oh well, there were also Vanya Materov, Seryoga Glazyev.

AVEN: Was Glazyev there, too?

LOPUKHIN: Yes, he was a deputy economic minister. He was a member of the team.

AVEN: What are you talking about? Glazyev was never a member of your government—not for a single day.

LOPUKHIN: I would never forget our appointment as deputy ministers on August 19, 1991. Glazyev said at about noon on August 19, "I have a small child; there is nothing to do here; I'm out of here, guys."

AVEN: He rejected the offer. He was offered a deputy minister's position, but he quit.

LOPUKHIN: The way he acted on that day was something you'd never forget. It was such a jolly day. Maybe he did have a small child.

AVEN: I see. About Saburov—

KOKH: If he really was so incomprehensible and unclear and his speech was tangled, how did he become economy minister?

LOPUKHIN: Because Zhenya was a professional above all.

KOKH: And who made that decision, if he could not explain what he wanted to the people in charge in an intelligible way? Who made him economy minister?

LOPUKHIN: I will speak for myself now. I realized that the country was finished sometime in 1990, when I was listening to speeches of RSFSR people's deputies on TV. They were presenting another program of reforms, and I was reading a book called *Fundamental Human Needs*. It said, for instance, that you cannot persuade an African not to destroy a protected plant or to eat a protected animal because he spends eight hours a day looking for something edible, then he grabs the first plant he can use as firewood or food. So I realized the way the country was going—we had to provide either bread or crude oil. Otherwise, there would be chaos. I knew nothing about bread, so I decided I would go back to the oil sector. I started writing a development program for the Tyumen region. Yurka Shafranik was the chairman of the Tyumen Executive Committee at the time. He actually hired me. By the time I met Saburov, and especially Yegor, I had a detailed program and I knew what had to be done in particular situations.

AVEN: So you became a deputy minister and then the minister?

LOPUKHIN: That was convenient for everyone. It was convenient for Zhenya because he didn't have to teach me what to do. A key sector had its program. And it was convenient for Yegor when I came to work for him, because there was clarity with what was done, when, with whom, and why.

PRICE LIBERALIZATION

AVEN: Vladimir, why were crude and petroleum product prices liberalized later than others?

LOPUKHIN: We agreed with Yegor from the start that 15 percent of everything I was in charge of would be sold on the free market. That helped us grasp reality, because we were constantly monitoring uncontrolled prices. And we were bringing the so-called fixed prices closer to uncontrolled prices.

KOKH: That lowered the free prices.

AVEN: And the idea of controlling petroleum product prices for a while, instead of just letting them go in January, was it your idea?

LOPUKHIN: Certainly not.

KOKH: Then whose?

LOPUKHIN: Yeltsin's.

KOKH: Then why petroleum products?

LOPUKHIN: Gasoline and fuel oil are basics.

KOKH: Coal is a basic product, and bread is a basic product, too.

LOPUKHIN: There was control over bread, too.

KOKH: No, bread prices were set free earlier than crude prices. The oil sector went completely free only in fall 1992.

LOPUKHIN: But prices were not fixed fully, I am telling you. Because we had that quota for uncontrolled prices.

KOKH: Everything was sold under that brand, I see.

LOPUKHIN: That was a purely political decision by Yeltsin.

KOKH: You brought a total price liberalization project to him, and he told you to stay away from the oil sector.

LOPUKHIN: That was the guideline.

KOKH: So you didn't hear the decision being made?

LOPUKHIN: That was a political decision.

KOKH: I see it this way. Gaidar was a good tactician. He realized that Yeltsin should be approached not with the most radical project but with something to prove its balanced nature. That is why some prices were left under control.

LOPUKHIN: Maybe. On the other hand, he permitted me to shift to fixed and partially uncontrolled prices before we did anything else. So everyone was waiting for new prices, and the supplies stopped. And it was winter. We could have frozen before the New Year. So we started to raise and set free prices. To some extent, we instituted the reform before everyone else, and there were no fights at gasoline stations.

When prices were liberated, Leshka Golovkov and I were driving to work in one car on January 1. We made a stop in Oktyabrskaya Square, where there was a food store. We climbed over a snowdrift, got our feet wet, and then we went inside the food store to see the prices and people's reaction to them. All was calm.

KOKH: The propaganda campaign had been going on for two months. People were prepared for the appearance of goods sold at high prices. So when people came, they saw what they expected.

LUKOIL, YUKOS, SURGUTNEFTEGAZ

AVEN: Vladimir, let's talk about how some particular oil companies were created.

KOKH: Formed when you were in office?

AVEN: Yes, and which appeared very different in their forms of ownership, management, and mentality. These are Surgutneftegaz, Lukoil, and Yukos. Surgut is led by a Soviet oil general. He has never changed. He has not become an oligarch or a billionaire—at least his lifestyle doesn't resemble that of our typical billionaires. Vagit Alekperov formed a large international private (and now public) company, and he is one of the richest people in the country, if not the richest. Finally, Yukos. It was formed by oil workers but fell into the hands of young men who had nothing to do with oil. Can you comment on each company? When were they established, and why were they so different?

AVEN: Just tell us the truth.

LOPUKHIN: Certainly, the truth and only the truth, but not the whole truth, as Comrade Nicolae taught us. The oil sector was told there would be vertically integrated companies. But they did not understand that—they did not understand what a company was.

AVEN: That is self-deception. It appeared Alekperov knew that better than you from the very start. And Khodorkovsky understood that, too.

KOKH: And Muravlenko. You think they didn't know what Western companies were? They knew that perfectly well: retail trade, refining, and production.

LOPUKHIN: As far as I understand, Alekperov was slightly offended for a while because he thought I wanted to fire him from the position of first deputy minister and send him off to set up some company. He believed at first that I didn't much like him.

AVEN: When he was still a Soviet deputy minister?

LOPUKHIN: He was my deputy, too. And he wasn't thinking about any company.

KOKH: So you shouldn't have appointed him if that was so. You could have appointed somebody else.

LOPUKHIN: I think that was a rather clever decision. As Vagit was the informal leader of the oil generals, it was important that he should be the first to form a company.

AVEN: Was that your idea?

LOPUKHIN: Certainly. Who else's?

AVEN: And who was structuring the Lukoil company?

LOPUKHIN: That was Vagit, and he did well although he had no legal framework. He used only his personal charisma.

AVEN: So you gave him the idea and suggested he put together a vertically integrated company?

LOPUKHIN: They were preparing something, an association or God knows what. He was given the suggestion to transform it into a company, and he did that.

AVEN: As I understand it, he personally selected the companies that could be merged.

KOKH: By the way, he did not choose the best companies. Being a professional, he must have realized there were better companies. For instance, the Noyabrskneftegaz enterprise was obviously better than any of his three.

LOPUKHIN: He did that wherever he could reach an agreement. Any agreement creates a totally new culture, a culture of partnership.

AVEN: It was a partnership at first, and then Alekperov actually became the boss.

LOPUKHIN: That is not the point. The point is that Lukoil had a structure completely different from other companies. For instance, Yukos was a totally different story.

AVEN: I remember you were friends with Khodorkovsky. Nevzlin and Khodorkovsky practically lived at your dacha.

LOPUKHIN: Let us start from the end. After Khodorkovsky joined Yukos, I left. I never was there together with him. I had a rather active position in Yukos. And their joining meant my leaving.

AVEN: What was the year?

LOPUKHIN: The year of loans-for-shares auctions.

AVEN: And did you cooperate with Yukos closely?

LOPUKHIN: With Yukos, not with them.

KOKH: With Muravlenko.

LOPUKHIN: Muravlenko was there. But Muravlenko took their side and I quit.

AVEN: Was the company established in the same way as Vagit's?

LOPUKHIN: That was a completely different story. The Yukos structure had been planned at the Economy Ministry since August 1991. We wanted to make a model company and were thinking about ways to do that.

AVEN: Did the generals support you?

LOPUKHIN: Volodya Zenkin, who was killed, was more enthusiastic than Muravlenko—that is, about refineries. A union of refineries, Samara, Kuibyshev …

KOKH: And when was he killed? Was it after the loans-for-shares auction?

LOPUKHIN: No, before that. There were really severe wrangles there.

KOKH: Muravlenko was champing at the bit to be with Khodorkovsky, and Zenkin was against that.

LOPUKHIN: Zenkin, may he rest in peace, was a rare kind of self-sufficient man. So, here was Lukoil and its charismatic leader, who did not quite understand what an oil company was. But in spite of that he gathered it into a single whole, reached agreements, settled formalities, and made a company. On the other hand, Yukos was nursed by lots of people—me, Grushevenko, Samusev, Zenkin.

AVEN: So, unlike Lukoil, the company was formed on the orders of the authorities, from above?

LOPUKHIN: Yes. And here is a different situation—Volodya Bogdanov. He was perceived as the youngest Soviet oil general at the time. He was good, but he stayed on his own. He is still on his own. I will tell you a very typical story about Volodya Bogdanov. The then director of the Kirishi refinery came to Surgut, and I happened to be there to discuss something about the company with Volodya. I arrived there, and I was having trouble sleeping.

AVEN: Were you the minister then?

LOPUKHIN: No—I was already a banker, and had a contract with Volodya concerning his company; I was paid for this work. So I came to discuss certain issues with Volodya. I just could not fall asleep. So I decided to go for a walk and get some fresh air. I went out. It was 3:00 a.m. The hotel was a remodeled 1930s barracks. I saw a shadow in a sheepskin coat. I wondered who could be out walking at such an odd hour. It was Volodya Bogdanov. I asked him what he was doing. And he said, "See, he"—the Kirishi refinery director—"is drunk, and he smokes in his bed. There may be a fire."

KOKH: Was he protecting him?

LOPUKHIN: He was protecting the barracks from fire. Alone, in the middle of the night—an oil general.

AVEN: Interesting.

KOKH: What can I tell you? It's probably right that Bogdanov became the master of the company he had built.

LOPUKHIN: And is he the master?

KOKH: In effect, yes. I don't know, the Pension Fund formally owns Surgutneftegaz. But he is the fund manager.

LOPUKHIN: We don't understand everything about property in Surgut, but when the company was being formed, Volodya spent days trying to grasp which rules were applicable, and what they could do and what they could not. So here are three different stories.

WORK AND DISMISSAL

AVEN: Now, to conclude the oil and gas theme: What do you rate as your biggest achievements from August 1991 through May 1992?

LOPUKHIN: First of all, I co-chaired the commission drafting the mineral development law. I drafted the law with all those limitations, and the modern system of mineral development was brought to life.

AVEN: Next?

LOPUKHIN: Second, we started the restructuring of the fuel and energy sector. The formula for vertically integrated companies was invented then and implemented later. Third, we managed to preserve the financial stability of the fuel and energy sector.

AVEN: To protect the system and to preserve it?

LOPUKHIN: To preserve the market, thanks to price maneuvering, quotas on uncontrolled prices, and so on.

AVEN: You gave us a very clear answer. Now tell us: we've been discussing the possibility of hunger with everyone, so was there any threat of cold in winter 1991–2?

LOPUKHIN: Actually, no. I had to deal with the threat of cold only once. A number of people froze to death in Khabarovsk.

AVEN: Was it because of democracy?

LOPUKHIN: Yes, it was because of democracy. Khabarovsk is a peculiar city. It stretches out for 50 kilometers along a riverbank. And it gets cold there rather early. Seasonal repairs used to be done early, and the heating system used to be started up because it was not very stable due to its long length and complex hydrodynamic characteristics. When the democrats took office, they decided to postpone the repairs on the heating system until October or November instead of starting it up in September. They tried to start up the system when it was already cold, but it refused to start up and began to rupture. They kept repairing it, and it kept rupturing.

AVEN: It was democrats, not democracy, at fault.

LOPUKHIN: Democrats, good or bad; but many new leaders of 1991 were simply ignorant. Hopefully, despite our lack of administrative experience, that can't be said about us.

AVEN: Vladimir, I had a feeling, and Shokhin told us in his interview, that the environment, the oil industry environment, was very alien to you. You were a boy from a family of Moscow intellectuals. Your father was an intelligence general, and then you had to deal with oil generals. Were there communication problems?

LOPUKHIN: No. First of all, I had experience with such communication. When I was writing a program for the Tyumen region, we stayed in touch with all the generals to discuss what we were doing and why we were doing it.

Besides, thanks to my family I was used to communicating with high-ranking officials from my childhood. Andropov gave me life advice. So communication was not a problem.

AVEN: That is not what I mean—I mean the attitude of oil generals toward you. When Yeltsin announced your dismissal and the appointment of Chernomyrdin, Churilov, the former oil industry minister of the USSR, who was seated in the first row, started to applaud.

LOPUKHIN: Yes, and he supported the GKChP. That was interesting to me.

AVEN: Do you remember him applauding? He was the only one.

LOPUKHIN: He was. And I wondered why. I think Churilov was the only one in the oil sector to support the GKChP. He ran to me later because, naturally, he shat his pants, scared he would be fired.

AVEN: And was he fired?

KOKH: He was fired due to the disintegration of the Union.

LOPUKHIN: He could have been fired for much worse reasons, as you understand.

KOKH: We harbored everyone who buried us. But that was the usual thing.

LOPUKHIN: Get this: the program I drafted was approved. No one but him applauded. Note that, will you? Other oil generals were also there, and none of them applauded.

KOKH: But somebody must have lobbied for your dismissal.

LOPUKHIN: It was lobbied by time.

AVEN: But why were you the first?

LOPUKHIN: I was not the first. I will remind you if you do not remember. We took a walk—Gaidar, Tolya, you, and me. I don't remember who else was there, but there were not many people in Arkhangelskoye when Gena Burbulis was gone, and someone called Petr Aven said, "They fired Gena without discussing that with us. It will all end badly."

AVEN: I knew that from the start.

KOKH: But Petr said we were talking about your dismissal.

LOPUKHIN: No, I remember that walk perfectly. The weather was gorgeous.

AVEN: Burbulis was not a member of our team, although I really did say it would all end badly.

LOPUKHIN: And when Gena was fired, you said it was not bad that he was fired per se but bad because the dismissal was not coordinated with the government. You said they could continue doing that.

KOKH: And I remember Gaidar's reply: "And what would you suggest? Shall we all resign?"

LOPUKHIN: For all else you may say, Yegor had impeccable morals. After I was fired he called for me and asked, "Do you want me to step down?" We had a one-on-one conversation. And I said no.

KOKH: That's not a conversation, that's nothing. He knew that there was no chance you would say yes. That was a ritual. I'm not arguing—Gaidar was a decent and fair man—but your example does not illustrate that.

AVEN: Even if Burbulis was the first, you were the second.

LOPUKHIN: Why? A key sector. The key to everything at that time.

KOKH: And what, do you think, Gaidar and the whole team should have done for you to keep your position? Do you have the feeling that your post could have been saved with a fight, but no one bothered to do it?

LOPUKHIN: Alfred, the first contract I got when I joined the fine bank Lazard was for the establishment of Gazprom. My first contract was with Chernomyrdin. Some conclusions may be drawn from that.

KOKH: Chernomyrdin was a subtle psychologist.

LOPUKHIN: Who thought I understood something.

AVEN: That's not what we are discussing.

KOKH: I can tell you a lot about Chernomyrdin. I watched his last interview for a whole hour. That was a good interview. And it had an important episode, when Chernomyrdin spoke about his several meetings with Yeltsin, when he tried to force him to pay a pension to Gorbachev. Yeltsin categorically refused even to discuss that, but he kept coming back. Chernomyrdin understood that people who might be your opponents should be kept close. Keep your friends close and your enemies even closer. Don't push them away to be on their own.

AVEN: Vladimir, did the dismissal disappoint you?

LOPUKHIN: I was disappointed because I didn't get to finish things—although I finished some of my work when I was employed by the bank. That work was related to Rosneft, Yukos, and Gazprom. In fact, I am an idealistic person, and from my idealistic point of view, God gave me a wonderful gift—I was in Moscow and I did my job using my knowledge and skills.

AVEN: Am I right that you were so busy with your industry sector in government that you practically took no part in our general economic discussions?

LOPUKHIN: To begin with, the atomic energy industry was added to my job: some 10,000 enterprises, eight and a half million employees, the paramilitary regime, and the minister able to reprimand a silo section head.

AVEN: Wasn't there an atomic energy ministry?

LOPUKHIN: Not at first. I used to meet with Yeltsin to create it. I also recommended Mikhailov.

KOKH: Distinguished.

LOPUKHIN: You know, Alfred, I was told after my appointment that I would have to sign every directive for the atomic energy industry. They brought the documents, and wherever I looked it was Beria, Beria, Beria. I told them, "I would not put my signature under Beria's. Go and draft something new." They returned and said, "Extend them for five years." I said, "To hell with you," and put my signature above Beria's.

AVEN: You were so engrossed with fuel and energy affairs that you participated less in other issues. I can remember that. What do you think we should have done that we didn't?

LOPUKHIN: There was a lot we didn't do. But I would phrase the question in a different way. What do we understand now, and what did we not understand then?

AVEN: Answer that question.

A CHANGE OF ELITES

LOPUKHIN: We did not understand, and therefore underestimated, what Carlyle wrote about only a revolution of morals being a true revolution. It did not happen, and it is still pending.

KOKH: A revolution or simply an evolution of morals is primarily an evolution of morals inside the elites. The elites did not change, and therefore there was no moral evolution.

LOPUKHIN: Right.

AVEN: The elites were not quite the same. They intermixed to a large degree.

KOKH: The administrative elite remained the same. The cultural elite remained the same. There was a new business elite, but it was incorporated by the older elites. The elite quality did not change. So here is the question I have been asking myself and everyone else: Do you think that elite could really be changed? Why did the Bolsheviks last for so long? Why did they take power in 1917 and last until 1991? That was because they changed the elite. Completely. They either banished or killed the old elite. And we did not do that. That is why we were all replaced very quickly—the old elite was back in practically ten years. We didn't ban the KGB elite, and it returned—that's all. The evolution of morals did not take place.

LOPUKHIN: It has not.

KOKH: Did the authorities of 1991–2 have the resources to introduce a law on lustration?

AVEN: They could have simply opened the KGB archives. That would have had a fundamental significance, and bans on certain kinds of work would have been unnecessary.

KOKH: So the KGB archives should have been opened by people who knew 100 percent they were part of those archives?

AVEN: Yes, but not all of them.

KOKH: They never would have made that decision. The problem was that people listed in those archives were supposed to open them.

AVEN: Yeltsin—

KOKH: He was there, a million percent—a million! The first secretary of a regional party committee simply had to be in there.

AVEN: What do you mean?

KOKH: Sure, he signed their papers. He would have had no chance of being the first secretary without regulating his relations with the committee.

LOPUKHIN: I don't know.

AVEN: I think, Alfred, you are exaggerating. Our KGB has been under the party's thumb since the Khrushchev era, and not vice versa—although in all the East European countries and the Baltic republics truly new elites took power. Those people had nothing to do with the former authorities. Václav Klaus was our guest yesterday. He had been working for the Academy of Sciences for years and had no right to travel abroad, being a semi-dissident. Havel was a dissident. Mazowiecki or Balcerowicz did not work for the party regional committee or the *Kommunist* journal, either.

KOKH: Okay, Yeltsin. He could not make that decision alone. Can you vouch for Gaidar? Or for Chubais? Can you say, "You can chop my head off but I am sure Gaidar did not cooperate with the committee"? I would not do that. I love Gaidar, and I would forgive him even if that really happened, and that was highly unlikely—but I would not vouch with my head.

And there were so many people who nominated Yeltsin as their leader: Sobchak, Popov, Ryzhov. Can you vouch for them?

LOPUKHIN: Alfred, calm down.

KOKH: Take Sobchak, who made Putin his first aide and entrusted him with operational work without concealing that Putin was a KGB lieutenant colonel. Can you vouch for him? A professor of the Leningrad State University Department of Law. It was a KGB outlet after the Leningrad case, and the law department above all. They didn't even admit students without recommendations from the police or the KGB, much less the teaching staff.

AVEN: One way or another, 1991 was not quite a revolution.

KOKH: A revolution is primarily a revolution of the masses.

AVEN: I agree. And still, in spite of your assertions, the stability of elites, and so on, I think we could have had a leader capable of discarding the Soviet past and heading the new elite. Yegor did not become that leader. Neither did Yavlinsky, although I think he was the closest to doing it. Walesa and Havel did. Speaking of economists, there was Václav Klaus, who was ten years older than Yegor. Balcerowicz too. These are leaders symbolizing the new generation. Why didn't we have any? Was it only because the revolution had not been genuine?

KOKH: The whole Soviet elite was affiliated with the Soviet system in one way or another. There was more of a civil society in Czechoslovakia and Hungary. There was the Church in Poland, which created alternative elites. We had dissidents, but there were very few of them here, and I have trouble imagining any of our dissidents, like Lera Novodvorskaya—whom you and I love very much—as a manager, a person making a balanced decision. I think if Lera is ever given a chance to manage anything, even a town, she'd make such a mess, they would have been better off beforehand. We had no source of new people.

AVEN: And where did such people come from in the Baltic republics?

KOKH: The Baltic republics have awful elites now—unprofessional.

LOPUKHIN: The basic difference is whether you have 70 or 40 years of Soviet power.

KOKH: Yes, and the scale of the country. This is a huge country, and one needs to know how to rule it. I will give you a simple example. Gavriil Popov attempted a drastic change in a part of the Moscow elite. He appointed Arkasha Murashov as the city police chief. Ridiculous. He also made Zaslavsky a district prefect. What happened? Naturally, Murashov's successor was a nominee of the old police force.

AVEN: The fact that we did not have a Klaus reveals a lot about the post-Soviet intelligentsia and the personal qualities of its best representatives. Naturally, that was the consequence of our entire history and those 70 years.

KOKH: Yegor asked me once: "Who on our team has never been a member of the Soviet Communist Party?" I said, "Petr, me, Manevich, and Borya Nemtsov." "That won't do. Not enough," he said. We mostly had people affiliated with the party and the Soviet *nomenklatura* in some way—Chubais, Shokhin, and so on. And that was on the team that personified the most liberal transformations.

AVEN: What about Nechayev?

KOKH: Nechayev was a party member.

LOPUKHIN: Not just a party member, but also a member of the institute party committee.

KOKH: And Borya Fyodorov? A Central Committee instructor. And Gaidar? The *Kommunist* journal was an organ of the Central Committee. We are talking about the new elite. And what about their objectives?

LOPUKHIN: Alfred, you are not listening. Half of the government belonged to our institute party committee: Shokhin, Nechayev, Saltykov, and I.

AVEN: I still think there could have been a person ready to break with the past.

KOKH: First of all, Yeltsin should have done that.

AVEN: He broke with a lot of things.

KOKH: Gaidar was ready to break with the past.

AVEN: He did not have enough power.

KOKH: You do remember Gaidar, don't you? Gaidar was ready to make the most serious governmental decisions, but in a personal confrontation.

AVEN: Obviously Gaidar was not prepared to be a political leader. But in every country that achieves something, they appear.

KOKH: I started working in Moscow in August 1993. Before that I had been working for the St Petersburg administration for two years. I can tell you that the St Petersburg administration had a completely different power balance between the influence of the staff and that of the industry committees. Industry committees had the lead. So I was amazed how easily the staff could override a ministry in Moscow. For example, we had the state property management committee, government administration departments, and the presidential administration. A resolution required coordination with some of the departments.

LOPUKHIN: Naturally.

KOKH: The departments meant people. Take, for instance, the Department of Defense. Its staff came either from the Central Committee or from the Union Council of Ministers.

LOPUKHIN: Lyosha Golovkov selected them.

KOKH: Yes, he did. But there was no one else to hire. Lobov, Skokov, Ilyushin, and Korabelshchikov were the regional party committee people. Yuri Vladimirovich Petrov was the first secretary of the Sverdlovsk regional party committee after Yeltsin. And he didn't replace any of them.

AVEN: We were rather comfortable with those people—much more comfortable than with democratic dissidents.

KOKH: Certainly. And in 1917 a sailor came to a ministry, kicked everyone out, and hired a new staff.

AVEN: And those kicked out were killed.

KOKH: We acted differently. We took office, hit the tree with a stick, and crows flew up, circled, and perched in the same tree. People like us made up 10 percent of the staff on Staraya Square or in the White House, or in the Kremlin in 1993, even though we headed all the departments. But all the rest came from the Soviet government and the Soviet Communist Party Central Committee.

AVEN: We have deviated from the fuel and energy theme a lot. A change of elites was not our focal point, that's for sure. Nor was the establishment of a political party, which we discussed in the previous interviews.

LOPUKHIN: If anyone had told you, Petr, the foreign trade minister, that in 1992 you would be forming a party, you would have laughed it off. You were busy with quite different things.

AN EXTREMELY DECENT MAN

AVEN: Vladimir, give us some personal memories—the most illustrative episodes of your work in our government. Do you remember us taking down the portraits of Lenin in the offices of the White House?

LOPUKHIN: Lyosha Golovkov had a remarkable episode with a Lenin portrait.

KOKH: Were Lenin portraits in place until 1991?

AVEN: Certainly.

LOPUKHIN: Lyoshka took down the portrait and left it in the back room. He came to work the next day and saw the portrait in its place again. He thought, "Hell, they put it back." Then he went to the back room and saw that the portrait he had taken down was still there.

KOKH: They had hung up a new one.

LOPUKHIN: Yes. He took down the portrait again, and they put up a third one. Golovkov summoned the administrative department head and asked, "What's this?" He said, "The manual says you must have a portrait. You have the right to take it down, but I must hang up a new one."

KOKH: I chaired the Sestroretsk district executive committee in 1990. I took down Lenin's portrait and no one put it back.

LOPUKHIN: There must have been no manual. But the White House had one.

CRAZY TEMPO

AVEN: Let us talk about more personal things—about Gaidar. How did you meet? What impressions did you have about him? Did you like working with him?

LOPUKHIN: There is always a drama in major reforms. The drama is that neither the government nor the laws determine the way the system operates. The system is regulated by a bunch of unwritten rules, customs, and customary relations. Whenever you replace system X with system Y, the drama is that you are unable to accumulate a critical mass of decisions to create a single whole in just one day. It takes thousands of decisions, tens of thousands of decisions, before something more or less integral is made. It takes a lot.

KOKH: Again, you are not answering the question about Yegor.

LOPUKHIN: Lots of things happened to Yegor the way they did because we were under constant time pressure. He had to make lots and lots of decisions in a wild tempo.

KOKH: Speaking of the idea that Saburov (and Yavlinsky) had about the gradual liberation of prices, that was simply impossible.

LOPUKHIN: The problem is that as soon as you say "X," the cockroach races begin. You need to appoint a load of new people and make a load of new decisions at a wild speed.

KOKH: The tempo of reforms is set by life, not by the reformers.

LOPUKHIN: By life, true.

KOKH: And you cannot choose your own tempo if acceleration is needed and life demands you implement decisions immediately.

LOPUKHIN: And then life carries you away.

KOKH: Unless you keep up with the tempo.

LOPUKHIN: Petr says, "You did not take part in general discussions." I slept three hours a day. I lost a tooth for every month in my ministerial term of office. Because I was not just the minister. I had to keep up with the tempo. And that was a challenge. When I took office, there were no borders and no regulatory norms: Soviet norms had been abolished, and Russia had no norms of its own. Export quotas and licenses exceeded production, by eight times for fuel oil. It was the winter season, and people paid money for those quotas and licenses. You could not simply annul them, but you had to: the country was freezing. That was a bone-breaking machine.

Kokh: About Yegor.

Lopukhin: Yegor was an extremely decent man. I think he was trying to do his job honestly and at the necessary tempo, because he realized he was in office temporarily.

Kokh: We all knew that. Did you meet much in the last ten years of his life?

Lopukhin: We met, but not often.

Kokh: And what do you think?

Lopukhin: I think he found his path. Academic research and indirect involvement in politics. That was a wonderful path. He continued defending his views. If God had granted him more health, in ten years the pain associated with him would have been forgotten and his historic role would have lived on. But he died too soon.

6

STANISLAV ANISIMOV

"It Was a Nightmare"

STANISLAV VASILYEVICH ANISIMOV was not a member of the Gaidar team. He did not work at the Academy of Sciences, took no part in clandestine economic seminars, and received no training abroad. While young associates of Gaidar were poring over the works of Kornai and Hayek, Anisimov was working at the Soviet Communist Party Central Committee, the Union Gossnab (charged with the primary responsibility for the allocation of producer goods to enterprises—a critical state function in the absence of markets), and the Soviet Ministry of Material Resources.

Anisimov eventually joined the Gaidar team, and became one of its most important members. We had three former high-ranking Soviet officials in the government—Anisimov, Fadeyev, and Bulgak. Anisimov says he learned a lot from his younger colleagues. But, in fact, it was we who learned from our senior colleagues, and acquired the experience we were missing in bureaucratic work and in personal life.

I happened to work closely with Anisimov in 1991–2. Both of us were responsible for market supply. True, I was in charge of only a small part of it—imports. He was responsible for everything—the food deficit, high prices, the breakup of economic relations, and deficient supplies of whatnot. I think that right up to the summer of 1992 it was the most nerve-racking and thankless position in the government. And no one knew the real market situation better than Anisimov. That is why his story is so interesting now.

Anisimov was a wonderful associate. Highly competent, very calm and thoughtful, he listened closely and was always prepared to help. He was a very decent and dependable man. It is a pity we worked together so briefly.

Petr Aven

PETR AVEN: Stanislav Vasilyevich, thank you for meeting with us. Given your position in the 1991–2 period, we would like you to tell us about the real condition of markets in 1992 and earlier. We should probably start with the food market. You must be aware of the discussion of whether or not hunger was possible in autumn 1991 and winter 1992.

And could you tell us first about the positions you had held before you joined the Gaidar government? Please, comment on the events up to the last meeting chaired by Gorbachev; I think that was on August 3, before he departed for his Foros dacha.[1] You were there, and your recollections would be extremely interesting.

FOREIGN PRACTICES OF THE USSR

STANISLAV ANISIMOV: I was the Soviet minister of material resources in 1991. Before that I was the first deputy chairman of the Soviet Gossnab, and then Gossnab was transformed into the Soviet Ministry of Material Resources. They were waiting for the retirement of Pavel Ivanovich Mostovoi, a deputy prime minister. As soon as he retired, they transformed Gossnab into a ministry, and I was appointed as minister to replace Pavel Ivanovich.

AVEN: How old were you?

ANISIMOV: Fifty-one. Actually, I never missed a government meeting after Pavlov became premier, because Mostovoi did not attend them. He did not want to work with Pavlov, and Pavlov did not want to work with him. Pavlov became premier in December 1990.

ALFRED KOKH: And by April 1991 he had already instituted that bizarre monetary reform.

ANISIMOV: Mostovoi announced he would not attend meetings until he turned 60 and could retire. And I had to attend them.

The ministry was supervising current supplies, as well as reform of itself and the entire logistics and procurement process. We started fulfilling that mission when I was still a deputy chairman of Gossnab. Together with Pavlov, I was working in every commission, including Abalkin's. There was another commission before that, and I attended its meetings, where we discussed reforms.

---

1. Foros, in Ukraine, where Gorbachev was held under house arrest in his summer dacha.

KOKH: What year was that?

ANISIMOV: After Nikolai Ivanovich Ryzhkov was transferred from Gosplan to the Central Committee as a secretary and economic department head, he started discussing reforms. He created lots of commissions.

Ryzhkov began to form the commissions as soon as he was appointed premier in 1987. That was when the Abalkin commission was formed. We mostly worked on that project in Barvikha. When we were forced to hand over materials to Yavlinsky, we moved to Arkhangelskoye. I also visited Arkhangelskoye to write my section of the program, about logistics and procurement.

I don't know if it's worth talking about the essence of those reforms. We were mostly discussing the transition from centralized distribution to more-or-less market mechanisms. Katsura and I visited Switzerland and Austria to study their markets, and I also made a visit to China (with another group) to study their reforms. We made proposals based on our experience. The focus was on the shift from centralization to the market. There were heated disputes, but the direction was consistent: from centralization to decentralization. We wanted to give more freedom to industries.

AVEN: The two-sector economy—a plan-based public economy and a market economy (private and state).

ANISIMOV: There was a great difference between the two sectors in China. There was a market sector: 30 percent of all metal was sold on the market, and 70 percent ordered by the government. Each type of resource had its own selling ratio.

AVEN: Was there something to learn from China?

ANISIMOV: Certainly. I visited China many times. Deng Xiaoping started enacting the reforms earlier, and, naturally, we were skeptical about the two-sector economy reform at first. It seemed to us that the two-sector model would invariably lead to corruption and other "delights."

But it turned out that plenty of enterprises got a breath of fresh air because they were able to buy resources. The Chinese evaluated the pros and cons, and started to create organized markets for selling resources. I thought, "Well, well—180 metal exchanges! That is crazy." But then I saw them trading.

A few things were disturbing. For example, we learned that China had a big shortage of grinding machines. They had a rule: if a grinding machine could be exported, it would be exported—even though they had none for themselves. So they sold grinding machines to Japan, Switzerland, and America. And they had none! That was the Chinese policy: export went first, to earn hard currency.

KOKH: A free economy needs hard currency. That is the priority.

ANISIMOV: When Silayev was the Russian prime minister, everyone discovered that everyone was exporting and undercutting each other's prices; it was chaos. You saw that, Aven, when you became the minister. Meanwhile, China had authorized trading companies. There weren't many of them, but still. You started to do the same later on.

AVEN: Authorized exporters was my mistake of 1992.

ANISIMOV: You know, that probably was not a mistake at the time.

AVEN: Maybe not.

ACADEMICIAN VELIKHOV AND COPPER EXPORT

ANISIMOV: The need for authorized exporters might have ceased later on, when the market took control of exports, but it was total confusion without them at first!

For instance, Academician Yevgeny Velikhov came to me and said, "Give me a license for 900,000 tons of copper. We want to sell scrap abroad." I asked him, "Do you know what 900,000 tons of copper means?" And he said, "I need to buy food." "Why are you buying food?" "You should mind your business." This is not a joke!

KOKH: He should have done thermonuclear synthesis instead.

ANISIMOV: He obtained Yeltsin's signature for it and came to me again. I refused to grant the license. Then I told Yegor, "Listen, Yeltsin has just permitted exports of 900,000 tons of copper. They may loot the whole of Russia."

KOKH: That was larger than Russia's annual copper output!

ANISIMOV: The cable output of the Soviet Union was 600,000 tons. We had the following balance: Norilsk Nickel produced about 600,000 tons of copper, and 3–400,000 tons more were produced in the Urals. The total production neared one million tons. And then Velikhov decided to export the entire annual production. He didn't understand that—

KOKH: He understood that perfectly!

ANISIMOV: He came to me again, with a more insistent resolution, which said, "You will be fired unless you give the permit." My response was, "I disagree strongly. Stick to what you do best. Don't try to do what you can't." I went back to Yegor. Yegor grabbed the paper and went to Yeltsin. Yeltsin crossed out the previous resolution and wrote, "Cancel."

KOKH: He did not allow the oligarch of those days to make money!

ANISIMOV: The school of Pavel Ivanovich Mostovoi. He was the Gossnab chairman and Soviet deputy prime minister. Before that he headed the Ukrainian Gossnab. It so happened I had been inspecting his work for ten years, and then he became my boss.

KOKH: And why did he refuse to work with Pavlov?

ANISIMOV: Mostovoi knew industries, agriculture, and the construction sector, but he knew nothing about the economy and finance.

KOKH: And did Pavlov know?

ANISIMOV: Pavlov had another characteristic feature: he generated ideas. He was generating them constantly, and perpetually switching to new ones. When he was working in groups, he suggested an idea in the morning and group members started analyzing it. He would leave the group meeting and return later on to discard the idea he had suggested in the morning and to offer a new one. And they were back where they'd started.

He was an extremely impulsive man and could corner anyone. He loved doing that, but, naturally, it was not a very good method for the premier: once the premier chooses a platform, he should stick to it till the end. We had arguments with him even at government meetings. He demanded that I present a concept, but the policy was uncoordinated with the Finance Ministry and the State Pricing Committee—and how could I do that without coordination?

The year 1990 was a year of research. Reforms were delayed, and there was an endless struggle among concepts. Meanwhile, the crisis was deepening.

AVEN: Did the so-called Pavlov reforms start in January 1991?

ANISIMOV: Pavlov was appointed premier in late December. He chaired the first meeting in January, and we started to reorganize Gossnab. We also relaxed centralized governance and wanted to increase the number of freely sold commodities year on year. We managed to get it to 30 percent.

We wished to relax centralization for metals and all listed resources. We started forming commercial centers. Gossnab entities were evaluated, and (something for which I was criticized severely) commercial centers opened in all regions at metal procurement authorities.

AVEN: Where did the commercial centers obtain their commodities?

ANISIMOV: We gave quotas to metallurgical plants, the commodities they could trade. That was when we realized what the initiative was and how far it could go. It was also when I got acquainted with Gaidar; I was writing and publishing articles, mostly in journals: *Planovoye Khozyaistvo*, *Materialno-Tekhnicheskoye Snabzhenie*, and certainly *Kommunist*. I met Yegor at *Kommunist*. Before that I had known him through his articles in the central press and journals.

AVEN: Were the articles your own initiative?

ANISIMOV: Usually he asked me to write them. If *Kommunist* rejected them for some reason, I published them in *Planovoye Khozyaistvo*. Naturally, that caused protests at Gossnab board meetings, especially when regional representatives were in attendance: they claimed we were undermining the system! Yet we took that path. Unfortunately, when Russia announced its own position about independence—

HOW THE SYSTEM BROKE DOWN

KOKH: The declaration of independence was adopted in June 1990. Did it have a real effect?

ANISIMOV: Until summer 1990 the Union procurement system, and the planned economy in general, had still been working. Orders were fulfilled at 95–7 percent. Naturally, some needs were not met. Whenever there is a plan, there is always a deficit. As always happens in a planned economy, when resources are given to everyone, demand is overstated.

AVEN: The last five-year plan was met at 50 percent, or even 46 percent. You say state orders were fulfilled at 95 percent, and that was simply impossible. The actual fulfillment was much smaller than what was planned.

ANISIMOV: I would say the plan was fulfilled at approximately 97 percent. You may say there were amendments, or even doctored records. But I am telling you about official statistical reports.

After the declaration of independence was adopted, rather serious problems began. I gathered republican ministers in Kiev in late 1990, and we agreed on the yearly plan. But stock discipline loosened, and the Baltic republics were doing whatever they wanted.

AVEN: That is, everything collapsed in spring 1991.

ANISIMOV: I would say yes. Even the Kiev agreements were neglected in spring 1991, although the Baltic republics had originally entered into them. It was already difficult in fall 1990, but we still found a common language in the movement of goods. But that was only until the money stopped moving. Once that happened, nothing could help us. That was why Shcherbakov was shouting at the meeting Gorbachev chaired on August 3, 1991: "Make a decision already!"

AVEN: We will talk about the last meeting later. As I understand it, it became obvious in fall 1990 that the republics no longer regarded Moscow as their absolute superior and commander.

ANISIMOV: Or as a partner.

AVEN: Or even as a partner. So you still had meetings and reached agreements, but your commands were disobeyed. Was that obvious? Was there a trend of slow separation?

ANISIMOV: Certainly. After all, I didn't meet only with ministers. I remember a meeting with the directors of all the metallurgical plants in Chelyabinsk in

1990. I also met with chemical plant directors, and we agreed to reform the system. True, I only spoke to the biggest industries.

AVEN: I can imagine how difficult it was to reach agreements with directors. In the 1970s and 1980s the Gossnab first deputy chairman gave orders to directors. And in 1990 you had to obtain their consent. Certainly there had been bargaining even earlier, but the force of commands had been larger and the tools of Gosplan and Gossnab had been much stronger. Things changed, and their persuasive power substantially declined.

ANISIMOV: Absolutely.

KOKH: They held elections and it was impossible to fire a director. When did the breakdown begin? Was it when directors were elected, or when Russia declared its sovereignty?

ANISIMOV: The first outbreak resulted from the election of directors, true. But I must say that the majority of elected directors were incumbent directors. In fact, the directors did not change, and neither did their mentality. But when sovereignty was declared and the financial and banking systems started to decompose—

KOKH: But that was a different story, although the commanders had not changed. It happened in summer 1917. It was decided to elect military unit commanders, and they could not give orders any longer; a decision whether to hold positions or not was made at a general meeting of the military unit. The front went to ruin. Yet commanders of military units were the same. Our case was similar. A director could tell you, "You cannot fire me—why do I have to obey?"

ANISIMOV: Why did Mostovoi prefer to retire? Because it was hard for him to see that. With Ryzhkov in office, Mostovoi told me, "You're behaving improperly. They come to your office and you listen to them and explain things. Smash their faces on the table and send them packing." The "smash their faces on the table and send them packing" formula did not work with those directors. That is what you are saying. It seemed nothing changed, but we had to make deals. You made a deal, and everything looked fine, but they were still in charge.

KOKH: I remember an episode from the film *At Home Among Strangers* in which Bogatyrev tells Kaidanovsky, "I will kill you, you dog!" And he responds, "No, you won't. You will carry me in your arms. You cannot kill me now. I am the only one who knows where the treasure is."

ANISIMOV: There was a vice premier. He had been the head of a motor pool earlier. I was chairing a meeting he attended and discussing matters with directors. All was well—we held the discussion, made a decision, and it was executed. The vice premier, who was later sent to Canada—

AVEN: Makharadze.

ANISIMOV: Makharadze. He told me, "I will chair the next meeting." I said, "Please do." He chaired the meeting in the style of Mostovoi. The directors listened to his speech, told him to go to hell, and left. And he was at a loss: "What shall we do now?"

The situation was different, and our style had to change. I may have had a gentler approach because of my Central Committee schooling. I spent ten years at the Central Committee economic department supervising Gosplan and Gossnab. All I was doing was analysis, analysis, analysis. People in the Central Committee would kill you if you interrupted them. You were supposed to listen and ask questions, but never comment. If you made a report, you were the only one to sign it. The signature of a department head meant only that he had read the report—he had no right to edit it. Naturally, the signatory was 100 percent responsible for the report. It did not depend on us where the report would go, either to the Communist Party Central Committee, the chief of state, or anyone else. So we developed a habit of listening intently, asking questions, analyzing, comparing, finding new documents, analyzing, and comparing—and only then writing. That must be the reason for my style.

KOKH: That was academic rather than managerial activity.

AVEN: I would say analytical.

ANISIMOV: Analytical. You had to analyze everything regarding the matter before expressing your opinion.

The year 1990 was difficult, and 1991 started with constant disruptions in logistics, procurement, and food supply. We tried to reach agreements, and met with the presidents instead of the premiers. But the result was no different—the system no longer worked.

AVEN: You keep talking about disruptions in 1991, but Moscow shops were already empty in 1988–9.

ANISIMOV: I am talking not only about shops. I can tell you there was no food—there was nothing on the eve of the events of late 1991. When the agreement declaring the Union disintegration was signed, we did not have a single food contract, and you shouldn't forget that we had imported 18 million tons of grain for the entire Union. We had nothing to pay with; the grain contracts became invalid, and so did the meat contracts became invalid.

"THERE WOULD HAVE BEEN HUNGER"

KOKH: We are gradually moving toward the hunger theme.

ANISIMOV: Western contracts became invalid, as did Union contracts. Ukraine halted supplies. Belarus halted supplies. Everyone did. If one had commodities, one made barter deals; if not, then, alas, not. Large industrial enterprises and big cities were affected most; regions were unwilling to exchange food for machines or tanks.

AVEN: Do you think there was a real threat of hunger in December 1991?

ANISIMOV: No doubt. Yeltsin raised the food question with the government on November 20. He wiped the floor with me: I took office only on November 10, and ten days later he was giving me hell. And then he said, "We'll all go see for ourselves what's happening in the cities." I can't remember now if you went on those tours or not, but Barchuk did, that's for sure. We flew to Nizhny Novgorod, Bryansk, Buryatia, Altai, and I cannot remember where else. We also visited Sobchak [then the mayor] in St Petersburg.

It was a nightmare. No one had food; there was nothing to sell and nowhere to get it. I didn't have a single contract for bringing supplies to the regions. Yeltsin was killing me there. We arrived, the gate opened, and we saw thousands of people standing and waiting for Yeltsin. He stepped up, the crowd enclosed him, and I was left behind. They were so hard on him! He called for Anisimov, and Anisimov was not there! He let me have it afterward: "Where should the minister be when the president meets with the people? Especially on those questions!" The only thing that saved me was that Soviet Gossnab administered not only procurement but also state

reserves. Naturally, I knew what the reserves were. When the new government took office, unfortunately, Burbulis had no idea about state reserves.
He never had to deal with them, and we were not too talkative about the
reserves. So when we encountered that situation, I said to Yeltsin, "There is
no other way, we must use state reserves." "Do you know what the reserves
mean?" he asked. "I do, but still." Yeltsin ordered the drafting of a decree.
Burbulis did that immediately, and we started supplying reserves to the
market. I was given a list of presidential trips. I planned how many tons
of food must be sent to that region, and Yeltsin was informed about the
number of trains carrying that food. When we came to see Sobchak, we had
to use the back door—it was winter and snowy. We couldn't use the main
entrance because too many people were standing there. So we had to use the
back door.

AVEN: To Smolny?

ANISIMOV: Yes. And we climbed some back stairs. We came to Sobchak's
office, and Sobchak said, "That's it, I don't know what to do! The city
has nothing. I can sell nothing to people, and I don't know where to get
supplies!"

AVEN: How long could the reserves last? Or would starvation have come one
way or another?

KOKH: Prices were liberalized, and it didn't happen!

ANISIMOV: Right. I think there would have been hunger if not for the January
decree on price liberalization. After our return from those trips, especially
after the meeting with Sobchak (and he was the last one we visited), Yegor
realized our weakness, and that our stock of confidence was running out.
He said, "That's it. We have to stop controlling prices and issue a free trade
decree. We cannot delay it any longer."

KOKH: Would hunger have set in otherwise? When? By April or March?

ANISIMOV: I think sooner. There is no doubt. In February or late January,
approximately. As soon as the decree on free trade was signed, food was
being sold along all the roads.

KOKH: Where did it come from?

ANISIMOV: From people's freezers. Some people were trading.

KOKH: I can tell you that Petr and I have a constant discussion about this. Actually, I side with your opinion.

AVEN: I agree there was a threat of hunger, but I say there was no hunger. There was no hunger! Consumption did not fall, which was confirmed by Illarionov's numbers. There was a threat, but there was no hunger.

KOKH: Why should I trust Illarionov's numbers rather than my own eyes and experience? I was working for the St Petersburg administration at that time, and I was aware of the food situation. I knew for sure that consumption had dipped, and it had dipped a lot. And numbers—what about numbers? We still don't know how many people died in World War II.

ANISIMOV: Why do I say there was a real threat? The food-supply system was being ruined recklessly and totally unnecessarily. For instance, we were visiting Bryansk, and Yeltsin suddenly said, "What do trade departments do? Why do we need them?" Something was being withheld by the trade departments, and he decided there must be no trade departments. I tried to reason with him: "Trade departments are a link—they know who needs what and where." "Buyers and sellers will find each other somehow," he responded. And that was it. Trade departments were liquidated. And what happened? There was food somewhere, but the question was: Who had it and who needed it? No one dealt with that issue anymore.

KOKH: They should have been liquidated after price liberalization, not before.

ATTEMPTS TO KEEP THE UNION

AVEN: May we go back to the conference Gorbachev chaired before his departure for Foros on August 3? Some say he told a conference speaker, "Do you want the state of emergency? Try it." This shows Gorbachev knew about putsch preparations. You were at that conference.

ANISIMOV: I was.

AVEN: What happened?

ANISIMOV: Somebody might have made the remark, but it is now difficult for me to remember.

AVEN: What decisions were made?

ANISIMOV: Presidents of the republics were there, and all of them raised the same issue: "Either we act as a single country, and then we need to ensure centralized movement of goods and financial and other resources, or do not keep us and let us solve our problems on our own."

KOKH: Am I right that the question was put this way: "Either restore the former administrative system, the discipline in movement of goods, the plan-based system, or we will separate and act as independent states"?

ANISIMOV: Certainly! Everyone was openly saying that at the conference.

KOKH: Gorbachev could not tell them, "We're restoring the former system." That was impossible.

ANISIMOV: Sure, he could not say that outright. Neither he nor anyone else could say that.

KOKH: That is a sneaky dilemma.

AVEN: Which one?

KOKH: Either a single country with centralized planning of everything or the breakup into several states, each of them building a market economy for itself. No one discussed the preservation of one country with a market economy. You must agree that was an odd dilemma. It offered two bad variants and did not even consider the optimal one.

ANISIMOV: August 17 gave me the answer to all the questions, more than all the conferences chaired by Gorbachev before that.

AVEN: And was it not clear on August 3 when Shcherbakov demanded that Gorbachev must make a decision?

ANISIMOV: That was practically Shcherbakov's cry of despair. When everyone finished speaking, he stood up and almost hysterically pleaded, "Make a decision, already! You cannot simply hold a conference and decide nothing!" He exploded when Gerashchenko, the previous speaker, said, "No money is being supplied to the Central Bank." The finance minister said, "The Union has transferred all the money it had to the regions—there is no money left." Every person who took the floor at that conference said the same: the country was finished de facto.

AVEN: Wasn't Pavlov supposed to have a solution?

ANISIMOV: After Shcherbakov's speech, Gorbachev told Pavlov to make a decision, and Pavlov gathered us again. I think that happened on August 9 or 11. The premiers of all the republics but Russia showed up. Oleg Ivanovich Lobov joined us. He was Silayev's deputy. The conference was attended not only by the premiers but also by the presidents. Mutalibov was there, and Nazarbayev.

AVEN: But Yeltsin was absent, wasn't he?

ANISIMOV: Yes, he was. Everyone came, took a seat, and went silent. Pavlov said, "Let us continue our discussion. What Gorbachev said—" And then Nazarbayev interrupted him and said, "Why should we listen to everyone? Let us hear what Russia has to say. There are 11 items requiring decisions. Who represents Russia?" Lobov stood up and said, "I do." "See—Russia did not even send its premier. Well, Lobov then. What can you say?" "Russia agrees with none of these 11 items." Then our dear friends said, "Why continue the discussion?" They stood up and left. It made no sense to hold discussions without Russia, its voice, and its decisions.

KOKH: What were the 11 items?

ANISIMOV: They were linked with the movement of commodities. We needed to make a decision. Mutalibov said, "The country owes me a certain amount of money. The Central Bank does not provide it, nor does the Finance Ministry." And the Finance Ministry replies, "We have no money because we have received none from Russia." "And how can I buy anything at centralized prices without money? Prices must be liberalized if you have no solution." Nazarbayev joined in: "Although it is a pricing absurdity, Kazakhstan is believed to be a subsidized republic. If pricing principles won't change, we will need money, too. You owe us." The same answer: "Sorry, no money." "Then stop controlling prices."

1. Yegor Gaidar, Moscow, 1993.

2. President Boris Yeltsin and Yegor Gaidar in Moscow, March 28, 1993.

3. The last picture in the office of the prime minister. Gaidar and his advisers in December 1992.

4. Yegor Gaidar in the office of the Institute for the Economy in Transition, 1993.

5. Sergei Filatov, Yegor Gaidar, Ruslan Khasbulatov, Boris Yeltsin, and Yuri Yarov at the Congress of People's Deputies of the Supreme Council in the Kremlin.

6. First Deputy Prime Minister of Russia Yegor Gaidar at a meeting of the Supreme Council of Russia, March 1992.

7. Boris Yeltsin and members of the Presidential Administration of Russia, 1994.

8. Rally in support of Boris Yeltsin in Moscow, March 1993.

9. Rally in support of Boris Yeltsin and Yegor Gaidar in Moscow.

10. Director of the Institute for the Economy in Transition, Yegor Gaidar, at a press conference on March 19, 1997.

11. Russian Deputy Prime Minister Alexander Shokhin, 1992.

12. Boris Fyodorov, Anatoly Chubais, Alexander Shokhin, and Vladimir Shumeiko at the IX Extraordinary Congress of People's Deputies of Russia, 1993.

13. "Burbulis was the founding father of the Government Reform," 1992.

14. "We all came from science," Alexander Shokhin, the Academician Stanislav Shatalin, Gennady Burbulis, and Yegor Gaidar, 1992.

15. Alexander Shokhin, Edward Dnieper, Tatiana Shokhin, and Mikhail Poltoranin at Alexander's dacha in Arkhangelskoye.

16. Yegor Gaidar, Petr Aven, and Alexander Shokhin at his dacha in Arkhangelskoye, 1992.

17. Negotiations on external debt. Horst Koehler (Deputy Minister of Finance, 1992, and President of Germany, 2004–10), Petr Aven, Alexander Shokhin, and Boris Yeltsin, 1992.

18. Minister of Foreign Economic Relations Petr Aven, 1992.

19. Press conference of First Deputy Prime Minister Yegor Gaidar, 1992.

20. Yegor Gaidar and Andrei Nechayev, December 1, 1992.

21. First Deputy Minister of Economy and Finance Minister Andrei Nechayev, 1991.

22. Chairman of the Russian State Committee for State Property
Management, Anatoly Chubais, during a press conference
at the White House regarding privatization.

23. Minister of Foreign Economic
Relations Petr Aven and Deputy Prime
Minister Anatoly Chubais (left).

24. Deputy Prime Minister Anatoly
Chubais, September 18, 1992.

25. Petr Aven, presidential representative for relations with industrialized countries (G7), Boris Yeltsin, and George Bush, Munich, 1992.

26. Petr Aven and Boris Yeltsin in negotiations, 1992.

27. Yegor Gaidar and Gennady Burbulis at the Congress of People's Deputies, April 18, 1992.

28. Boris Yeltsin and Gennady Burbulis at the Davis Cup tennis tournament, 1992.

29. Sergei Shakhrai, Gennady Burbulis, and Mikhail Fedotov at the VII Congress of People's Deputies of the Russian Federation, 1992.

30. Deputy Prime Minister of Russia Sergei Shakhrai and Mayor of St Petersburg Anatoly Sobchak at a meeting to discuss the issues of constitutional reform.

31. Russian Defense Minister Pavel Grachev during a visit to the 31st Airborne Brigade of the Bundeswehr, Germany.

32. Boris Yeltsin presents the Minister of Defense Pavel Grachev with an order "For Personal Courage."

33. Vladimir Mashchits, Chairman of the State Committee for Economics 1991–6.

34. Stanislav Anisimov, Minister of Trade and Material Resources of the RSFSR, 1991.

35. Minister of Economy and Finance of the Russian Federation Yegor Gaidar, and Minister of Fuel and Energy of the Russian Federation Vladimir Lopukhin at a meeting of the government of the RSFSR, December 5, 1991.

36. Russian President Boris Yeltsin, Russian Foreign Minister Andrei Kozyrev and Moldovan President Mircea Snegur at a conference in Istanbul.

37. Chairman of the Supreme Soviet of Azerbaijan Heydar Aliyev at a meeting with Russian Foreign Minister Andrei Kozyrev.

38. Alfred Kokh (left) and Anatoly Chubais.

39. Boris Nemtsov, Alexander Kazakov, Alfred Kokh, Yevgeny Yasin, Anatoly Chubais, Yakov Urinson, and Oleg Sysuyev at the funeral of Viktor Chernomyrdin, 2010.

40. Yegor Gaidar and Alfred Kokh (left).

41. Michael Manevitch, vice-governor of St Petersburg. Behind him, Alexander Kazakov, then deputy prime minister, Alfred Kokh, and Anatoly Chubais.

42. Boris Nemtsov and Alfred Kokh.

43. US Secretary of State James Baker speaks at the
Supreme Soviet of the USSR.

44. Minister of Economy and Finance Yegor Gaidar and Deputy Prime Minister and
Finance Minister of Poland Leszek Balcerowicz at a press conference, December 1, 1991.

45. Barricades in front of the Supreme Soviet of the RSFSR.

46. Journal *Ogonek*, no. 36, dated August 31, 1991.

47. October 4, 1993. The storming of the White House, Moscow.

AVEN: Those were debts in old, low prices.

ANISIMOV: So the 11 items were transformed into a document, which suggested what decisions must be made for the economy to keep running while economic and political reforms were implemented.

AVEN: It would be interesting to learn the 11 items.

KOKH: They may be reconstructed; it's more or less clear what was discussed.

ANISIMOV: Those items are well known. They were included in the premier's protocol.

KOKH: The important thing is that a conference was held on August 9. Yet Russia had refused to fulfill the 11 items on August 8. It had stopped fulfilling them about a year earlier, and the debt Mutalibov and Nazarbayev were talking about had been amassed since then. Actually, Lobov, Silayev, and similar people were the Russian economic authority, and they deliberately acted to dismantle the system. They were rather experienced and skilled people, and they had to be aware of the consequences. Am I right?

ANISIMOV: Yes.

KOKH: Although Pavlov thinks that the main reason for the disintegration of the Soviet Union was the transfer of the ruble disbursement rights to republican central banks, the Russian government's conduct could not be neglected, either. The entire system was working for the disintegration of the Soviet Union. And those people had to be aware of the fact that they were breaking up the Soviet Union. How come Grisha Yavlinsky, who had done his best to break up the Soviet Union a year before, decided suddenly in fall 1991 to head the Union government and, what's more, bet on preservation of the Soviet Union?

AVEN: That is a question for Grisha.

ANISIMOV: I don't think he framed the issue that way.

KOKH: How else could he have done it? He was the first vice premier supervising the economy.

ANISIMOV: Yes, he was the first vice premier for economic affairs. Silayev appointed him so that he could implement the 500 Days program. That was his mission.

KOKH: Did he accomplish it?

ANISIMOV: No. But he felt he did not have the powers needed to implement the program. Therefore, he quit that position and the further continuation of economic reform. Of course, he hadn't even started that reform.

AVEN: You said August 17. What happened then?

ANISIMOV: Yes, August 17. I gathered the ministers at the Kremlin again on August 16. What should we do? Really, what could we do? We were trying to connect things that refused to be connected.

AVEN: Was a Russian representative there?

ANISIMOV: Vladimir Vozhagov. He was in charge of Russia's Gossnab. And we had one more roundtable and confirmed there were no common rules, but that we would honor commitments to each other. I had gotten permission from Pavlov to visit my mother, because my father had just died and she needed support. But he suddenly called me and ordered me to be in Moscow in the morning. I told him, "You let me take leave." "No discussion. The government presidium will have a meeting, and you will make a report." "All right." The government presidium convened, and I (a non-member of the presidium) was there.

Somebody was talking, and then Pavlov stood up and said, "We have two items on the agenda. The first one is about the Union treaty and the second is about the relations between Anisimov and Russia." "That's quite an item," I said to myself.

They started discussing the first item. Pavlov said that, as premier, he had no objections to the Union agreement, but lots of things were being overlooked. He also said that the Union agreement needed an appendix so that it did not have to be rewritten. What would the appendix be about? First of all, the common disbursement center and the common banking system. Second, the common financial system. Then the common foreign policy and the common foreign trade policy.

AVEN: There was nothing about that in Gorbachev's Union agreement?

ANISIMOV: Nothing about the common foreign trade policy and the free movement of material and technical resources and food between the republics. Those were six items. And he made every person sitting there stand up and clearly state if he was pro or con, and if you were against a given point, to explain why. But it turned out that everyone there was for it.

He asked everyone, and me too. I told him, "I am not a member of the presidium." But he said, "You are here, you heard what was said, you have to give your opinion." So I gave my opinion and supported it. Then he said, "The document must be signed immediately and couriered to Foros." General Varennikov took the document to Foros. So whenever they say that he went to Foros to seize Gorbachev, I doubt that very much—a decision was made to bring the document to him so that the Union agreement would not be signed on August 21 without the appendix that had been brought to Foros.

In my opinion, the main point of disagreement on August 3, 11, and 17 was the question raised in that protocol—the common movement of resources, the ruble disbursement, and so on. Even Ryzhkov made me study that; I visited foreign countries to learn their practices.

KOKH: What countries?

ANISIMOV: He sent me to Switzerland and to Austria—where there is a confederation and a federation. I think that was the reason for disagreements between our republics. They wanted to preserve the common policy, and so on.

AVEN: That is what the USSR wanted. And the republics—

ANISIMOV: The republics wanted that, too.

AVEN: Then who was against it?

ANISIMOV: Gorbachev held meetings on the Union agreement without inviting anyone—not even the premier. We saw only the final document, and we don't know what debates there were.

KOKH: It seemed the republics wanted to preserve the Union, too, but they would not abandon their new powers, either. And it was impossible to combine those two things.

AVEN: Do you think that all your partners in the republics were pro-Union?
ANISIMOV: They were neither pro-Union nor anti-Union—

KOKH: Actually, their position was the following: "Why would I say no when I was carpeted in Moscow? Why would I do that?"

AVEN: Besides, my area was procurement. That was a limited question. I should have said yes and tried to get something out of them. Politics was none of my business.

KOKH: I discussed that with Gorbachev. Even he said that the disintegration of the country was predetermined after August 19. Nothing could be saved. Those "fools," as he called them, thought their putsch would help save the Union. But they actually brought it down. That's Gorbachev's opinion.

He has the following position: "I was perfectly aware of the economic degradation and the looming collapse. But I also thought I would be able to stop that degradation by signing the Union agreement and receiving certain powers, and I would smother all those presidents in my arms in that renewed Union. I would have regained control."

ANISIMOV: That is impossible without political unity.

KOKH: He claims he would have restored unity.

AVEN: It was too late for that.

KOKH: He said, "I did not want to quarrel with them."

AVEN: There was no real unity. There was a position of the Union government, but the republics no longer wanted to stick together.

ANISIMOV: I cannot say that any of the republics attending our conferences were against that. They didn't mind the free movement of money and goods and a common emission policy.

AVEN: Then why did the Soviet Union break up?

ANISIMOV: Because they stopped transferring money to the center.

YOUNG REFORMERS

AVEN: All right, I think there is nothing to add about hunger and the Union disintegration. Let's change the subject. You must be the only Union minister to become a minister of the Gaidar government. You met Gaidar at *Kommunist*, you wrote articles and worked together. Do you have a positive impression of the Gaidar team or not? Some of our former colleagues are hard on us nowadays. Are you still with us?

ANISIMOV: Absolutely.

AVEN: How did you feel, and what was the attitude of your former colleagues toward your decision to join us?

ANISIMOV: Certainly I was totally indignant at first. It was not because they had invited Gaidar. Before that Lobov called me, brought me to the meeting room, and told the board that I was removed from office. The (Union) minister had to leave his office and the building at once, and the board was dismissed.

AVEN: That was a Russian government reply to the putsch. It was quite common at the time.

ANISIMOV: I was practically under house arrest. I wasn't allowed to go anywhere, I had to stay at home, and so on. So I sat at home in September and October, unable to take off.
 Suddenly Gorbachev published a resolution in late October. It appeared that neither Lobov nor Yeltsin had had the right to fire me—that only Gorbachev had had that right. Then I was notified that I was dismissed, and that I would receive compensation for all that time. Several days after, I was invited to join the Russian government.

AVEN: Did someone call?

ANISIMOV: No. They sent a messenger, who said I was being summoned. It happened on November 7. It appeared Gaidar had invited me. I didn't yet associate him with the government.

AVEN: He was not *the* Gaidar then.

ANISIMOV: Eearlier, Silayev had wanted to appoint me as the minister and to remove Vozhagov. And I said in the presence of Vozhagov, "No. I understand it would be impossible to work without the Gossnab system, and I am ready to hand over its control; but I will not be a minister in the Silayev government."

When Gaidar made the offer, I told him, "That is totally impossible. We have had so many fights with Silayev, Lobov, and the others. This would lead to another humiliation for me, and everything would stop there. I have been through that before, and I've gotten over it." He started telling me that I had to—the country, and all that.

I returned to my office. But I couldn't just sit there, could I? And I also couldn't stay home; I had spent two months at home, and I was so bored. So I came to the Gossnab party committee room. I took a seat, and Yasin asked me to do some calculations for Yavlinsky. Yegor called on November 11 and asked, "Why are you not in your office?" I asked, "What would I do there?" "Yeltsin signed the decree, you must go to your office." I asked, "What decree?" And he said, "The president signed the decree on November 10. Go to your office and sit there." I learned on the same day that nearly half of the Supreme Soviet was against me. Burbulis summoned me in the morning and asked, "Tell me, are you pro-GKChP or anti-GKChP?" I said anti. And then he said, "Some deputies claim that you chaired a closed-door meeting of the Gossnab board on August 19. We want to know the board agenda." Pavlov had gathered the government on the evening of August 19 and ordered all ministries and departments to hold closed-door meetings before lunch.

AVEN: Did he do that on August 19? Right on the putsch day?

ANISIMOV: I gathered my board on the morning of August 20. Pavlov had evaded discussion of the state of emergency at the government meeting the day before, but focused on additions to the Union agreement, which made me dedicate the board meeting to preparations for the winter season. Board members asked me about the putsch and tanks, and I told them about preparations for the winter season. I could say nothing else. As always, board meeting records were encrypted, but the records were there, and I asked to have them deciphered and two signed copies brought to me. I took one copy for myself and gave the other to Burbulis. I took my copy to Yeltsin. We read the records. There was nothing suspicious there—only the sowing of winter crops and preparations for the winter season. Somebody had to do that, after all. All the speeches and reports were dedicated to procurement, no politics at all. The minutes showed there were questions about the current events. But my answers were also recorded: "Let us talk about our business now, and ask all the other questions later." Yeltsin read it and said, "Go back to your office."

And then I had my first impressions of you, Petr. I met Economic Minister Nechayev first, and then all the others. I was somewhat shocked by the procedures, which differed from what I was accustomed to. I started listening. After a very short time, I realized that I didn't know lots of things you were talking about. Although I had experience and age, there were many things I didn't know.

Then I realized that the young men brought new zest into our life. They were far beyond us on the question of reforms and their knowledge of the Western market economy. I understood that I would not show off but try to catch up with you. As for the tasks set by Yegor for preventing a total breakdown, I gathered directors and heads of city and regional administrations, and took some other steps for stopping the breakdown and helping Yegor. I was also writing a program of procurement reforms, which I think was accepted the way I wrote it, without major corrections.

AVEN: As you remember, correctly, price liberalization and the free-trade decree led to the immediate appearance of commodities.

"PUTIN PRACTICALLY COMMITTED CRIMES"

KOKH: There is one more important thing we keep underestimating—we touched upon it in our interview with Andrei Nechayev. The food supply in the country was insufficient, so the country was heavily dependent on imports. Free prices were not enough to stop the threat of hunger—which was not so acute and not so unavoidable, but still the food supply fell short of the demand. Free trade and price liberalization were accompanied by the liberalization of foreign trade, which was supervised by you, Petr, and imports started growing in absolute terms. That was another factor that helped stave off hunger. Just these two things: free prices and foreign trade liberalization.

AVEN: Thanks, Alfred.

KOKH: We sold everything! We sold everything to foreign partners and brought in food. Putin practically committed crimes. He authorized exports of rare earth metals; he had no right to sign contracts, but he did, and the Finns delivered food, and the hunger threat was gone in St Petersburg.

ANISIMOV: Surely that was an entire set of measures, not just free prices. What did free trade do? Not only could we trade freely, but we were also free to set our own prices. That is what the Union republics had demanded: "You cannot subsidize us? To hell with you! Just give us normal prices, and we will sell our commodities, to any of our partners in the Union or to foreign partners."

KOKH: I still want to ask my question. There was a series of conferences in summer 1991. The economy was degrading, discipline was decreasing, and everything was falling apart. Didn't Gorbachev see that? Did he refuse to see, or was he not competent enough to understand what was going on?

ANISIMOV: He didn't want to make a decision; that was his usual behavior.

By the way, the Gaidar government was a big surprise for me. I was accustomed to lengthy consideration of every issue. Even for Ryzhov—who climbed that administrative ladder, was a bona fide plant worker, and had rather good economic knowledge—every issue still had to be discussed at one, two, or three meetings of the presidium. He did that not in order to spare anyone's feelings, but because he was uncertain; as a rule, the decisions were unanimous.

And then there was Yeltsin. He signed 15 to 17 decrees at once, within two or three hours—he grasped things very quickly.

I even think that if he had stayed in office through 1993 and, God grant, 1994, we would already be living in a totally different country. We would have done the reforms much faster and better. He knew what had to be done.

I was amazed when he gathered us after we had announced our resignation at the congress and said, as if speaking to deputies, "Why are you celebrating? Do you know what to do? We gather twice a week and discuss things; we know what we are doing, but nobody else does." And then he called for a stenographer and dictated a program within one hour. He read out that program at the session. "What do you mean, we have no program? Here is our program." The program was developed later on. Remember, he had no written notes—nothing. But he dictated step by step. He knew what must be done—the necessary sequence of actions. I cannot say he never made mistakes; perhaps he did.

And look at Chubais. How firm he was in defending his position! His face was red, he was sweating, but he never gave up. It was simply impossible to score against him. He always had arguments to offer.

KOKH: Yes, the team was very different from the Soviet ministries.

ANISIMOV: Certainly. What amazed me about that government was that everyone knew what to do. A guy is only 33 years old, but he already knows what must be done.

AVEN: Not 33. Gaidar was 35, and I was 36. Chubais too.

ANISIMOV: Whatever, 35 years old.

AVEN: We were ready, and we knew exactly what to do.

ANISIMOV: Yes, you were ready. And that year taught me much more than the previous five years.

The only man I kept disagreeing with was Titkin. He had a very simple ideology: destroy everything, and that will make the reforms easier. Shall we discard the people, too? Destroy the country to make the reforms easier? That was the same ideology of forcing the republics out of the ruble zone: "We don't give a shit about the other republics. Let's save ourselves." I didn't agree with him.

KOKH: It was a forced position. We couldn't save everyone.

ANISIMOV: Actually, we had no internal conflicts. Oh, yes, the railroads minister strongly opposed the reform.

KOKH: Fadeyev?

ANISIMOV: He didn't allow us to reform the railroads. He said we could reform depots and other infrastructure, but not the railroads. Chernomyrdin insisted on Gazprom's keeping the entire pipeline network, so it did. Gaidar didn't argue with Chernomyrdin or Fadeyev. And he practically didn't argue with Bulgak, either, because Bulgak said, "I will present my ideology and then you may criticize me." He did, and—regardless of disagreements—his concept was basically approved 80 or 85 percent of the time.

AVEN: We knew what to do, and we trusted each other. We trusted other government members even if—like you or Bulgak—they were not our team members. That is why there were no intrigues.

COULD THE UNION HAVE BEEN SAVED?

KOKH: The economic model of the Soviet Union became obsolete. Saying that we had to replace the planned economy with a pro-market variant on the brink of the 1980s and 1990s is not very interesting. Anyway, Eastern Europe and China took that path. The question is whether the Soviet Union could have been saved.

ANISIMOV: I think it was possible, because breaking up the Union without an alternative—

KOKH: Who broke it up? Was it Gerashchenko or Belovezh, Yeltsin and Shushkevich?

ANISIMOV: Let's start this way. The Nineteenth Party Conference made a decision on pluralism and allowed a multiparty system. Was the country prepared for that or not?

KOKH: It was.

ANISIMOV: In my opinion the country was not prepared. There was a plurality of opinions, but one party was in centralized control. How was that possible? The Soviet Communist Party Central Committee was making every decision, and those decisions were mandatory, although it was permissible to criticize them. Just like today. The rule of one party is not the multiparty system. It may have a new and beautiful name, but it is still one party.

KOKH: Do you know the difference between today's one-party system and the Soviet one? Back then the party reacted to criticism. The modern party does not.

    Back to my question. I am interested by the technology. If it was possible to keep the Union, could we have kept the Baltic republics in it, for instance? They were prepared for anything, up to an armed revolt. That means it could not have been preserved.

ANISIMOV: I'm not saying it could have been preserved in its original form. As for the Baltic republics, it was obvious when Ryzhkov was still in office that they could not be kept in. He changed tactics—he was very polite with them, and he tried to solve all of their problems, but still—

Kokh: They would have left just the same. Those were not economic decisions.

Anisimov: I should stress that Baltic ministers did attend the last ministerial conference I chaired in Kiev. They agreed that economic contacts must not be cut. Certainly they left, but they had no other economic contacts at that moment. And the other republics wished to stay. They wanted cooperation, and they saw no other way out.

Aven: I think we have covered everything we wanted to discuss. Shall we talk about Gaidar again?

Anisimov: Unlike economists from the Russian Academy of Sciences, he was a man beyond comparison. While others were just wasting words, he knew what to do.

Aven: Yes—and he was not afraid of doing it, either.

7

VLADIMIR MASHCHITS

"We Were Like the Bourgeois Specialists of the Civil War Period"

HISTORICAL MEMORY IS NOT PERFECT. People often remember personalities of little significance and forget the really important ones. Vladimir Mikhailovich Mashchits is a fine example. He was the only full member of two competing teams, Yavlinsky's and Gaidar's, and enjoyed the absolute trust of both team leaders. He played a vital role on our team. That was only natural: Vladimir is a thoughtful and highly educated economist capable of theoretical analysis and practical work. No wonder he was a minister longer than any of us—for about five years. But he is remembered much less than our previous interviewees—Chubais, Nechayev, Shokhin. I think that Vladimir's modesty and dislike of publicity were not the only reasons; he is extremely thorough, and perfunctory interviews are not Mashchits's métier. (He even looks like a serious and unhurried merchant—an old believer.) After our session, he called us several times to clarify dates, the sequence of events, and somebody else's quotes. Vladimir has an exceptional memory. And his opinions are precise—he is a very calm person and, in my view, remarkably objective. That is why he is so interesting.

Petr Aven

PETR AVEN: We usually start with recollections. We are sitting here with you, and revolutions are taking place in Egypt and Tunisia. Could you compare them with our revolution or, if you prefer, semi-revolution of 1991? Then we will start our recollections.

Revolution is an Impulse

VLADIMIR MASHCHITS: Revolution is an impulse to development, but, like any impulse, it dies down as time passes. Alas, a single impulse is often not sufficient, and revolutionaries prove unable to follow one impulse with another.

KOKH: Where, in your opinion, did a revolutionary impulse have long-term consequences? Not in France and not in Russia. As Trotsky wrote, revolutionaries had been replaced with bureaucrats by the middle of the 1920s. Where did that happen? Was it in the United States? But that was not quite a revolution—it was rather a war of independence. A revolutionary surge is short-lived everywhere.

MASHCHITS: It doesn't have to be revolutionary. For instance, our system was replaced in 1953–7. Formally it was not a revolution.

AVEN: Alfred and I imply two things when we say revolution: first, a transformation of the social system; second, a change of the elite—a drastic change. The social system changed in Russia in 1991, but the elites did not. So it was not quite a revolution. But both things happened in 1917.

MASHCHITS: Yes. And in 1929?

AVEN: There was no change of the elite in 1929. It was cleansed a bit, but generally remained the same Soviet Bolshevik elite. And there was no fundamental transformation of the social system by the Marxist definition.

Certainly the "rules of the game" changed seriously with the death of Stalin; but the fundamentals were unwavering. And the elite changed to a minimal degree.

MASHCHITS: The "social system" term does not sound absolutely clear from the present-day position, because typological definitions are more detailed now than they were in the times of "the only correct teaching." The word "revolution" has developed an interesting connotation, which means we should shift from old customary concepts to new definitions. In its old meaning, a revolution implied the toppling of authorities. And what is happening now?

KOKH: "A revolt cannot be successful, otherwise it has a different name."

AVEN: And what is going on now? Comparing the present day and 1991, what similarities and differences do you see?

MASHCHITS: Between Russia of 1991 and the modern Arabs?

AVEN: Indeed.

MASHCHITS: There are a number of essential differences. The first difference is that the events of 1991 were provoked by a powerful and lengthy decay of the system competing with the West. The decay intensified in 1987 and became pronounced. Russia in 1991 was a country that had been through three years of the most difficult political concessions of the authorities to the people. The country had become addicted to politically conditioned loans—that is, dependent on the West; and that dependence was very serious. In exchange for the loans, the USSR undertook political commitments—to disarmament, and eschewing the use of force against Eastern Europe.

AVEN: That is, in contrast to Tunisia and Egypt, there was no spontaneous one-time action in the USSR; there was a long process.

MASHCHITS: Besides, Egypt and Tunisia are relatively peripheral countries, and we were witnessing the breakup of an empire! The stakes were totally different. One of the biggest blocs in the world was disintegrating rather peacefully, and by 1991 many decisions that predetermined the outcome had been made: the pullout from Afghanistan, the disbanding of the Soviet bloc, and the reunification of Germany.

So our first and main difference from Egypt and Tunisia was the end of confrontation between two systems. Second, the process was started up by Gorbachev. The system had become totally inefficient, and he realized that. That is, the whole perestroika happened because of—

AVEN: Because of despair.

MASHCHITS: Absolutely, because of despair, but consciously.

The third element that these countries are lacking is topics of major international concern, primarily nuclear and other weapons of mass destruction. Our case concerned the fundamental interests of all of humanity.

Probably one more serious difference is the breakdown of our ideology—a kind of secular religion. It broke down very rapidly thanks to glasnost. The Arabs are not showing such an ideological breakdown.

KOKH: Let us speak about similarities.

MASHCHITS: The similarities are also clear. We cannot permit a situation in the modern world where people have nothing to live on, to put it mildly.

AVEN: I don't quite agree. Tunisia had practically the biggest GDP growth rate in the Arab world.

MASHCHITS: That's immaterial. They had the rate, but what was the starting level? And what was the differentiation? I think the Tunisian regime was toppled because the younger generation—who made up the majority and had access to normal education—had nothing to live on.

KOKH: And there were Arabs in neighboring Italy and France, where they could spend their weekends. They saw how people were living in free countries, and how they could live.

MASHCHITS: It was the same here. Many in the USSR believed that education was the key to a normal life, a worthy public position. They were educated, but they never made it.

AVEN: You sound like a regular reactionary: they should not have been educated. If they had not been educated, they would not have taken to the street. Education gave them excessive hopes.

MASHCHITS: On the other hand, the country will have nothing without education.

KOKH: It takes secondary education to drive a tank. Especially a modern tank. And if Stalin had had no tanks, he would not have lasted for long—so he had to educate people.

AVEN: It's not about a formal education; it's about an adequate idea of the world. Education forms this idea. But in the 1980s, especially when computerization started, information barriers came down and the country was flooded with the truth about life abroad, our history, and so on. That made 1991 inevitable. Let's talk about it now. Why do you think our team joined the government then?

WHY GAIDAR?

MASHCHITS: They had been doing very well without us until 1990–1. But after programs of the 500 Days type failed to start, Yavlinsky quit. Abalkin changed after they started winding down his program of late 1989—

KOKH: Abalkin's program was approved, but not implemented.[1]

MASHCHITS: Yes, they did not implement it.

KOKH: Obviously Abalkin's program was a program of half-measures.

MASHCHITS: What do you mean, half-measures? Any program will have half-measures if your country is breaking up and you want to keep the power yet manage some refurbishment and modernization. They were frightened to take drastic steps—the top brass would never do it.

AVEN: You're right—they easily did without us until the winter of 1990–1. What's more, if you remember, we started talking about our possible appointment to government positions only in spring 1991.

MASHCHITS: Yes, something came up in the spring. The Novo-Ogaryovo process was on, more or less successfully. Gorbachev once again realized that something had to be done with the country. And then, as I understand, things happened that were not advertised broadly. That was the so-called *nomenklatura* privatization—the setting up of a bunch of dummy companies on the sly, without any documentation.

KOKH: We called it "Privatization à la Svyatoslav Fyodorov."

MASHCHITS: Lots of variants. Remember the ANT cooperative scandal?[2] There was more: there was creeping illegal privatization. Directors and the *nomenklatura* were looting the country and transforming ministries into concerns of the Gazprom kind.

And I think that was the time they decided to quit the creeping process

---

1. The first comprehensive Soviet reform program to update the Soviet economy and start market-orientated reforms.

2. Early in January 1990, a shipment of tanks was detained in the port of Novorossiysk, sent abroad by the ANT cooperative under the guise of industrial tractors. An arms-smuggling criminal case was opened, although it ended in nothing.

because they could sense the country's bankruptcy. They felt it was close. Then the roles were divided. Some urgently siphoned off assets, as they planned for their future life. Others wondered who would save the country. Who would do that? I think we took office not only because we knew something and were known—although we were secondary actors—but also because we weren't rooted in that system. We didn't present a threat to business interests.

AVEN: That's what they thought.

MASHCHITS: That's the way it really was. First of all, we had not siphoned off property. Second, the government was formed, and government workers were appointed at a critical moment, starting from November 6, 1991, when it was absolutely necessary to make final decisions. If I'm not mistaken, Chechnya declared its independence on November 5. Tatarstan had declared its sovereignty by the same time.

AVEN: You were close to Gaidar by then, but did you cooperate with Yavlinsky?

MASHCHITS: I was interacting with Yavlinsky rather closely. But I worked with him on the economic community agreement, which was signed in October. The Interstate Economic Committee (IEC) was formed and headed by Silayev, and I somehow stepped aside. I was already Gaidar's deputy at the institute.

So I did the work for Yavlinsky and moved to Dacha 15 to join Gaidar. That was my second arrival; I already realized it made no sense to play pointless games. By that time, almost everyone had declared their independence. The finale was clear: the country was breaking up.

KOKH: The declaration of Chechnya's independence in 1991 passed unnoticed, but it was actually when the whole Chechen story began. Or wasn't it?

MASHCHITS: I wouldn't say it was unnoticed—

KOKH: Tell us more.

MASHCHITS: They declared their independence on November 5, I think. Yeltsin introduced—

Kokh: The Supreme Soviet?

Mashchits: No, not the Supreme Soviet. Yeltsin declared a state of emergency and Spetsnaz flew down there. Spetsnaz flew, but it was blocked.

Kokh: Right on the airfield?

Mashchits: Either on the airfield or in some building. I cannot remember details now. Yeltsin tried to push the Supreme Soviet to adopt some plans, but they were denied support, and he had to back off.

Aven: But why did Gaidar appear then, not Yavlinsky? I thought Yavlinsky had the biggest chance. Unlike Gaidar, he is charismatic—

Kokh: Yegor had his own charisma. But Yavlinsky was much more popular. Could his popularity have made Yeltsin wary?

Mashchits: I was not a witness, but I think Yavlinsky still had illusions of the possibility of a Union economic reform. I also think that his idea contradicted Yeltsin's own plans.

Kokh: Chernomyrdin said he had asked him once, "Yeltsin, would you have let the Soviet Union break up if you were in Gorbachev's place in 1991?"

Mashchits: Of course not!

Kokh: Precisely! That is what Yeltsin told him: "Never!"

Mashchits: I know about that, too.

Kokh: And he was the man who put in a lot of effort to break up the USSR.

Mashchits: I was communicating with Yeltsin at that time. I was a permanent member of delegations to those negotiations. His public statements, at least, showed he was committed to retaining the maximum possible unity.

Public Politics

Aven: And what if Yeltsin had hired somebody else, not Gaidar, who thought differently and had other ambitions and goals? Could we have formed a broad and powerful liberal movement? Liberals formed influential parties and unions in Eastern Europe. They built a whole world! And we couldn't do it.

MASHCHITS: Yegor did not want it. That is my absolute conviction.

KOKH: Chubais thinks it would have been senseless to form such a movement without Yeltsin, and Yeltsin did not want us to join his party, which had one member only, Yeltsin himself.

MASHCHITS: Not quite.

KOKH: Yeltsin never publicly supported Gaidar's party, Democratic Choice of Russia. Not even once.

MASHCHITS: Gaidar realized that, politically, Yeltsin would try to disconnect himself from the "predatory reforms" and the people who personified them. So the political cover, thanks to which it all began, was not unconditional and totally unreliable. I don't think that was the only reason. Yegor was aware of his shortcomings as a public politician.

AVEN: He was not fully aware of them in 1991.

MASHCHITS: I think he was. He didn't like any of that. I talked with him a lot about that later on. He had no taste for public politics.

KOKH: Yegor gave me one of his last big interviews, for *Medved* magazine; that was a huge interview, which barely fit into two issues. He told me, "I was a political zero."

MASHCHITS: It seems that his cultural and psychological type was that of a loner rather than a leader.

KOKH: More an advisor than a leader. A responsible, educated, and clever person prepared to answer for his words. But he was not an orator or a leader.

MASHCHITS: Don't underrate him. I think he deemed himself somewhere between Keynes and Erhard, but he liked Keynes more. Yet the role he played in the end was more that of Erhard.

KOKH: We may argue further, but I'm telling you how Yegor described himself in our conversations. He said, "I realize that I like the advisor job more. I am ready to do research, to give advice and to bear responsibility for it, et cetera. But I happened to become a leader, not an advisor. I had to do the work myself. Being fully aware of my responsibility, I did."

MASHCHITS: Alfred, tell me what day he said that.

KOKH: That was a couple of years before he died, in 2007.

MASHCHITS: That was different. Remember the way he was in 1993? And earlier?

KOKH: Sure.

MASHCHITS: So, was that an advisor?

AVEN: He wanted to be the prime minister!

MASHCHITS: I will tell you more. I had a serious argument with him in 1992 after he refused to be the first deputy, at Chernomyrdin's. He didn't want us to stay because he wanted to be the prime minister. That was bad for our work.

KOKH: Everyone is wondering now why Yegor did not create an efficient liberal opposition. But how could he be the opponent of the new government when practically all of his associates were still government members?

I think Petr was the only one to quit after Yegor. You, Petr, told me recently that you had all agreed to write resignation statements. And you came home and wrote yours diligently, assuming that the others were doing the same. And it turned out in the morning that you were the only one.

MASHCHITS: We never said that!

AVEN: Sure you did. How many of us met after Yegor had been given the boot?

MASHCHITS: I was not there, and I simply could not understand why he told me, "You must quit, too," when I was engaged in preparations for forming the CIS. I told him, "Listen, we have to bring at least something to a conclusion!"

AVEN: Everyone was thinking about himself as well then. I think Yegor was waffling: stay or go. And then he decided to quit. He thought it was in preparation for a future flight. So he wanted to take all of us with him; he thought he would be out but he would keep his team. But Yegor didn't have enough fire to be a leader in the big political struggle.

MASHCHITS: Then why didn't he form a party after that?

KOKH: He started to form a party. It was called the Democratic Choice of Russia. A year later the party had the largest faction at the Duma after the 1993 election. Formally, it had the same number of seats, 64, as the Liberal Democratic Party; but considering that Shokhin's Party of Russian Unity and Accord [PRUA], with 22, and independent deputies tended to support Gaidar, it was the biggest faction in practice.

AVEN: Vladimir, when did you leave?

MASHCHITS: I was one of the last. Actually, Chubais and I were the only ones left. I was the acting minister up to March 1995. Then I spent a year as a first deputy minister, and only then did I move to Mezhgosbank. But I saw the projects we had started through to the end. They were accomplished after all, more or less successfully—the CIS still exists. You may have your attitude toward it, but it still exists!

AVEN: Let us change the subject a bit. You were the only one—or, to be more exact, you and Borya Fyodorov were the only ones—affiliated with Yavlinsky's team and ours. What would have happened if Yavlinsky, not Gaidar, had been chosen? Would Yeltsin have gotten used to Yavlinsky? Or would they have broken up more rapidly?

MASHCHITS: There was a little-known game played through the year 1990. What was the 500 Days program? It was kind of a compromise between the Union and Russian administrations on ways to pursue the reforms. And Yavlinksy played an enormous role, although Nikolai Yakovlevich Petrakov, Gorbachev's assistant, was also active. As I understand it, Yavlinsky viewed himself as the main coordinator—if not the premier, then the person in charge of the reforms. Like Balcerowicz, for example. I think this is right: not Mazowiecki but Balcerowicz. And his trip to Poland was not acciden-tal—actually, we both went there.

AVEN: Who else was with you?

MASHCHITS: Me, Alexashenko, Kostya Kagalovsky, Borya Lvin … Why was I so calm about shock therapy? It seemed to me our process would be slower but nothing different. And there was nothing scary in Poland.

How was Yavlinsky different, and what were his characteristic features in general? He is more social democratic then Yegor. Yegor was a bona fide right-winger, no kidding.

AVEN: Yavlinsky really is a social democrat.

MASHCHITS: He worked a long time at Goskomtrud.[3] He had a profound knowledge of labor. In that sense, he was closer to the people. What would he have done wrong? I don't know. Life would have forced him to do approximately the same, because you are under the pressure of time and circumstances. I think the question is about purely political rather than economic preferences.

AVEN: Was he prepared to be a mere executor in Yeltsin's administration who could have been sacrificed at a convenient moment, just to gain time? Yavlinsky was older and more independent. He would not have agreed to be under Yeltsin.

KOKH: That was why he was not appointed. The appointment of Yavlinsky was already impossible. Burbulis gave us a rather explicit and logical explanation.

MASHCHITS: As I understand it, Grisha would have set so many conditions for his involvement that half of them would have been sufficient for Yeltsin to stop communicating with him. And I kept thinking about a model that, from my standpoint, could have worked rather well. The model featured Yavlinsky as the IEC head, Yegor in charge of the Russian economic sector, and me the way I was, Russia's representative to Union organs. Was that actually possible? For all the "buts," I think it was.

KOKH: Gaidar and Yalvinsky? One could design plenty of such duos at that time. But the main thing was that the Gorbachev–Yeltsin tandem did not work, which made the model fail from the start.

---

3. The State Committee for Labor and Social Problems.

MASHCHITS: In my mind I have them in pairs that way: Gorbachev–Yeltsin, Yavlinsky–Gaidar.

THE COLLAPSE OF THE UNION

AVEN: Vladimir, you were in charge of the CIS. What was happening there? Did the republics believe in 1992 that they could survive, that they were independent states? Or did they think it was a dream?

MASHCHITS: Self-determination processes had their own dynamic. The three Baltic republics said outright, "No CIS, no confederations. Go to hell." Three countries had internal conflicts looming: Transdniestria in Moldova, South Ossetia and Abkhazia in Georgia, and Tajikistan.

KOKH: Plus the protracted Karabakh conflict between Azerbaijan and Armenia.

MASHCHITS: The Karabakh conflict is still a tricky thing. Karabakh looks like an internal problem of Azerbaijan, and it does not belong to Armenia formally. How could it be defined? Is it an interstate conflict between Armenia and Azerbaijan, or is it Karabakh Armenian separatism inside Azerbaijan? That conflict was several years old by fall 1991.

How did the self-determination process develop? It seems everything started with the economy. Secession from the USSR was not on the agenda, and no one contested the existence of the Union when Estonia suggested a concept of territorial republic self-financing. The concept penetrated everyone's mind. Then the question of political independence was raised. It was republic self-financing before separatism and popular fronts.

Back in the Andropov era they were thinking about remapping the country in order to preserve its unity. Volsky was doing that in Andropov's administration. A higher status for autonomous republics was being considered under Gorbachev. That was the source of Tatarstan's movement for independence.

AVEN: They wanted to raise the status of autonomous republics to counterbalance the separatism of Union republics? That is not trivial.

MASHCHITS: Yes. But "popular fronts" were still growing in the republics. Besides, certain republics accumulated and accentuated differences with the center. Take, for instance, the Gdlyan–Ivanov investigation team, the

Uzbek cotton case. When they went too far and imprisoned lots of locals, their actions stopped being regarded as a simple fight against corruption, or some other crime, but were taken as Moscow's humiliation of Uzbeks.

KOKH: Uzbekistan must have thought it was a reprisal, and innocent people were sent to prison.

MASHCHITS: Their hatred for the central authorities was growing out of the feeling of Moscow's injustice. I remember the coordination of interests within the 500 Days program. They had so many grudges, and it was just 1990. Everyone was already very touchy about the central authorities by the middle of 1991, before the GKChP coup attempt.

AVEN: Anisimov told us that all the republics attended conferences and wanted to reach agreement, up to the GKChP. None of them was thinking about the disintegration of the Union—except the Baltic republics, of course.

MASHCHITS: I think in 1990 that was true.

AVEN: Then why did it all break up in spring 1991?

MASHCHITS: When the so-called Novo-Ogaryovo process started in the spring with the idea of signing a new Union agreement, the situation got worse with every month.

KOKH: Could the Novo-Ogaryovo process have been the catalyst for disintegration? You know what people think: "If they talk to us, then they can't give us orders. Then we can fool around endlessly."

MASHCHITS: This is not the most important thing. The republican leaders saw that the Union was weakening. They saw what we were doing in Eastern Europe, and understood that we were bound by non-aggression accords with America and Europe. Humanitarian aid was already being supplied. They brought 26,000 tons in 1990, and ten times more in 1991. St Petersburg alone got 26,000 tons in the first week of January 1992. What did that amount mean? That was a large shipment. I remember distributing that aid between the republics at the IEC meeting—Bundeswehr food rations and other food.

AVEN: I have the impression that the republics did not realize at first that they were independent. They thought they would be forced back into the Union in 1992 and told to stay. I think the Ukrainian referendum put an end to that.

MASHCHITS: December 1991 was the hardest for me. Before Belovezh I had had the title of plenipotentiary representative for economic community affairs. And Russia was the leader in forming the new structure. We spent a colossal amount of time on the coordination and synchronization of reforms. Ukraine kept asking for deferrals—they must have been preparing to declare their independence. And it became obvious on December 8 there would be no coordination of reforms. Yegor said Kravchuk came to Belovezh with the firm intention not to sign anything or coordinate anything.

Each of the republics had two elites. Some made their careers in the Union and others did so locally. Their relations were not always smooth. But when the self-determination question arose, they all took the same position: independence.

AVEN: And what impressions did you have?

MASHCHITS: My impression was the following: imagine an encircled division and its three options—to scatter, to break through enemy lines in units, or to do so as a single force. Each of these options implies certain conditions. If you decide to break through as a single force, you will need commanders, armed commissars, security officers, and discipline. You need sufficient amounts of ammunition and fuel. You need lots of things—but we had none at that moment.

People were already scattering. Everyone who wished to leave the country did so. Some went to the States, some to Israel, some to Germany, and some to other countries. But that implied complete state disintegration in the end.

So the third option was optimal—to break through enemy lines in units. One group left and sent a signal: "All right, we are out." Others then followed, and so on.

KOKH: That was the way it happened. The Baltic republics left first. They seemed to be all right. Others followed their example.

MASHCHITS: That's right, the Baltic republics dropped out, and then the others said they were independent, too. The real flight started after the putsch. Importantly, the ideological factor was being added by that moment. Every republic had its own intelligentsia. There were lots of people who realized they could get new positions—at foreign ministries, embassies, and so on. They realized they would upgrade their status and take an office; grudges against Russia were also a factor.

There are plenty of great-power advocates in this country now, but the republics had their own great-power advocates. Like ours, they told their great-power philosophy to their people.

I had a huge sheet on which we listed all the issues requiring settlement, from strategic weapons to the recognition of pensions, education certificates, standards, "nuts and bolts." The work plan looked monstrous—so many problems to resolve! Those were not just political and foreign trade issues. You may have five items on the bilateral agenda with a foreign country: trade and practically nothing else—no other points of contact. And the number of problems was colossal in every field in our case. Plus we were bound by the foreign debt, which had to be divided (that was when we worked together with you, Petr).

AVEN: Domestic currencies?

MASHCHITS: They started appearing slowly in 1992.

KOKH: Kazakhstan got its currency in 1993.

MASHCHITS: Approximately in 1993, but correspondent accounts were divided in the middle of 1992.

KOKH: Okay, then. What was the main impetus for the Soviet Union's breakup?

MASHCHITS: I think the process in the USSR became irreversible with the disintegration of the Socialist camp.

KOKH: In 1989?

MASHCHITS: The USSR, as a more monolithic structure, lasted longer. First we had to decide on our withdrawl from Afghanistan, then on our attitude toward Poland's Solidarność and to those who pulled down the Berlin Wall.

KOKH: That was in 1989.

MASHCHITS: Actually, the events that triggered the USSR's breakup happened in 1988–9. Important military-strategic changes took place simultaneously. We reduced medium- and shorter-range missiles and engaged in negotiations, which yielded an agreement on conventional armaments. The military thought that was bad and that our concessions were unfounded. The elite started to split—

AVEN: When did Marshal Sergei Fyodorovich Akhromeyev commit suicide?

MASHCHITS: Shortly after the putsch, on August 24. But it was not about Akhromeyev; Gorbachev dismissed practically the entire military command in 1989. First he took advantage of Mathias Rust, who landed his plane in Red Square in May 1987. Defense Minister Sokolov was replaced with Yazov, and he brought his own team, as a new minister usually does.

KOKH: Khrushchev started the détente. He signed agreements with the West; we accepted the doctrine of peaceful coexistence. Wasn't that evidence that the Soviet Union was doomed to fall apart?

MASHCHITS: That is not what I mean. It is just that in 1987 preservation of the Union was paralyzed. What if the GKChP had been tough and energetic?

KOKH: Anisimov, who was working in the Union administration in the 1980s, told us they were closely studying the market regulation and price liberalization practices of China, and even of Western countries. They went on countless trips, studied stuff. But they did nothing. Why? Am I right that our leaders were more orthodox than the Chinese?

MASHCHITS: No.

KOKH: Or could the intellectual degradation of the administrative elite have been deeper than that in China or Eastern Europe?

MASHCHITS: I don't think so.

KOKH: Why, then?

MASHCHITS: They feared unpopular decisions. Besides, they still had some hope in 1988–9. The process had just begun.

KOKH: The Mazowiecki cabinet liberalized prices when Jaruzelski was still president. Am I right, Petr?

AVEN: Yes. Jaruzelski was still president.

KOKH: Thus, the Polish soviet elite were capable of doing that and ours was not. The Chinese Communist elite was capable, and ours was incapable.

The people who elected Chernenko chief of state in 1984 cannot be called sane. They cannot be called farsighted and responsible. They just wanted to keep the status quo at any cost. They didn't care about the country, its prospects, or the prospects of their own children; they just wanted to keep that status quo. That was stupid. Those elites were doomed.

MASHCHITS: As I understand it, Gorbachev tried to bring new people into the administration.

KOKH: Those were very timid attempts. And he had nowhere to get them. This is what Petr and I keep saying: there was no alternative to those elites. The present-day Russian elites are young, the best we have had, and capable of at least some renovation of the country. But those elites were not new—they were a part of the old elites, survivors.

Serious degradation of the Russian elite began at the start of the millennium. Compared with the Arabs, we are even stupider than the Egyptians.

MASHCHITS: Allow me to disagree.

AVEN: Elite or not, a lot depended personally on the leader, on Gorbachev. Judging by our conversation with Anisimov, no one in the administration understood what Gorbachev was planning or what he would do. There was no decision-making system—either political or economic. Back to our main subject: if Yavlinsky had been chosen as the main reformer, what would have been different? How did he differ from Yegor?

THE GAIDAR TEAM AS MILITARY SPECIALISTS

MASHCHITS: Grisha was more authoritarian. Yegor was more democratic and lenient toward people. Yavlinsky was touchy, and it was hard to restore relations with him after any altercation.

KOKH: I mainly saw Yavlinsky only on television. But I think the main difference between him and Yegor is that Yegor didn't worry much about his intellectual leadership and felt confident in any group. Grisha had doubts, and selected his circle carefully. Who was left in his party? It's a joke.

AVEN: The ability of Yegor to gather a bigger and stronger team was a factor. What was the 500 Days team? Just young guys, unknown students, aside from you and Borya Fyodorov, meaning—no offense—we would not have admitted them to our team.

MASHCHITS: If Grisha had been appointed, I think he would have gathered a team. Besides, acclaimed Westerners were helping him—Stanley Fischer, for instance.

KOKH: Probably he could have recruited skilled people, but he never made an efficient team. Yegor created a powerful institute, but no one followed Yavlinsky to his EPI Center think tank.

AVEN: With the exception of his boys. Speaking of resignation, you said you told Gaidar when he suggested that you quit with him, "We cannot quit. We must see the project through to the end." What was it?

MASHCHITS: First of all, we had to finish the drafting of documents needed for the total work of the organization called the CIS. Complex negotiations were in progress.

AVEN: Was that really so important? Gaidar offered you a real fight for power.

MASHCHITS: Imagine the big factory we once were. In spite of self-financing and bureaucratic bargaining, we were one factory technologically, with extremely narrow specialization and extremely broad geography. You know that the Volga car plant alone needed 240 partners who were making parts for Zhiguli cars. Some supplied rods, some supplied other parts.

KOKH: Do you think you could help them? Do you think VAZ wouldn't have reached agreement with its partners without you? Please—I spent ten years there!

MASHCHITS: Did you spend ten years there?

AVEN: Alfred's father was the VAZ's chief liaison with its partners; he was actually in charge of part supplies.

KOKH: He was building partner plants throughout the Union! I can tell you that you neither helped nor hampered their relations when you were building the CIS. Plants made agreements directly, and continued to make cars.

AVEN: So why couldn't you quit the government? Give us a better answer, Vladimir!

MASHCHITS: Listen. I had a clear work plan, and I knew that there was nothing left for me to do after it was fulfilled. But why would I quit while I still had the work plan? Would my successor do better than me? No, because he would waste time getting up to speed. This meant my resignation would be harmful rather than useful.

KOKH: Gaidar came to you and said, "This is all bullshit. CIS or no CIS, leave with me! If we take a break now, we will have full power later."

MASHCHITS: That's not how it was.

KOKH: And if he had put it that way, would you have gone?

MASHCHITS: Then I would have stood up and left.

AVEN: What did he say?

MASHCHITS: He said nothing. He said something like, "There is nothing here to do for you, either." That was it.

AVEN: You went your separate ways?

MASHCHITS: We did. Actually, Yegor was behaving oddly and illogically. Why did he decide that Chubais should stay because he had not finished with privatization and I must quit because the CIS was nothing? Was that so?

KOKH: I can tell you why, but everyone will take offense again.

MASHCHITS: Go ahead.

KOKH: Chubais will take offense. And it was simple. Chubais had a stronger personality than Yegor, so Yegor preferred not to quarrel with him, to keep at least a semblance of the team. He needed something to rebuild his team from. He also knew that no one (Chubais included) wanted to quit. But he thought he was stronger than you, and when it turned out differently, he might have been offended.

MASHCHITS: You know, I don't think he took much offense.

KOKH: I am positive he did. He thought everyone would quit if he left. But no! No one did! And he was offended. He was afraid to take offense at Chubais, but he was offended by you.

MASHCHITS: I don't know—it didn't seem that way to me.

KOKH: Let's take a glance at a later period, 1995–6. The wonderful story of Yeltsin's support or lack of support for the Democratic Choice of Russia. Yegor didn't want to support Yeltsin, I know that—because of Chechnya, because of the endless shameful drinking, and all that shit he had done with Korzhakov, such as the National Foundation of Sport, and other things. I don't want to lie, but now I seem to remember that he said, "We'd be better off supporting Grisha." But, you know, Chubais won him over. He did not persuade him, he pushed him, with his typical syllogisms.

MASHCHITS: I thought Chubais used other considerations to persuade him.

KOKH: Which ones? It is just that Chubais bullied him, reasoned with him. He made Yegor realize that a personal conflict would be unavoidable. And Yegor couldn't stand that—especially conflicts with people he was close to.

MASHCHITS: I think he gave him other reasons. The most important was, "We'll be giving up the country to the communists."

KOKH: Why not stake on Yalvinsky instead of Yeltsin? Yes, we would have lost power (we hardly had any), but we would have kept the communists away!

MASHCHITS: Was that alternative discussed?

KOKH: That's the point—it wasn't! But why wasn't it discussed?

MASHCHITS: I don't know.

KOKH: But I do, and I can tell you why: because we who held office in 1995–6 had another dilemma: "Maybe we will not give the country to the communists if we support Yalvinsky, but we will lose our positions." "We" are Chubais and his team, including me. I tell you that frankly.

AVEN: You were not involved. You were not a staff member.

KOKH: My involvement was not direct, but I fulfilled some of Chubais's orders. But another thing was more important: if they had asked me, I would have done what Chubais did. Because it's true that the choice was between the communists and the democrats, but it's also true that there was another choice inside it: whether we would hold office or not.

Don't think I'm condemning anyone. Fighting for power is normal—it's what men do. In the end, we are just males trying to prove through fighting that we are alphas. Thus I understand the objective conflict between Yegor (out of office) and Chubais (in office). The dilemma was simple for Yegor—the communists or the democrats; but it was more complex for Chubais—and, I must admit, for myself.

MASHCHITS: You know we had more than one or two choices of that sort to make in the 1990s.

KOKH: Right. The first choice was made in late 1992, after the resignation of Yegor. The second was at the end of 1993 when Gena Burbulis called on everyone to take part in Duma elections without seeking the support of Yeltsin (who was reluctant to give it), or even slightly opposing him. The third was at the end of 1994, when those drunks started the first war in Chechnya. The fourth was during the presidential election of 1996. And after that we had no chance to make a choice. We were all kicked out—that was the end of it.

AVEN: You know, that's right. At all those crossroads, personal things played a much bigger role than we try to convince everyone they did—including ourselves.

KOKH: And Yeltsin took it 100 percent personally. To be more exact, 90 percent was personal and 10 percent was for the country's sake. I feel some-times that he didn't care at all: if he could have defeated Gorbachev through the return to communism, Yeltsin would have returned to communism. But the electorate wanted change and freedom, so he rode that horse.

MASHCHITS: No!

KOKH: Yes!

MASHCHITS: Stop! Tell me, then, why did he call on us?

KOKH: Because the electorate wanted a market economy and democracy. Besides, there was no other way out but uncontrolled prices and the free movement of goods and capital—and that required specialists.

AVEN: Yes, that was simple: we were the ones to make him successful.

MASHCHITS: I don't think it's quite ethical to claim our contribution. What was Gaidar's team? It was what we now call a team of crisis managers. It was hired for a brief and strictly limited period of time. The period appeared to be longer than the employer expected. So what? And the team, which had worked for too long, imagined it could aspire to a share of political power. Yeltsin blew away that illusion very rapidly.

KOKH: Do you mean to say that you, like everyone else interviewed by us with the exception of Gena Burbulis, think we had no chance to be an independent political force?

MASHCHITS: We did not. No way.

KOKH: So we were Yeltsin's appendix and nothing else in the 1990s, weren't we?

MASHCHITS: "Appendix" sounds vulgar. Not just an appendix—a hired team, which may be fired.

KOKH: At any time?

MASHCHITS: Yes. And which was not paid, actually. They didn't pay us— they just threw us out without giving us severance pay.

AVEN: Some think they paid us too much.

KOKH: It's just that certain team members took their share, without asking for permission.

MASHCHITS: No, it's a different question that some team members did the best they could afterward.

We held high-ranking positions, but that didn't mean we had political significance.

AVEN: But could we have tried?

MASHCHITS: No—I think that would have been useless.

AVEN: Then why did Balcerowicz become a political figure in Poland? Why did Klaus become a political figure in the Czech Republic? He became the president! Why did young Hungarian economists become significant?

MASHCHITS: I think there were several reasons. If we had been reforming a small country that broke free from the big brother's hug, such as Georgia, we would have become the national elite. We would have been elite in practically every CIS republic.

AVEN: We were not a national, popular force—is that what you want to say?

MASHCHITS: There were bourgeois specialists—the military experts of the Civil War years, the former regime's army—helping the reds, and we were like them: a group of strangers the people's administration had to tolerate for a while.

KOKH: And Lobov and Poltoranin were commissars—a step to the left or a step to the right.

MASHCHITS: There were many more commissars. You cannot even imagine how many of them there were. I think each of your steps was carefully analyzed. Even in our closest circle. For instance, there was Shakhrai from the presidential administration's state and legal department. That department verified every document, as far as I know.

I feel all right about Shakhrai. He wanted to do something and he actually tried, but he was still controlling us. He became a vice premier later. But at first he was an opposition figure.

Remember the first government structure? There were so many controllers under Rutskoi. There was one controller for every step we made!

KOKH: I remember Rutskoi and his notorious briefcases full of compromising materials. He kept fooling us throughout 1993. He was telling us he would send us all to prison.

MASHCHITS: There were none of those briefcases in 1992, but each of us had a controller of our own.

KOKH: They were analyzing us under a magnifying glass. It's crazy how many parasites grew fat in the years they were looking for the least little thing—just to catch us doing something bad!

MASHCHITS: We failed to become a part of the "people's administration." That was the main reason, I think. The other reason is that we had no strong party to back us up.

AVEN: Concerning the party: if there was none, and it was necessary, why didn't we build one? Right then, in 1992. I think—I keep saying this to Alfred—we could have tried to become an independent political force at that moment.

MASHCHITS: Well, if anyone had taken that seriously.

KOKH: Let's take a critical look. In 1993, in the election held immediately after the adoption of the new constitution and the October putsch, Gaidar's party, the Democratic Choice of Russia, formed the biggest faction at the State Duma, 14.2 percent; and Sasha Shokhin's PRUA had 6 percent. Actually, pro-government parties had more than 20 percent in the State Duma. Such a result was achieved again only in 1999.

MASHCHITS: Like United Russia now.

KOKH: Alas, no. United Russia has the constitutional majority. We had no more than 25–30 percent, including small satellites and independent deputies. But that was a good start. Instead, we declared the 1993 election a failure. And, as far as I know, we didn't even negotiate a possible merger with PRUA. The 1995 election was totally illogical, due to the parallel existence of Our Home Is Russia and the small parties of Borya Fyodorov, Kostya Borovoi, and Ira Khakamada.

AVEN: I remember well the walk we took with Gaidar and Chubais in 1993. We were walking along side streets, close to Tverskaya. Chubais was still a government worker, and we were already out by then. When we stopped at a red light other pedestrians applauded us! You won't believe it now. We were quite popular young men, supported by the public. The liberal idea had not been discredited at that time—that happened in the second half of the 1990s. But we didn't even try to make a normal political party. I think the reason was the absence of a leader.

Why couldn't we become a political force? We weren't anti-populist intellectuals wearing glasses! I look at you, Vladimir, and I see a typical Russian merchant. You are not Latvian, or a Jew, or a German, or a Tajik mixed with an Uzbek.

MASHCHITS: My last name is no good. I have a Belarusian surname.

AVEN: A Belarusian surname is all right. How can you be non-folk? Kokh and I don't belong to the people—that's how it is. Neither does Chubais (and he admitted that himself). But what's wrong with you? Nechayev, Shokhin, Gaidar—whose real last name is Golikov—why didn't we try to fight for power? We were grown-ups, almost 40 years old.

KOKH: Borya Fyodorov was a leader of the Choice of Russia. And then he formed his tiny party, Onward, Russia. He was quite a charismatic Russian man.

MASHCHITS: I think the problem is that our folk trend fluctuates so much that it requires thorough analytical work to trace it. It's unclear if there is any trend at all, or it is simply a chaotic vibration of the nation. Could people have moved toward freedom because they were simply hoping for a miracle? But no miracle happened, and we had what we had. We may forget about stable political support for the liberals. I also think that happened in many republics.

KOKH: That wasn't statistically significant. Not so many people left—only one million left in the 1990s.

There was no statistically significant emigration. Certainly it did colossal intellectual damage, but not electoral. There was intellectual damage because the best people left. Out of a million biologists, perhaps ten were gone, but they were the best ten biologists in the country. But one million were still there. The structure of the nation was unchanged.

AVEN: Let's return to our government.

KOKH: What were your relations with key members? With Yegor, Petr, Chubais?

MASHCHITS: We had a working relationship. Everyone minded their own business. For instance, I easily transferred the question of the USSR's foreign debts to Petr: that was the right of succession. A memorandum of joint and several liability had been signed before, on October 28.

KOKH: What was the memorandum about?

MASHCHITS: I put down its correct name somewhere—I no longer rely on my memory. This was the name: the Memorandum of Mutual Understanding with Regard to the Debt of the USSR and Its Legal Successors to Foreign Creditors. Monday, October 28, 1991, Moscow.

KOKH: Who signed it?

MASHCHITS: The USSR plus eight republics. All members of the future CIS, excluding Ukraine.

KOKH: And who didn't?

MASHCHITS: Ukraine, the Baltic republics, Georgia, Moldova, and Armenia. That was the last document Yavlinsky worked on.

KOKH: Was the debt divided proportionally?

MASHCHITS: No—there was joint and several liability. Actually, it was divided, but it was implied that Russia would pay it the event that any others failed to do so.

KOKH: How interesting. And why did Russia sign that document?

MASHCHITS: That was the G7 ultimatum: aid will stop if you do not sign it. And our leaders feared a humanitarian catastrophe—grain and drugs were supplied daily from the West.

KOKH: I shouldn't have criticized Petr. I thought we had had a proportional formula at first, and then Russia assumed the debt, under Western pressure, when Gaidar was in office. And it appears that before Gaidar the Russian government had signed a paper that made Russia the end payer. So Petr's decision to assume the debt fully was a better solution. At least we got the entire property of the USSR abroad, a place at the UN Security Council, and so on, while the October 28 memorandum gave us nothing. We were end payers, no more.

AVEN: Thank you, Alfred. Volodya and I got them to agree only in December that we shared not just the debts but also the foreign assets of the former Union. And that debt story was a graphic example of the West's petty and shortsighted position on Russia and our government.

KOKH: As I understand it, the West actually conned Russia. It gave certain hints about integration, and we rode before the hounds. After we had covered the whole distance, the West told us, "You will have to wait for integration and assistance a little bit." "And why is that?" "You have already covered the distance for free. Why would we pay you now?"

MASHCHITS: The West could have been much more adamant.

KOKH: Could it really? I remember well the abortive attempts of Kostya Kagalovsky to wheedle $3 billion from the IMF. NATO started its eastward enlargement. There was no integration for us either with the European Union or even with the WTO. What else could they do? Occupy us?

AVEN: We weren't eager to integrate, either. If we had told them, "We are ready to give you East Germany on the condition we are admitted to NATO, and we will set free the Baltic republics on the condition we integrate with the EEU," that would have been perfect. But we preferred to be autonomous. We actually stuck to the two-bloc logic, and to our "special way."

Vladimir, please, say a few words in conclusion about Yegor.

MASHCHITS: He was a grand man; there was no doubt about that. He was a grand and fearless man who foresaw many processes that others didn't understand, or even notice. But he understood them and, no matter what, he took the punches, throughout his life.

Unfortunately, people have been very unjust to Yegor. They ascribed things to him that he never did. In fact, they even blamed him for problems that were not in his purview, or were beyond his control. We know that while we were working on economic reform, no other reforms were instituted—but judicial, military, administrative, and constitutional reforms should have been implemented simultaneously. Lots of other reforms should have been put in place, because the entire administrative system had broken down. Yegor was just one cell in a huge organism.

And I totally disagree with the assumption that the failure was complete.

8

ANDREI KOZYREV
A Bona Fide "Kamikaze"

Some of Gaidar's associates and admirers believe that the dismissal of Yegor in December 1992 was a sign of a serious deceleration of the reforms started by Yeltsin, if not a change of course. But I realized from my conversation with Andrei Kozyrev that the resignation of the foreign minister at the end of 1995 may have been a much more significant event.

For in fact, the Gaidar reform fundamentals (privatization, macroeconomic stabilization) continued even without him, and no one reversed his accomplishments (the convertible ruble, uncontrolled prices). There simply was no serious alternative to Yegor's economic reforms—one could discuss the rate of reform, but not its essence.

Foreign policy was different. Kozyrev attempted a drastic change in the fundamental of Russia's foreign policy—a shift from confrontation with the West, albeit peaceful, to an allied relationship. As he brilliantly put it while being approved for his position by the Supreme Soviet, "Democratic Russia should be and will be as natural an ally of democratic countries of the West as the totalitarian Soviet Union was a natural enemy of the West."

Kozyrev's attempts failed. The Russian elite and the Russian president were not prepared for this turn. The West was not quite prepared, either. Russia did not become a part of the Western world, but returned to its traditional course of confrontation and "cooperation" when Yevgeny Primakov came to the Foreign Ministry.

Possibly Kozyrev was somewhat naive; possibly he was ahead of his time. Either way, he paid for his choice with his future. Back then we described the Gaidar team as a "kamikaze government." That definition was clearly an exaggeration for the majority of us (but not for Yegor). Andrei Vladimirovich Kozyrev was a bona fide "kamikaze." He was accused of betraying "national interests," rejected by the majority of his former colleagues, and effectively banned from practicing his profession.

Kokh and I liked Andrei very much. A remarkable and subtle narrator, he recalls events that happened 20 years ago as if they were yesterday. We didn't want the conversation to end. I regret that we had spoken so little before. I also hope that Kozyrev's story will be of interest not only to us.

Petr Aven

PETR AVEN: Andrei, let's start with your career—with the Soviet Foreign Ministry, where, as I remember, you were a true star, a young star.

AT THE SOVIET FOREIGN MINISTRY

ANDREI KOZYREV: I am a career diplomat, and my career at the Soviet Foreign Ministry truly was successful. It all started slowly, but by 1990 I headed the Department of International Organizations. Since we are bragging here (and why shouldn't we?), I was the youngest department head at the Foreign Ministry.

AVEN: I assume there was no influence involved on your behalf?

KOZYREV: There was no influence at all.

AVEN: Your appearance is not quite Russian, either, and that was an issue for the Foreign Ministry.

KOZYREV: In spite of my appearance (and your hints do have some substance), I had an ideal personnel file. Your file was the first priority in the Soviet Union. They could beat you up for your looks, but appointments were based on your personnel file. Both of my parents were communists. My personal details were studied under a microscope when I applied to the Moscow State University Institute of Foreign Relations (MGIMO). I was a dedicated communist myself at first, and experienced a sort of inner revolution in approximately 1976.

AVEN: How did you get into MGIMO? That was practically impossible without pulling strings.

KOZYREV: MGIMO is a separate story. After I finished high school, I made a conscious decision not to apply for admission to an institute, but became a worker at the Moscow Kommunar Machine Building Plant. I was curious to know what it was like to be a plant worker. My parents were intellectuals, but I decided I would work at a plant first and then join the army (I had a year left before the draft). I finally decided I would apply for admission to an institute the next spring.

AVEN: So you didn't apply anywhere the first year?

KOZYREV: No. I did the social entertainment work at the plant; in fact, I was doing that my whole life. I organized parody shows and contests. We had lots of fun. When I finally decided to be a student, the workshop party organizer told me, "The best thing for you is to have a reference from us. I will give you a plant reference, which will get you into any institute." I said, "Fine. Terrific." I was happy.

ALFRED KOKH: What did the Kommunar Plant make?

KOZYREV: It made vacuum cleaners. But that was just one workshop, and the plant had over 50 workshops in all. Those were not making vacuum cleaners.[1] Getting a job there required as much paperwork as going on a foreign trip—and I had been a worker there, and I had the reference. But where would I go? I had missed regular preparatory courses, and I didn't have much time to prepare, either, because the work was hard. It was exhausting learning the job. So, which institute would I choose, without a good preparatory education? Someone, probably at the party committee, gave me a smart hint: "Try Patrice Lumumba University, where students are admitted only by references. No one cares about your knowledge—all you have to do is to be cleared for interacting with foreigners. Our plant is high security. You can be trusted, and that's how you may become a student." I gladly went to the Patrice Lumumba University, and it appeared they had no admission tests—there was only an interview. They interviewed me and said everything was all right, but then the party organizer for our plant showed up and said, "Listen, we have a problem. The security clearance of plant workers is so high that you cannot go abroad for three years." Admission to Patrice Lumumba University is just a direct pass for foreign trips.

---

1.   They made air-to-air missiles and launching systems for fighter jets and aircraft cabin instrument and components, according to the Russian Defense Business Directory, US Department of Commerce.

Kokh: Direct contact with foreigners.

Kozyrev: Yes. I was bound by security restrictions, while the admission meant direct contact with foreigners. So that broke down, and I had nowhere to go. It was June, too late to do anything, but I started studying math—for some reason I wanted to try a math course. So that was the situation I found myself in, but the party people—and, I think, not only them; there was a certain organization monitoring security clearances and other things—happened to be normal guys, and even had some liking for me. They made some telephone calls to find out alternatives. Then MGIMO popped up, because it was the other institute that admitted students based on such references.

Kokh: But you had to take MGIMO admission exams—especially the language test?

Kozyrev: I did, but I had good language skills.

Kokh: How is that?

Kozyrev: I went to a Spanish-language school. Spanish is a rare language, and I think it was rather difficult to evaluate one's knowledge of Spanish. In fact, there was a combination of lucky factors—and, to be frank, the KGB guys did the whole thing themselves; they sent my documents to their colleagues at the MGIMO. I don't know whether this is now a state secret or not, but MGIMO had a parallel administration—the dean, for instance, and the class tutor.

Kokh: Were they the real people in command?

Kozyrev: Yes, that's exactly what they were. But all of them were of retirement age; they must have been retired colonels. We knew them well, and they knew us well, because they were the other administration. So it all happened through them. I don't know what role they played at the admission exams, but I passed the exams very easily. In fact, our year tutor was a decent man, like many others from that agency I worked with, especially on the middle level.

Aven: When did you graduate from MGIMO?

KOZYREV: In 1974.

AVEN: It must have been very hard to get a job at the Foreign Ministry.

KOZYREV: It was. There were lots of students (including my friends) in my class with rather influential parents. Some strings were pulled that took me out of the appointed job and put me into the Foreign Ministry—that was it. It was done by people who could do that easily and did it on their own initiative.

AVEN: So, you came to the Foreign Ministry with the help of your friends?

KOZYREV: Yes. But, as always happens in life, on the one hand I was glad, but on the other I was sad, because I guessed that they would stop taking care of me now. That was a one-off event.

KOKH: And you could rot away as a clerk somewhere.

KOZYREV: That's what happened. I spent the next six years in the lowest-level job, because no one paid any attention to me. I could understand the people in personnel. They were waiting for instructions. It's like Petr guessed—you couldn't just take a job at the Foreign Ministry, and the HR person understood that. He looked through my file. But still, there should have been one. Like any other bureaucrat, he was waiting for a phone call or some other signal. And I was totally uncomfortable going to the people who had helped me, even though we were on friendly terms; the terms had a specific character then, and then that specific character ended, and I could no longer turn to them, and I ended up on hold. My beginning was very difficult.

AVEN: What changed your status?

KOZYREV: The Foreign Ministry, and the entire Soviet system, had an element of selection of personnel that was not only based on influence. Those who pulled strings had already moved abroad as attachés. By the time I became an attaché, the majority of our guys had already become third secretaries, if not second. But then a person has to start working. The department is large—about 60 or 70 people; but only five or six of them actually work. We had to send lots of notes to the Central Committee; there was other work requiring knowledge and writing skills, and so on. Bosses tend to appreciate those who can do the work quickly and well. So my career started moving up, and then I had a stroke of luck. It was almost like a joke. I must have been a first secretary by then, when the man taking shorthand at board meetings fell ill and my boss told me: "Take a seat at the corner of the board room, so no one sees you. Your rank is too low to take shorthand at these meetings. Write down primarily what the minister says." It was our issue—they were discussing the work of international organizations. "So, write down the minister's words, and turn the document around quickly." The minister was an elderly person. He spoke off the cuff, and rather schematically. I had three pages transcribed, which I sent upstairs on behalf of the minister. There were no computers in those days.

AVEN: Gromyko was the minister.

KOZYREV: Exactly. My boss looked through what he said; he might have corrected something or not, but we sent the speech to the secretariat very quickly. I barely slept all night, because it had been an important assignment. My boss was a very decent man—I knew he would never take credit if they said it was good. If they didn't like it, the possible reprimand would be mild because it was not my job, after all. In fact, I knew I would not be punished if they didn't like it, and if they did, he wouldn't take credit, or at least not all of it. They really liked it, and the minister approved my writing and sent it directly to the Politburo, the way it was always done.

My life changed at that moment. I started attending board meetings, writing down the minister's words, having meetings with him. In general, life was totally different. As a rule, this kind of participation in ministerial affairs begins at the department head level. So my career was on the rise. Then Gromyko left and Shevardnadze came, and I was even more successful. The article I published in *Mezhdunarodnaya Zhizn* in 1989, sharply criticizing our foreign policy, also helped. The point was that we needed to review our opinion of our so-called revolutionary friends, the West, and so on. The *New York Times* reprinted it immediately, and it was even discussed at the Politburo. The party strongly criticized me at first, and Honecker wrote a letter against me in the name of the Socialist Unity Party. But Shevardnadze apparently sympathized with my ideas. I became department head.

AVEN: Tell me about the evolution of your viewpoint.

KOZYREV: I made my first trip to the West in 1975, and it was right to the US. We worked for the Department of International Organizations, and attended the annual sessions of the UN General Assembly in New York.

Then I went to a supermarket. The shock I experienced came not from what I saw on the shelves, but from the fact that the customers were ordinary people, not capitalists. They were Latinos, African Americans, and not white-collar workers. They were filling up their shopping carts with food.

Kokh: That was so different from the shops for Soviet apparatchiks only!

Aven: I know from Samoteikin, a Brezhnev aide, that when Brezhnev came to America for the first time, Nixon took him to a supermarket. They spent a couple of hours there, and when they left Brezhnev said, "Zhenya, they may have solved the consumer goods problem here, but all that food was brought in just before our arrival. It simply cannot be otherwise."

Kozyrev: Yes, yes, yes. That is true. People from our mission told me that a Politburo member had visited and they could not convince him that a supermarket was not a Potemkin village. Yeltsin also had a shock. He started swearing after a visit to a supermarket in the US, and he usually never swore.

Aven: Khrushchev had the same shock. He launched his huge housing program after a trip to the United States, where he realized that people could live, if not in private homes, then at least in their own flats. He started sowing corn after the same trip. Surprisingly, our people (even the most educated ones) still mythologize the West without understanding Western life. At least they are not surprised by supermarkets any longer.

Kozyrev: The cultural gap is enormous. The supermarket was the first shock, from which I almost recovered, but the second shock was stronger. I went to a bookstore. I spent a lot of time there, and then saw Russian classics. "That can't be!" I said to myself. There were Chekhov, Dostoyevsky, Tolstoy—the regulars. And *Doctor Zhivago*. It was impossible to read the book in Moscow, so I bought *Doctor Zhivago*, went to Central Park, and spent the whole day reading it in English. Then I recalled that it was a forbidden book, and left it on the park bench. The question "What was so anti-Soviet about it?" tormented me for three months after I returned to Moscow.

Kokh: That question tormented everyone. But, as far as I understand, the main affront was not the content of the book. The main affront was that Pasternak was rejected by a local publishing house, and he published the book in the West without asking for permission.

KOZYREV: That is probably how it was formulated, but I had a slightly different conclusion. I concluded that the problem was that he wasn't with us—with the communists, with the party. He did not mind the party—

AVEN: But he was not a supporter, either.

KOZYREV: That's even worse—because a totalitarian system is unable to tolerate not only rejection but—

KOKH: People who go their own way.

KOZYREV: Exactly! I concluded that that system did not tolerate any personal freedom. And it led to my absolute internal dissidence. I had not the courage to become a true dissident, a human rights defender or something. I kept working at the Foreign Ministry, but the more I thought about what I was doing, about our foreign policy and its essence, it all collapsed like a house of cards, and in the end I became an anti-Soviet person. I knew my job well, and I probably did it very well, but I was also well aware of my thoughts.

When Gorbachev took office and glasnost and perestroika started, we were very suspicious. There were a number of guys of approximately my age at the Foreign Ministry—we knew each other, and I suspected their opinions were similar to mine.

Here's what the young career men were doing at the Foreign Ministry at that time. Say Gorbachev goes on a trip somewhere. We prepared his speeches, papers, and so on. So he says, "Glasnost." We summarize reactions to the trip and give him the following hint: "Glasnost is good, but the UN adopted the Human Rights Declaration of 1947. It does not speak about glasnost—it speaks about freedom of speech, freedom of media, freedom of opinion, of assembly, and so on. If you say that, that would be wonderful because such things are universal, they are spelled out in the declaration." So we kept on saying that, and Gorbachev finally spoke about freedom of speech in 1989; I remember we were very happy. We prepared his speech, and he delivered it at the UN; the occasion was immediately used by sharp-witted dissidents, the *Moscow News* and others, who started making references to his statement: "Well, Gorbachev said 'freedom of speech,' therefore there are no more restrictions; I can write what I want."

We intentionally engaged in those subversive activities, but we didn't dare to go further. Then the Russian Supreme Soviet came into existence, and it was much more radical than the Soviet congress—especially after they elected Yeltsin as Supreme Soviet chairman, and he took part in direct elections under very radical slogans. He was backed up by Democratic Russia. Here, I finally felt, as many of us did: "What if this really is a chance for genuine transformations?" We didn't think that Gorbachev was such a chance, but Yeltsin looked like one. So I moved heaven and earth to be introduced to him.

THE RUSSIAN FOREIGN MINISTRY

AVEN: What year is this?

KOZYREV: Nineteen-ninety. My friends helped. Lukin helped—he was an RSFSR people's deputy, after having worked at the Foreign Ministry for some time. Seeing that he was a deputy—and, more important, the chair of the International Affairs Committee—I went to him as my only acquaintance there. I told him I badly wanted to work there. He looked at me and said, "Fine, fine"—and he recommended me.

AVEN: What was the Russian Foreign Ministry doing at that time?

KOZYREV: For a person who at retirement age could not take a good ambassadorial post, the RSFSR Foreign Ministry was a very good option. It had a residence on Prospect Mir, which I successfully inherited, and while there was absolutely nothing to do, it all looked real—there was a second government-switchboard phone, a personal car.

KOKH: Were there any foreign trips?

KOZYREV: There were some, but they were easy and pleasant trips on the economy or cultural ties; to Alberta, Canada, say, or a German land—a twin province of the Russian Federation. People working for the Russian Foreign Ministry weren't politicians; it was a sort of cultural center or God-knows-what. I went on such a trip only once, because it had been scheduled in advance, and I liked it very much. It was a little vacation, with beer-drinking and nothing much else.

AVEN: But the Russian Supreme Soviet appointed you for a totally different purpose. When was it?

KOZYREV: In fall of 1990. Together with Shoigu—who, funnily enough, was rejected at first, while I was confirmed.

AVEN: Did you realize what was in store for you?

KOZYREV: I realized that I was joining the opposition, because relations between the center and the RSFSR were already awful. On June 12 the Supreme Soviet adopted a declaration on state sovereignty, and from that moment, Supreme Soviet chairman Yeltsin and the Russian government actually turned into a legal opposition.

AVEN: Did you have a feeling you would take power sooner or later?

KOZYREV: I very much wanted that to happen—not for the sake of seizing power, but to make our project successful and achieve a certain dynamic. I couldn't resist the temptation to be part of it.

KOKH: But you were skeptical, weren't you?

KOZYREV: I was very skeptical; to be frank, I did not trust Yeltsin much. I had fewer doubts about Yeltsin than about Gorbachev, but still. I never had a real talk with Yeltsin before my appointment. But I was appointed immediately, in the very first round, despite the radical nonsense I babbled. It was the first time I made this statement in public: "democratic Russia should be and will be as natural an ally of democratic countries of the West as the totalitarian Soviet Union was a natural enemy of the West." I've stuck to the formula for the rest of my life.

KOKH: But the West does not think so.

KOZYREV: I think so. And so does the West. The point of this formula is the proportion. Once again: democratic Russia will be as natural an ally of Western countries, Western democracies, as the totalitarian Soviet Union was their natural enemy.

KOKH: Did they view us as a natural ally when Yeltsin was in office?

KOZYREV: Were we a democratic Russia then?

KOKH: Very much so under Yeltsin. I can name a lot of the so-called natural allies of the West with much less democracy now than what we had not only in Yeltsin's Russia, but even in the present-day Putin–Medvedev Russia.

KOZYREV: Then we must have lived in different places. I don't think we ever became a truly democratic country. We didn't strive to be a true, sincere ally of the West for long. That's why we aren't one.

KOKH: That is a casuistry: "The West rejects Russia because it has not become a genuine democracy." Genuine democracies do not exist at all.

KOZYREV: That's not true. There are no ideal democracies, but there are real ones. Basically, they are called the West.

KOKH: Was there freedom of speech under Yeltsin? Yes, there was. Were there free elections? Yes, there were. Was there separation of powers? Yes, there was. Did the principle of checks and balances work? Definitely! And so on and so forth. How is that not a democracy?

KOZYREV: When was it?

KOKH: In 1995, for instance.

KOZYREV: Correct. I must say that the West was rather benevolent to us in 1995. But the war in Chechnya was an obstacle.

KOKH: I didn't feel the West was amicable—there was no embrace. By contrast with the Baltic republics, which they accepted immediately.

AVEN: The Baltic elites had an inner consensus about movement toward the West. We never reached any consensus of that type. What did your former colleagues at the Soviet Foreign Ministry say about the change of your political views and departure?

KOZYREV: I came to Shevardnadze the day after the Supreme Soviet approved my appointment, and told him, "Eduard Amvrosiyevich, here is the situation." He was not in the know. So he asked whom I could recommend. I told him, "Seryozha Lavrov." He appointed Seryozha and that was it—a new life started there.

AVEN: Did anyone at the ministry try to discourage you, or did you just present them with a fait accompli?

KOZYREV: No one in the ministry was aware save for my close friends—young men who left together with me. The Soviet Foreign Ministry boycotted us very quickly; they severed every possible contact, and no one stayed in touch with me. But the people in the small Foreign Ministry proved to be decent, and stood up against the GKChP.

CHANGE OF COURSE

AVEN: People think that politicians have a wide window of opportunity: you may go left, you may go right, you may go anywhere. Those who have really been to the high places are well aware that the choice of options is usually extremely limited, and it's rare to be in a situation where you choose between fundamentally different strategies. For instance, any reasonable liberal government in the place of Gaidar's government would have taken practically the same economic course.

You, like us, are accused of anti-Russian activity. To what degree was your policy set by Gorbachev in the first place? Can Yeltsin's foreign policy be said to have truly differed from Gorbachev's? Being an amateur, I can practically tell no difference between the foreign policies of Yeltsin and Gorbachev.

KOZYREV: We put the question in a new way. We wanted—and Yeltsin fully supported this—to shift from détente between adversaries to a partnership of allies.

AVEN: Do you think that Gorbachev and Soviet Minister of Foreign Affairs Alexander Bessmertnykh (and before him Shevardnadze) had no such goal?

KOZYREV: Never. Gorbachev had no such goal; nor did Bessmertnykh, naturally.

AVEN: You're expressing two completely different positions. The first is that we are enemies but we try to coexist peacefully, and the second is that we are friends and we are trying to become a part of your world. That is a fundamental turn. How was it manifested—in what practical steps?

KOZYREV: The implementation of any policy takes time. The most representative case was that of so-called "mutual assured destruction"—of all those nuclear missiles built by the Soviet Union, America, NATO. Present-day Russia and America may annihilate each other at any moment. That is what the world is built on: we presume they can and even want to attack us, and they presume the same about us. In order not to make that happen, one needs to be sure of being able to destroy the other side, and rather quickly, under any circumstances. It's about the missile defense issue; disagreements persist, as we all know.

Our logic was very simple: Russia remained a nuclear power—that was normal and good, but you can be a nuclear power like, for instance, France, which also has nuclear missiles but does not aim at the assured destruction of America. It doesn't think this way at all. For France, nuclear weapons are simply a question of defense against everyone. Whoever attacks will get it. Having just a few bombs is enough to keep everybody off. So why don't we take the same strategic position as France or the UK? Even China doesn't have the goal of building an arsenal sufficient for destroying the United States under any circumstances.

That was the most typical remnant of the Cold War, a confrontation between two systems, and we wanted to get rid of it. First of all, we had to be rid of it ideologically. I was the first to say it; then Yeltsin started saying that the United States and NATO were not our potential enemies but allies; and then we signed the Charter for American–Russian Partnership and Friendship in Washington, in summer 1992, and both sides adopted that statement. We simultaneously worked on a START treaty, which was supposed to minimize the confrontation. It was impossible to remove everything at once.

KOKH: Now wait, Andrei, all you said is just the continuation of Gorbachev's tradition. It's peaceful coexistence. But where is the new trend?

AVEN: Did you move beyond Gorbachev in disarmament?

KOZYREV: Much further. But there were other things we did not have time to finish.

KOKH: So that was not a fundamental breakthrough. The integration phase was supposed to begin later.

KOZYREV: The fundamental breakthrough also implied accession to all international organizations, from the World Bank to the IMF. We did that. We tried to join every organization possible.

KOKH: I remember the IMF had a Soviet observer.

KOZYREV: I'm not saying we took a different direction; certainly it was a continuation. There was an attempt to do it all more radically, and also to do, eventually, what Gorbachev had not wanted to do.

AVEN: You think Gorbachev was still an adversary in the eyes of the West? As the West was in his eyes?

KOZYREV: Yes, certainly. He said recently that Kozyrev's Foreign Ministry was a branch of the Department of State. Meaning that we could never take positions as a part of the West, or as allies.

KOKH: Was Yeltsin an adversary of the West?

KOZYREV: Not at that moment.

AVEN: Am I right in assuming that economic deficiencies had no great significance for Yeltsin and you? That is, you were acting out of ideological considerations, and not because you couldn't afford a different policy?

KOZYREV: Yes, that's absolutely true.

KOKH: Do you mean, for example, the withdrawal from the Vietnamese base?

AVEN: From Yemeni Socotra, and from Cuba. Lourdes and Cam Ranh did not fit the Kozyrev doctrine.

KOZYREV: We repudiated our "old friends," stopped supporting the Syrians; but I wanted to keep Cam Ranh as a base for rest and repairs. It was abandoned after my office ended.

AVEN: So it wasn't about money? I have always thought we simply had nothing to pay for all that.

KOZYREV: You know better about the money. But, for instance, there were never money problems with the nuclear arsenal. In 1992 there was no worry about losing all of that—they were under control and in our hands. The nuclear arsenal created to destroy the enemy was located in four republics:

the RSFSR, Kazakhstan, Belarus, and Ukraine.

Kazakhstan and Ukraine had very serious missiles, SS-18 Satans. Those were heavy missiles with multiple warheads, and each was capable of carrying up to 12 individually targeted and extremely powerful payloads. Actually, one missile was sufficient for doing away with the United States—and we had hundreds of them. Yet an interesting question pops up under these circumstances. We wanted only Russia to keep nuclear weapons. The Ukrainians and the Kazakhs had a different view, which was based on international law. By international law, the disintegration of any state makes all of its parts its legal successors; they must convene an international conference with third states to share the legacy. That is the essential approach, and we adhered to it, because otherwise you would be stuck forever: you keep what's on your territory, and the other keeps what's on its territory. External obligations are shared in a different way. Depending on economic factors, contribution …

KOKH: And population?

KOZYREV: Yegor thought so, yes. I don't know. Did Petr take part in that?

AVEN: I did.

KOZYREV: So, nuclear weapons are an asset, just like anything else, and they were left on the territories of Kazakhstan, Ukraine, and Belarus. After Chernobyl, the Belarusians said they didn't want any nuclear weapons on their territory. There were practically no arguments with them over nuclear weapons. The others felt differently.

We spent three years settling that question. We talked Nazarbayev into it in 1992. Ukraine gave up last, and the final document—as Professor Preobrazhensky put it in *Heart of a Dog*, "the real document"—was signed only in 1994. It was signed by Yeltsin, Kravchuk, and Clinton in Moscow. This is an example of the Western attitude. In nuclear arms issues, their attitude was definitely that of a partner. Yet they could have blackmailed the potential enemy.

THE ATTITUDE OF THE WEST

AVEN: For purely rational reasons, it would have been better for the Americans to concentrate all the arms in Russia. It's impossible to control many countries, and it's hard to reach agreement with a large number of states. I think they helped by persuading Ukraine and Kazakhstan.

KOZYREV: It wasn't exactly persuasion.

AVEN: They pushed them—I understand. But I think there's nothing friendly about that. It was a very rational political decision. It is better to deal with one than with one plus three others. I think that was the reason. In fact, for us, the Gaidar team, the absence of real assistance from the West was shocking, no matter what the communists and other vicious critics of ours may write today. We thought that we, the first pro-Western government in Russia in decades, would have access to diverse economic support: IMF loans, written-off debts, and so on. But all we had after a year was $1 billion and, with great effort, a reasonable rescheduling of foreign debts. That was it.

KOZYREV: That's true.

AVEN: It seemed to me they were personally much more comfortable dealing with the Gorbachev people, who were about the same age and had experience. Bessmertnykh was much more understandable to them than you, Andrei. They understand him well—they know him. He is a reputable person, not a boy; there's a certain history of relationships and trust.

KOZYREV: Western leaders were strongly opposed to the disintegration of the Soviet Union.

AVEN: Andrei, your ideas look somewhat naive to me. Obviously the problem exists on both sides—it exists in Russia; but the West was and is in no hurry to integrate us, even just economically. Understanding that came as a big disappointment to us. We realized it quickly. We realized that our professor friends, like Jeff Sachs and Stanley Fischer, wanted to help us very much. But the Western bureaucrats didn't. Bureaucrats knew how to deal with the USSR, and they had no idea what was going on here, and didn't give a damn about us and our change in the paradigm "from confrontation to integration." Did they think better of Yeltsin than they did of Gorbachev? No.

KOZYREV: That came later. First, they were accustomed to Gorbachev; and second, a peaceful, calmer, more normal and sane adversary is psychologically more convenient to deal with at the transitional moment in a crisis (which, they realized, would stretch out for a long time) than a new and difficult ally. It's true that I, as foreign minister, convinced Yeltsin to integrate and to be an ally of the West, rather than to hold a pistol. But we had a long road to go from point A to point B.

AVEN: Correct—they hadn't had time to develop confidence in our turnaround.

KOZYREV: We weren't homogenous. The country didn't change with the appearance of this foreign minister, this prime minister (such as Gaidar—we had a detailed discussion of that with Gaidar), and another 15 good ministers. Missiles were still in their silos. It takes a certain time to travel from the moment when Aven decided to open a bank to the moment when that bank could have an IPO. No matter what you say, even Aven cannot do that in one day.

AVEN: I agree.

KOZYREV: And it takes lots and lots of effort. Even if you work in an emergency regimen, I think the process will take several years. As far as I can tell, that requires audit, international accounting standards, and a couple of years to make sure that our accounting statements are something real, not just digits on paper.

It's absolutely the same for a country. The most primitive audit done before 1993 would have shown that the country did not have a new constitution or a normal separation of powers: the congress had turned into a reactionary force that changed the constitution any way it liked; the privatization program was announced but not yet started; and all the transformations were a mere declaration, but the reality was a far cry from that. I wonder who would have given a loan to Alfa-Bank without an audit when there wasn't even a hint of international accounting, and when Ruslan Imranovich Khasbulatov, the chairman of the board, said, "Who is that boy in short pants? We'll kick him the hell out of the bank tomorrow." Do you think anyone would give it a loan, or open a credit line?

AVEN: Sounds convincing.

KOKH: Totally unconvincing.

KOZYREV: Why? Because Western banks hate Russia? No. Why wouldn't the West be happy to see a normal Russia? After World War II, America occupied and in fact freed Europe, but allowed Germany to become a real rival—an absolutely independent country; allowed France to make an atomic bomb; allowed the UK to make an atomic bomb. Why wouldn't they be happy with the appearance of, say, a new Canada?

I saw the situation very simply. If we were lucky, and managed to do something right, we could become a new Canada. You can't get rid of dependence on resources—but you can be a Canada or a Venezuela.

KOKH: Gorbachev told me something interesting—he felt he could get anything he wanted from the West in 1988–9. But as we became weaker, economically in particular, the tone they used with him got tougher. New conditions kept being added, and a final decision on every bit of assistance was delayed. I think Gorbachev's viewpoint has its merits. They wanted to integrate us while we were strong, and once we grew weak they became indifferent to us and simply wanted to do away with the danger. Once the danger was eliminated, they simply forgot that this country existed.

KOZYREV: The danger was not eliminated—that is just what Gorbachev thinks.

KOKH: Well, it was lowered significantly. Pakistan, India, and finally Israel also have bombs. That is a danger. But a quite tolerable one.

KOZYREV: No, these are different dangers. The Pakistani bomb was made to counterbalance India's. The Ukrainian one could have been used to counterbalance ours, especially if our patriots had made claims on the Crimea. That would have been a fine playing field for the United States if they had hated us.

KOKH: I say again that when you talk about having a new audit, and making sure about your clients' creditability, and so on, I can't get why we've been negotiating admission to the WTO for 18 years already. Ukraine was admitted within a year. Who held an audit there in the time of Yulia Tymoshenko? Who checked their competitiveness or solvency? Or the independence of their judicial system?

KOZYREV: WTO negotiations are not my area.

KOKH: Sure! Because that was and always will be an absolutely political decision.

AVEN: Alfred, you oversimplify the problem. Ukraine was much more willing to come to terms than us.

KOKH: The Baltic republics were admitted not only to NATO but also to the European Union, the WTO, and so on. Shall we conduct an audit of Latvia?

KOZYREV: They met their obligations.

KOKH: What did they meet? What did they promise? What were the Latvian banks doing? And, by the way, what are they doing now? They launder money, and everyone knows that, but nobody cares. Claims against us are endless—new claims replace the old ones. When I took part in the WTO negotiations 14 years ago, we were given a list of questions; we were told it was the final list.

AVEN: You are partly right. They demand much more from us than from the Baltic republics: that's a historical given. The reason is our bad credit history, and the attitude toward us really is more serious. They close their eyes to lots of things in the case of the Baltic republics; but not in our case. They have always considered Latvia, Lithuania, and Estonia as a part of the West—that's the difference.

KOKH: I think they have a very clear idea of the borders of the West, and Russia is not within them.

AVEN: Is Ukraine in?

KOKH: Ukraine is. And Turkey is.

KOZYREV: And why?

KOKH: I don't know.

KOZYREV: Because they hate the Russian people.

KOKH: I didn't say that.

KOZYREV: Is there anything else? Why, then? Is there an international conspiracy? Why do they treat us with prejudice?

AVEN: Andrei is saying a simple thing. The West has a bad experience of interaction with Russia. Without delving into the more distant past, Russia tried to become a part of the West in the early twentieth century, and for three or four years under Yeltsin and Kozyrev. Then we curtailed these attempts once again. So their prejudice and fear are only natural.

KOKH: I think totally new leaders are necessary in the West to overcome that prejudice—the stereotype that Russia is not the West—leaders with imagination and scale. Otherwise, any integration attempt by Russia will fail. You need a mind like that of Churchill, who saw an ally in Stalin. There are no such people. I can tell you, it was a big problem that Bush Senior—a man of experience and imagination, who actually made peace with China—was replaced by Clinton, a totally cynical, pragmatic, and petty person. He is a coward, too, who minds only his own business. Strobe Talbott, the man in charge of Russian affairs in the Clinton administration, is a banal and narrow-minded man of colossal self-importance and overconfidence.

KOZYREV: That's absolutely correct. Bush and Jim Baker, my first partner in America, understood the Soviet Union very well.

KOKH: Its scale—and the scale of the task of Russia's integration with the West, and the colossal gains for the whole world coming from this integration.

KOZYREV: Bush was CIA director and an ambassador to China—they knew us very well. They took care of Gorbachev like nannies during those last three years. They spoke every day—and Gorbachev is surprised that they stopped giving loans.

KOKH: They didn't give him any at all.

KOZYREV: Toward the end.

AVEN: Gorbachev created our foreign debt. It was not catastrophic, but, still, it was $100 billion. And he did nothing. When things are headed for collapse, how much money can one lend?

KOKH: Listen, if they had given us at least $50 billion in 1992, the Gaidar government would have survived, and that would have been much more beneficial to America. When Mexico fell into crisis in 1994, the West gave it $50 billion immediately.

AVEN: It's easy to lend money to a neighbor or a family member, but not to a little-known person who has also been your enemy for many years. The lending of $50 billion requires public support. American society didn't know us and feared us in 1992, as it still does—and so did American bureaucrats. So, no matter how great Bush might have been, it was simply impossible to give a serious loan. The Germans received unprecedented aid after the war—but they formally acknowledged their capitulation and started de-Nazification; and the new leader was Adenauer, who had spent time in a prison camp, and not the former first secretary of a Soviet Communist Party regional committee (Yeltsin). I would have liked to see them granting a Marshall Plan if Goering or Bormann had taken power in Germany. We didn't even condemn Bolshevism, either in 1992 or now. So any Marshall Plan was out of the question.

KOZYREV: I had a many-hour conversation with Baker in Brussels immediately after the putsch. I left the White House [in Moscow] on August 20, 1991, with the powers to create a government in exile, should it be necessary. Luckily, that didn't happen—but I met with Baker in Brussels. I told him, "The situation is very simple. It is the Cold War in reverse." Our conversation kept returning to Churchill, and I said, "We're waiting for Bush, or you, or I don't know who, to make a Fulton speech in reverse."

KOKH: The curtain being lifted?

KOZYREV: Yes. The Soviet Union disappears, and normal guys—good guys, fools, idiots, whoever—have come to power in Russia, and they want to be in the same place as you. You need to support them; there is a need for a new Marshall Plan. You just shut your eyes and give them money, political support, ideological support—full support. Lots of things happened after that conversation; and after the Belovezh deal was made, in December 1991, Baker spoke before the US Congress and said exactly that, word for word: "There was the Fulton speech, the declaration of the Cold War, and now I declare a crusade to help the democrats who took power in the former Soviet Union. Certainly we shall see how democratic they are and how their words comply with their deeds—but this is it, there will be assistance." We started the discussions—Yegor took part in them. That was a historic moment.

KOKH: Tell us the details.

HUMANITARIAN AID

KOZYREV: This is very important, because there is no anti-Russian conspiracy at all. One must understand what happened. We started working with Baker to at least put down the guns, to remove them from each other's temples. We started discussing what to do—to agree on lowering the threat level, and so on. Then we discussed aid. Baker flew in right after the Belovezh meeting, in mid-December. It was a horrible month in terms of all the work to be done with the former republics. Now Baker stomped in. He was totally out of place at that moment, because we had to deal with internal affairs. But there he was. He repeated every word he had said in America. Yeltsin brought Baker over to talk with us. We had no protocol—we improvised everything. We didn't have a normal government—nothing. Yegor was totally wrapped up in his business; we had a brief conversation on the run about Baker's speech. I had expected Yegor to approach Boris with the economic aid question beforehand. I never was a profound economist, but I assumed Yegor was handling it. I told him, "I will fully support you. If you want, I can go to Yeltsin myself." I had a much closer relationship with Yeltsin back then, and later on, too, so I often offered my help to Yegor. I told him, "Yegor, if you are unable to get through to him, you tell me what to say, and I'll memorize it and tell Yeltsin." Yegor said, "Okay, you briefly tell him to give me the floor." So we agreed. That was logical, because I could get something wrong, or Yeltsin could, and we'd end up with a mess. Logical and wonderful. But Baker went off to engage in complex diplomatic ballets with Gorbachev, who was still in the Kremlin.

KOKH: He hadn't given up the nuclear brief.

KOZYREV: It created all this confusion, and that left very little time for talking to Yeltsin. Yeltsin started talking rubbish—that he felt himself the complete master of the Kremlin, and so on. That's called small talk, which is essentially a normal part of diplomatic communication; but it simply left no time for the rest. It's unclear why Baker's conversation with Gorbachev took such a long time, as Gorbachev was no longer in office. Yeltsin was not quite in office, either, and in that total chaos Baker was trying to find out what we needed and what was going on. In short, our conversation ended when Baker finally led us to a serious conversation and a serious moment, and said clearly, concretely, directly: "Well, fellows"— addressing Yeltsin, naturally—"what is the top priority for our help? Clearly, we cannot do everything, we cannot give you billions, because there is the Congress, but we can do something; just tell us what you want." Yeltsin said, "Humanitarian aid." That was recorded.

KOKH: What can you say? That had scope!

KOZYREV: Yes, humanitarian aid. Baker asked, "Just to you?" Yeltsin answered, "Why, no! Humanitarian aid to Ukraine, to all the republics." Yegor and I nearly jumped out of our skins when he said that. I asked him, "Yegor, is that what you wanted?" He said, "No." I said, "Let Yegor talk." Yeltsin made a regal gesture indicating, "Who is this Yegor who will talk?" No one else could talk when he talked. So everyone got up and left. Baker left with my hat, which I had given him at the airport. It was freezing cold, and I gave him the beaver hat I'd bought at the special shop for Soviet Foreign Ministry staff. So he left to prepare humanitarian aid with my hat on his head. They declared the granting of humanitarian aid and convened the Lisbon conference—I think that was in May (very quickly, within five months)—and even more humanitarian aid than before started flowing in.

In Lisbon, we adopted a keynote declaration with Baker and Genscher; it was called KGB—Kozyrev, Genscher, Baker. It was on the nonproliferation of nuclear weapons, and stated that Russia would be the only nuclear power. That was the first time that Ukraine agreed to sign.

KOKH: Genscher? Why was that? Germany has no nuclear weapons.

KOZYREV: That's not the point; the Western heavyweights were pressuring Ukraine, and their pressure brought results. By agreement with Yegor, I told Baker in Lisbon, "Certainly Yeltsin told you about humanitarian aid. Certainly humanitarian aid is very important, but we need economic, not humanitarian, aid—what you said in your speech, so to say, a Marshall Plan. Where is that?" Baker said, "I get it, I know, you think I'm that stupid?" (We were on very good terms.) "We're working on that as well, but it's not that easy. It's a big package, and since he said 'humanitarian aid' we have to do that first." In other words, while we were dancing around humanitarian aid, Bush started experiencing serious internal problems in America. He was ideal for us, and Baker was ideal, but then came our friend Clinton, who didn't care about us at all. Russia was not on his horizon, nor was Europe or NATO. There was a slogan associated with Clinton: "It's the economy, stupid." It's the only thing Clinton cared about.

KOKH: Even that was not his concern; he only cared about himself.

KOZYREV: I agree.

AVEN: I can tell you that the personal intercession by Bush and his friend Robert Strauss, later ambassador to Moscow, was of fundamental help in our negotiations with the Paris Club. I will tell you more about it later. There was nothing like that in Clinton's era.

KOZYREV: We could do colossal things with Bush and Baker. Baker was a partner to Gaidar and me because he understood economics, he was the secretary of the treasury once. Baker became head of Bush's presidential campaign and left the post of secretary of state. It was clear that they would lose to Clinton, so they stopped talking about aid—they were too busy. So the incumbent administration went on the defensive in early summer 1992 and could do little for us, and then Clinton became president. He didn't care about Mexico or Canada—much less Russia, wherever the hell it was.

AVEN: I think you mentioned something fundamental. There was a bad credit history, and then changes began. We needed time to prove to ourselves and to them that Russia was really building a new life. Rapprochement is a two-way process. But then Kozyrev was replaced with Primakov—and Primakov didn't want to integrate with the West. The Marshall Plan was accompanied by de-Nazification of Germany and fundamental liberalization of the German economy. Without that, it is very difficult to hope for assistance.

KOKH: I fully agree with you, but I think these elements are intertwined. Say Erhard started liberal reforms and Adenauer began de-Nazification. And then imagine a change of administration in America and the absence of the Marshall Plan. Both Adenauer and Erhard would have failed.

INTERNAL CONTRADICTIONS

KOZYREV: Primakov replaced me in January 1996; before that he had headed the Foreign Intelligence Service and called himself a friend of Saddam Hussein. Can anyone presume that the American president and other Western leaders didn't know that the same people continued doing the same things in our intelligence service? So he sits there and knows that my agents, whether charming like Ms. [Anna] Chapman[2] or ugly, work against him. I come to him and say, "Bill, just stop paying attention to it. That is only

2. Arrested by the FBI in New York in 2010.

natural. Besides, I have my revolver pointed at you. I clean it every morning and load it every morning, but that doesn't matter either. Please give me a Marshall Plan."

KOKH: Andrei, that is not so. You could have come and said, "As you can see, there are two Russias. One Russia is represented by me, and the other cleans its revolver and does the subversive work."

KOZYREV: I represented the whole of Russia. I was the Russian foreign minister.

AVEN: Alfred, one must be very brave to bet on those who are unable to handle their own country.

KOKH: May I ask a question? Why was Primakov put in charge of the Foreign Intelligence Service?

KOZYREV: That was Yeltsin.

KOKH: You knew him well. Can you tell us why he did that?

KOZYREV: Why did Yeltsin do lots of things? Fire Gaidar—

AVEN: And then Kozyrev?

KOKH: Let's suppose that Gaidar was his compromise with the congress, but Primakov wasn't even a question.

KOZYREV: He didn't have to make the Gaidar compromise at the congress. I'm absolutely positive about that. I said so to Yeltsin.

AVEN: Certainly he could have kept Gaidar, no matter what the congress said.

KOKH: Then why did he give him up?

KOZYREV: That man, a regional party committee secretary, came to America and saw a supermarket; and then people came to him from Democratic Russia, people such as Sakharov, Burbulis, Gaidar, Kozyrev, and so on, and that democratic riffraff told him all this stuff. He honestly believed it at that moment. Certainly it was an instrument of struggle against Gorbachev.

KOKH: Decide which you mean: either he honestly believed it, or it was an instrument.

KOZYREV: It was both. There was an element of honesty; and then he became a tsar and fought the Supreme Soviet. He also needed it because democracy was a banner, although Gaidar irritated him, and I—although we were very close for a long time—irritated him.

KOKH: You didn't fit his idea of a civil servant.

KOZYREV: We were simply people with two different circulatory systems.

AVEN: And how did you cope with the alcohol?

KOZYREV: Just as badly. I just can't do it, and it's obvious—you can't hide it. Do what you can; but if you skip drinks, after the first or second round you stand out, you don't belong. This is meant to be a party, fun—correct? Everyone is having fun, and one person is clearly uneasy and clearly skips drinks.

KOKH: He's not at ease with us.

KOZYREV: He's not at ease—he's faking it. Is that normal? No.

AVEN: That was what I said about myself.

KOZYREV: That was an important circumstance, too. Clinton, who didn't care—at least at the start—took office, and then Ruslan Imranovich Khasbulatov decided to play an active game. Plus there were personal factors, and I was the next to share Gaidar's lot. The only reason I stayed during the congress was the number I pulled in Stockholm. That was it.

KOKH: What number was that?

KOZYREV: I went to Stockholm for an OSCE conference, which was during our Seventh Congress. I wrote my speech while on the plane on the basis of an article by our friends from the very moderate opposition, based on the Civil Union program. I copied an extract and read it out as if it were my speech, without giving any explanation. Before that I agreed with the council chairperson, a Swedish woman, that I would take the floor twice. My first speech would be very short, but I also wanted to take the floor again, about 40 minutes later, although that was inconsistent with the general procedure. So she allowed me to speak again, about 40 minutes later. The first time I read the two paragraphs from the Civil Union program. It almost triggered a Cold War. The media were agitated.

KOKH: What exactly did you say?

KOZYREV: I said a very simple thing, which is now the official policy: that NATO and Russia are not on the same path. Not that we are enemies—but we don't need them, or the West. As for the former socialist camp, particularly the CIS, this is our sphere of influence, and we would like them to keep from sticking their noses in there. I said it in an extremely polite way. Just two points.

KOKH: And who liked it? Yeltsin or the congress?

KOZYREV: Nobody liked it. It caused an explosion of fear in the world.

AVEN: It was hard for Yeltsin to fire you after that.

KOZYREV: You are absolutely right. And I waited for 40 minutes, until the temperature reached practically 40 degrees centigrade, and then I said in my second appearance, "That"— my first speech—"shows what it would have been like if the opposition, specifically the moderate opposition, had won at the congress. But since the moderate opposition did not win, I will tell you what I really have to say, and what really represents the opinion of the Russian government and the president." They took it as an act of hooliganism, but, first of all, I wanted to wake up the West, including Clinton. Second, I wanted to put Yeltsin in a position where he would have to say very simply: "No, we are not taking this turn." Really, he was pressed from every side—correspondents besieged the Kremlin, ambassadors, and all that Western mercenary imperialistic pack with questions, and certainly our reporters were there, too: "Yeltsin, what Kozyrev said first—is there really such a turn?" He said, "Kozyrev is panicking. Nothing of the sort is happening. Where did he get that? The policy is unchanged." That is what I needed: "The policy is unchanged." "And why did you dismiss Gaidar?" Gaidar was dismissed that very day. He said, "Gaidar is dismissed, but the economic policy will not change, either. Nothing will change." I hoped my action would save everyone, save everything, and not just force Yeltsin into justifying himself.

KOKH: Judging by what you say, Yeltsin had no firm political convictions. Or did he have any? Chubais thinks that Yeltsin was a man standing with one foot in the old world and the other in the new world, and that he was sincere about both new and old. Seryozha Shakhrai thinks that he used the new rhetoric only as a way to take and keep power.

AVEN: There is one more reasonable point of view, in my opinion. Yeltsin had no considered ideological preferences (neither in the economy nor in foreign policy), but he believed in democracy. Despite his authoritarian urges, he had profound democratic instincts. That's why he didn't limit media criticism of the regime and of himself; that's why he listened so intently to the Congress of People's Deputies. It was *vox populi* for him. The people didn't want Gaidar, and he was ready to dismiss Gaidar even if he disagreed. When the people didn't want him, he listened less attentively— but in everything except personal power he was prepared to listen to the opinion of the people.

KOZYREV: I agree, to an extent.

KOKH: And I do not. I think Yeltsin didn't want Yegor.

AVEN: To continue: the people were not prepared for the turn in foreign policy Andrei is speaking about. The army was not prepared, because every military unit had a poster depicting the potential enemy—the United States and NATO. Intelligence agents and diplomats were not prepared. Alfred and I have said many times that there was no change in Russia's elite. You, Andrei, were ahead of your time. The backlash was inevitable. It could have been avoided only if Yeltsin had firmly and sincerely shared your convictions. But he didn't believe in them, and listened to the "people."

KOZYREV: I think everyone here is right—Chubais, Shakhrai, and Petr. Speaking of Yeltsin, it is important to distinguish between periods. Seryozha is right to say that, starting in 1994, Yeltsin fully concentrated on his hold on power and switched to a wholly opportunistic policy; then the bureaucratic revenge came. But it was not so in 1991 or, partially, 1992.

Yeltsin underwent a major internal evolution—he started to enjoy power. He originally had a sincere desire for change, but the elite didn't share it. There were either politically neutral people or people from the past, such as Primakov. The *siloviki* were mostly absolutely neutral, brave, and personally rather good people, but not equipped with ideology or understanding of what needed to be reformed. That was wrong in the revolutionary situation. Leaders must be prepared ideologically and politically. Deputies and staff don't need to be—you can have military specialists, but the leader must have a political turn of mind, like Trotsky. And you needed a party from which commissars can be recruited to supervise the military specialists. Yeltsin had no party.

KOKH: And he deliberately refused to build one.

HOT SPOTS

KOZYREV: Since the *siloviki* did not understand what to do, I had to stay in touch with the military and visit hot spots—Transdniestria, Tajikistan, Karabakh. I had to personally convince the border guards on the Afghan–Tajik border that the border must be protected. I came almost monthly and told them, "You are protecting Russia." They were just Soviet troops, and we told them they had become Russian.

I flew to those places because I thought that the border guards needed that, and so that they and the rest of the army saw that Kozyrev, although some claimed he was an American emissary, was not afraid: "He comes under fire together with us." If the border had been opened during a civil war moment, they would have crushed us here, because millions of refugees from Tajikistan would have come to Russia. And who would follow? Uzbekistan, and then all the other places, because there were no borders. Those new states were even weaker than us at that moment. The only stronghold of greater or lesser stability during the first few months was Turkmenbashi, who had become a dictator very quickly and enforced peace and quiet at home; and then Islam Karimov did the same in Uzbekistan. When our human rights activists (and the liberals in the West) started pecking at us for supporting dictators—and they were dictators, of course; they had taken that path—I thanked God that at least Uzbekistan and Turkmenistan were under some sort of control. When I went there, there was some sense of civilization. People walked down the street, and I did not expect all those people—the Russians, the Uzbeks, who had the same Soviet passports as us—would show up in Moscow tomorrow as refugees, and then a civil war would break out throughout the Union. Then I met a state farm director in Tajikistan. His name was Emomali Rahmonov. He was a political figure to an extent; he had populist ideas—although, to be frank, just one gang supported him. In short, people supported him, and things started to settle down with our assistance.

AVEN: There were proposals to interfere in the affairs of the republics more actively—not just protect the border, but also use our troops in internal conflicts. You were categorically opposed. Tell us about it.

KOZYREV: In the Supreme Soviet they started saying in April 1992 that force should be used, and not only in Tajikistan (remember Rutskoi and company). We were on the brink of practically the Yugoslav scenario through all of 1992—that is, the use of force against the republics, or, actually, a war in the former Soviet Union. I flew to various hot spots to say, "Yes, I am against starting a war by the Milošević scenario"—that is, I do not want Russia to use military force to try to take control over, say, the Crimea.

KOKH: Was there such an intention?

KOZYREV: Yes—the Moscow mayor who was in favor of the Crimea proposal.

KOKH: That was just idle talk.

KOZYREV: That was very dangerous idle talk. Remember, Rutskoi, an Afghan War hero, was vice president.

KOKH: And what did he say?

KOZYREV: For instance, he planned to bomb Georgia. Here is a striking episode. While I was hanging around in Tajikistan, I heard the radio in some village square (I had no phone, no communications) tuned to Mayak, which was reporting that Rutskoi was visiting Transdniestria, and they gave a piece of his speech. He addressed a huge crowd, according to the radio—this was where the officers of Lebed's Fourteenth Army were stationed—and essentially said it was a stupid idea to break up the Soviet Union, and it should now be restored. That meant, "Officers, go into Chisinau and start putting things in order." That was exactly what Milošević did: "The hell with sovereignty. There is great Serbia. There is great Yugoslavia. Our tanks will restore it. Move on."

I kept a close eye on the Yugoslav situation; it was a nightmare haunting me. I realized that we could fall into a similar situation any day, and that it would happen unnoticed—it would have just started in one place, and that would have been it. The Yugoslav people's army was subordinated to Belgrade, and army units were in the republics. There was no need for an intervention—they were already there. The question was, "Will they intervene or not? And which side will they take?" As soon as they get involved, then bandits of all kinds will get involved, too, and here is the Yugoslavian situation. A bloodbath. Under our circumstances, a nuclear war. Tactical nuclear weapons were everywhere—actually, no one could say exactly where they were and where they were not. Yugoslavia would have looked like a kindergarten compared to what might happen in our country.

So, Rutskoi makes his speech. I use a phone booth to call Yeltsin in Moscow and tell him, "Here is the situation." "So what?" he said. "What do you mean, so what? It means war!" Meanwhile, the Supreme Soviet is discussing the need to take the Crimea. Certainly Ukraine will take that as our first step in a military campaign. That was the purely Yugoslav scenario. It would start in some district and then spread everywhere. He listened to me and said, "Yes, you are right. What would you propose?" "What would I propose? Recall Rutskoi!" "How can I recall Rutskoi? I did not send him there." That was not true; he had, I later learned. He gave him spoken permission. Rutskoi caught him in a hallway and said, "I will go there to put things right." Yeltsin said, "Go," because he wanted Rutskoi to leave. And certainly they didn't discuss the political position—they discussed nothing. Yeltsin and I agreed to the main elements—that is, that the army must not interfere under any circumstances, that the army must be neutral, and that the maximum the army could do—and what we would like it to do—is to become a peacekeeper, to take positions between the conflicting sides, as in Tajikistan, and give shelter to refugees. But there must be no campaigns in Chisinau or anywhere else. The Chisinau campaign was viewed as just the first step. So I boarded my Tu-135 and flew with stopovers for refueling, and so on, dropping everything in Tajikistan, and I flew to, what do you call it—

KOKH: To Tiraspol.

KOZYREV: To Chisinau, because it was hard to land in Tiraspol—there were hostilities there or something. So I came to Chisinau and talked to President Mircea Snegur, and I told him, "We're not going to conquer you, naturally, and I'm going to put a stop to all this now, but you must stop your bandits, too. You probably don't have complete control, but you must pull out your forces, otherwise I can't guarantee anything." He ran off somewhere to deal with it. It's not that he changed his political views, but they at least pulled out the police units from there. So I took a helicopter to Tiraspol.

They were waiting for me. Rutskoi had left only a few hours earlier. They gathered a rally, similar to the one Rutskoi had addressed—about 3,000 people, mostly women. The women were aged from 25 to 55, and their dema-goguery was tough: "Rutskoi is a fine guy, but who are you?" He dispar-aged the government—including, naturally, Gaidar and all of you—and the foreign minister who sold God-knows-what to the Americans. My body-guards, only five or six men, came to me and said, "We should leave—we are unable to protect you from that crowd. What can we do? Even if we start shooting, that would be senseless because they would simply crush us."

I disembarked from the helicopter, and there was that crowd with red flags, aggressive and warmed up, and probably drunk, and what was I to do—should I go back? I say, "You people do not have to come with me, because, naturally, you are unable to help me. I will be sorry if they beat you or kill you." I go straight into the crowd and say, "Where is the stage? Let me say a word." I climb to the stage, where some woman is demonstrating against the traitors in Moscow. How could I explain the Yugoslav scenario? I just said, "You know, women"—most of the people here were women, although there were a number of our military men in the crowd, blending in—"raise your hands if you are ready to send your children to a civil war." Somehow that had an effect. I do not know what gave me the idea—I just blurted it out. And they were at a loss. Luckily, a woman suddenly jumped up and said, "He's right, you know. Just think what we are shouting about here? Do we want war?" And the heat was gone—they calmed down.

That was the expression of the public mood in a conflict zone: on the one hand, the people are aggressive, and on the other hand, they listen and can be talked to. They held an officers' meeting three hours later. Lebed was in Moscow at the time, intriguing against Pasha Grachev. I must have been lucky or something, but probably, if Lebed had been there, there would not have been such chaos; I mean, the army was not controllable at that moment. I entered and they lazily stood up—although the commander, Lebed's deputy, ordered them: "Stand up!" They stood up either to greet me or to follow his order, but the discipline was half lost. And we also had a meeting, a conversation of several hours—and there we saw another mood, that of military professionals: colonels, majors, even generals, were repre-sentatives of the people and the army. We started our talk. The questions were aggressive, and I explained about Yugoslavia. It all lasted for several hours. People were able to listen—they needed to have these explanations, they had to be spoken to. They had listened to Rutskoi and supported him; they were preparing to start their campaign. They listened to me, and they cancelled their decisions; they adopted a resolution, and the peacekeeping mission of the Fourteenth Army started at that moment. It was a decision of the officers' meeting—not to engage in the conflict, not to side with the demagogues from the Russian-speaking population although the officers were ethnic Russian; and that was a colossal decision for them. Here was a real situation—there were really casualties there. There were bandits on both sides, and atrocities, because the ethnic dimension was strong. But they understood—they gained control of themselves, they put things in order, they adopted a resolution not to get involved, but to protect the civilian population and perform the peacekeeping mission.

I left them in a calm state. I knew that the army would not move on anything; but if it had, I would not be here now talking with you. I think history would have been different. The civil war Russia suffered once would have looked like child's play.

KOKH: Child's play?

KOZYREV: Yes, child's play. Although they buried people alive, there were no nuclear power plants, nuclear weapons, or chemical weapons all over the country.

CIS AND NATO

AVEN: There are people who think that Yeltsin could have raised the Crimea issue in Bela Vezha. Kravchuk was prepared to discuss it.

KOZYREV: No—if he had even mentioned that, there would have been no CIS. It was hopeless to try to discuss the Crimea. And everyone has forgotten that we managed to sign the CIS document, which Gaidar and I—two lousy intellectuals—wrote all night. Just three pages, but those three pages say a lot: the absence of borders for citizens, a common economic area, a common army, and so on.

AVEN: That did not happen.

KOZYREV: Some of that did not happen, but it is a fact that we not only broke up peacefully but also immediately laid down the idea of, at least, cooperation, a certain rapprochement, integration—that was very important, because the republics not only avoided a war, but also continued the dialogue, which was held in the context of the CIS agreement. It's a shame the creation of the CIS is underestimated.

AVEN: Now say a few words about your position on relations with NATO. As far as I understand, NATO and Yugoslavia are the two most sensitive subjects, on which your enemies attacked you and over which you had the biggest altercations with Yeltsin.

KOZYREV: NATO is a fundamental issue. I thought that NATO was our potential ally. What is NATO? That is London, Paris, Madrid. If this bloc is inherently hostile to us, then it's over—just turn off the lights. I didn't raise the question of Russia's accession to NATO, because that was as unrealistic as the building of communism (although some hotheads here wanted that). But we can and should have amicable, partner, or maybe even allied relations with NATO.

KOKH: And what about the admission of new members to NATO?

KOZYREV: I have always opposed the accelerated, too rapid expansion of NATO. I thought we should first build a new relationship with NATO, and then they might start the expansion. But I didn't mind their expansion as such—it would have been absurd to oppose that. NATO cannot reject Poland if it wants to be a member.

KOKH: We signed papers to declare that there would be no eastward expansion of NATO.

KOZYREV: Who? With whom?

KOKH: Bush and us.

KOZYREV: No one made such commitments, ever.

AVEN: There were verbal assurances.

KOZYREV: The most they could have said was, "We have no such plans so far." There were no legally binding documents.

AVEN: And yet by 1995 our official position had slid down to being against any expansion of NATO (which was stupid because we could not influence that). NATO was declared an enemy again, and you were gone.

KOZYREV: Yes. Concerning the rapid enlargement of NATO, I said publicly,

"That is a mistake of the partner." I also told Yeltsin that harboring Yugoslavian criminals, if they were Serbs, was our temporary mistake that would pass, while NATO was a fundamental mistake—a mistake in our policy.

RESIGNATION

AVEN: To a certain extent, your resignation was more significant than the dismissal of Gaidar. It meant a real change in foreign policy, although some integration with the West continued. In the case of Gaidar, no one retracted fundamental things—liberalized foreign trade, unregulated prices, the convertible ruble. The reforms slowed down, but there was no drastic reversal.

And now let me recall some personal information. You were 39 when you became minister.

KOZYREV: I was 44 when I retired.

AVEN: And in fact you were banned from practicing your profession. How did you handle it? It killed Gaidar. Alfred and I found an occupation for ourselves—we make money and interview people. How was it for you?

KOZYREV: Very hard. I am really a career diplomat, and I have done nothing else in my life. I did, however, run for the State Duma in 1995, and spoke to Yeltsin in September. I was loyal to him, but I said, "I don't want to participate in the realization of the 'new course.' I think that is your personal mistake, that you are obliterating your historical role. It's a colossal mistake for the country, a fatal mistake, and I don't want to be part of it. I'm going to Murmansk to run in the elections there. Here is my request; by law you have to give me six days off." According to the constitution, you can't combine being a deputy and being a minister. Yeltsin said, "Let me think." He thought for a week, and in a week's time I had to start my election campaign. Yeltsin wouldn't respond, so I called Ilyushin. "You have a green light—go ahead and work on the election." Basically, that was the decision on the question of my leaving. Officially, he released me only on January 5, 1996. Before that I had been in the elections, gone on vacation, and was no longer working, but I was still considered a minister. On January 5 he called and said, "I guess you're right. Let's stay friends, and so on." I practically leaped out of my chair. It may not have been very nice, but I shouted into the telephone, "Thanks a lot!"

KOKH: And then?

KOZYREV: I was completely isolated in the State Duma. I tried to do something for my district, but couldn't do much. I was suffering for four years, then quit and was offered a job in an international pharmaceutical corporation. I embarked on self-education. So now I do business—I'm gradually figuring it out.

AVEN: When we were looking for you, Andrei, we couldn't get your phone number at Lavrov's liaison office, or from Igor Ivanov, or any of your former colleagues. Are you out of touch? Why?

KOZYREV: The reason is ideological, as far as I understand. They don't feel comfortable communicating with me officially. They were my deputies—we worked together. But after I left they shifted to a different course, which closely resembled the old one. At first they followed Primakov, without any essential change of policy afterward. The Foreign Ministry is essentially a non-ideological organization. When I worked there I believed that 15 percent of my colleagues fully supported me, 15 percent were ideological enemies, and 70 percent were mere technocrats, professionals. My former deputies are future ministers, outstanding specialists. But this new–old course is what separates us ideologically. It's nothing personal.

9

SERGEI SHAKHRAI

"Those Events Made Yeltsin More Isolated, Angry, and Vindictive"

LIKE ANDREI KOZYREV, SERGEI SHAKHRAI was not a member of the Gaidar team. He had begun engaging in public politics 18 months earlier than we did, and had developed into a "political heavyweight"—a popular phrase now—by November 1991. That circumstance created an initial atmosphere of mistrust between him and the team. He was suspected of being Yeltsin's "eye," and certainly the presidential distrust was insulting and painful. I think Yegor felt it most of all.

But there is something else that's hard to define. Before, I used to think that the atmosphere of your youth—music, books, events, and idols of school and college years—made you a member of an unspoken fraternity of people of the same circle and of the same generation. If that were so, it would have been easier to explain the team spirit and solidarity with Sergei that was rooted in the sense of belonging to the virtual order of the people of the 1970s. It seemed to me then that being born in 1956 and graduating from Moscow State University were sufficient to develop bonds of friendship. But experience showed there was no such fraternity, and people who grew up listening to Deep Purple could easily betray the celebrated "ideals of youth."

Apparently both the horizontal bond between people of the same generation and the vertical bond with parents are important. Your roots, your ancestors, your kinship matter. Shakhrai had the right roots: the roots of a Cossack and the roots of a soldier.

Motivation was even more important. Sergei's readiness to move to the background for the benefit of the cause appealed to me strongly. It was the feature that made him akin to Chubais and, primarily, to Gaidar. All of us have a certain degree of vanity. Neither Petr nor I am an exception. But we were always ready to play for the team and to behold a nobody basking in the sun of glory (which should rightly belong to us). We thought we could disregard our ambitions for the benefit of the cause. Maybe we were wrong.

In any case, those features made Sergei much closer to the Gaidar team than any of Yeltsin's old apparatchiks. The obvious became clear slowly: he—and, in fact, all of us—had nothing in common with that group of respectable and quite meaningless old men. They hated him and branded him a parvenu, and they felt the same way about us. None of us ever learned to drink with them.

Being a career lawyer (while we were economists), he knew more about psychology than any of us. He had a keener feeling about people's motivations and reactions. Probably that was why he was less radical than many of us. But every time Yeltsin found it difficult to cope with a problem, he passed it along to Gaidar, Chubais, or Shakhrai. That happened, for instance, during the Ossetian–Ingush conflict. His first impulse was to give the mission to the "experienced manufacturer" Khizha. But Khizha failed, and it turned out that the younger could be much more useful than the impotent elders.

Sergei had so many ups and downs that he must have lost track of whether he was in favor or an outcast. When he wasn't needed, the Kremlin forgot about him, and then called for him again as soon as they needed a constitution. "Where is Shakhrai? Bring him here at the double. You sit down and write." Gaidar told me once that he had counted 16 ups and downs in his career. And every time he came to a meeting he saw his status immediately. Whenever people greet you cheerfully, surround you, and ask you about your family, you are up. Whenever there is an empty circle two meters in diameter around you in a crowded room, you are down: you are a shot-down pilot, you are a loser.

Sergei had even more ups and downs than Yegor. Thus his wisdom is hard-earned. Socrates said once, "By all means marry. If you get a good wife, you'll be happy; if you get a bad one, you'll become a philosopher." The same principle applies to the civil service. Any successful courtier bores me. He is intellectually meek, and the success makes him a primitive obscurantist. A person who has had his share of ups and downs is different. Such an interlocutor knows more about people, about high splendor and about nasty meanness, about fear and about cowardice, about courage and about fortitude. He knows more about life—and more about death. It is more interesting to deal with him, and there are more things to learn from him.

Alfred Kokh

ALFRED KOKH: Petr and I are writing a book. We agreed originally to write a book about Gaidar. But, as often happens in real life, it has gone beyond Yegor's formal government work, and we have touched upon some earlier events.

We have inevitably touched upon later events, too, such as the putsch of 1993 and the First Chechen War. We have not taken a look into Yeltsin's second presidential term. Gaidar's trail is less visible there, so to speak, although we did touch on the election of 1996. And we have not probed a more distant period, of the stagnation before Gorbachev.

PETR AVEN: We have mostly spoken with economists, with the exception of Gena Burbulis, who was an exclusively political figure. We are interested in you and Gena as non-members of the Gaidar team. We are interested in an outside view of the Gaidar team. Why and how did it come into existence? What did it do?

Besides, you undoubtedly played a fundamental role in the Belovezh events, the constitutional process. It is of paramount importance to remember these events now.

KOKH: How did you become acquainted with Yeltsin, and how did your relations develop?

PARLIAMENT WORK

SERGEI SHAKHRAI: I saw Yeltsin at the First Congress of Russian Deputies, but we didn't meet then.

KOKH: Was it in summer 1990?

SHAKHRAI: It was still spring; the First Congress opened on May 16.

AVEN: Who elected you?

SHAKHRAI: The Moscow region, the tenth national territorial district, approximately 1.35 million voters. That election was held in territorial districts with no more than 450,000–500,000 voters, and in national territorial districts with one million voters on average. I got the biggest district. It included all towns of the Moscow region. I could not understand what it was for a long time—a bagel, territories around Moscow but excluding Moscow. And it was the line of defense—the locations of military units.

And air defense commander General Vladimir Vasilyevich Litvinov was supposed to become their deputy. Naturally, we were not admitted to the premises of military units to do our canvassing. We had to climb over the fence to get inside garrisons.

AVEN: Who were your other rivals?

SHAKHRAI: Alevtina Fedulova, the former number one Soviet Pioneer, and a couple of astronauts. A celebrated athlete, the weightlifter Vlasov. In fact, I had 16 rivals.

AVEN: They didn't expect you to win, did they?

SHAKHRAI: Probably I didn't expect that myself. I was nominated by Kaliningrad, now Korolyov—the location of the Strela, Kompomash, and Energomash defense plants. I visited that town to deliver lectures to the Knowledge Society, and they knew me there for a couple of years as a pedagogue of Moscow University's Department of Law. Researchers at those plants had a scientific approach. They made a list of 26 candidates and held a number of meetings in huge rooms attended by 1,500 people. There were direct debates, actually the first primaries à la russe. And I made the short list.

KOKH: Did the defense plants outnumber the soldiers?

SHAKHRAI: They did. I took part in the runoff election and became a deputy. I didn't know Yeltsin or Democratic Russia before my election. And then my skills appeared to be in demand. I was a lawyer with a professional knowledge of parliaments, including parliaments of federative states. Second, I was an expert who developed an electronic ballot system at the Soviet Supreme Council for Anatoly Ivanovich Lukyanov. Actually, it was not I who developed it—computer programmers did that, and I wrote the algorithm because I knew the procedures, the sequence of speakers, and the voting regimes: soft, rigid, and qualified majority voting. We had to consider every option so that it was in the system. I was seated at the Council of Nationalities, near a huge electronic device, and made sure the procedures were observed. I also made voting results known to the general public on the same day, or the next day.

Surprisingly, deputies voted one way when they knew the results were not to be published and the completely opposite way, irrespective of their party, when they knew that tomorrow's newspapers would publish the voting results by name. In fact, the electronic ballot changed the entire political system.

Being aware of my work, the congress put me in charge of the procedural commission. We designed an electronic ballot system for the Russian parliament, and made the voting results accessible to the general public on the same day. News agencies and newspapers learned the voting results immediately. Deputies tried to ban such publications, but they could do nothing.

In fact, it is only a small stretch to say that Yeltsin became the RSFSR Supreme Council chairman and deputies made many important decisions for the sole reason that the voting results were published by name, and they could do nothing about it.

I met Yeltsin personally after the First Congress, when the Supreme Council started working. I was made the chairman of the legislative committee. This probably happened because the best-known legal experts had shifted to the Union parliament and I was the last "big man on campus." There were not so many lawyers at the Russian Supreme Council—especially those knowledgeable about parliamentary affairs. Besides, they learned about me even before the congress, after I had written a big article for *Izvestia* on the Russian parliament, its structure and operating mechanism. That was how I caught their attention.

After I had been appointed as the committee chairman, I was introduced to Yeltsin and Burbulis.

Kokh: I see. And how did your relations develop? When did you join the executive branch?

Shakhrai: I moved to the executive branch in December 1991.

Aven: Our government was already in place.

Kokh: I see. Shall we go back a bit, to the August putsch?

Shakhrai: There was all of 1990 before the August putsch, and lots of interesting things had happened.

Kokh: Tell us, then.

Shakhrai: Everyone was talking about economic reforms, but no one gave a thought to their political security. I was not an economic expert in 1990, but I understood that anything was possible amid drastic changes: either you would have a civil confrontation and a revolution, or you wouldn't.

I consider this my main achievement: when all the deputies took off after the First Congress, I collected two or three experts, several members of the legislative committee, and at the legendary Dacha 15 at Arkhangelskoye, we wrote the Referendum Law in six weeks. I still think that the law was the core of the transformation of the political system and our victory.

AVEN: Did you really believe a revolution was possible?

KOKH: And when did you get that impression?

SHAKHRAI: When the congress opened and when Yeltsin was elected. The logic was simple: if the situation was seriously exacerbated, it was better to send people to polling stations than to the barricades. But that required a system, a certain mechanism the world calls "referendum." I think this invention has saved the situation many times. In particular, it saved the economic reforms.

AVEN: Were you interacting closely with Yeltsin at that moment?

SHAKHRAI: There was no personal interaction in 1990; we just met from time to time as members of the Supreme Council Presidium.

AVEN: And who sent you to Dacha 15? That must have been an administrative decision.

SHAKHRAI: I sent myself. I was inspecting the Supreme Council of the old RSFSR, including its administrative department, from March through April 1990. I already knew that the department had real power, because it controlled garages, dachas, and so on. In the end, I chose that dacha for our committee. I had to isolate the experts so that calls or meetings did not disturb them. They were supposed to sit down and write. They also needed a certain degree of autonomy—conference rooms, offices, recreation rooms.

AVEN: I see.

SHAKHRAI: In short, I will keep insisting on my thesis: the Referendum Law saved the political and economic systems and gave the president time to maneuver and for negotiations.

Aven: You had a feeling that a revolution could happen. But there are different kinds of revolutions. Some happen due to the lack of freedom and others due to the lack of justice. There are revolutions of the poor, when people take to the street for the sole reason that they have nothing to eat. What were the main reasons in our case?

Shakhrai: In Russia, everything happens in cycles, I believe. The waves happen because nothing is done until the situation becomes extreme. The revolution of the 1990s was the creation of only a part of the society. Actually, only Gorbachev and the Politburo team realized that the country was in hot water, and started to act. And people just didn't care. It was not a classic revolution where the authorities can't and the people won't. Only the authorities did something in our case.

Kokh: Why would the authorities want it?

Shakhrai: They had information, and they knew that the country would collapse, say, next Monday, if they did nothing.

Aven: And the people would rip their guts out.

Shakhrai: They really would. The authorities simply tried to pursue a preemptive tactic.

Aven: What, in your opinion, was the main problem? What could have galvanized people into revolutionary action? Was it poverty, or justice, or freedom?

Shakhrai: The absence of prospects and poverty. The *nomenklatura* was degenerating because of the lack of social mobility. There was no prospect for young or old, for engineers or poets.

Kokh: Do you mean we may have a revolution now for the same reason? The Americans just supplied 60 million barrels of oil to the market. The crude price will fall, they will supply more, and it will dip again. The Americans will win and we will lose. Hello, poverty.

Shakhrai: I think that people would have stayed quiet if they still had vodka. They would have been inert for a long time. Farms have their own food; it doesn't matter to farmers if they have money or not. They have homemade vodka, and life is good.

KOKH: By then the majority of people had already moved to towns. Villagers were immaterial, but also they were passive till the very end.

SHAKHRAI: By no means did all the people who had moved to towns remain there permanently. Their parents still lived in villages, and their old homes were still standing, although they were shaky—vegetable gardens, dachas, garden plots. I am not speaking about the masses. I mean that the reform of the mid-1980s started because the authorities realized how disastrous the situation was, and had to do something; it was not a question of a revolution.

The difference in 1990 was the failure of the anti-alcohol campaign, the food deficit, and the food coupons. Still the society, primarily its political segment, had a certain equilibrium. The democrats were not the majority—that was clear. But they had initiative and a following wind.

For instance, Vorotnikov told the Politburo that the communist majority had never been bigger than it was at the congress of RSFRS people's deputies—96 percent. Vorotnikov described our congress as an ideologically proper communist monolith.

AVEN: Radical deterioration started in fall 1990. Did you have the same impression?

SHAKHRAI: It started to deteriorate physically—I recall that from my personal experience. I had two children, and I had trouble feeding them. Everyone felt that. And people started to turn political.

KOKH: The unwritten social contract between the people and the authorities—"You feed us and we do not meddle in your affairs"—was breached. Do you remember that wonderful joke about Gorbachev? Once I told it to him: A call from a Siberian regional committee wakes up Gorbachev in the middle of the night. The committee secretary is hysterical: "Send us a trainload of vodka!" "Are you out of your mind? We have an anti-alcohol campaign in progress." "Then I'm not responsible for what happens!" "What's going on?" "The men have sobered up, and they're asking where the tsar is!"

SHAKHRAI: That is good! I had forgotten that one. Actually, it was important for me to point out that I tried to create certain elements of the political system, as I was not a member of the economic team.

AVEN: Were you still doing that in 1990 and early 1991?

SHAKHRAI: I called it the political security of the reforms. They needed legal and political security and appropriate instruments. People gathered and talked on the street or in their kitchens, but nothing happened.

THE YELTSIN TEAM

AVEN: You were a member of the team of Burbulis and Yeltsin from fall 1990?

SHAKHRAI: Yes.

KOKH: And what was the team hierarchy? What were the roles of Lobov, Skokov, and so on?

SHAKHRAI: One may say that Yeltsin had several teams. But I believe that there was only one team—though he also had plenty of connections, commitments, and favorites, each of them acting on his own, without a team. Neither Lobov nor Skokov had a team.

KOKH: There were also Petrov, Ilyushin, Korabelshchikov …

SHAKHRAI: You're right about Petrov. But Ilyushin was different: he was an apparatchik, an administrator, a sacred cow. But he had one team: Burbulis, Gaidar, Shakhrai—with all their contradictions, disorganization, and all that. That was his team. And all the others were a counterbalance.

KOKH: To his team?

SHAKHRAI: To his own team.

KOKH: That was the Yeltsin trait that always amazed me.

SHAKHRAI: Nothing has changed.

AVEN: And did you feel that counterbalance personally?

SHAKHRAI: Not at that time. I was 34 years old. I was simply trying to do my job well. And Gena was sort of a dispatcher and shock-absorber.

KOKH: Do you mean the situation had been the same before Gaidar?

SHAKHRAI: Yes—it had been like that even before your team took office. What was Gena's problem? Having some knowledge of conflict resolution and psychology, I told him that he should not control everything. He became the only umbilical cord, which could be cut off easily, sending everything to ruin. I said he should not be afraid to create additional channels for obtaining information, and simply keep an eye on them. But he had everyone connected to himself, and brought the information obtained at brainstorming sessions to Ben[1] after he had interpreted it, being certain that he was the only one capable of persuading and motivating Yeltsin. In the end, this policy ruined him, the team, and the Gaidar government!

AVEN: Who were the members of "Yeltsin's Politburo" before the Gaidar team appeared? There was Burbulis, there was Yeltsin—and who else?

SHAKHRAI: Gena, I think, even though his role was decidedly that of a dispatcher. And that was correct from the psychological point of view—he didn't make decisions himself, he prepared things so that Ben could make the decisions. He never said, "The Tsar made the decision. Yeltsin said so." No. Gena listened to us and collected our opinions; sometimes we visited Yeltsin together and spoke as best we could, and Yeltsin made a decision. Sometimes Gena prepared him in advance, and sometimes he didn't.

AVEN: Burbulis, you, and who else? Stankevich?

SHAKHRAI: No, Stankevich wasn't there. Ilyushin was there all the time, because every decision needed to be formalized properly. There was also Lev Sukhanov.

KOKH: Poltoranin?

SHAKHRAI: Poltoranin was always there then. He describes it slightly differently now, for some reason, but he was an active participant at that time. Silayev? No.

AVEN: Who else from the deputies?

SHAKHRAI: Yuri Alexeyevich Ryzhov—

---

1.   Ben — B.N. Yeltsin, the staff nickname for Yeltsin. He was also nicknamed Granddaddy or, more rarely, the Tsar.

Kokh: Sobchak?

Shakhrai: From time to time. He was in St Petersburg.

Kokh: Gavriil Popov?

Shakhrai: Popov attended meetings of the Presidential Council.

Kokh: Khasbulatov?

Shakhrai: No. He wasn't a member of the team, after all.

Kokh: Wasn't he?

Shakhrai: He didn't like anyone, and no one liked him.

Kokh: Then why was he elected?

Shakhrai: Why? There was a primitive idea of Russia as a multinational state and Russia as a leftist state. So Rutskoi represented the left-wingers, and Khasbulatov represented nationalities.

Kokh: But there are Tatars and Bashkirs. Why a Chechen?

Shakhrai: When the GKChP putsch happened, the presidents of all the autonomous republics—the Tatars, the Bashkirs, and all the rest—came to Yanayev's office within an hour. Yeltsin didn't want any of them after that. And there were no Chechens there.

Aven: Gena said he was shocked when Yeltsin told him that he would not be the vice president, in spite of their earlier agreement, because he had chosen Rutskoi instead. Did that surprise you, too?

Shakhrai: That's a separate story. To begin with, I drafted the law on the presidency, and there was no vice president in that law at all. The worst thing that can happen to Russia is diarchy. Burbulis and Yeltsin were in France, and I had a session to attend in the morning—I had to speak to the deputies, to persuade them of the need to do this and that, and to promote the law. During the night I had a call first from Burbulis and then from Yeltsin: "Add the vice president!" None of them reacted to my meek objections that we must not do that. I might have been able to convince them at a personal meeting, but I couldn't do it by phone.

KOKH: Gennady was picturing himself?

SHAKHRAI: Naturally. So, I added the article about the vice president by morning. Naturally, Gennady saw himself in that position because he had always been close.

KOKH: But not Yeltsin!

SHAKHRAI: He always acted according to the situation. ... Speaking of the eternal question about mistakes and non-mistakes: Ben was often slow. He was far from being the decisive man everyone imagined him to be. Months were wasted because of that—precious months, during which the situation continued to deteriorate. Things could have taken a different turn.

AVEN: Why was time wasted? Did he drink, disappear?

KOKH: That's what I wanted to ask. Was he already drinking heavily?

SHAKHRAI: I think he enjoyed drinking even before that. But his system was able to process alcohol rapidly until 1996–7. I think biochemists call that "active alcohol dehydrogenase." An hour or two later, he was fit as a fiddle. That quality deteriorated with age. Yeltsin in the early 1990s was king. Everyone would be suffering from a hangover, and he'd emerge an hour later, wearing a fresh shirt, and ask, "What's the matter with you? Let's get back to work!"

AVEN: Tell us how the vice president was elected.

SHAKHRAI: When we started to prepare for the elections (and time was running out), we were feverishly looking for a running mate for Yeltsin, because both the president and the vice president were elected at the same time. Everyone was saying that a leftist candidate was necessary to win over the communist electorate. They suggested Rutskoi. The Russian Communist Party had discredited itself seriously by then, and Rutskoi, although he was a member of the Russian Communist Party Central Committee, represented a more or less sane faction, the Communists for Democracy. Besides, he was a pilot, a young hero, he had a moustache, and he was handsome. He was expected to win many female votes. As a result, Gena got no vice presidency, which had not been hard to predict.

KOKH: Everyone was so naive then.

AVEN: Burbulis was very disappointed.

KOKH: You see, he wouldn't have been disappointed if Yeltsin hadn't promised that position to him. And Yeltsin did. Then he invented the position of state secretary for Burbulis, but that was a half-measure.

SHAKHRAI: The State Secretary was not a half-measure. The State Council was a variant of a collegial advisory body. The Soviet Communist Party called that body the Politburo. There was no party or any other organization in 1991, and we had to bring together five to seven decision-makers somehow. So we had the State Council.

KOKH: Why did Yeltsin not make a party for himself? It would have been a great help.

AVEN: He didn't understand that. He thought he had a direct link to the people, without any party. Like a monarch.

KOKH: The concept of being the president of all Russians is a total absurdity. You studied parliamentarianism—you must understand that well.

SHAKHRAI: I do understand that, but I also understand other things. It's 2011. Well? Has anyone formed a party here?

AVEN: No one.

SHAKHRAI: Neither could Yeltsin.

KOKH: Wrong! He didn't even try—while Putin (to be more exact, Berezovsky) created United Russia.

SHAKHRAI: That's not a party—it's a mechanism.

KOKH: Wonderful. Yeltsin could have created the same mechanism.

SHAKHRAI: No, he couldn't. There was no state machinery then. Union officials stepped aside and waited for the entire structure to go down so that they could return with clean hands.

KOKH: Really, we still have no normal parties. I think this is why Putin sticks to the "president of all Russians" formula.

SHAKHRAI: Basically, yes.

KOKH: But that's a dead end.

SHAKHRAI: One could hardly say it better than Chernomyrdin: "No matter what party we try to make, we end up with the Soviet Communist Party."

THE PUTSCH OF 1991

KOKH: Let's talk about the putsch.

SHAKHRAI: It seemed to us that the Union situation had been settled somehow and we had created normal mechanisms, such as referenda, conciliatory procedures, and the presidency. It seemed we would have no more political struggle in the form of a putsch. But it appeared the mechanism contained a certain coil, or spring.

AVEN: Do you mean you didn't expect that? Or did you?

SHAKHRAI: The situation was not surprising considering the historical context. The surprise was that, although tensions had seemed to be easing, the explosion happened.

AVEN: When you learned about the putsch, were you, a political analyst, surprised by their capacity for violent action?

SHAKHRAI: Who knows? I was just scared.

AVEN: Were you surprised?

SHAKHRAI: Yes. And I will explain why. There had been two significant plenary meetings of the Soviet Communist Party Central Committee—they were held in November 1990 and in April 1991. They were interesting both for their public front and their behind-the-scenes events—and the main behind-the-scenes event was the dethronement of Gorbachev. The party administration was displeased with Gorbachev, and branded him a traitor—he had become the president, and separated from the party.

KOKH: Did you have insiders to tell you what was going on behind the scenes?

SHAKHRAI: There were both insiders and eyewitnesses. In short, in April they decided to hold a Soviet Communist Party Congress on September 3, 1991, to replace the secretary general, and a Congress of Soviet People's Deputies on September 4 to replace the Soviet president. The period from April to September gave Gorbachev a choice: either give up or try to defend his position. And he had rather good advisors—Shakhnazarov, Revenko, and others.

KOKH: And he decided to sign a new Union agreement, didn't he?

SHAKHRAI: Yes. There was a meeting with four republican leaders.

KOKH: Four leaders. Who were they?

SHAKHRAI: Nazarbayev, Yeltsin, Shushkevich, and Kravchuk. The format resembled the Belovezh meeting, but Gorbachev was also there. They met in July 1991, a month before the GKChP.

AVEN: Was there the idea of building a new state with Gorbachev and those four leaders?

SHAKHRAI: Yes.

KOKH: Was it you who proposed that?

SHAKHRAI: No, not me. Gorbachev's team.

AVEN: Was the Union agreement their idea? Did they suggest that Gorbachev and those leaders should build a new structure, avoid the Soviet Communist Party Central Committee's vengeance, and break up with the orthodox communists?

SHAKHRAI: Right. The entire power structure would have changed—there would have been a new Union agreement and a new constitution. Actually, Gorbachev agreed to be a president of a practically German kind.

KOKH: I see—like the British queen?

AVEN: Not quite.

SHAKHRAI: That would have been impossible in Russia, but he would have transferred most of his powers to Union republics. A genuine confederation would have been built.

KOKH: And?

SHAKHRAI: Kryuchkov recorded their conversations and played them to other Politburo members: "There's no place for us in this structure! Are we supposed to just leave? The choice is simple: either we are all betrayers of the great Soviet Union or we have to do something!" That is how the GKChP was born. A decision was made that they did not need Gorbachev in such a capacity: they called him a traitor on the leash of the "separatists." The text of the Union agreement was coordinated in late July. The signing was scheduled for August 20. That's why the putsch started the day before.

We met Yeltsin at the Vnukovo airport late at night on August 18; he had arrived from Kazakhstan. We met him and went to Arkhangelskoye, where we lived. Ilyushin and I agreed to leave for work early on August 19, and Arkhangelskoye was blocked at 7:00 a.m. We walked to Yeltsin's dacha and started thinking what to do.

AVEN: When you were at the airport, did you already know what would happen, or not?

SHAKHRAI: No—I learned about that only on the morning of August 19. The GKChP trick caught us by surprise!

AVEN: Let's finish the discussion of the Novo-Ogaryovo process. Did you realize that the formula wouldn't work?

SHAKHRAI: I visited Novo-Ogaryovo many times and attended conferences. The Novo-Ogaryovo process kept running into an impasse, because of the autonomous republics. There were 16 autonomous republics in Russia at the time, and Gorbachev and his team were flirting with them. I came across the so-called autonomization plan in 1992 in a special file of the Soviet Communist Party Central Committee. The Union authorities planned to make the autonomous republics equal parties to the new Union agreement in order to keep Yeltsin in check.

KOKH: Did they want to establish a direct relationship, bypassing Yeltsin, and make them full constituents of the new Union?

SHAKHRAI: There was a legal time bomb—Article 72 of the Soviet Constitution, which declared the right of Union republics to secession. And Gorbachev—or, I would say, Shakhnazarov—proposed instead of a Union of 15 republics that could secede freely a Union of approximately 35 constituents without a right to secession. That would be the 15 Union republics plus 20 autonomous republics (in addition to Russia, autonomous republics also existed in Uzbekistan, Georgia, and Azerbaijan).

The process was endless. Yeltsin kept asking: "Shall I sign on behalf of all of Russia or do I sign as Yeltsin, and my 16 republics sign separately?" The Union authorities told him: "You and your 16 republics." And Yeltsin said no. He realized that the formula implied the secession of the 16 republics from the RSFSR. And that was 20 million citizens, 51 percent of the territory, and practically the whole bulk of strategic resources.

They reached a strange compromise in the end: Yeltsin would sign the agreement and the Russian autonomous republics would sign, too, but their signatures would be put under Yeltsin's, not next to it—all the 16 republics.

In the end Yeltsin signed the Union agreement on August 17. I bore witness to that—it happened in my presence.

KOKH: But some did not sign it, and the agreement didn't enter into force, did it?

SHAKHRAI: Right, it didn't enter into force. As you understand, that happened on the eve of the putsch. That was why the putsch took place on August 19, no earlier and no later. They might have been not quite prepared, but the signing began.

Why am I talking about the autonomous republics? The declaration of Russian sovereignty was a forced step. We had to override the autonomization plan of the central authorities. The Declaration of Sovereignty even had an article that said the rights of autonomous republics must be broadened in compliance with Russian laws—that is, without external interference. Why did 96 percent of communists vote for the declaration at the congress of RSFSR people's deputies? Because they understood that Gorbachev's playing up to the autonomous republics would lead to the breakup of Russia. And now they're trying to blame the declaration.

AVEN: Gorbachev really tried to build a structure: him, the Union authorities, and the republics. But we have heard many times that Russia kept breaking the model.

Stanislav Anisimov told us how economic conferences were held. The Union republics sent their top-ranking officials, the presidents, to those meetings (Anisimov was a Union minister at that time), and Russia didn't send anyone higher in rank than Lobov.

What was Yeltsin's attitude toward the Gorbachev structure? Burbulis said that Yeltsin took the course toward secession in 1990, and wanted Russia to be absolutely independent from any unions. Or is that wrong? What did actually happen?

SHAKHRAI: Yeltsin didn't share such ideas with me. I had a slightly different impression.

KOKH: Let's go back to the putsch chronology. You came to Yeltsin's dacha in Arkhangelskoye in the morning?

SHAKHRAI: He was wearing a white shirt, jogging pants; I think he had slippers on his feet and had not combed his hair: "What shall we do?"

KOKH: Who was at the dacha at that moment?

SHAKHRAI: There were Burbulis and Ilyushin at first. Sobchak, Khasbulatov, and somebody else joined in later. Poltoranin dropped in.

KOKH: When did you decide to oppose the GKChP publicly?

SHAKHRAI: The decision was made right there, within 20 or 30 minutes.

KOKH: There were no doubts?

SHAKHRAI: We had some doubts. There is a brook in Arkhangelskoye—you must know it. There was an idea to cross it and to escape through the territory of an adjacent health resort. But our security guards told us that we were blockaded—there were men from the GKChP waiting, and there was no point in disgracing ourselves by going into the water and getting arrested.

KOKH: And?

SHAKHRAI: Then we decided to do it Russian-style.

KOKH: To break through?

SHAKHRAI: Just drive to the White House. The guards at the gate didn't dare to stop us. Either they had no such command or there was another reason—but we rode on to Moscow!

AVEN: Was there any arrest order at all?

SHAKHRAI: Who knows?

KOKH: Probably there was none. Or the putschists were not really good at it.

SHAKHRAI: But the impression made by tank columns moving along the Moscow Circular Road, Kutuzovsky Avenue, and around the White House: that was something. The tanks were real.

AVEN: And then you flew down to bring back Gorbachev. How was he?

SHAKHRAI: He looked as though he had just come out of a nervous break-down.

KOKH: And who else went there?

SHAKHRAI: Rutskoi.

KOKH: And what about Primakov?

SHAKHRAI: Primakov, as he tells it, was flying together with Gorbachev, because he had been vacationing nearby.
    I didn't go in first class; I had a seat in the back. I didn't see Primakov. We arrived in Moscow at night. Kryuchkov and Yazov came with us. They had been interned, and we were told to bring them to their dachas in the

Moscow region so that they couldn't communicate with each other. They were considered sort of under house arrest.

KOKH: Were they arrested?

SHAKHRAI: They were later. But at the time we were told to meet them on the tarmac at Vnukovo airport and to drive them home, where they were put under house arrest. I was lucky enough to chat with Yazov.

KOKH: He was my neighbor later. We lived next door on Tverskaya-Yamskaya. Quite a decent old man. He went shopping and stood in lines. A normal pensioner—a war veteran.

AVEN: What impression did he give, and what comments did he make?

SHAKHRAI: He was swearing. He swore at Gorbachev—but he stayed calm, and he was not drunk. He behaved courageously. I tell you, I was lucky.

AVEN: And did he swear at Yanayev? Or just Gorbachev?

SHAKHRAI: Yanayev was at the top of his list! But he let Gorbachev have it, too.

The Collapse of the USSR

KOKH: I want to comment on the possible plans of Burbulis and Yeltsin to break up the Soviet Union and to achieve full independence. I have the impression, in particular, from what Sergei is telling us—

SHAKHRAI: Sorry for interrupting you. I would like you to listen to me: the constant use of the verb "to break up" keeps us in a psychological trap. "To break up" means to be active and focused in one's actions. Take a look from another angle: did anyone want to keep the Union, or was everyone indifferent and prepared to let go of it? In fact, only the GKChP group (for personal reasons, to put it mildly) and Gorbachev (probably for loftier but still personal reasons) were trying to save it. The overwhelming majority did not give a damn about the Union! It was gone not because somebody broke it up—it was gone because nobody needed it! No one took to the streets or rushed to its defense at the parliament or in the media. No one cared. Such a union stood no chance.

KOKH: That is an important idea. I agree.

I have the impression that Burbulis certainly desired Russia's complete sovereignty. But I think they would not have dared to unilaterally denounce the Union agreement—neither he nor Yeltsin. The key factor was Kravchuk's election victory and the choice of full sovereignty and secession from the Union at the Ukrainian referendum.

AVEN: Alfred is right. Neither Burbulis nor Yeltsin had a clear vision of the future.

KOKH: Their concept was to gain as much power as possible. They got lucky before the Belovezh meeting: the Ukrainians made a decision for everyone. And they breathed a sigh of relief: "There is nothing we can do. Let us bury it—it's dead anyway." Burbulis told us that, as soon as they started speaking about a Union structure in Belovezh, Kravchuk interrupted them and said, "Guys, you shouldn't discuss anything in my presence—I will sign nothing."

SHAKHRAI: That really did happen.

KOKH: And there is no Union without Ukraine, obviously. That was the end of it.

SHAKHRAI: There were some more important circumstances. We all realize that the USSR was a federation de jure, and the Soviet Communist Party was the state mechanism de facto. If the state mechanism called the Soviet Communist Party breaks down, the entire structure is incapacitated.

KOKH: Indeed. Soviet administrative structures and the government were so shaky and underdeveloped.

SHAKHRAI: Gorbachev returned from Foros in a sulk. The first thing he did as secretary general of the Soviet Communist Party was to relieve himself of his duties and urge all communists to tell that party to go to hell. And the leaders of the Union republics, the first secretaries of the republics, and regional executive committees said, "As a matter of fact, what would we need Moscow and your democracy for?" They held their power and their property on their territory, while the center was plunging into anarchy.

KOKH: I did not see the party as the state mechanism at that time. I chaired a district executive committee in 1990–1, and the party district committee was next door—

SHAKHRAI: Was that in Tashkent?

KOKH: No, in St Petersburg, in Sestroretsk.

SHAKHRAI: Right—and I am telling you about Almaty, Tashkent, and Askhabad.

KOKH: Understood—but let me finish. I want to tell you that the district party committee had been reduced to nothing, even though we still lived in the Soviet Union and everything was more or less in order. We, the district executive committee, stopped obeying the commands of the district party committee much earlier, right after Gorbachev crossed out the constitutional article about the party as the leading and guiding force.

SHAKHRAI: Correct—you ignored the district party committee, but you built nothing to replace it!

KOKH: That's why power still belonged to the Soviets, even though the Soviet Communist Party was blown away.

SHAKHRAI: There was no power—come on.

KOKH: Certain Soviet bodies were still operating. You shouldn't dramatize.

SHAKHRAI: In fact, we had anarchy. But I would like to emphasize another point. The first secretaries—and some of them are still presidents—fled Moscow to fight for their independence.

AVEN: You're absolutely right!

SHAKHRAI: Certainly Kravchuk struck the last blow—but actually Kazakh and Uzbek leaders were no less efficient in fighting for their sovereignty.

KOKH: They said neither yes or no, with truly Asian cunning. They were independent de facto, but curtseyed to the central authorities de jure. And Kravchuk was the only one who said, "I will sign nothing. Ukraine has become an independent state—we have had our referendum. Period."

SHAKHRAI: They behaved differently, but had seceded from the Union de jure before December 8.

AVEN: No, not Nazarbayev.

SHAKHRAI: Nazarbayev seceded on December 16. And the others declared their sovereignty much earlier than the Belovezh meeting. And we congratulate them on their independence days from spring to December 1 (Ukraine) and December 16 (Kazakhstan).

KOKH: Wait, what about the Declaration of Russian Independence adopted on June 12, 1990?

SHAKHRAI: Are you talking about the Declaration of Sovereignty? It didn't use the word "independence" even once. It said: "A democratic and law-governed state within the renovated Union of Soviet Socialist Republics." Claims that our declaration started the disintegration of the USSR are a myth.

THE BELOVEZH ACCORDS

AVEN: Let's talk about Belovezh. I learned Burbulis's opinion about the Union just yesterday. He drew charts for me. He said the putsch put lots of things in order. He spoke about four states within a union, primarily about Ukraine and Belarus, and about a milder variant of association with Kazakhstan and, probably, with Kyrgyzstan. He also said they would have taken another path if that one had proved abortive. It was clear they had no definite plan.

SHAKHRAI: We departed a day earlier because we had an official visit to Moscow. Burbulis and Gaidar arrived on the next day.

AVEN: And you traveled with whom?

SHAKHRAI: With the president. It was an official visit. However, nothing special had been planned. No one knew about Kravchuk—whether he was coming or not. And suddenly the task was set after dinner! And we had nothing—no ideas or drafts. When we came from Minsk to Viskuli on the next day, Kravchuk was already there. He went hunting in the morning and was out for the whole day. He walked in from the frosty outdoors; we sat down to dinner and started our discussion.

KOKH: Did you know Kravchuk was there?

SHAKHRAI: Certainly. We learned that after we had come from Minsk to Viskuli.

KOKH: Who invited him? Or did he come on his own?

SHAKHRAI: Shushkevich invited him.

AVEN: A troika meeting was planned, with the possible participation of Nazarbayev.

SHAKHRAI: Then somebody said "a Slavic union" (I don't remember who said that, but it sounded so good). We realized quickly that the effect would be the opposite, and Yeltsin and Shushkevich started to call Nazarbayev in the morning.

KOKH: Nazarbayev never showed up.

SHAKHRAI: He made a stopover in Moscow to seek advice from Gorbachev. The latter promised him the premier's position in the Union government, and he never joined us.

AVEN: When did you realize that Ukraine would be adamant?

SHAKHRAI: When we started to discuss the formula and its name. Nobody wanted a union; everybody said, "No union." The word "commonwealth" was chosen quickly. "Association" was suggested before that. But Yeltsin didn't like the word "association"—he probably didn't know what it meant.

KOKH: A foreign word.

SHAKHRAI: We had dinner first. We were discussing the possibility: should it be just the three of us?

AVEN: Without Gorbachev?

SHAKHRAI: Without Gorbachev.

AVEN: Without the center. Everyone on his own. Did you speak about common administration?

SHAKHRAI: We discussed the form at first. The words "confederation" and "association" were rejected: they couldn't have been legalized under our circumstances. The single state was unrealistic. Nobody was prepared for that and nobody wanted it. So we agreed to "a commonwealth." Legally, we were speaking about a confederation—but that didn't sound Russian.

KOKH: There's a Russian word for commonwealth, *sodruzhestvo*.

SHAKHRAI: The commonwealth. Then we began to paraphrase the Novo-Ogaryovo document. The Commonwealth of Independent States. We discussed nothing else that night.

AVEN: What did the commonwealth mean? Was it the common army or the common foreign policy? What was it? What were you supposed to describe in addition to economic matters, about which Yegor knew everything?

SHAKHRAI: Yegor was writing and I was helping him. We could sense what the commonwealth could have in common and what it could not.

AVEN: What was it supposed to have in common?

SHAKHRAI: Common nuclear forces, common currency, common money disbursement—

AVEN: And what about foreign policy?

SHAKHRAI: Rather, a coordinated foreign policy. And all the rest was supposed to be separate.

AVEN: What about the army?

SHAKHRAI: Just the nuclear forces; somehow, we discussed nothing else. Wait, we had the joint staff.

KOKH: In the end, there was no common currency—

SHAKHRAI: In the end, there was little of what we had written about. I had to visit Kazakhstan practically every month to wheedle our warheads from them, and do the same in Ukraine later on.

AVEN: In short, the structure was contradictory from the very start. It was not a confederation, because foreign policies were coordinated but there was no common foreign policy. A confederation implies one disbursement center, one foreign policy, and one army.

KOKH: Do you mean Switzerland?

AVEN: That is a classic example.

SHAKHRAI: Confederation is what Switzerland is called formally. In fact, it is a very solid federation.

AVEN: What's the difference between a confederation and a federation?

SHAKHRAI: A federation is a single state, while a confederation is a union of states; at least, that's what we have been taught. The CIS defined Ukraine, Belarus, and Russia as independent states, and the CIS itself as a commonwealth that united them.

AVEN: Then why do you call that a confederation? A confederation implies voluntary delegation of powers to the center—regulatory powers in defense, monetary disbursement, and foreign policy. But the document you have just described looks like the Union agreement drafted by Gorbachev in Novo-Ogaryovo. Nuclear forces? Didn't the Gorbachev document say that?

SHAKHRAI: Yes, it did.

AVEN: And the common currency? Didn't Gorbachev and Yeltsin sign that already?

SHAKHRAI: Yegor crossed out the word "disbursement" later; he replaced it with another word. But, actually, the common currency was mentioned.

AVEN: What about coordination of foreign policy?

SHAKHRAI: And coordination of foreign policy. I added Article 5 to the agreement, which said that the existing borders between CIS member states would be recognized as long as they stayed within the Commonwealth. I meant the Crimea and other lands. If you want to have a problem with the Crimea, quit the CIS. And the converse—you will have no border problems if you join the CIS. I wanted to bond the CIS countries: as long as you're in the CIS, no one will divide up Crimea or anything else.

AVEN: Is it still so?

SHAKHRAI: It was so for a year, but then Kozyrev, Lukin, and others signed the Russia–Ukraine border agreement. They shouldn't have done that!

KOKH: Why not?

SHAKHRAI: Because the absence of internal borders in the CIS is a political bond.

AVEN: I still see no essential difference between the Novo-Ogaryovo and Belovezh documents. Every fundamental problem was settled in the same way. What do they criticize Yeltsin for? Actually, there was no difference between the two documents, but the interpretations were so different.

SHAKHRAI: Three of four states that founded the USSR in 1922 met in Belovezh. The fourth state was the South Caucasian Federation, but it split into three republics in 1936. Hence, we had the formula: the founding states would declare the death of the USSR and would create a new common-wealth. The king is dead, long live the king. And the single state had already died in the Novo-Ogaryovo process.

KOKH: As I understand it, the historical drama is that you had absolutely no agenda when you came to Minsk. The question simply popped up when you were having dinner. Did you go there just for the sake of a meeting?

SHAKHRAI: Yes. To chitchat: What are we going to do? Probably we should have had our discussion and left. But we realized that we might never gather again. We had that feeling because an officer from the Ninth Department of the Union KGB was standing by each cottage, and informed Moscow every minute that we were sitting there and having a conference. Formally, they were protecting us, but actually they put us under surveillance.

All of us were surrounded. But, just as they thoughtlessly let us go from Arkhangelskoye in August, they were useless there, too.

KOKH: This means they didn't care about the Union.

AVEN: Did the Belovezh meeting push the disintegration, or did it simply certify the state of affairs?

SHAKHRAI: I would put it differently: it accelerated the breakup of what was still standing because there could be no state without a single political center. That was the difference between Belovezh and Novo-Ogaryovo.

KOKH: You're right—there is no state without a single political center. I would add that there is no state if its parts have different goals. A single state is senseless without a common goal. That would be an artificial state. And the state had no common goal by then.

SHAKHRAI: Without a single mission—it had none by then.

KOKH: Central Asia had its mission, the South Caucasus had its mission, and the Baltic republics had theirs.

SHAKHRAI: There had been seven or eight republics ready for a confederation before August 19—but not after.

AVEN: I've learned a lot from this conversation—the picture is absolutely clear.

SHAKHRAI: In fact, I kept trying to convey just one idea to you, ministers-economists.

AVEN: Alfred was even a vice premier.

SHAKHRAI: We needed to buy time for economic reforms with legal tactics. That is what I was doing.

AVEN: What was the public reaction to Belovezh?

KOKH: Did the overwhelming majority of parliament deputies say yes?

SHAKHRAI: They were practically unanimous. There were three emotions. First, there was clarity and, to a certain extent, relief: "It happened—we've got it." Second, there was fear and concern about what might happen. Third (and it may be linked with the first factor), there were constant claims of taking advantage. They kept saying on the streets that Georgia was a parasite, Central Asia was a parasite, Moscow was a parasite, the Baltic republics were parasites—an "information virus" of sorts. And it seemed that you would survive for sure only if you did not have to take care of others. Those claims were transformed into economic realities. No one regretted that the USSR was gone. And I learned from the Politburo "special file" that 88 kopecks out of every ruble were spent on the defense sector.

KOKH: The Soviet Union had become a machine that transformed money into hardware, and that hardware was totally unnecessary. They kept making weapons for God knows what purpose.

SHAKHRAI: There is a town, Tchaikovsky, in the Perm region. It is a beautiful town. And there are rows and rows of tanks three kilometers away from it!

KOKH: Yes, Nechayev has told us about that. Tanks and guns. Senseless, idiotic waste of money, resources, and labor.

SHAKHRAI: And underground cities? They can be neither destroyed nor maintained. An economic dead end. We just overextended ourselves.

AVEN: How can you explain that now?

SHAKHRAI: We should put these documents on the table; and others—not us, not the participants—should talk about them. Whenever we present facts, no one believes us because we took part in those events. There must be no link between individuals and information. Then they may finally hear.

ABOUT THE GOVERNMENT

AVEN: Let's focus on our team, the Gaidar team. When did you learn that there were new people at the dacha in Arkhangelskoye?

SHAKHRAI: I told you we had lived there for a long time—we had been writing laws. I simply dropped in on you one night, and we started our parallel work at that dacha.

AVEN: And you joined the government in December 1991 as a—

SHAKHRAI: A vice premier.

AVEN: Were you wary of us?

SHAKHRAI: Absolutely not. I had sat on so many Union parliament committees, the Council of Nationalities with all its impotence, that I was happy. For the first time I saw people with shining eyes who wanted to do something.

AVEN: Right—you are one of the Moscow University alumni; you could not have felt differently. You had no allergic reaction to us. I remember the traditional Tuesday tea at Burbulis's. You came, and Burbulis said there was a proposal to appoint Sergei Mikhailovich Shakhrai as a vice premier. Everyone burst into applause. That happened in December. Why didn't they appoint you earlier?

SHAKHRAI: I have my own theory. Before that I had been a state advisor, probably since summer, and I had had to attend government meetings. There was an impression of a certain duality—a commissar overseeing the government. I had that impression, and so did everyone else.

AVEN: We thought at the beginning that you were a commissar. You stayed apart and took notes.

SHAKHRAI: Gorbachev offered me a job as the Union Committee for Nationalities chairman in September 1991. I said it was too late to do that, and declined the offer. I told Yeltsin, but he took umbrage anyway, for some reason. The Union structures were finished in December, and I had to choose between remaining a deputy and a state advisor and doing real work.

AVEN: Our government was a motley crew: there was the Gaidar team, but there were also Poltoranin, Lobov, and others.

First, what do you think about the effect of personal incompatibility and diversity on our work? Second, how did that match up with Yeltsin's mentality? Did it show that he himself had no idea of what was right, and therefore selected such different people? Or could he take pleasure in watching their disagreements? What did Gaidar and Poltoranin have in common? How were they able to stay together? How was that related to Yeltsin's character?

SHAKHRAI: Ninety percent of the situation was Yeltsin's character. I think, first of all, he didn't quite understand the essence of Yegor's economic ideas.

He must have had a gut feeling that those ideas were not only necessary but also the only possibility at the time, because all the other alternatives were missed in 1990 and 1991. Yet it was a gut feeling, not understanding. He constantly needed interpreters, translators, interfaces—people who could calm him down and confirm that the proposed measures would be correct and appropriate. He also needed people to catch the ball and keep the government going if this team blew it.

Second, the great principle of "divide and rule" was important for him. The first secretary of the regional party committee, who had been to every level, up to the Politburo and the Soviet Communist Party Central Committee, never would have bet on one team or one source of information only.

KOKH: So the "divide and rule" principle was secondary, was it?

SHAKHRAI: In that particular situation, yes. Because he had tried lots of people. He had tried Silayev, he had tried Yavlinsky—

AVEN: Which didn't work.

SHAKHRAI: Which didn't work. Later, in the second half of the 1990s, these two factors might have switched places. But this is the way it was at the moment we are discussing. It's natural for Russian tradition. Gorbachev had a team from Stavropol, Brezhnev from Dnepropetrovsk, and Yeltsin from Sverdlovsk—there were Petrov and Lobov, and nothing could be done about that. It was insurance. Certainly it was not a single team. There had not been so many moments in history when the economic and political conditions gave carte blanche to a leader for a number of years and he could pick whomever he wanted. Usually everything happens in a situation of a crossroads or a crisis, and the leader moves people and structures around.

KOKH: Certainly, the alternative team of "Sverdlovsk apparatchiks" didn't have broader electoral support than Gaidar did. We cannot call it the fruit of a compromise with the parliament or public opinion.

SHAKHRAI: I would like to make two additions. No one thought about the electoral potential of particular government personalities at the start. Yeltsin came, and Yeltsin won. He was a charismatic leader, and all the others were standing behind his back.

But as the Supreme Soviet and his team shared power in 1992–3, he had to invite industrialists and "red directors," to hold preferential voting, to bring in Chernomyrdin, and so on. In effect, there was no period of a "pure reform government."

AVEN: That period was over in April 1992.

SHAKHRAI: Second, I think that our recollections are somewhat linear. But a team with its outlook, proposals, and even bills (the main distinction of the Gaidar team) was still not enough. There was no administration or staff to implement those ideas. The party administration was gone: some went into business and others joined the opposition. Soviet administration heavy-weights preferred to lie low—and that was probably why your academic supervisors lay low, too.

In the end, the government building had no middle story. There was the government, there were the people, there was the economic crisis, and there were ideas of how to fix that—but there were no operating mechanisms.

Why did I quit in spring 1992 after I had quarreled with Burbulis and Gaidar? I kept asking the question, "Who is going to do the work?" I proposed to win over Soviet bureaucrats, and even wrote a concept paper to that effect.

There was no one to implement the reforms. Only the ideas that had a direct effect for Yeltsin or the people proved viable. And we had no administration for a very long time.

KOKH: That is the great achievement of Chubais's: building the Goskomimushchestvo[2] vertical.

SHAKHRAI: Right. That was the first new vertical.

KOKH: It reached every district of every town. Sasha Kazakov did that.

SHAKHRAI: It proved viable and reached out everywhere precisely because it was new. We couldn't have used the old vertical—it wasn't working.

KOKH: Old apparatchiks had respect for Chubais. What he did sounded important in their slang: "He created an industry." We laughed at their phrase then, but now I understand what it means.

SHAKHRAI: Yeltsin, like all men of this caliber, if he was taken by an idea,

---

2.   State Committee for State Property Management.

made it his creed. Take, for instance, freedom of speech. He let in the market and private property. He believed in several things and made them materialize.

KOKH: The free-market rhetoric allowed him to surpass Gorbachev.

SHAKHRAI: Yes. As soon as it stopped being a factor in his popularity, he stopped using the term, but that didn't change him personally.

KOKH: You're absolutely right. But tell me, why didn't he believe in Gaidar fully? He kept inventing counterbalances till the end. Was it the traditional Russian peasant's mistrust of the intelligentsia?

SHAKHRAI: You may say that. That's what I said in the beginning, but I formulated it differently. The word "alien" has a connotation of rejection. He didn't have that. On the contrary, he accepted us—but he didn't fully understand either our ideas or our mentality.

KOKH: He didn't trust us?

SHAKHRAI: He did not. Lack of understanding implies lack of trust.

KOKH: So it wasn't about Yeltsin. It was the standard attitude of the Russian people toward the intelligentsia and various kinds of smart people. What is Putin's gimmick? He is one of them through and through. He is not an intellectual, but people are sure that he could show up those eggheads. Just listen to him gabbling away in German! Bravo!

SHAKHRAI: I think that Yeltsin's duality, inconsistency, and blowing hot and cold helped keep him in power. If he had stuck to one policy, he would have run into a social protest, a revolution, or a conspiracy to overthrow him. They simply could not decipher him. He took a step forward and then a step back, forward and back. He was flexible.

KOKH: Ideology was secondary to him.

SHAKHRAI: Situational.

KOKH: The core task was to retain power—at any cost.

SHAKHRAI: But that was real politics. If you look, you see that beyond pros and cons and the purity of concepts, there is the concrete factor of time: if you get from point A to point B in time, you win—no matter how many ideological fluctuations you have had on the way, you beat that factor!

AVEN: And who else but Gaidar and our team (and, obviously, we were highly ideologized) had a clear ideology? Did Khasbulatov have any ideology?

SHAKHRAI: Absolutely none—even less than Yeltsin.

AVEN: What about Zorkin? The opposition of Zorkin and the whole policy of the Constitutional Court are well known.

SHAKHRAI: By law, the Constitutional Court is supposed to be above ideology and politics. But before making any comment on it, I can tell you that the Constitutional Court played a historic role in the end because it solved the task no one else in the world had ever solved. The confrontation between Yeltsin and the State Duma (after Khasbulatov) made it impossible for six years to pass a single normal law on state-building, federative relations, and other spheres of public life. Meanwhile, the Constitutional Court interpreted the constitution, explained principles of laws to legislators, and temporarily filled in legal gaps with its decisions. They deserve a monument for that.

But in the early period, when Yeltsin had his "young team," the Gaidar government, the Constitutional Court really played a rather tragic role. It not only buried a series of presidential decrees, but also gave legal backing to his opponents. Do you remember the decree about a special administrative regime? Yeltsin hadn't even signed it—he just spoke about it on television. And the Constitutional Court immediately responded to Khasbulatov's inquiry: "Yeltsin is acting unconstitutionally." It condemned the president for a document he hadn't signed.

KOKH: When was it?

SHAKHRAI: In March 1993, after the Eighth Congress, when deputies refused to compromise with the president and carry on the reforms, and when the country was paralyzed. Yeltsin made a direct address to the people—he told them that party apparatchiks were contemplating revenge, and that he had decided to enact a special administrative regime.

KOKH: Did it happen before the "Yes-Yes-No-Yes" referendum?

SHAKHRAI: Yes, it did. The April referendum was the result, because the Constitutional Court actually enabled Khasbulatov to claim they "had grounds to impeach the president," and to convene the Ninth Special Congress. The Constitutional Court exceeded its authority and interfered in politics—

KOKH: And what decision should the court have made?

SHAKHRAI: None at all. The Constitutional Court by law is not involved in politics. It verifies the constitutionality of existing documents. If there is no document, it had nothing to discuss. The decision was political, not legal, and Khasbulatov and his team had an illusion that the impeachment was possible. They almost made it. They fell short by only six votes. The "Yes-Yes-No-Yes" referendum held in April was a compromise—the referendum was a motion of no confidence in both the president and the parliament. That was one of the most tragic periods.

KOKH: There was still a shootout in the end.

SHAKHRAI: It might have been avoided. Few people remember that the warring sides met at the Patriarchal residence in the St Daniil Monastery on October 1. Khasbulatov's representative, Yuri Mikhailovich Voronin, and Yeltsin's representative, Sergei Alexandrovich Filatov, attended that meeting. And we were there, too. We convinced Yeltsin to agree to the zero variant—simultaneous early presidential and parliamentary elections. Voronin was supposed to bring that document to the White House on Krasnopresnenskaya Embankment, but he never delivered it.

KOKH: Why?

SHAKHRAI: I can't answer this question. Peaceful solutions were possible until the very last moment, until hostilities ensued. As far as I remember, Burbulis and Khasbulatov were holding direct negotiations.

AVEN: So Voronin never delivered the document?

SHAKHRAI: Maybe he did, and even showed it to Khasbulatov, who stashed the offer and never discussed it with the presidium. Actually, fatalities could have been avoided if a simultaneous early election had been held three months later—just as the document had suggested.

GAIDAR AND YELTSIN

AVEN: Do you want to say anything else about Gaidar? How did you meet? What was your opinion about him? And what role did he play?

SHAKHRAI: I remember Gaidar as two or even three different people. One of them is an egghead leader of the reform team seated at Dacha 15—with shining eyes, constantly explaining, and explaining clearly. That is a rare quality for a scholar, to speak clearly to deputies. I must say that is not an easy task.

The second Gaidar lived next door to my dacha. Our wives—my Tatiana and his Masha—constantly shared their concerns, and naturally passed the information on to their husbands. So Yegor and I also had communication between our families. The tradition continued later, when we moved to the same building on Osennyaya Street.

I remember the third Gaidar from when I worked at the Audit Chamber. I frequently visited his institute, usually to ask for some analytical report. Stepashin and I kept asking for his opinion about the budget. And he met our requests gladly. I visited him; we talked and had some tea. That was analytical work with scholar Gaidar.

KOKH: What is your impression of those three Gaidars?

SHAKHRAI: They were all positive. We were the same age. He was born in March and I was born in April. We were born under different zodiac signs, but we had something in common. I felt he liked me.

AVEN: Gaidar really liked you very much. Besides, Gaidar said he knew two Yeltsins—before and after 1994. Would you say the same about Yeltsin? Did you see him after 1996? Or did you two stop meeting after 1994?

SHAKHRAI: We kept meeting until 1998.

AVEN: Did he really change so much?

SHAKHRAI: That's why I have three Yeltsins, too.

KOKH: We speak about Yeltsin the way he was before fall 1993, before and after the White House shooting. There was a tense period during the adoption of the constitution; then he dismissed Fyodorov and Gaidar, and started to form his own power on totally different principles.

SHAKHRAI: I had absolutely different periods in my evaluation of Yeltsin. I think the White House events made him more isolated and angry, but his power strengthened. He used force, and he became stronger.

KOKH: Everyone realized he was prepared to persevere to the end, and they stopped the polemics.

SHAKHRAI: He became more isolated, angry, and vindictive. I realized that from the amnesty situation. I viewed the events of October 3–4 as a civil war episode, in which neither side was right or wrong. And I proposed political amnesty for Khasbulatov, Lukyanov, and others as a measure of conciliation. I explained my standpoint to Yeltsin, and he seemed to have heard my arguments and let the prisoners go. And then he asked Korzhakov to tell me that he would never forgive me for that.

AVEN: What was your position at that moment?

SHAKHRAI: I was a vice premier and chaired a faction at the First State Duma. There were 33 deputies in my faction.

KOKH: Was Sasha Shokhin there?

SHAKHRAI: Yes, we had Shokhin and Kalmykov and Melikian. It was the Party of Russian Unity and Accord (PRUA). Our faction promoted the amnesty resolution at the State Duma.

AVEN: Sasha Shokhin was a vice premier at the time?

SHAKHRAI: Yes, he was a vice premier, too. We had a strong faction—two vice premiers.
   Maybe 1994 was a year that was important for Yeltsin's transformation, but my idea of Yeltsin has 1996 as the landmark. Even his looks changed.

KOKH: There is a very simple explanation: a new stage of his ailment. They told us he was sound as a drum earlier—he could booze all day long and be cheerful in the morning.

SHAKHRAI: Not even in the morning, just two hours later.

AVEN: Did you have a period of fascination with Yeltsin or not? When I came to Moscow and started working for him, I was not fascinated by him. But Chubais told me that both he and Yegor were charmed. Were you charmed?

SHAKHRAI: I was not charmed or enamored, for two reasons. First, I was not raised that way. Second, Yeltsin had to withhold support from me in a lot of small things, and he did that with—or maybe without—pleasure.

He nominated me to be a vice chairman of the Supreme Soviet. The voting day coincided with the anniversary of Sakharov's death, and 118 democratic deputies went to the cemetery.[3] They boarded buses by the Kremlin Palace, and as soon as they departed my nomination was put to the vote. Obviously, "our" deputies were gone, and we lacked votes. Was it a coincidence?

But I didn't bear a grudge. Because he was a real politician. I was aware of his limitations and abilities, and his historic role.

AVEN: Could you tell us briefly what his historic role was?

SHAKHRAI: He had to govern the country amid the breaking apart of the economic, political, and social system. By Russian standards, that breakage had minimal costs. Our transformations led to a bloodbath—it might not be immediate, but it would happen just the same. What was the October Revolt? Just a few people running around a square—but we had the Civil War later on!

KOKH: This war is still on.

SHAKHRAI: Actually, yes. It goes on, judging by the ruined lives, and the schizophrenia in our heads.

KOKH: Giant groups of people have different opinions of fundamental things, and different goals.

---

3.   They were kept under tight Soviet police surveillance, and he was removed to hospital and force-fed for months at a time after two separate hunger strikes. Released from exile in 1986 by Gorbachev, Sakharov was elected in March 1989 to the new parliament and co-led the democratic opposition, the Interregional Deputies Group. He died on December 14, 1989, at age 68 of a heart attack while taking a nap before preparing an important speech he was to deliver the next day in congress.

SHAKHRAI: The most terrible thing is that the Civil War and later years cut off the historical memory. Families preserved something, certain people preserved something, emigrants preserved something. But I couldn't force my own family to remember. One of my grandfathers was a victim of repression, and the other lived long.

AVEN: Was he executed?

SHAKHRAI: No, just exiled to Siberia.

AVEN: Did he survive?

SHAKHRAI: No—all was over when he was 28. And I couldn't make either my father or either grandmother tell me what happened after 1917. They feared that knowledge might hamper my university studies.

AVEN: Were they Cossacks?

SHAKHRAI: No. My father's family was Cossack. My mother was born in the village of Savinskoye, near Rybinsk. Grandfather Alexey came to St Petersburg in 1914; he was working at the Putilov Plant, and was then assigned to the unit of 25,000 specialists who went to the countryside in 1928 to assist with the collective farms. He was a technician, a blacksmith, and he worked at machine and tractor stations of collective farms. He was a jack-of-all-trades. And memory of him was lost: a whole generation without memory, without roots.

KOKH: What haven't we discussed?

SHAKHRAI: Well, I think there was one more interesting episode related to the "Yes-Yes-No-Yes" referendum. I told Yeltsin that the referendum shouldn't simply be about "like or not like" and "trust or no trust." I said we should publish a draft of a normal constitution.

AVEN: Did you work together with Oleg Rumyantsev?

SHAKHRAI: Geographically, yes, we were members of the same commission; but not in content or ideology.

KOKH: Did you write the new constitution?

SHAKHRAI: Sergei Sergeyevich Alexeyev and I wrote the new constitution, just the two of us.

KOKH: What did Rumyantsev have to do with it?

SHAKHRAI: Nothing, actually. It was not so much about writing a text. The Rumyantsev commission had plenty of such texts—all of them were variants of the Supreme Soviet. But Alexeyev and I wrote the presidential constitution, and a constitutional assembly was convened to adopt it. At that assembly I presented the draft constitution prepared by the Constitutional Commission—Oleg was its secretary—and compared it with the draft constitution written by Alexeyev and me.

AVEN: Article by article?

SHAKHRAI: Article by article, and item by item. And in some cases we used the draft of the Constitutional Commission—we admitted that their text was better. I have said that many times, and I have praised the commission because it consisted of highly skilled lawyers.

And now people try to calculate the percentage of each draft in the present constitution. Specialists know that it is simply impossible to write a totally new fundamental law—the main principles and ideas were coined centuries ago.

AVEN: Still, did you have a personal relationship with Yeltsin?

SHAKHRAI: There was no relationship. If I visited his dacha, it was to attend some meeting.

KOKH: You must have been alien to him.

SHAKHRAI: Probably. Now we're almost the same age he was then, but back then we were in our thirties and forties. Yeltsin saw us as a different generation, a different civilization, and a different planet.

PAVEL GRACHEV

"I, the Defense Minister, Did Not
Allow the Army to Break Up"

DEFENSE MINISTER PAVEL GRACHEV was no more popular than the Gaidar team. There were countless accusations and foolish nicknames. Yet Grachev was a real general with combat experience. He spent five years in Afghanistan, and was promoted from major to major general. He was a Hero of the Soviet Union. He was also the youngest commander of the Airborne Forces.

The armed forces were coming apart, just like the whole country, due to their unavoidable and sudden reduction, the homelessness experienced by many former officers, serious problems (not created by Grachev) in the withdrawal from Warsaw Pact countries, and attempts to involve the Russian Army in conflicts in former Union republics. Disgruntled former officers inevitably became an active part of the opposition to the Yeltsin regime. How could Yeltsin's defense minister be popular?

Nevertheless, Grachev retained control of the armed forces. Russian servicemen never took part in internal disagreements in CIS states (despite the appeals of Alexander Rutskoi). Grachev also set a new course in relations with the traditional "potential aggressor."

Grachev had been to Afghanistan, and had little to fear. Yet he risked his life more than others, even after the Afghan War. He could have been court-martialed for his refusal to storm the White House (the seat of the Russian parliament) in August 1993, and for his direct involvement in the suppression of the putsch in the same year. Grachev would have been one of the first men executed by the coup leaders if they had won.

Grachev knew all about war and, unlike many who had never smelled gunpowder, was not eager to fight. He was the main opponent of the First Chechen War, and few remember that now. It was he who talked to Dudayev, who pulled weapons out of Chechnya (as much as he could), who tried to convince Yeltsin to start negotiations. Had he succeeded, Russian history could have taken a different turn.

I always felt at ease with him. I was at ease when we were members of the government in 1992 (and worked together in the arms trade, an area of mine), and now when Kokh and I interviewed him. I was at ease because Grachev was not only a brave person but also very serious, independent, and thoughtful. These qualities made a boy from the village of Rvy, near Tula, a general. Also, Grachev is an extrovert. It was very interesting for us to speak with him.

Petr Aven

PETR AVEN: You are the last of our planned interviewees. Everyone knows that you were the Airborne Forces commander at the putsch moment, but tell us a little about your life before August 1991. Then we will ask questions about the putsch. Who knows—maybe you'll tell us the hitherto unknown truth.

PAVEL GRACHEV: I can tell you the whole truth. Indeed, my book is practically finished, too. I had planned to write one book only, but then so many people interviewed me that my book became a three-volume edition, instead of one volume about 1991. I graduated from the General Staff Academy in 1990, and was appointed as the Airborne Forces first deputy commander.

SERVICE BEFORE 1991 AND THE GKCHP PUTSCH

AVEN: Did you fight in Afghanistan?

GRACHEV: Yes. I had been on two Afghan missions by then, for a total of five years. I was there from 1981 to 1983, and from 1985 to 1988. I went on the first mission as a major, and became a major general by the end. I was awarded the Hero of the Soviet Union title in 1988. I was admitted to the General Staff Academy, and graduated with merit in 1990. There was a choice: to appoint me as the commander of an army based in Chernigov or as the first deputy commander of the Airborne Forces. My former commander, who was like a father to me, Dmitry Semyonovich Sukhorukov, headed the main personnel department at the time. He called for me two or three months before my graduation, and offered me the opportunity to return to the Airborne Forces. That was in July 1990. I had been the first deputy commander for no more than six months before Commander Vladislav Alexeyevich Achalov was promoted to the position of Soviet deputy defense minister, and through the joint efforts of Achalov and Yazov I became the Airborne Forces commander in approximately March 1991. Naturally, I had not expected such rapid promotion.

ALFRED KOKH: Were you in Afghanistan with the Airborne Forces?

GRACHEV: My mission in Afghanistan started (after my graduation from the Frunze Academy) in the rank of the first deputy commander of the 345th Separate Airborne Regiment. The mission lasted from 1981–3. I was the chief of staff of an airborne division based in Kaunas in 1983–5, and was summoned back to Afghanistan in 1985. They told me I must go there for at least a year. They promised me a new rank, a new position, and other benefits. They kept their promise—but I was there for three years instead of one.

And I really didn't expect the promotion to the position of the Airborne Forces commander. I was inspecting troops in the Far East, in Ussuriysk, when Achalov summoned me urgently. I asked, "Why the haste?" And he told me, "I have good news for you." I came to his office the next day. He said, "I have been appointed as the deputy defense minister, and you will be the Airborne Forces commander. Let's go and meet with Yazov." Yazov congratulated me, and I told him, as a military man should, "I'll do my best to justify your trust." I didn't know then that such a grandiose plot as the GKChP was looming.

KOKH: Was it then looming already? I don't think so.

GRACHEV: Yazov made an interesting remark. He said Russia was witnessing serious events, that I was the best paratrooper and a man who had been in action, and that he expected me to execute any order to keep the country safe.

Yeltsin was out of favor, and Yazov, Achalov, and especially the party bosses thought negatively of him. I had not known Yeltsin personally. Once in late March—

KOKH: Were you the commander by that time?

GRACHEV: Yes, I was. I had a call; they told me, "Yeltsin will speak with you." He said, "Hello, I have heard about you and I would like to visit the Tula airborne division." I told him, "We will need the permission of the defense minister." "Can't you give permission yourself?" "Certainly not—but I will make a call and ask." "Then call Yazov and Achalov." I called Achalov and said, "Yeltsin wants to visit the Airborne Forces, in particular the Tula airborne division." He thought for a while and said, "I will ask Yazov for advice." He called me back in about 15 minutes, and said, "Okay, we have Yazov's permission, but you must be careful. Give him a cool welcome—don't wine and dine him, and say little." I went to Tula the day before the visit, and we started to prepare a training show. Yeltsin and his entourage arrived the next day. I made a report. "Now show us your paratroopers." I showed him shooting, parachute jumps, and our hardware. And while we were talking I realized that he was a rather pleasant, smart, and independent man. Frankly, I liked him, although Achalov kept calling me and saying, "Mind, you must follow our instructions." But I said, "He is a normal man. Why shouldn't I show him what the Airborne Forces really have?" "All right, but don't feed him or offer him drinks." We saw the shooting training, and I showed him around and then Yeltsin asked, "Shall we have lunch?" And I had already ordered the support services chief to make a good lunch and to serve it in a tent. One tent was put up for the commanders and the other for the entourage and journalists. When he was done looking, I brought him to the tent and he liked the food. I asked him, "How about a drink?" And he said, "With pleasure!"

Naturally, there were informers to report the warm welcome. Achalov called and said, "You will suffer the consequences." My answer was, "You do what you think is best. I simply had to welcome him as a hospitable host." So we had our lunch and our drinks, and there was a lake there, and the ice had just melted. He suggested we take a swim. We undressed and jumped into the lake. And all the bodyguards jumped in after us.

KOKH: Did Korzhakov do that?

GRACHEV: What else could he do? Korzhakov was nobody at that time—a senior lieutenant picked up in the street; his own fellow servicemen had gotten rid of him. So we met, hugged, and parted as friends.

Yazov and Achalov summoned me. They said they were completely displeased with my welcome of Yeltsin, and told me I had not been supposed to do that. I said, "I am not a politician, I am a military man and I follow orders honestly and scrupulously." Things started. I did not meet Yeltsin frequently, but you, Petr, must remember that I became a very close acquaintance of Yuri Vladimirovich Skokov—a very good friend.

KOKH: Was he in the Yeltsin entourage during that first visit?

GRACHEV: He was a member of that delegation—he was a man close to Yeltsin, like Burbulis and Petrov.

KOKH: Do you think they were courting you?

GRACHEV: No doubt! That was not easy to do, but Yeltsin wanted to make an acquaintance, and he made one. I was mostly communicating with Skokov.
  Yeltsin was wise, cunning, and clever; he kept asking how the Airborne Forces were doing and what problems we had. I pretended I didn't notice his courting: I just liked him, and I decided to befriend him.
  What happened next? Achalov called for me in June or July 1991, and we went to see Yazov together. Yazov was calm, and told me, "Kryuchkov wants to meet you." I asked, "Why is that?" "You are an apt commander, and he wants to meet you." I thought, "There must be some reason: the KGB chairman would not want to meet some commander for no reason." I asked, "When shall I go?" "You go now—he is waiting for you." I went to the Lubyanka, an uncomfortable place. Have you ever been there?

AVEN: I have.

GRACHEV: Have you been to his office? So creepy.

AVEN: I was there at a different time.

GRACHEV: I was met at the gate and politely shown to the elevator and to the reception area. As soon as I entered the reception area, a door opened and he greeted me personally. He looked so quiet and modest to me—

KOKH: A knight of the cloak and dagger.

GRACHEV: Aha. So, he showed me into his office and called for his deputy. I took a seat and started shivering. I was a paratrooper, but I was so uncomfortable. The room had such a gloomy atmosphere.

KOKH: With a portrait of Felix[1] on the wall?

GRACHEV: Sure, there was.

"The country's situation is unclear. Gorbachev is sick at such an inappropriate time. The Politburo has no leader. People are disturbed." I was listening intently. "You see, it may happen that …" He took a roundabout approach and said, "I just wanted to ask you; there may be a situation requiring support of the armed forces." I asked, "Why?" "What do you mean, why? To prevent disturbances." And I asked, "What do the Airborne Forces have to do with it? There is Yazov, there are the armed forces. What do the Airborne Forces have to do with it?"

KOKH: There are also the Interior Ministry forces.

GRACHEV: He said, "Compared with the Interior Ministry forces, the Airborne Forces are elite, and they may be of use." I asked, "For what?" "Maybe people will not understand all this. We will have to protect the most important facilities. But the reason I asked you to come here is to work on a possible plan for the peaceful transfer of power from Gorbachev to the Politburo if he is unable to work any longer." I was surprised. I said, "I know nothing about such plans. I can shoot and I can fight." "That is all right."

KOKH: Interesting, to use the army for a peaceful transfer. There's no need to use the army if the transfer is peaceful.

GRACHEV: He told me, "We will assign two men to you, and you will go to a countryside residence. You will take some rest and draft a possible action plan. They are smart fellows." I called Yazov and said, "Here is the situation." He said, "Do what Kryuchkov tells you." "Yes, sir." We agreed on a meeting on the next day. A car was parked at a corner in Khimkhi, and there were two young lads in it. I remember one of them, Zhizhin—he was from my hometown.

AVEN: The deputy head of the KGB First Main Department. He took an active part in GKChP planning.

GRACHEV: Right. I joined them in their car and let my car go. They said, "We may have to spend the night there."

---

1.   Felix Dzerzhinsky, founder of Soviet State Security.

Kokh: Were they young?

Grachev: They were.

Aven: Just about my age—younger than Pavel.

Grachev: We came to a luxurious dacha in a forest. A table was laid; there was just one waitress there, nobody else. "We will be working here." "And what do we have to make?" "A peaceful transfer plan." And I asked, "What do I have to do with that?" "The Airborne Forces may play a role." They started planning and looking through documents on power transfer in various African countries, but nothing was good for us. I was sitting silent. I saw that the others were not very active, either—they seemed to be at a loss.

Kokh: Or they could have been using some Aesopian language to make you set a task for yourself: to seize Moscow rapidly and, if possible, without fatalities. And you pretended you did not understand what they wanted.

Grachev: Sure!

Kokh: I see.

Grachev: In short, we spent three days there but did not draft a clever plan. The only thing I insisted on was that the Airborne Forces should come to Moscow and protect the main buildings from damage, just as in 1917.

Kokh: Post, telegraph, telephone, and bridges.

Grachev: Television, radio, telegraph, post, the City Hall, the White House, and so on. Three days later they presented the plan to Kryuchkov. I asked them, "Give me a copy—I will make a report to my commander." Yazov called within several hours. "What were you doing there?" I said, "Here is the plan—I do not know what they want." "No, this plan is no good." "But I don't know what they want." In short, he was displeased. "Be prepared to lead divisions." I said, "I will do that on your orders." That was it. Two weeks passed. And I thought that was all over. But then, what day of August was it?

Aven: August 17.

GRACHEV: The day before, Achalov called me and said, "Here is the order. Prepare two divisions for possible relocation to Moscow, listen to the radio, and watch television." I ordered the Tula division to prepare for a march, and the Bolgrad division to be ready for landing at the Chkalovsky airfield.

KOKH: What was the other division?

GRACHEV: Bolgrad. Bolgrad is a town near Odessa. The 98th Bolgrad Division.

When they started playing Tchaikovsky music on TV, Achalov called and said, "Bring in the Tula division." I asked, "What is the mission?" "To protect the most important facilities, and so on." The facilities were listed in advance. I gave the order, "Onward." The division accomplished its mission rapidly. Yeltsin called some time later: "Where are your forces?" I told him, "One division is marching to Moscow, and the other is in Odessa, preparing to land at the Chkalovsky airfield." "Will you shoot at me?" "Yeltsin, what shooting? No one will be shooting." "Can you inform me about what you do?" "Sure." "When shall I call you?" We had a normal conversation. He was afraid that—

KOKH: Shooting?

GRACHEV: No. There would be a command to seize him, personally. We came to Moscow, took positions (in particular, near the White House, where Yeltsin was), and secured the City Hall perimeter. Then Luzhkov got nervous. He called me. I said, "Calm down. Why are you shouting?" "What are these troops?" "We are protecting your building, the City Hall." "I do not need protection; we can protect ourselves." "Okay, what do you want?" "Pull out your troops." "Okay, as you wish. But be prepared for possible attacks."

AVEN: The tanks that crushed three men, were they yours?

GRACHEV: No. Moscow District Commander Nikolai Vasilyevich Kalinin brought in the Tamanskaya and Kantemirovskaya divisions on the orders of Yazov. Those tanks were from the Kantemirovskaya division.

AVEN: Did anyone else give you orders? Or did you just stay there? Was there an order to seize Yeltsin, or somebody else?

GRACHEV: No, there was no command to seize anyone. I kept communicating with Yeltsin via Skokov. He finally believed that I had no intention of sending my battalion to storm his White House.

AVEN: Actually, there was no such order—am I right?

GRACHEV: Right, there was no order.

KOKH: And why didn't they give the order?

GRACHEV: They were scared. They realized that events had taken an unexpected turn. They expected universal support, but no one supported them.

KOKH: How could they have screwed it up like that?

GRACHEV: Well, they did.

KOKH: The KGB was monitoring public opinion constantly.

GRACHEV: So what? It was an impromptu act.

AVEN: You helped Yeltsin a lot. You were holding negotiations with Skokov, but you were generally executing orders. Did you receive any orders to begin the storming?

GRACHEV: There was an order to storm the White House in the morning.

AVEN: There was?

GRACHEV: Indeed, next morning.

AVEN: Was it on August 18?

GRACHEV: My mistake—the order was given in the evening of August 17.
Achalov called me and said, "You will have to seize Yeltsin." I said, "Give me a written order. Blood will be spilled. They will start shooting. They won't give him to us without a fight." "You will get your written orders." "The order will be executed if it is given in writing, but not otherwise." Then I gathered my guys, my deputies, at the Airborne Forces Staff in Sokolniki. They were experienced men, we had fought in Afghanistan together. So

we talked and decided that we would not spill blood or storm anything no matter what orders might be given.

KOKH: Was that your decision?

GRACHEV: Ours. Yes. We called for our Spetsnaz[2] to protect the perimeter from possible attacks. Yuri Vladimirovich Skokov came to see us. I told him, "You tell Yeltsin that I would not storm you even if I have such orders. Blood will be spilled, and it will be the fault of the drunken Politburo, but they will hold me responsible because I am in charge of the military. I do not care about dying, but I have my family and children. They will seize them. No—we all have families, I will not do that." He thanked me. I sent [General Alexander] Lebed to accompany him. I said Lebed could stay with them. Lebed chose a somewhat wrong tactic to deal with Yeltsin. Skokov called and said, "Recall Lebed, he will seize us personally if there are such orders."

AVEN: Seize?

GRACHEV: I recalled him and sent him to the Chkalovsky airfield. "You can receive the 98th Bolgrad Division better than anyone else." I had another call later—they said, "The storming must begin in the morning. At 7:00 a.m." I kept insisting on my condition: "I will do nothing without written orders." It was 7:00 a.m. already, but I did nothing. Staff Chief Podkolzin— you must know that general—told me, "None of us wants the storming, but you should call the defense minister and ask whether those orders will be given. You should define your mission like a military man in order to avoid misunderstandings in the future." I called the minister's office. A man told me that the defense minister was resting and had asked not to be awakened. I thought, "A fine time for taking a rest." I called Achalov, and his office also told me, "Vyacheslav Alexeyevich is resting—he asked not to be disturbed." I said, "Please, tell him Grachev called about written orders. We kind of had an agreement—we are on hold here." They promised they would tell him. And I said, "Okay, we won't storm—we will wait for the orders."

KOKH: So there was no written order.

GRACHEV: Right! They didn't even define the mission orally at 7:00 a.m. And I had a call at 8:00 a.m. Achalov asked, "So, Commander, have you

2.   Special operation forces.

stormed it?" I said, "I didn't even try!" "How? Why?" "Because I asked for written orders. I had no confirmation. You were asleep. So was the defense minister. I could have been put on trial before a tribunal, or even executed, for acting on my own!"

"Now, prepare to suffer the consequences." We breathed a sigh of relief: the consequences. They were simply scared.

All was clear by the morning, and we understood there would be no orders. So we drank cognac.

KOKH: Did you drink a lot?

GRACHEV: We did! And they surrendered at about 9:00 or 10:00 a.m.

KOKH: We know what happens to those who don't surrender. One was torn into pieces by a crowd just recently.

GRACHEV: Who was that?

KOKH: Gaddafi.

GRACHEV: Well, yes. Then Yazov explained he was an old fool to have got involved.

MINISTERIAL RANK

AVEN: Pavel, you have given us a very detailed account of the putsch. When the putsch was over, what was the condition of the armed forces in 1991? The country was falling apart—the economy was falling apart.

GRACHEV: Military units in Russia were still combat ready in 1991. Especially the units in the Moscow region: the Kantemirovskaya division, the Tamanskaya division, the Airborne Forces, others, the Air Defense Forces—they were still in good shape. That was before salaries were delayed for several months.

AVEN: And outside of Russia? In Tajikistan, Ukraine?

GRACHEV: The decline had already started outside of Russia. But military units deployed in Russia belonged to the second strategic echelon. They had worse armaments and weaker officers, because the first strategic echelon, which was supposed to deter the enemy on the border—the Baltic district, the Belarusian district, the Ukrainian district, and the South Caucasian district—was in the hands of independent states, which were not even CIS members at the time.

AVEN: That happened later.

GRACHEV: Yes—and the strongest forces were certainly deployed in those republics. And what did we have? Just the Moscow district, and, probably, the Far Eastern district.

AVEN: But did the Soviet armed forces function normally?

GRACHEV: The armed forces were still functioning at that time.

AVEN: In Russia, yes. But what about Ukraine and Belarus?

GRACHEV: They were also capable of combat; they were staffed and well provisioned.

KOKH: Here is my question. I have read plenty of interviews with various heroes and anti-heroes about the slow leak of armaments into the hands of the Chechens. As far as I understand, that process started in summer 1991?

GRACHEV: That happened later, when we, our government (including Petr Aven), and our friends Sergei Shakhrai and Andrei Kozyrev convinced Yeltsin not to negotiate with Dudayev. Rutskoi was particularly angry: Why should we negotiate with him? Who is he, anyway? And Dudayev was elected president and started talking about independence. He started talking about independence not because he actually wanted to break free from Russia. But, as a highlander, he was offended that he, a president elected in a universal ballot, was not reckoned with, was not invited to the Kremlin, but was treated like 100 percent trash. And he was a Soviet army general, a remarkable pilot, and a divisional commander. I spoke to him a lot. He told me, "Nobody wants to speak with me. And I am still the president, no matter how bad a president I might be. People elected me. To hell with you if you don't want to speak with me. Then I will raise with my people the question of separating from Russia." I told the government about that so many times. I said, "We must speak with him." But everyone was adamant: Yeltsin should not receive Dudayev!

KOKH: Why were they so selectively hostile to Dudayev? Why were others who talked about separatism, such as Shaimiyev, received? Take, for instance, Murtaza Rakhimov.

GRACHEV: Their separatism was mild, soft. None of them raised the question of secession.

KOKH: First of all, they did. But I want to understand the sequence of events: did they stop meeting with Dudayev after he started talking about separatism, or did he start talking about separatism because nobody wanted to speak with him?

AVEN: Those were parallel processes.

KOKH: Still, what came first—the chicken or the egg?

GRACHEV: He talked about broader autonomy at first. He didn't speak about secession.

KOKH: So, he didn't differ much from the other regional leaders, did he?

GRACHEV: Absolutely, absolutely. But those regional leaders were received and spoken with; but not he.

KOKH: That is what I am asking: Why was it decided not to receive Dudayev?

GRACHEV: I don't know. I've always thought it was silly.

AVEN: That was done by many, among them Khasbulatov.

KOKH: Did Khasbulatov deem himself the main Chechen and oppose negotiations with Dudayev?

GRACHEV: Yes—and you may also ask Sasha Rutskoi why he never visited Chechnya, although he was supervising it. He said, "To hell with Dudayev. I, the vice president, will not talk to some Dudayev." That produced an adverse effect on Dudayev's behavior. I visited him when it was decided to pull out our training center from Chechnya, in 1993, after tensions had already started to escalate. They didn't seize anyone back then, but tensions had already been escalating. And they started to abuse Russians in Chechnya, too.

KOKH: They had armed themselves by 1993. Hadn't the depots been looted by then?

GRACHEV: Not yet.

KOKH: You can find some documents, photocopies of certain orders on the internet.

GRACHEV: Lots of things have been posted on the internet. I visited him in 1992 and asked, "Dzhokhar, what are you doing?" We met at his home. All those guys, Basayev and others, were there. They treated me normally.

KOKH: Had you already been acquainted?

GRACHEV: I had only met Dudayev before.

KOKH: Did you meet in Afghanistan?

GRACHEV: Yes. The table was full of food. I said, "Dzhokhar, what are you doing?" And he said, "Nobody wants to talk to me. Rutskoi sent me to hell over the phone. If I don't react, my guys, my people, will not understand me." And I asked, "Do you know why I am here? I will pull out our forces." "Why? Aren't they all right here?" "You know there have been attacks on our forces—some have been wounded; and our families have been terrorized."

KOKH: There had been many Russians in Grozny, and all of them were evicted, and some were even killed.

GRACHEV: I said, "I will probably pull out our forces." "No, I will not let you do that." "How is that? I will open fire." "You open fire, and we open fire." "Come on, how can you do that?" In short, he was offended, and that was it.

AVEN: Did he allow you to pull out your forces?

GRACHEV: Yes, he did. But the forces were unarmed. Actually, we pulled out some of the weapons. We decided we would share the weapons 50/50, and criminal charges were brought against me for not taking the entire stock. Those dogs, prosecutors, could not understand that I was lucky to pull out at least half of the firearms. Certainly lots were left behind.

KOKH: When was this?

GRACHEV: Either in late 1992 or in early 1993. We need to look this up—there are documents. They started criticizing me: "You left the weapons to Dudayev." "You must thank me for pulling out heavy armaments." I pulled out the entire artillery stock first. We knocked out the wedge breechblocks and drove them out quietly. Then I stealthily withdrew all the mobile radio stations. I brought out everything that needed to be brought out.

KOKH: So, were you really pulling forces out of Chechnya?

GRACHEV: Under the guise of exercises.

KOKH: In fact, you were aware that you were operating on enemy territory, weren't you?

GRACHEV: I couldn't believe it was enemy territory. I was hurt that our leaders had pushed on Yeltsin the idea that war was right.

AVEN: You were very close to Yeltsin. Kozyrev and you were his closest political advisors.

GRACHEV: Come on—Kozyrev was not the closest!

AVEN: To whom did Yeltsin listen most closely at that moment?

GRACHEV: Of the ministers?

AVEN: Yes.

GRACHEV: No one!

KOKH: And other than ministers? Personally, who was the closest? Was that Korzhakov?

GRACHEV: Korzhakov was not strong enough yet.

AVEN: Who, then?

GRACHEV: Well, he listened to Petrov, to Skokov.

AVEN: Lobov?

GRACHEV: No—who was Lobov? There were Petrov, Skokov, Gaidar, later Galya Starovoitova, me. Actually, Yeltsin asked my advice. But only when we were hunting in Zavidovo—we spent two days there and discussed everything. Then we called for Petrov. He came gladly, saw a deer herd, and shot about 15 deer with his submachine gun. Yeltsin gathered us and said, "There is a killer among us. Petrov, fall out. Get out of here—you won't be hunting with us anymore."

AVEN: Kozyrev told us the main problem was Rutskoi pushing Yeltsin to interfere in the internal affairs of the republics. Rutskoi tried to engage troops in conflicts in Transdniestria and Tajikistan, and wanted to solve every problem with the help of the Russian Army. Kozyrev said he had stopped the Lebed army from marching on Chisinau.

GRACHEV: Well, maybe—I don't know.

AVEN: He said Rutskoi tried to send Russian troops stationed in Transdniestria to Chisinau.

GRACHEV: Certainly not. How could he do that if the Fourteenth Army was subordinated to me only?

AVEN: Yes—and Kozyrev says that Lebed was intriguing and playing his own game.

GRACHEV: Lebed marching to Chisinau? Are you nuts?

AVEN: That never happened. Is that what you think?

GRACHEV: There was the shaky, broke Fourteenth Army in Transdniestria. A march to Chisinau? No. Who could have fought there?

AVEN: The Fourteenth Army could.

GRACHEV: You must be joking. There was no one to fight. Maybe Andrei was taking some diplomatic steps there.

AVEN: And what about Tajikistan? He said he had the sole task of keeping servicemen from deserting. Everyone in Tajikistan was prepared to desert—border guards and, in the first turn, the army. He told us he had to convince the border guards to stay. What can you say?

GRACHEV: I don't know about border guards, but I know all about my troops in Tajikistan, Turkmenistan, and other republics.

AVEN: No one was trying to desert?

GRACHEV: They never tried. I visited military units and spoke to servicemen. But I wasn't in charge of border guards.

AVEN: I understand. But were you in full control of the army?

GRACHEV: I was in full control of the army. Absolutely. There were no vacillations.

AVEN: Were there attempts to interfere in the internal affairs of Tajikistan, Uzbekistan, or anywhere else?

GRACHEV: No.

KOKH: So, you pulled forces out of Chechnya, but firearms had been left there, which complicated the situation because Dudayev formed his own armed units loyal only to him. Further escalation of tensions was just a question of time.

GRACHEV: Yes. That is right.

AVEN: Kozyrev told us he saved the country from the Yugoslav scenario. You think there was no such threat at all?

GRACHEV: No! Certainly not.

KOKH: I also think this is sort of an alarmist theory, claiming we could have plunged into war for restoration of the Soviet Union. I think there were no significant social groups prepared to fight for that.

AVEN: But that is what Kozyrev told us. We are not specialists in that field—

we are economists, and we know nothing about that. Kozyrev told us one more thing: he said he had tried to change the foreign political doctrine. The former course, Gorbachev's, identified us as enemies of America and the West, although we had détente, and Kozyrev tried to become a Western ally or even a part of the West. Did you see any change of the defense doctrine with regard to NATO, or not?

RELATIONS WITH NATO

GRACHEV: Certainly, the doctrine changed.

AVEN: Toward alliance?

GRACHEV: We took a course that was not yet an alliance, but toward better understanding with NATO.

AVEN: And that course was called?

GRACHEV: Partnership for Peace. I visited Brussels several times. We were discussing the so-called flank limitations—the amounts of hardware.

AVEN: Kozyrev claims the non-enlargement question was never raised.

GRACHEV: Non-enlargement of NATO? It wasn't, at the time—although we said we could do nothing about the wish of certain countries to join NATO. Yet there was supposed to be a buffer zone between our borders and the former borders of NATO. And countries in the buffer zone were supposed to remain such, even if they decided to join NATO. NATO forces were not to be deployed on their territories.

AVEN: Was that the question of Ukraine?

GRACHEV: No. The Baltic republics, in the first instance.

AVEN: So the issue was discussed after all?

GRACHEV: Certainly.

KOKH: Did they promise not to deploy forces?

GRACHEV: Yes. We agreed on that.

KOKH: And were any documents signed?

GRACHEV: I saw it, yes.

KOKH: And how do they explain the deployment of NATO forces in the Baltic republics?

GRACHEV: You should ask this question of other ministers. That didn't happen when I was in office.

AVEN: Kozyrev says there were no legal commitments. He said the West had never promised not to enlarge NATO.

GRACHEV: What? They certainly did!

AVEN: Did they?

KOKH: And did you sign any papers?

GRACHEV: Sure. Agreements.

AVEN: Kozyrev says no such documents were signed.

GRACHEV: There were written commitments. You tell him about the agreement on flank limitations, and the agreement that set limits on armed forces in various strategic sectors. That's what I can remember. But the actual number of these agreements must have been bigger—those agreements set the amount of NATO forces and their locations. I repeat: there was no commitment to deny NATO membership to those countries; NATO really didn't pledge to do that. But they pledged not to deploy forces in those countries even if they became NATO members.

AVEN: All right—and what about new members?

GRACHEV: No agreements were signed with regard to new members; that question hadn't even been put on the agenda.

AVEN: So the most important question, of whether Poland would be a NATO member, wasn't raised?

GRACHEV: That question wasn't asked when we were in office.

KOKH: All right. Poland could have joined NATO, but not its military component—like France, for instance.

GRACHEV: There was no serious discussion of Poland, I can tell you that. Actually, we didn't think about new members of NATO at that moment. That happened later.

KOKH: So we may say that the West didn't undertake any serious commitments?

GRACHEV: No one did—neither they nor we. There was no such question— there was no question of missile defense or anything else.

KOKH: But the Treaty on Conventional Armed Forces in Europe was still in force, wasn't it?

GRACHEV: Yes, it was.

KOKH: But it doesn't work!

GRACHEV: That's different. But it worked when I was the minister. And then NATO started their enlargement, and retracted that accord unilaterally. Because the West was moving silently.

AVEN: Did you take part in foreign political discussions, including discussions about NATO? I mean, Kozyrev was negotiating in Brussels.

GRACHEV: Sure, I went there together with him. Kozyrev and I frequently traveled together. But I was negotiating on purely military issues. I never gave much thought to political issues.

AVEN: Did Kozyrev hold those negotiations himself?

GRACHEV: Yes.

AVEN: Do you think he was not close to Yeltsin?

GRACHEV: They were, but not as close as we were. Yeltsin respected him and loved him; but the president was close to no one. Except, maybe, me.

AVEN: So you were the person closest to him for a certain period?

GRACHEV: As I was told: "You are not number one in Russia but you are not number two, either."

AVEN: Right. You did not expect your dismissal, did you?

DISMISSAL AND AFTERWARD

GRACHEV: Actually, no. When Russia became effectively independent, in August 1991, we took a walk in the woods. There were six or seven of us. Yeltsin said to us, "Let's swear allegiance to each other. I will never let you down. Let us take an oath on our blood." We had a knife, and we cut each other's hands and licked the blood.

AVEN: Who else was there?

GRACHEV: Me, Korzhakov, Kozyrev—

KOKH: Did Kozyrev cut his hand? He told us nothing!

GRACHEV: There was also Viktor from the KGB—he passed away recently, what was his name? I remember: Barannikov. Not Rutskoi. Skokov and two others were there.

AVEN: Was Burbulis there?

GRACHEV: I don't remember. We found an old tire and made it our table. The tire might have belonged to a Belarus tractor. We swore blood oaths on his initiative. And then he let us down. That was sudden. Why was it sudden? Because after Yeltsin had failed in the first election round in 1996, that team led by—

KOKH: Why did you say he failed? He won the first round.

GRACHEV: He didn't win the election in the first round—there was a runoff election. He failed to gain 51 percent of the votes. Zyuganov ranked second, and Lebed was third. And then his team, led by Vitya Ilyushin, Yumashev, and Tatiana, that trio, and the other mafia, decided to win over Lebed's electorate—although Lebed had always been against Yeltsin. They summoned Lebed and told him he must give them his voters.

AVEN: That was Berezovsky's idea.

GRACHEV: Berezovsky? Could be. "You give us your voters, and we will give you a position." "Which position?" "The position of the Security Council secretary." "All right, here are the voters." But he made one condition. Lebed bore a grudge against me: I dismissed him after he had gone wild in Tiraspol.

They persuaded Lebed (I don't think it took them long), and Lebed said he would give his voters to Yeltsin, fighting Zyuganov in the runoff election. He was given the position. But Lebed insisted he must have the right to give orders to the law enforcement ministries and the defense minister. Yeltsin summoned me after they had made the deal; I knew at once that something was wrong. Food was on the table and we had a drink, a second drink, and a third drink, and he told me: "I have decided to appoint Lebed as the Security Council secretary." "Why is that?" I asked.

KOKH: A second drink, a third drink? Yeltsin had just had a heart attack!

GRACHEV: Yes—he was already losing control, and he got drunk quickly. Yumashev and Tatiana were in control—mostly Tatiana. She was the one who always filled his glass. I saw that outright: his drunkenness was to her advantage. We were alone that time, though. And he was still quite sober. "Why would you make him the secretary? He was your election rival!" "But he promised us his voters." "How could he promise that? He doesn't have voters in his pocket. What if people who had voted for him would now vote for Zyuganov?" "Come on, Lebed promised." "Now, Yeltsin, your team works badly. But that is none of my business. What can I do for you?" "You see, I recently called you the best minister of all times and of all peoples." "You should not have said that." "Why? All right. Let me ask if you are ready to be subordinated to Lebed." "Why? By law I am subordinated only to you and, being a government member, to the prime minister within the limits of government powers." "I know that, but what shall we do?" I said, "I understand. Don't bother—I quit." Yes. I saw he was expecting me to say that. "And what would be the wording?" he asked. "Why make anything up?" And he said, "Shall we say that you failed in your duties? But I just called you the best. Shall we say for health reasons?" "Please, you should fear God. I am as healthy as a bull—I am a sportsman." "True." "Don't worry," I told him. And we drank a bottle or two and said our goodbyes and embraced and cried. Yeltsin's guys—Tanya, Yumashev, and some others—were already waiting behind the door. "Write your resignation statement," they told me, and gave me paper and a pen. And I wrote, "To the Supreme Commander, the President. I hereby tender my resignation from the position of defense minister in connection with ..." And then I stopped, because I could not think about the reason. I was drunk but my brain was still working, and I wrote, "In connection with the circumstances." Period. I signed it, and told them to hand over my statement to him. They were so glad, and rushed off to publish that same night a decree relieving me of my duties in connection with the circumstances.

AVEN: Strange wording.

GRACHEV: Some lawyers, especially Lukyanov's daughter Katya, are still trying. They say to me, "Let us win this case. Your dismissal was absolutely unlawful. What were the circumstances? What were the reasons?" She keeps telling me, "You are still the defense minister de jure. We can win so much money." "Let it go, Katya, I do not need anything."

KOKH: Let's return to the beginning. What were your relations with Gaidar?

ON GAIDAR'S GOVERNMENT

GRACHEV: Good. We came to an understanding immediately. He comes from a military family, after all. I certainly had respect for him. His lack of knowledge of industry was a disadvantage, but he was really full of those new market ideals. And he was so intelligent. In fact, I often couldn't understand what he was saying—he spoke breathlessly and used his smart economic terms.

AVEN: If you often didn't understand Yegor, then you must never have understood me at all.

GRACHEV: I liked Gaidar. At least he had aspirations. He probably needed a little practical work. He had no source for his knowledge in Russia, so he might have taken it from the West, from sources uncharacteristic of Russia. But he really had a wish to build a market economy in Russia and make this country strong. I can vouch for that.

AVEN: Was he decisive, bold?

GRACHEV: He was bold all right. He feared nothing, although he was so young. I think he was younger than you, wasn't he?

AVEN: A year younger.

GRACHEV: And I liked Petr Aven.

KOKH: Everybody likes Petr.

GRACHEV: Petr is a fine man, so handsome. His wife frequently accompanied us on business trips. He talked so well to that Deutsche Bank. Like any clever man, he was a bit absentminded. He could easily forget his jacket or toiletries at a hotel—

KOKH: He was just very rich.

AVEN: I was not rich at that time.

KOKH: But you already had the manner!

GRACHEV: I lent him my shaver several times. I think that was in Dresden. But that is a normal weakness of every smart person—they are all absentminded. Why did I gladly accept your interview offer? I would not have spoken with another person. But I respected and still respect Petr a lot.

AVEN: Thank you—it's mutual.

GRACHEV: We never quarreled.

KOKH: And I have a question about December 1992. There is an opinion that Yeltsin simply had to give up Gaidar. There is also an opinion that he could have avoided that, but Yeltsin simply preferred not to fight for Gaidar. What is your opinion?

GRACHEV: I think he did not fight for Gaidar. Because Gaidar—due to his numerous reforms, which were not clear to many people—was strongly disliked by the population. Besides, the media covered the government policy badly. The media team were poor, that's for sure.

AVEN: Poltoranin was in charge.

GRACHEV: What could he do? Probably he didn't have a full understanding himself. If the media coverage had been normal, there might have been less criticism. But they kept saying, "This is Gaidar; Gaidar is the root of all problems; Gaidar is responsible for every misfortune"—and there was nothing to be done about that. Could they have been doing that on purpose? Could Poltoranin have been doing that? Shifting the blame to Gaidar and shouting, "He's the one, again"? Sure, that was done on purpose. I understand now: a Führer is a Führer, he cannot be fully predictable. And I couldn't understand him (Yeltsin), even when he dismissed me.

AVEN: Did you communicate with Yeltsin after he fired you?

GRACHEV: Of course. He promised me a position. Did they do that? Like hell they did. Two or three months afterward, I had a call from that bearded man—he was the head of the personnel department: Savostyanov. He said, "Yeltsin told me to find you a good position." I asked, "So, did you do that? What position can you offer me?" Three months had passed and I had forgotten about that promise. "We want to appoint you as an ambassador." "Great! I know German rather well, and I am ready to be the ambassador to Germany, Austria, or even Switzerland." "No. These positions are taken for many years to come." "Then, what do you have to offer me?" "There is New Zealand, for instance." "And where is this country situated?" "This is such a wonderful country." "No, that's too far, I won't go there." "There are also a number of African and Latin American countries." "Are you trying to stash me away? I see you are mocking me. And why do you want to send me so far?" And then he said that phrase: "We have to hide you from the people for two or three years." "From which people?" "Well, everyone knows that you were the main ideologist of the war in Chechnya." And I said, "What?!"

KOKH: That is not so—everybody knows that is not so!

GRACHEV: "What? Go to the archives and pull up all of my speeches! Even the Chechens know that I was the main and practically the only opponent of that war!"

THE CHECHEN CAMPAIGN

KOKH: What a stupid thing to say. Even the media said it wasn't you. The initiative belonged to Vice Premier Yegorov.

GRACHEV: You know the media was cautious—Yegorov and a few other comrades.

KOKH: Who else?

GRACHEV: Doku Zavgayev.

KOKH: Sure, but he was a clerk, a department head …

GRACHEV: Yegorov and Doku mostly. I won't tell you who else—they are my colleagues. It doesn't matter who. And then I told him, "No, tell Yeltsin I don't need your positions." I left, and a month later Zhenya Ananyev called me and said, "It is time to stop being idle. Will you be my advisor?" I said, "Right, downgraded from the marshal's position to the sergeant's. But what shall I do? All right, I will." That was how I took the sergeant's position. It's all right—I have got over my pride, and I feel fine now. It turned out later that plenty of others needed me.

AVEN: What are you doing now?

GRACHEV: I chair the board of directors at a Ryazan plant, and I am a member of the board of directors and the chief advisor of an Omsk plant. I do what I can—no complaints. Are you planning to hire me—is that it? I don't need a job right now. I will call you if things get tough.

AVEN: They won't—you are not that kind.

GRACHEV: Then we will just be friends.

KOKH: I am interested in the beginning of the Chechen war. Especially in the story of Stepashin's volunteers, Avturkhanov and others. Why did they fail? They actually reached the presidential palace. Why were they not supported?

GRACHEV: And who was supposed to support them?

KOKH: As I understand it, Yerin was supposed to support them with the Interior Ministry troops—or was he not?

GRACHEV: As far as I know, they didn't ask Yerin for advice. That was the plan of Sergei Vadimovich and his security services. Doku Zavgayev orchestrated the whole thing. There was also my Krasnodar friend, Kolya Yegorov, the vice premier. Those guys secretly decided to organize a march to Grozny. They formed a battalion, and the Defense Ministry gave them as many tanks as they needed; Yeltsin gave me that order. Armored personnel carriers; officers and soldiers in reserve were invited to be volunteers, and many of them agreed. The hastily and wrongly formed battalion marched easily into Grozny, and relaxed. Meanwhile, Dudayev's boys got organized to beat the shit out of them. It was a close escape.

KOKH: I thought practically all of them were killed.

GRACHEV: Some escaped, but 80 percent of them died. That was a thoughtless act. After that campaign there was no way out: the desire to start the war was very strong.

KOKH: So you think there was no way back after that?

GRACHEV: Sure there was. We could have admitted that we did wrong, that we shouldn't have used force. After all, no one had declared war or given the order to attack. We should have invited a delegation led by Dudayev to Moscow and negotiated with them—but nobody wanted that. I was the only one to go there once, and I made the second visit before the war. In short, no one wanted a peaceful solution. They felt humiliated. They told me to begin a storm. They put the blame on me until the Chechens told them, "Grachev has nothing to do with it—he was the only one to object to that war." But they made me the scapegoat, and I was branded as such for a long time. To this day, there are people who think I started the war.

KOKH: Gaidar said, in an interview he gave me shortly before his death—he was absolutely clear—"I know Grachev had nothing to do with it."

AVEN: Our team had an ideal relationship with you.

GRACHEV: Right—it was ideal. When people accused me of starting the war, I asked Lobov, "Listen, Lobov, everyone is accusing me—why are you silent?" "What can I do?" "Take archive documents, my speech and others, and we will publish them. Let the people know that the decision to wage war was made by Chernomyrdin and you!"

KOKH: And did he want war?

GRACHEV: Sure—he even wanted to dismiss me. After I had said no,

Chernomyrdin said, although we had been friends, "Yeltsin, we do not need this defense minister. I propose to dismiss him and appoint another man to this position." Yeltsin announced a break in our conference. They recessed: Lobov, Shumeiko, Yeltsin, and Rybkin. They recessed to decide what to do with me. Ten minutes later, Yeltsin returned and said, "We will not dismiss you, but you must prepare for hostilities within ten days." I said, "It is almost winter. How can we fight when the roads are muddy, the fog is thick, aircraft cannot fly, and artillery crews cannot find a target?" "What do you suggest?" "We can fight in spring, and hold negotiations until then." I wanted to drag things out; I thought we might still reach an agreement—but there was no way. I said, "Chernomyrdin, you will bear personal responsibility for this." Then our relations cooled off.

AVEN: This is news.

KOKH: News, indeed. He always told us he was against.

GRACHEV: He was the initiator, and others supported him. Shakhrai kept silent.

KOKH: Chernomyrdin was the leader? I'll never believe it.

GRACHEV: It was Chernomyrdin, all right. Lobov supported him. I told Lobov, "Let us publish my speeches." And he said, "I don't know—I think we don't have them in the archives."

KOKH: No, no, no—that is a lie. Everything is still there.

GRACHEV: I said, "What? All the speeches must be there." "Well, we cannot find them." "I see," I said. Then they dismissed me. Chernomyrdin was the leader.

KOKH: Look, Petr, this is another view of the problem.

GRACHEV: What view? This is not a view. This is the truth.

AVEN: Listen, Pavel, lots of people read our interviews—there will be a book. What you are telling us is very important. And what else do you think it is important to tell people about you, about those times, and about the army?

KOKH: Especially about the early 1990s. The most important things.

THE ARMY AND THE PUTSCH OF 1993

GRACHEV: What is important? First of all, the failure of the GKChP and the revolt, and the civil war that nearly happened. It was about to start both in 1991 and in 1993—no doubt about that. Especially in 1993. Groups were spontaneously forming around the country: one of them supported the GKChP and another supported Yeltsin in 1991; in 1993, one was for Khasbulatov and Rutskoi and the other for Yeltsin. The country was on the brink of a civil war—and I think that the resolute stand of the armed forces didn't allow it to happen.

AVEN: Please, specify the role of the armed forces in 1991 and 1993.

GRACHEV: In 1991 the armed forces didn't allow ... No, it would be more correct to say they didn't imprison Yeltsin. That was the most important thing.

AVEN: Practically, they refused to engage in the conflict.

GRACHEV: They didn't get involved in the conflict, and thus prevented a squabble—first on the local level and then on a broader level, across Russia. Although the fight across the country might have been insignificant, because Yeltsin was still unknown to many. And in 1993 only the determined stand of the armed forces—six inert projectiles fired by a tank at the White House and the capture of those guys, Rutskoi, Khasbulatov, others, as well as Dunayev, Barannikov, and so on—prevented a civil war in Russia. Why? Because local leaders and certain military commanders were on standby. Who wins? If the other side had won, there would have been a fight immediately.

AVEN: Were you sure? Rutskoi called and tried to send aircraft to bomb the Kremlin. Were you sure of your troopers? Were you sure that no one would attack the Kremlin?

GRACHEV: Sure, absolutely! Because I had good commanders. Petr Stepanovich Deinekin, my friend, was the air force commander; my friend Semyonov was the army commander; Prudnikov was the air defense commander; and the navy commander was also our friend. Yevgeny Nikolayevich Podkolzin was the Airborne Forces commander. I had appointed my friends to those positions, and I was sure none of them would betray me.

KOKH: How did you make the decision to open fire at the White House?

GRACHEV: Yeltsin, with Korzhakov and a few more men, came to the Defense Ministry at about 3:00 a.m. on October 3. We drank a little.

KOKH: The day before Ostankino was stormed and Interior Ministry soldiers were killed?

GRACHEV: Yes.

AVEN: You say you drank a little.

GRACHEV: We drank a little, and everyone was so agitated. Yeltsin said, "The City Hall and Ostankino have been seized. I think we should capture those men from the White House in order to stop them." I said, as always, "Give me a written order, and I am ready to execute it." Korzhakov retorted, "What written order? Yeltsin, I knew they would be scared!" I told him to shut up. Yeltsin was furious and replied, "You will get your written order!" He lied, though—there was no written order. Then he sobered up a bit, and called me at about 5:00 a.m. (I had been prepared for the storm) hinting that I would have to execute a verbal order.

KOKH: I don't understand why they so feared giving you a written order.

GRACHEV: I told him, "Certainly, I will execute the order. What shall I do?" "Capture these men." "Yeltsin, the 119th Airborne Regiment is stationed near the White House. There will be no problem." But there were plenty of snipers on the right and on the left—there were houses nearby, and there were snipers on every roof.

AVEN: Their snipers?

GRACHEV: Yes, theirs. I said, "No problem, but we will have casualties." "What do you propose?" "I propose to scare them." "How?" "A tank will fire inert projectiles straight at them. They will run away. At least, they will go down to the basement, and snipers will flee the roofs. We will find them in the basement later." "Okay." So I ordered a tank to take a position on the stone bridge near the Ukraine Hotel. I came up to that tank and put a captain in the seat of a gunner and a senior lieutenant in the seat of a mechanic; bullets were flying around: bang, bang, bang. "They won't get us—they are about to fall," I thought. I told them, "Do you see these roofs? Now start counting. One, two, three, four, five, six, seventh window. That must be Khasbulatov's office—they are all there. You must hit that window. Can you do that?" "Comrade Minister, the tank has just had shooting practice—it's all right." "And do you have projectiles?" "Live or not?" "Live? Are you out of your mind? Inert." "Sure, we have some—we came here right from the training range." "Now target the window." And lots of people were standing nearby. The bystanders loved it—they watched us as if we were onstage. I said, "Guys, don't you hit them, or people will die. We will be torn to pieces." And I asked the captain, "Can you hit the target?" "I can. It is less than a kilometer away." "And do you see the American embassy building nearby? There will be a scandal if you hit it." "Comrade Minister, it will be all right." "Fire, one," I said. And then I saw the projectile hitting the window precisely. A fire started. It was beautiful. Snipers fled the roofs in an instant. When the snipers were gone and the tanks were done, I ordered the 119th Regiment to storm the building. They smashed the doors and there was some shooting inside. Nine of my men died. There was a clash inside the building after all, but we also killed many.

AVEN: How many?

GRACHEV: A lot.

AVEN: About 200.

GRACHEV: Maybe so—nobody counted. A lot.

AVEN: From 200 to 400, by various estimates.

GRACHEV: Many, in short.

AVEN: White House defenders.

GRACHEV: Yes, defenders. A lot.

AVEN: And who were they? Conscripts or volunteers?

GRACHEV: What conscripts? They were mercenaries, bandits.

KOKH: Where did they get their guns?

GRACHEV: The government, the Supreme Council, and any other building of the kind has armories storing submachine guns and munitions, which are used in case of attack.

AVEN: What about snipers? The same?

GRACHEV: I don't know. They might have been professionals.

KOKH: There were career officers there. Terekhov's Union of Officers.

GRACHEV: There were career officers who had been bought, or who had been fired from the armed forces. They could shoot. And plenty of them were killed.

AVEN: So tank officers opened fire and obeyed your order implicitly.

GRACHEV: Implicitly.

KOKH: And some said they were paid for doing that.

GRACHEV: What money? That might have happened later.

AVEN: They were paid for storming the White House.

GRACHEV: No!

AVEN: As far I remember, some bankers close to the authorities were raising funds from big business. It's unclear where the money went.

KOKH: To repair an abyss, so that it didn't grow bigger. They must have pocketed the money.

GRACHEV: There was no money. We expressed our gratitude to those officers differently. One way or the other, Khasbulatov's forces raised their hands when they saw that we were serious—that we were determined to get them.

AVEN: Did you give the captain an award?

GRACHEV: We made him a Hero of Russia. And the senior lieutenant received a Courage Order, I think. Their names were classified, and they were transferred to other units. That was beautiful. The White House was ablaze. Pavel Borodin congratulated me and I asked why. "Funds have been assigned, and I will make repairs." I asked: "How much did you snatch?" "No, no, no—not a single kopeck!" As I understand, they spent 20 million on repairs.

KOKH: Nothing is said about that now. This is not a big sum by modern standards.

GRACHEV: It may sound insignificant now, but the sum was huge for 1993!

KOKH: Petr, was that a good story?

AVEN: An impressive story. The man has things to recollect. Those were fundamental historic events. The country was on the brink of a civil war, but the solution was so simple. By the way, was Achalov there?

GRACHEV: Yes, he was there. He was also arrested—all of them were arrested. Korzhakov and Mikhail Ivanovich Barsukov went inside when the danger was gone and shooting had ceased, and imprisoned the "defenders." And I was watching Korzhakov and Barsukov leading them to a bus to take them to Matrosskaya Tishina prison.

AVEN: And some said that forces were ordered to march to Moscow when the putsch was on, but they were in no hurry to get there.

GRACHEV: Some hot shots must have thought our troops ride in Mercedes or Toyotas; we have tanks, armored personnel carriers, or infantry combat vehicles. Their average speed, especially in a convoy (and we had a huge convoy stretching several kilometers), is approximately 20 kilometers per hour. And those civilians claimed we were too slow, and nearly sabotaged the orders. Combat vehicles are not a means of transportation or a taxi—they are built for fighting; and a new tank's service life is only 200 kilometers. What can I say? Our people love to talk. Normal countries bring their combat vehicles to the battlefield by special trucks or by rail. And in this country we are ordered to ride along a highway on caterpillar tracks—and they say we are slow! You know, guys, what hurts most? So many people claimed to be the winners after the events of 1991 and 1993! So many tore their shirts claiming they had won.

KOKH: That's not surprising.

GRACHEV: I know that a victory has many fathers, and a defeat is always an orphan. So many people were shouting in 1991: "We defended the White House—we organized the defense!" So many good-for-nothing servicemen claimed they had been dismissed illegally! And then they established some councils and trade unions. I had trouble keeping them off. Zhenya Shaposhnikov couldn't do that, and I could. And I thought, "Where were you in 1991, when our boys stood there and our staff decided not to storm the building under any circumstances—even if we had written orders? Which of us, you or me, could have been court-martialed? Why did no one but the armed forces defend Yeltsin in 1993? Where was the KGB? Where were their Alpha troops? Alpha refused to storm. Where was the Interior Ministry?" But then everyone waved their hands and shouted, "We were the winners."

The third major event was international—the beginning of Russia–NATO partnership negotiations. That happened at the end of 1992, when tense relations with NATO developed into a dialogue. I could drink vodka with an American secretary and an American general. We had a normal, human conversation and argued about which armaments we would have and where they should be placed in NATO's territory and ours. Only Zhukov and Eisenhower could do that in 1945! And we were allies in that year. I made six trips to Brussels in 1993 for one-on-one meetings. That is the third achievement, in my opinion.

The fourth achievement was that I, the defense minister, did not allow the army to break up. Certainly it was not because I was so talented as a commander—it happened thanks to my subordinates, especially the commanders in military districts who understood me and trusted that things would be fixed sooner or later. We didn't allow the army to fall apart—and we didn't allow the looting of weapons, nuclear arms.

KOKH: Did anyone try to do that?

GRACHEV: Of course—such attempts are still being made. But we kept everything safe. That was the fourth achievement.

The fifth achievement may not look important to some people, but it looks important to me: Patriarch Kirill and I signed an agreement on cooperation between the armed forces and the Church. He was in charge of the Russian Orthodox Church's external relations department at that time, and we became friends.

AVEN: He and my wife are godparents to Shokhin's children. So my wife and the Patriarch were fellow sponsors!

GRACHEV: He is a terrific man.

KOKH: How would you rank the Chechen campaign among those events?

GRACHEV: The Chechen campaign? It may rank after the preservation of Russia and the armed forces. You went on visits with me a thousand times— I remember you, but you didn't have a beard then.

AVEN: Do you think the Chechen episode was your achievement?

GRACHEV: Certainly not. That is a shame of our domestic policy.

KOKH: The problem could have had a peaceful solution, couldn't it?

GRACHEV: I could have persuaded them! I could have brought Dudayev and organized a meeting, just the three of us: me, Yeltsin, and Dudayev. Talk!

KOKH: Did Yeltsin refuse?

GRACHEV: Yeltsin was ready, but they kept whispering into his ear. I don't know who it was, boys or girls supervising domestic policy. I don't know with whom he met.

AVEN: But who was impeding the peace talks?

KOKH: I can't find that out. I keep asking this question, and everyone says it was Yegorov. Could it be because he is dead? Now they say it was Chernomyrdin. Probably also because he is dead.

GRACHEV: Chernomyrdin in terms of the war?

AVEN: This is news to us.

GRACHEV: He supported that war—and I think even Kozyrev supported it. Although he always was timid and undecided.

AVEN: Do you stay in touch?

GRACHEV: No. We met several times. We have normal relations. He once called on me to move to America.

AVEN: To do what there?

GRACHEV: Live. They have a council of defense ministers led by William Perry. Kozyrev sent letters inviting me to join their council. They were ready to give me a residence, a dacha, and a good salary—after I had been dismissed here. They were bombarding me with letters for the first two years. They told me, "You were insulted in your country, and you did so much for rapprochement with NATO."

AVEN: You did a lot for rapprochement with NATO and the United States. Kozyrev and you made those relations completely different.

GRACHEV: A month after my dismissal I started to receive letters from Perry, Cheney, and Powell. They wrote me, "Pavel, you have done a lot for our relations. You are an outcast in your own country, and no one needs you. We invite you here for permanent residence." And I replied, "Guys, I would not understand your lifestyle. I won't be able to tell anyone to get lost there. And I won't be able to grill my kebabs there, either."

KOKH: They call it barbecue.

AVEN: Do you visit your home village frequently?

GRACHEV: Yes, I go there often. I have plenty of time. And it is only a two-hour ride.

AVEN: Does any of your family still live there?

GRACHEV: A brother. I took care of the repairs on his house. And you, Petr, when did you stop being the minister?

AVEN: In December 1992, together with Gaidar. To be more exact, a week after Gaidar.

GRACHEV: You were good guys. At least our team—and I say nothing bad about today's team, either—but our team was much stronger. It had a stronger spirit.

AVEN: Spirit and ideas. What do you think about the current army reform?

GRACHEV: I have a negative opinion.

AVEN: Why? Do you think the idea is wrong? Is the ideology wrong?

GRACHEV: First of all, they have reduced the army beyond recognition. Military standards say there must be one solider for every six meters of the borderline (and all countries, including the United States, stick to these standards). I mean the border perimeter. You count how many soldiers we need if the standard says six meters per soldier. That is the first thing. Second, a certain amount of hardware is needed for frontline deterrence: tanks, artillery, and I also had some nuclear artillery units, and so on. Nothing is left now. Third, districts were transformed into commands. How is the commander supposed to cover the whole eastern zone, from the Pacific Ocean to Baikal? There is no such territory. Even China is half the size. The command system has been lost, absolutely. There is some small stuff, too—though it's not really small stuff. Practically all the support services—logistics, clothes—were handed over to civilians. There are civilians everywhere. But civilians are different. They report for work at nine and go home at six, war or no war, and you will have to look for them, while military people are on duty permanently. That is totally wrong. Besides, they are reducing the benefits given to servicemen, such as health care, health resorts.

AVEN: And who is behind these reforms, do you think?

GRACHEV: I don't know. That must be the General Staff. Serdyukov simply approves the plans. Being the defense minister, he sets the guidelines. And he receives his guidelines from the supreme commander, and the staff makes detailed plans. Take, for instance, the order to form brigades in the armed forces. Who can say this structure is good? The Americans. So, everything goes the American way.

JAMES BAKER

"You Still Have Not Built a Free Market Economy"

JAMES BAKER PLAYED AN ENORMOUS ROLE in Soviet and Russian politics. Chief of staff and secretary of the treasury in the administration of Ronald Reagan (1981–8) and secretary of state under George H. W. Bush (1989–92), he enthusiastically hailed Gorbachev's new course. Thanks to perestroika, Baker entered the political landscape: on June 1, 1990, he and Eduard Shevardnadze signed the Russia–United States Maritime Boundary Agreement, ceding some of the Bering Sea to the US, along the Baker–Shevardnadze line.

The secretary of state supported the Russian reformers, often promoting the interests of an independent Russia to his own detriment. Russia's first minister of foreign affairs, Andrei Kozyrev, considered Baker his most reliable partner aboard. However, even the efforts of Baker and Bush were not enough to change the direction of relations between Russia and the West.

Petr Aven

PETR AVEN: Mr. Baker, thank you for agreeing to this interview. My colleague Alfred Kokh and I are writing a book about the events of the 1991–3 period in Russia, and the role of the West in these events is still not completely clear. Did the West, especially the USA, influence the process of the collapse of the Soviet Union? Was the West prepared for this collapse? How far were the decisions of the Western leaders correct about aid to the republics of the former Soviet Union in this period—or, on the other hand, denying aid? How did these decisions affect our lives?

JAMES BAKER: Have you read my book?[1] In it I cover a lot of what you have pointed out.

AVEN: I will certainly read your book. But since it has not yet been translated into Russian, it would be fascinating to hear your opinion on a number of constantly discussed topics in Russia today. For example, my first question is: To what extent was the American government ready for the collapse of the Soviet Union? Zbigniew Brzezinski made predictions about such a collapse long before it happened. However, as it seemed to us—the Yeltsin government—in the autumn of 1991 the American bureaucracy was very surprised by events in the USSR. The West was totally unprepared for the collapse of the Soviet Union.

BAKER: I don't think that we were not prepared. I believe that we were ready, but we were still surprised when it happened. No one expected the collapse of the Soviet Union's empire to be so rapid. However, also no one in the USSR, maybe except Yeltsin and some of his employees, had any idea about what happened in Minsk—I mean the declaration of the dissolution of the USSR and the creation of the Commonwealth of Independent States. And yet we were ready to respond—we quickly established contacts with the leaders of the new countries, and within a few weeks opened embassies everywhere.

AVEN: That is correct. But if we go back to the year 1989 or the 1990s, had you among yourselves discussed the possibility of the collapse of the Soviet Union?

BAKER: Oh, no! At least for me it was a surprise—and as well for everyone in the administration. But had anyone expected it in Russia itself?

AVEN: In our economic circle, in the spring of 1991 we had come to the conclusion that the collapse was inevitable and began to prepare for it.

BAKER: In the spring of 1991, six months earlier.

AVEN: Yes, six months. What were you thinking about at that time?

---

1.   J. A. Baker and T. M. DeFrank, *The Politics of Diplomacy*, 1995.

BAKER: I will repeat: we were ready for the collapse of the Soviet Union, but we were still surprised. There is a difference between a principled readiness and an expectation of a specific period of time. We had already clearly understood that the US would remain the sole superpower, as did happen. And at the time everyone tried to move closer to America—in particular, Yeltsin and his government. In fact, he was ready to agree with most of our actions. We had disagreements, but not too many. There were very few differences between Yeltsin and Bush.

AVEN: As you know, Russians believe in plots and conspiracies. In particular, the drop in oil prices in the spring of 1986, which was a disaster for Gorbachev, was explained by the machinations of Americans. They say it was you—that is, the CIA—that pushed Saudi Arabia to increase oil production and thus lower prices, in order to make the USSR collapse. I have discussed this matter with Donald Rumsfeld, former US secretary of defense. He told me that we are extremely overestimating the intellectual abilities of the American bureaucracy.

BAKER: I will agree with Rumsfeld, and will put it this way. It is in our national interest to have a lower price of oil—it helps our economy. But we never pushed the prices down to make the Soviet Union collapse.[2]

AVEN: Let's go back to the "surprises" of 1991—in particular, the August putsch. The question of whether Gorbachev knew about preparations for the putsch is strongly debated. They say that you (you personally, or George Bush) warned Gorbachev two or three days earlier. Is this true?

BAKER: Yes. I think it was not two or three days earlier, but back in June.

AVEN: From where did you get the information? From the CIA?

---

2.   After my conversation with James Baker, I discussed the topic of the fall of oil prices in 1986 with the most famous world expert, Dan Yergin, author of the bestseller *The Prize*. In his opinion, the Americans did not expect this fall; it caught them by surprise. The decision to dramatically increase the production was taken by Saudi Arabia because, firstly, Saudis believed that their partners in OPEC were "cheating" with the output by significantly outperforming quotas that were illegally obtained from the organization. Secondly, there was a fast growing production outside OPEC, making strict control of quotas within OPEC largely meaningless. In addition, according to Yergin, the oil lobby in the United States is so strong that the government is unlikely to ever dare to seriously fight for a decline in oil prices.—P.A.

BAKER: I don't remember. I also don't really remember whom I called. I think actually not Gorbachev, but Bessmertnykh. We really had information. And we also heard rumors, that Gorbachev might be prosecuted after the failed putsch. People in his circle said so. When meeting Yeltsin in December 1991, I said that the prosecution of Gorbachev would be a mistake.

AVEN: I don't think that Yeltsin had such plans. Anyhow, concerning your readiness for the disintegration of the Union, when we started working in the government, we, the Gaidar team and I, being in charge of foreign economic relations, evolved a strong sense that Western officials did not want and feared this collapse. What they wanted, what they felt more comfortable with, was to continue to work with Gorbachev. This desire to work with the Soviet Union, which in fact no longer existed in autumn 1991, was clearly manifested in the Paris Club. By inertia, your officials tried to interact with inter-republic institutions, and for a long time looked upon us (the government of Russia) as interlopers. The United States was represented in the Paris Club by David Mulford; he behaved accordingly.

BAKER: Mulford worked for me when I was the secretary of the treasury.

AVEN: We also had the feeling that, in terms of mentality, Gorbachev was closer than Yeltsin to Western bureaucrats. You knew Gorbachev better— you were used to him. And you understood Bessmertnykh better than Kozyrev. By the way, when talking to us, Andrei agreed with this opinion— even though he noted his exceptionally close personal relationship with you.

BAKER: But I do not agree. Starting in June 1991, whenever I visited Russia (as Andrei knows), I always met with Kozyrev and Yeltsin. Did we support Gorbachev? Yes, because he was a reformer—we had experience working with him, and believed that he would not leave the path of reform. We did not want the return of hardliners, it's true. But we also saw what was happening. Therefore, in my official visits to the Soviet Union I, the US secretary of state, always met with Russian leaders.

AVEN: Kozyrev told us that when you arrived in Moscow on December 16, 1991, you spent a long time with Gorbachev. It was pointless, since Gorbachev no longer had power. However, you were friends with him— you were personally close and obviously wanted to support him. Andrei believes that you lost a lot of time with Gorbachev, and therefore during that visit you did not have time to discuss with him and Yeltsin issues about aid to Russia from the West.

BAKER: I do not agree. I spent a lot of time with Yeltsin, I spent a lot of time as well with Kozyrev—we regularly communicated with the Russian leaders before the collapse of the Soviet Union. In the spring of 1991 we met in Moscow with the opposition, which was not welcomed by Gorbachev's staff. However, we had worked with Gorbachev for several years—we had seen his efforts and wished for the success of his reforms. We did not want the reforms to drown. We worked with both Yeltsin and Gorbachev. And when it became clear that power had been transferred to Yeltsin, we built the same close and effective relationship with him and Kozyrev as we had with Gorbachev and Shevardnadze.

AVEN: All right, but when we began negotiations with the Paris Club at the end of November 1991 and the delegation arrived in Moscow, it wanted to deal only with inter-republic institutions and Gorbachev. This was two weeks before the official collapse of the Soviet Union.

BAKER: At the end of November Gorbachev was still the official leader. And it would have been a mistake not to work with Gorbachev. Yet, possibly, you may be partly right—bureaucracy does not look into the future. I, however, as secretary of state, always met with both the Soviet and Russian leaders at that time.

AVEN: I truly believe that there is a gap between the position of the leaders (at the time, you and Bush) and the position of mid-level bureaucrats. Bureaucracy is late—David Mulford realized that the debts should be discussed with the Russian government, not with the structures of inter-republic economic committees, only after considerable delay.

BAKER: Probably. My own closeness to Yeltsin can be demonstrated by our conversation at the end of December 1991. Do you know what Yeltsin told me?

AVEN: He asked for humanitarian aid—

BAKER: What?

AVEN: According to Kozyrev, Yeltsin asked you for humanitarian aid. And you did not have time to discuss anything else, as you were held up with Gorbachev.

BAKER: That's what Kozyrev thinks. And this is nonsense. If you look at my records, you will see that we had a serious discussion. And let me tell you what Yeltsin said. He told me, the US secretary of state, with unprecedented frankness, how the nuclear program and the control of nuclear weapons would develop within the Commonwealth of Independent States; how new missiles would be located, who would have the button, and who would not; what the leaders of Ukraine, Belarus, and Kazakhstan thought about it—how they believed that they would have the nuclear weapons, but in fact they would not. Yeltsin said all this, not Kozyrev. So I do not agree that we did not have a serious talk.

AVEN: Gaidar and Kozyrev remember that at this meeting they wanted to raise the issue of large-scale Western aid to Russia—about something that looked like a Marshall Plan. And then they didn't manage to articulate it precisely enough, because there was not enough time.

BAKER: They're justifying themselves.

AVEN: Perhaps. Incidentally, this visit to Moscow took place two weeks after the Belovezh meeting. As we found out after talking with the participants in this trip, on his way to Belarus, Yeltsin was not even sure that he would meet Kravchuk there. He primarily went to meet with Shushkevich. But they subsequently dissolved the Soviet Union there—without having any advance preparations, any documents—

BAKER: And you say that we had to be prepared, had to know. They knew nothing themselves.

AVEN: True, but maybe you were wiser and could have foreseen this.

BAKER: No, it was a surprise. Both for us and for them. Although both we and they (Yeltsin, Kravchuk, Shushkevich) somehow prepared for it.

AVEN: On nuclear weapons: Kozyrev told us that, in his opinion, you were the most useful figure among all of the Western politicians with whom he had to deal—that you understood the reality better than anyone else.

BAKER: We were just good friends, and worked well together.

AVEN: And he said that, thanks to you, the USA played a crucial role in the withdrawal of the nuclear weapons from Ukraine and Belarus.

BAKER: This is true. I spent three months on this—particularly struggled with Zlenko. Nazarbayev in Kazakhstan, Zlenko in Ukraine, I do not remember anyone in Belarus—they all wanted to keep the nuclear weapons. They did not trust Russia.

AVEN: And why were you so keen for the weapons to remain only in Russia? Is it because it's easier to deal with one country than a few countries? Or is it because you trusted Russia more than, say, Ukraine?

BAKER: No, trust has nothing to do with it. We certainly wanted to deal with one country instead of four.

AVEN: Because it is easier to control and come to agreements?

BAKER: Easier to control. And also there was a problem not only of strategic nuclear weapons but also of tactical weapons. We did everything to make these weapons also remain only in Russia. On this topic we worked together with Kozyrev, as well as your nuclear scientists. Scientists had lost their field of action; they had nothing to do after the closure of the nuclear programs. And we were afraid that as a result they would be in the wrong place. I met with your scientists in the city—what is it called?

AVEN: Arzamas. Was the policy that nuclear weapons must remain only in Russia solely the position of the US, or of all the Western leaders?

BAKER: Well, they all agreed that it was not good after the collapse of the Soviet Union to get four nuclear powers instead of one—although discussions did take place. And there were discussions about who should get the Soviet veto power in the Security Council. All these things have been resolved the way we wanted them to be. And I think the way in which the issue of nuclear weapons has been addressed fully reflects the Russian interests and those of other former Soviet republics. There is no doubt about it.

AVEN: The decision to accept Russia into the UN was unanimous?

BAKER: Nobody seriously questioned it.

AVEN: We asked Andrei Kozyrev, what was the difference between Yeltsin's and Gorbachev's foreign policy? Kozyrev gave a clear answer—under Gorbachev the West (as throughout the entire Soviet era) was seen as an

enemy, albeit peaceful, but an enemy; the USSR and the Western democracies, by definition, were in different blocs. But under Yeltsin the West was
viewed as a real partner; Russia wanted to become a part of the Western
world. Thus Kozyrev attempted to radically change the traditional direction
of Russian foreign policy, almost for the first time in our history.

BAKER: I completely agree.

AVEN: Then a question: Were you ready to view Russia as a part of the West?

BAKER: Well, yes.

AVEN: Integrate Russia into NATO? Not just with words, but with real
actions?

BAKER: I wrote in the *New York Times* in 1993 that Russia should become
a part of NATO. If Russia was to continue to build democracy and a free
market, then we must ensure Russia's entry into the North Atlantic alliance.
I was heavily criticized for that article.

AVEN: In this sense you truly differ from the majority of Western politicians. In fact, maybe you were the only one. Or you and George Bush. After
Clinton came to power, everything changed. And we remember not only
your article from 1993, but also your speech to the Congress in 1991.
    One way or the other, we were Russia's first post-communist govern-
ment. And, once we came to power, we really hoped for Western assistance.
We were surprised and disappointed that we were getting extremely little.
In 1992 we received $1 billion from the IMF and nothing from Western
governments. When the Mexican crisis occurred in the late 1990s, Mexico
received $50 billion from the USA within a couple of days. Fifty as opposed
to one. Besides, we thought that Russia was a more important country than
Mexico—a nuclear power, the military containment of which costs just the
USA hundreds of billions of dollars annually. But first we couldn't even
agree on standard conditions with the Paris Club, on terms similar to, say,
the ones that Poland got. We were able to agree only after direct intervention
by the US ambassador in Moscow, Bob Strauss. Strauss played an important
role: at my and Gaidar's request, he flew to Washington and managed (by
meeting either with the president or with you) to change the US negotiating
position. David Mulford's position—very negative at first—was completely
changed within a week. American negativism, in the case of the Paris Club,

made little practical sense—the United States had little to gain. Whereas Germany, our major creditor, had a much more positive mindset.

For Gaidar, Kozyrev, my colleagues, and me, the absolute unwillingness of the majority of Western politicians to view us as partners instead of enemies—you, I repeat, were an exception—initially proved to be a real shock. Yet we quickly adapted to this situation. Why were the majority of Western politicians not ready for the integration of Russia into the West? Sorry for the hint, but there are several answers: they did not want to see a stronger Russia, regardless of what happened within it; they did not trust Yeltsin; they did not believe that Yeltsin would be able to hold on to power, or that he could change Russia; they had domestic political constraints.

BAKER: We, of course, wanted to support Russia. And we trusted Yeltsin and Kozyrev. But politically, yes, you're right, it was very difficult to justify economic assistance to Russia, with which we had fought for 40 years.

AVEN: So domestic political constraints were the main factor?

BAKER: Yes, but nevertheless, we understood the importance of attempting to integrate Russia into the European or Eurasian model. We in the US—Kozyrev knows it—wanted this. Other countries may have been more careful. In Germany, for example, the memory of World War II still remained; France and Russia had their own problems. We strongly wanted to cooperate with Russia, wanted to move away from confrontation to, if not a partnership, then in any case to cooperation.

AVEN: Not to a partnership—this is very important. Kozyrev sought precisely a partnership; you, however, speak about cooperation. Yet a partnership, given US public opinion, was impossible. A Marshall Plan for Russia was impossible.

BAKER: A Marshall Plan at the time was absolutely out of the question. The American public would not support it—neither then nor later.

AVEN: Even if Bush had remained the president?

BAKER: Who knows. Perhaps, if Bush had stayed, our cooperation would have been better. In fact, many things could have turned out differently. If we had remained and there had been no attempt on the life of Yitzhak Rabin, then the peace agreement between the Arabs and Israel would almost certainly have been signed.

AVEN: In his interviews, Gorbachev speaks very badly about Kozyrev.

BAKER: Naturally. He was among those who deprived Gorbachev of power.

AVEN: Gorbachev says that under Kozyrev the Russian Foreign Ministry was a branch of the US State Department. What do you say to that?

BAKER: Under Yeltsin and Kozyrev the views of Russia and the USA were truly very close. But to say that the Russian Foreign Ministry was a branch of the State Department is unfair. I don't think so.

AVEN: Gorbachev also says that as the USSR was becoming weaker. He received less and less Western assistance. He basically believes that the West betrayed him.

BAKER: All documents on this are available. There is nothing he was promised that he did not receive.

AVEN: That's possible, but according to him, he was even promised less and less; as he was becoming weaker, he became less interesting to everyone.

BAKER: I do not agree, no. In my book I write how much money he got with our help, for example, in Southeast Asia. I personally spent a lot of time on this until his retirement.

AVEN: And what did you see as the main difference between Yeltsin and Gorbachev? Who was easier to work with?

BAKER: Contrary to the popular opinion, I do not see such a dramatic difference in working with Yeltsin and Gorbachev. Gorbachev stayed at the top of the party *nomenklatura* for longer, and maybe because of that was less decisive. We talked about the dissolution of the Soviet Union in Minsk, about the fact that it was done without any preliminary plan, suddenly. That's typical for Yeltsin. Gorbachev would never have done this—he was more cautious. And, also crucially, he was a lawyer. I am also a lawyer. Lawyers do not hurry.

AVEN: Who did you trust more?

BAKER: We trusted both of them—trusted, but verified—although I do not recall any cases of Yeltsin saying something and then not doing it. Yeltsin and Kozyrev never deceived us. Shevardnadze, too. And Gorbachev, even though it was often difficult for him—he was always under attack from either hawks or liberals.

AVEN: Kozyrev told us that Yeltsin's big mistake was not firing people known for their anti-Western mentality—for example, Primakov and a number of other people from the KGB. This made it more difficult to build a normal relationship with you.

BAKER: Perhaps, to some extent. More importantly, neither Gorbachev nor Yeltsin was able to seriously reform your country. They were reformers and democrats, but they still didn't manage to make economic reforms. You still have not built a free-market economy.

AVEN: I participated in the economic reforms, and don't agree that we haven't built anything. That's not entirely the case. Nevertheless, we have been accused of building the "wrong thing" for almost 20 years.

BAKER: I remember the first time we allowed Soviet citizens to travel outside the 25-mile zone from New York. And I invited Shevardnadze with a couple of his colleagues to fly down to visit me. He took an economist with him, so I could tell him about the free-market economy.

AVEN: Who was it?

BAKER: Not very young. His last name begins with an S.

AVEN: Shatalin? Stanislav Shatalin?

BAKER: Yes, Shatalin.

AVEN: He was my teacher, and later my boss.

BAKER: I told him about the free-market economy. I recall that Gorbachev did not commit to large-scale market reforms. He always hesitated. The problem was not a lack of ideas, but rather his indecisiveness. I know that the 500 Days program, or the Shatalin Plan, was prepared as early as August 1990. But after a month of reflection, Gorbachev emerged with a completely different plan—one that did not signal a transition to the free market.

Virtually under prime minister—what is his last name?

AVEN: Pavlov.

BAKER: Yes, under him the Soviet economy became not more but less free, more centralized. Although on the plane with Shevardnadze I advised Shatalin differently.

AVEN: Alas, to some extent it is a vicious circle. We did not carry out the necessary reforms, and because of that you did not provide the necessary assistance. But without this assistance the standard of living (due to the reforms) inevitably fell, which led to the curtailment of the reforms. I still believe that if the Gaidar government had received, if not a Marshall Plan, then at least $10–$20 billion in 1992, we could really have passed liberal reforms. In reality, a liberal economic reform was never really made—and yet the liberals are to blame for everything bad that has happened. Although the economy is deeply anti-liberal.

BAKER: Yes, Russia today is anti-liberal. But it is very difficult to build a free economy in a country that never had it before. You are not the only ones who experienced a very slow process of change. Mongolia and several other former communist states are also examples.

AVEN: Still, in 1992 some financial assistance from the West (despite the fact that we ourselves, of course, had to enact the reforms, and enact them more decisively) could have made a difference. We already recalled Mexico, which received $50 billion. What would have happened with Mexico without your help?

BAKER: We did not have a 40-year-long Cold War with Mexico. And I am sure that, together with George Bush, we did everything we could to help you, within our limitations. But you were not ready to help yourselves. Did Russia want to join NATO, which I thought was right?

AVEN: There were different views on this in Russia.

BAKER: Exactly. We, of course, made mistakes. Mistakes are unavoidable. But we did what we could—both economically and diplomatically. After all the years of the Cold War, to spend billions of dollars of taxpayers' money was impossible. But, most importantly, you yourselves were not ready. And you yourselves did not know where to go.

AVEN: Thank you. I think not everything is yet lost.

BAKER: Thank you. Good luck.

12

YEGOR GAIDAR

"I Made a Bad Public Politician"

PETR AND I THOUGHT HARD ABOUT WHETHER OR NOT TO INCLUDE an interview with Yegor Gaidar in this book. There were lots of pros and cons. We decided in the end it would be the right thing to do—to let the reader hear Yegor's answers to the questions discussed in the interviews of his friends and government colleagues.

I interviewed Yegor two years before his death on behalf of *Medved* magazine. The interview is interesting not only because of his answers to the questions and reflections. I think the interview reveals Yegor Gaidar as a human being: a delicate, ironic, and kind man. He does not pejoratively evaluate anyone (but himself), and tries to put himself in the place of all the people mentioned in the interview one way or another.

This is Yegor Timurovich Gaidar, with all his strengths and weaknesses. He spent too much of his potential on pitying his opponents. And they were absolutely unwilling to repay him in kind.

The biblical truth: "A prophet is not without honor except in his own town, and among his relatives and in his own home" (Matthew 13:57) has practically become a cliché. People (never!) believe in the talent, farsightedness, and honesty of a person by their side.

But now the man is no longer with us. Shall we finally open our ears and listen to what we refused to hear when he was still alive? We will hear the voice of a genuine patriot—the man whose love for his fatherland did not secure him millions in Swiss bank accounts, and who sacrificed his life to it.

His life could have been happier and luckier if he had been calculating and pragmatic. But Yegor had the life he had—and we are grateful that he was strong enough to live his life the way he did. Petr and I think that, among other things, he added some special meaning to our own lives that we would have lacked without him.

Alfred Kokh

FIRST CONVERSATION: ON THE RESIGNATION

ALFRED KOKH: My interviews never concern current events; to use high-flown language, they exist in the context of eternity. So I will ask nothing about the poisoning attempts we have discussed many times in private. I am interested in the following: it's Brezhnev's centenary, and I wish to compare his epoch with the time when you were making reforms in Russia—and especially the time after your resignation.

We grew up with the idea that high-ranking politicians, from the premier and up, should leave their posts in a natural way: they either died like Brezhnev, Andropov, Chernenko, or quit due to their retirement age. I think you were the first politician removed from power at the age of 36.

You were the first who had to think, "What's next?" after your retirement. I'd rather not anticipate your feelings; I would like you to dwell on this subject. You must have felt peculiar: you had held a position comparable to a strong drug, while other occupations, with the possible exception of skydiver or lion tamer, could not give you so much adrenaline. Thus, I want to know how you felt, how you coped with withdrawal pains, how you tapered the dose, and whether you broke free from your addiction or not.

YEGOR GAIDAR: When I stopped being the premier, I had no withdrawal pains. My first feeling was that I was bone tired. I also had subconscious apprehension. It seemed my phone would ring and I would have to go somewhere, to make decisions, to argue with someone, to punish someone, to force someone to do something, and to wrangle—and that they would sling mud at me again.

I understood that I was no longer responsible for the country—my phone would not ring, and I would not be told that an OMON battalion[1] had been attacked on the Ossetian–Ingush border, hostilities were on, and we had to do something. I understood that, but every phone call sent shivers down my spine. I was tired and I was nervous—and that was it. I had no withdrawal pains. I had no craving to take the controls again. Right before I quit, I had

---

1.   *Otryad Mobilny Osobogo Naznacheniya*, Special Purpose Mobile Unit.

been settling the Ingush–Ossetian conflict. That was hard, and forces had to be relocated. Military men could never reach an agreement: one said he could not relocate troops because he had no planes, and another could not do something else. Practically, the situation required manual control. At the same time I was settling the situation in Tajikistan: there was a civil war, and more than 100,000 Russians, the 201st Division, and border guard units.

After my resignation, every phone call made me jump. I wanted to get some rest. And, most importantly, I didn't want to be responsible for everything.

KOKH: Absolutely everyone says it is extremely difficult to force oneself to work again after a resignation. That is the main thing.

GAIDAR: This is true. You know I am a workaholic: I am used to working, reading professional books, taking notes, and writing. It was hard to re-establish a work rhythm. I was forcing myself, but then I took a sober look at myself: I sat at my desk, but I needn't have bothered; I reread my writings and realized that they were worthless. My head would simply refuse to work. And at first I was completely exhausted. I was sleepy all the time—I slept when standing, sitting, or lying down.

KOKH: Your tiredness eventually passed.

GAIDAR: I don't know what would have happened to my sleepiness, but I never had a chance to rest properly. I decided soon after my resignation that my life would be calm and there would be no phone calls. But one phone call woke me up early in the morning. I was told about a difficulty requiring immediate action.

KOKH: What was it?

GAIDAR: While I was in this "twilight" condition, Chernomyrdin froze prices. In the first two weeks without me, the government was in a state of chaos. The money supply to the economy was larger than ever before in any two weeks of the previous year. Then they decided to freeze prices—not fully, but just a bit. The weekly inflation rate spiked to unprecedented levels and, worst of all, we had a deficit of commodities again—the situation we thought we had already settled! And I was in a suburb of St Petersburg, sleeping and ignoring newspapers and the radio. Chubais called and asked,

"Do you know what is going on here? It's just awful, a nightmare."

And I suddenly woke up. I was aware of the consequences, and I knew that I was able to intervene in situations where I deemed it necessary. I called Yeltsin and told him it was important and I would send him a brief note listing the urgent measures. He read my note and gave the orders. In short, we preserved a more or less responsible monetary policy and free prices—but not without losses.

My retirement was a slow process. I couldn't just wake up and start living a normal life. True, I stopped being the acting prime minister responsible for my work and holding others responsible for theirs. But I was fully integrated into the political elite—I knew that I could inform the president about my opinion anytime I chose. I knew that he read my notes. And colleagues from the government's economic bloc frequented my dacha in Arkhangelskoye.

KOKH: Didn't they take away your dacha and everything?

GAIDAR: That happened later. Another time, Andrei Vavilov gave me a panicky call, in summer 1993: the Central Bank was withdrawing old banknotes from circulation and introducing new ones. That was summer, and people were on vacation, but they were told their old banknotes were invalid—that they could exchange sums equivalent to no more than $10, and the rest would be wasted. He called and said that the Finance Ministry had not been warned, and Yeltsin was taking a vacation somewhere. I had to engage in that fight.

KOKH: Did Gerashchenko do that?

GAIDAR: Yes. As you can see, I was in a peculiar position at that moment. I was out, but I was not fully disengaged from the decision-making processes. Besides, a confrontation between Yeltsin and the Supreme Council was building. He was trying to reach an agreement, there was a referendum in the spring—in short, we were having fun. The Presidential Council held a meeting, and Yeltsin asked me to return as first vice premier. Do you remember the atmosphere of my appointment?

KOKH: Frankly, no.

GAIDAR: I gave my consent. While the decree was being drafted, I decided to visit Rostov—I had been promising to do that for a long time. Yeltsin planned to announce my appointment at a meeting with bankers, but something went wrong. He visited the Tamanskaya division the day before, and said, while he was standing near a tank and looking straight into the camera, "Gaidar will be the first vice premier for economic affairs."

Then I had my second government job. It was completely different. I had a totally crazy start: the events of October 3–4 and the extremely complicated situation of late 1993. The putsch was over, and the State Duma election was pending. Many people saw me as the next premier: the State Duma election would take place, and the democrats would get the majority of seats. You can imagine how enthusiastic Chernomyrdin was about me. On the one hand, he was my boss; on the other hand, I was his former and future boss.

And then we lost the election. To be frank, I still don't understand why they claimed we lost the State Duma election in December 1993. Our faction was the largest in the State Duma. The democrats have never had such good results as in the first State Duma election. I have my own opinion on that.

But it was not the question of the end result, or the election campaign. In my opinion, the Supreme Council should have been dismissed in April instead of September, and the election should have been held immediately after the "Yes-Yes-No-Yes" referendum, instead of in December. The results would have been different, and the damage suffered by the economy would have been smaller. No doubt those were mistakes.

Back to my government work. I had little influence on the situation after my return to the government, and everything bypassed me.

Kokh: And why did that happen? You were the first vice premier for economic affairs, after all! Was it a direct order from Chernomyrdin?

Gaidar: Naturally. Nobody said that out loud, but when key decisions costing $20 million get made without my endorsement, you know that could not have been accidental. You worked in government, and you knew that a document could not be validated without your signature or the signature of our deputy unless there was a direct order from the premier. There must have been such an order. And the administration executed it gladly. I didn't want to involve Yeltsin, and I never told him what was going on.

It was senseless to stay in the government after the election, and I decided it would be better to join the State Duma. We actually had a workable parliament. We also had a constitution, which gave colossal powers to the president, and he was in the mood to pass reforms.

Kokh: Thus, it was the beginning of 1994. Did you quit together with Fyodorov?

Gaidar: No, it was more complicated. Fyodorov hoped he would be offered a major position for his decision to stay on. So I quit first, and he quit when he realized there would be no offer.

Kokh: Finally, it was over—you were absolutely nobody.

Gaidar: Not quite—I was still at the State Duma. The faction leader and all.

Kokh: You were elected to the State Duma again in 1999–2003, weren't you?

Gaidar: I didn't head the faction then. I didn't have to perform those rituals: speak at plenary meetings, make fiery speeches.

I had to do my job. It was a pleasure due to my relations with the government and the government's implementation of our program. I could get key documents signed by decision-makers, including the president, within two or three days. I didn't have to make public speeches; instead, I had the opportunity to do something useful, and that opportunity was the biggest in my government career. But that opportunity started shrinking rapidly.

Kokh: Back to 1994. Your slow withdrawal from power continued. You were the faction leader, which meant you had those meetings, direct phone lines, flashing lights on your car, dachas, and so on. Most important, you retained the status of "the entourage."

Gaidar: I had all that until December 1995, when we lost the State Duma election. Although we failed to pass the 5 percent threshold, we still had 11 deputies elected in single-seat constituencies, and I remained a public politician as the party leader. My scope for action was narrower then, but Chubais was appointed as the presidential chief of staff and I was invited to narrow-circle meetings whenever they had vital issues on the agenda.

They had taken away my dacha earlier, after I left the government. They didn't stand on ceremony. They also took away governmental phone lines and the car. The administration saw their chance—they knew Yeltsin wouldn't interfere. I didn't remind him about me. The classic situation of silent phones and the cold shoulder from former "friends" were my realities in late 1995.

KOKH: Sure. Apparatchiks are delicate people. They knew Yeltsin would not issue an order to take away your dacha—but he would not tell you to keep it, either. And Gaidar was not the kind of a person to call Yeltsin and make complaints. So they would take it away. You had it coming. Did you receive government job offers in spring 1997, when Governor Boris Nemtsov became a vice premier and Chubais was transferred from the presidential administration?

GAIDAR: No, we didn't discuss that question. Yeltsin mentioned the expediency of my return two or three times after my second resignation, but he was never specific. I said I would hardly be useful in a government led by Chernomyrdin.

KOKH: And did they discuss Chernymyrdin as the premier?

GAIDAR: He was walking on thin ice in spring 1997. Chubais played the key role. Tolya could have become premier at that moment. But he thought that Chernomyrdin had behaved decently during the presidential election campaign, and it would be wrong to scheme against him.

KOKH: Did your relationship with Chernomyrdin go wrong from the very start?

GAIDAR: No—I can't say that. We had normal relations when I was his boss, quite peaceful. He was decent and did not aspire to the premiership. There was a moment when my position became shaky, and certain people started to fuss. But not Chernomyrdin.

KOKH: Actually, my dealings with Chernomyrdin were rather positive. He was quite a normal man.

GAIDAR: Yes. The only moment when he and I had some trouble was in late 1993 and early 1994, when we were put in a complicated situation: I was practically his legal successor, and worked as first vice premier. Nobody would have liked that. Our relations were tense at that point.

KOKH: And when he was setting the administration against you.

GAIDAR: Yes—and before and after that, our relations were fine.

KOKH: Let's go back to your final resignation in late 1995—that feeling of being given the cold shoulder.

GAIDAR: Naturally, they were silent. That silence was tangible.

KOKH: And no people rushing to shake your hand.

GAIDAR: Interesting—even if you are not appointed to an important position but they know you are listened to and you have influence, every time you attend an event in the Kremlin you are surrounded by directors, governors, and others saying hello and telling you, "We are so glad to see you! It has been a long time!" And the next day the situation changes, and you can see people recoiling and staying seven meters away from you. And it has happened more than once.

KOKH: And for so many centuries!

GAIDAR: Usually, a person experiences that once or twice in his entire life. I had eight such experiences—and I started seeing them as a jolly show.

SECOND CONVERSATION:
ON MORALITY AND EFFECTIVENESS IN POLITICS

KOKH: Let us speak about morality and effectiveness in politics. I am warning you I will provoke you—I will be politically incorrect on purpose. In short, I will be a hard-boiled newshound.

GAIDAR: Go ahead—do it. Morality and effectiveness in politics? In my opinion, the overwhelming majority of moral politicians are ineffective.

KOKH: I understand what you mean. And still, aren't there any examples of highly moral but effective politicians? The first example that occurs to me is Pope John Paul II.

GAIDAR: Yes, John Paul II was a moral man. But I cannot call him a politician—that is different. He was not elected by the people.

KOKH: Do you mean it is easier to be moral for a politician who is not elected by the people?

GAIDAR: This is so. It is strange, but I am afraid it's true.

KOKH: So, should I look for moral politicians among tsars or dictators?

GAIDAR: Why not? I think that Alexander II had some moral principles.

KOKH: Especially with regard to his first wife.

GAIDAR: That happens—but it has nothing to do with his political qualities.

KOKH: I'm not so sure. Alexander III was a highly moral man. He fought on the Balkan front during the so-called liberation campaign of his father, and Russia did not fight at all as long as he was the tsar. He had had more than enough of frontline truth.

GAIDAR: Yes, probably. But he also halted his father's reforms, which Stolypin resumed only many years later. And Russia missed its opportunities and advantages. He was highly moral, but he was not effective. That is what I meant. Everything we had in the twentieth century—the revolution, the Civil War, and the Stalin genocide—was the price we paid for those decades of stagnation.

KOKH: Right—he had that "small deeds" theory. In other words, Alexander III was the first politician of stagnation and stability in Russia.

GAIDAR: Precisely.

KOKH: What about Roosevelt?

GAIDAR: That is a hard question. I do not know his personal story well enough.

KOKH: Let's assume it is impeccable.

GAIDAR: I would like to think so, because Roosevelt gives the impression of a moral politician.

KOKH: He was a pragmatic politician, to put it mildly. Just remember his playing up to Joseph Kennedy, who was suspected of relations with the Irish mafia, which was always linked with the Italian mob.

GAIDAR: Really? That is why I do not dare to say that he was a highly moral politician. I can hardly imagine what highly effective moral politicians are like. I've never met one.

KOKH: Yes. But I still have an example: Margaret Thatcher?

GAIDAR: Well, this is interesting. She was really very effective, practically never lied, tried to hold a policy based on her beliefs, and did not intrigue her way to power—at least we know nothing of that. I agree, there is Margaret Thatcher.

KOKH: Then do we get the reverse: truly effective politicians are always moral people? But what is effectiveness? Margaret Thatcher does not leave the impression of a bona fide winner. She did her job and left.

And Reagan had an image: he pulled apart the Soviet Union. But look here: he did it with the assistance of Islamic fundamentalists, the Taliban, bin Laden, al-Qaeda, by creating the issue of religious terrorism. The present-day Islamic renaissance was born in the 1980s, with US financial backing.

The Soviet Union had been the Evil Empire—a monstrous totalitarian regime subordinating other states to itself, and a terrible and inefficient economy endangering global ecology; but one could still reach an agreement with it, with Brezhnev and Andropov. They were ready to negotiate, and honored their agreements. There was a dialogue, and one could live in that world.

And what have we now? There is no one to agree with, because decision-makers are untraceable and cannot be negotiated with; they don't keep their promises, and they even lack real control over armed terrorists. An attack is possible at any moment, at the metro, in a food store, in your office—a bomb, a poison, whatever.

Is that a good substitute for the Evil Empire? Are these people winners? Are these people effective politicians?

GAIDAR: And still we may call Reagan an effective politician. He wanted the communist regime to be gone, and he achieved that; he wanted to do that quickly, and it happened. I know people who did not like him, but he is an example of an effective politician, from my standpoint.

KOKH: So, there are no effective highly moral politicians, are there?

GAIDAR: I think there are situations in which moral policy wins. But that is an exception. Pardon me, but I think I am a moral person.

KOKH: But you say you are not good at politics—

GAIDAR: I am a total zero as an elected politician.

KOKH: I'll tell you something unpleasant: what you were doing in the early 1990s was not politics. It would be senseless to discuss your political effectiveness.

GAIDAR: Certainly. I was simply playing certain political roles at the crucial moment, and did what I had to do.

KOKH: That was not politics, because you did not seek power. Because if you had wanted power, just like Chernomyrdin did, you would have ordered your administration to overlook someone. You would have known that you could easily banish a person capable of intriguing against you. And you calmly worked together with Chernomyrdin while Yeltsin could have given you full premiership. You didn't put pressure on Yeltsin, although you could have done. You are not a politician. There is one serious claim that our government of young reformers can make—the first or the second in which we both worked, or the third: we never wanted full power.

GAIDAR: This is true. There was only one exception in the government of young reformers: Boris Nemtsov. He is a politician, and he wanted power. In our midst, he stood out. He was different.

KOKH: It was a big mistake not to seek full power. But I always say Yeltsin would have given us none. I felt that tone, the atmosphere of 1996–7, better than you, because I was inside—and you were outside, to a degree. The young reformers no longer had the influence on Yeltsin they had enjoyed in 1991–3. Yeltsin was completely controlled by Tanya, who in turn was charmed by Berezovsky and Gusinsky. And they told her there were dozens of such Chubaises, and they would be in full control.

Berezovsky said on a live television program that the government should listen to big business—but he actually meant himself. Apparently he personified big business.

Amazingly, the *siloviki* claim victory over Gusinsky and Berezovsky, but in the days when those two wandered through government cafeterias and opened the door to Yeltsin's office with a kick, they obeyed their orders and didn't fight them at all. Chubais, Kokh, and other powerless people were fighting, while the *siloviki* supplied Berezovsky and Gusinsky with compromising material about us.

GAIDAR: You started a revolt, and you were shown who was the real master. There, you see—Gusinsky and Berezovsky were not highly moral, but they were effective!

KOKH: And Yeltsin didn't support us, but did what those aces wanted. He gave them media resources and actually started serving them. What do you call that, regarding Yeltsin? "Rejection of morals for the sake of effective policy" or "I am ready to sacrifice anyone for security, personal power, and a quiet old age"?

How could that happen? Two men were given control of the main channels for free, without any right or excuse, and they started running the country the way they wanted. Was it done by the charismatic politician who was holding on to power at any cost, and sacrificing everyone, even his own blood brothers? The politician who betrayed his friends and allies in order to give power to Berezovsky and Gusinsky?

Putin may be forgiven a lot of things just because he tamed those two ruffians. His rejection of morals for the sake of effective policy at least illustrates our point.

GAIDAR: I have a feeling that I know two Boris Nikolayevich Yeltsins. One of them ceased to exist on October 4, 1993. I know that man well; I worked together with him. There was another man called Boris Nikolayevich Yeltsin, but he was completely different. You could never have imagined the Yeltsin of 1992 listening to Berezovsky and Gusinsky! That's not even funny.

KOKH: But that very early-period Yeltsin put a certain Poltoranin and then Mironov in charge of PR support for the liberal economic reforms—that is, television.

GAIDAR: Well, Mironov came later.

KOKH: And what about Poltoranin? There is little choice in rotten apples.

GAIDAR: Certainly Poltoranin was not better, but he was politically close to Yeltsin.

KOKH: But he was not effective. He gave no PR backing to the reforms—quite the opposite!

GAIDAR: Certainly, he didn't do that—but when he wrote the text of Yeltsin's speech at the plenary meeting, that was a funny story. The plenary meeting was held in October 1987, and Yeltsin was dismissed as first secretary of the party's Moscow city committee for opposing himself to the party. And he opposed himself by announcing his resignation plans in disagreement with party policy. His speech was rather rambling. It could not have been published the way it was, because it would have caught no attention. No big deal—a first secretary is dismissed. He was not a celebrity then, and his dismissal would have passed unnoticed. And Poltoranin wrote all about Raisa Maximovna and privileges—everything the people wanted to hear. That text was distributed. He was a highly effective person for his time. Yeltsin simply did not realize that time had changed drastically.

Listen, I'm not saying that Yeltsin was an ideal man in 1991–3, that he did not drink or smoke—although he never smoked. No, he was a complicated person, with whims, hard to work with, and inclined to sudden decisions and disregard of everyone's opinion. He sometimes went ballistic in our discussions.

I do not say that Yeltsin had been a knight without fear and reproach before fall 1993; but he was a different man after 1993. And then the events you are talking about started.

KOKH: What was it—the weakening of his will? Or old age? Or did he have a moral breakdown?

GAIDAR: It was sort of a breakdown, moral and physical.

KOKH: Was the drinking habit interfering with his work?

GAIDAR: That didn't surprise me when I was leaving in 1994.

KOKH: Do you think the breakdown happened after the putsch?

GAIDAR: Yes, I think it happened after the events of October 3–4, 1993. Although such processes are always protracted.

KOKH: Could it have been the Chechen war?

GAIDAR: No, the war started later. His entourage and administration were fooling him. He was very tired, and they played him this way: "Don't worry, this is beneath you! Soskovets or somebody else will do that. That is not important, really. Why don't we do some paperwork?"

KOKH: I understand that, but how could he allow them to destroy the Chubais team and never give us, Chubais, and Nemtsov a chance to defend ourselves? That was his only pillar! Neither Interior Minister Kulikov nor Prosecutor General Skuratov was his supporter—they were all FSB men, who were worth nothing! Especially those left after Korzhakov—they had no personal loyalty to Yeltsin, and were not personally indebted to him. Could he think after the meeting with Gusinsky and Berezovsky that he had a new team, a more effective one?

GAIDAR: I know less about his attitude to Chubais in the latter period, but he was cold to Chubais in the early 1990s, when we worked together. He was cordial to me, although we had some disagreements, but he always seemed aloof toward Chubais.

KOKH: This is not about cordiality. He involved Chubais in his election campaign of 1996 when he was in trouble. When Korzhakov and Soskovets thought no better than to dismiss the parliament again.

GAIDAR: Indeed. To lose Chubais and his team was a poor decision, which cost the country a lot, including the default. But I think he was cautious about Chubais personally.

KOKH: Still, he did that. Could he have thought he had a new Chubais?

GAIDAR: You know, there's a reason Yeltsin was called unpredictable. For instance, everyone was positive that he would never give up Korzhakov. Even Berezovsky believed that. I heard him saying six months before the dismissal of Korzhakov, Barsukov, and Soskovets that Yeltsin would not fire Korzhakov even if he executed a hundred people near the Kremlin Wall.

I think the decision to dismiss those three men was really hard for him, but the stakes were too high. He must have regained some of his old fighter's qualities at that moment, and realized that it was a question of power—he could either become a banal dictator jointly with Korzhakov, the army, and the security services, or become a real president. When the question was put that way, he dropped Korzhakov.

KOKH: Then why did he withdraw from power? Then it looks like: "I love power so much I can sell even the man who saved my life several times; but then, just a few months later, I dislike power so much that I'll hand it over to some car dealer."

Speaking of abandonment: we can make an endless list of personalities, but there is a key group of people, very different people, who played a very big role in his life. Alexander Korzhakov is a striking example of one group, and Anatoly Chubais of another. Those two groups were at odds, but they played a very big role in Yeltsin's life. Being a member of one of the groups, I realize that we must not underestimate Korzhakov's role in the suppression of the 1993 putsch. He played an important and positive role. It is also hard to overestimate his role in August 1991, when he was actually shielding Yeltsin with his body.

They were true friends, blood brothers—they drank vodka together and they played tennis. But he gave him up. Although he had more delicate ways to do that—not so public and not so irrevocable.

It is possible to deprive a person of power and to remain friends, especially as the presidential security service has rather limited powers—and it was Yeltsin's fault that he gave practically unlimited rights to Korzhakov. It wouldn't have been hard to bring him back to reality. Yeltsin didn't do that: he dismissed Korzhakov loudly, publicly, and humiliatingly.

Now take Chubais and his team. He fired everyone, although Chubais had done so much for Yeltsin. Yeltsin would not have been reelected without him—that was clear. There is an opinion that he did that for the sake of Russia, and no sacrifice would have been too much for it. There is another opinion—that it was about personal power and nothing else. At least, personal power and the security of his family and himself were the absolute priorities, and other people were trash he made use of in the achievement of his goal. His last gesture, of transferring power to his successor, had the same value: he betrayed the cause he had long worked for. Which of these points of view are closer to you?

GAIDAR: I am a bad judge. He did nothing bad to me personally, and he had to dismiss me. He was always honest in our personal relations. At least, with me.

KOKH: You were lucky to be fired in the early period, because he changed completely. It was hard for Yeltsin at first to give up his people; but he got used to it, and never gave it a second thought later on.

GAIDAR: Speaking of Yeltsin, he really did want power. Remember how he overruled the decree that had appointed Chernomyrdin as acting president as soon as he regained consciousness after the heart bypass surgery?

But I think he had a sense of mission: he didn't just occupy that position, but felt he had the right to occupy it because he was saving Russia.

KOKH: It is a rather common idea that everything done for the sake of Russia is moral, including immoral deeds.

GAIDAR: There is such an idea, and it doesn't contradict what I have just said.

KOKH: I have been doing a lot of journalism lately, and have been meeting with journalists often. They are convinced they have their own morals, journalists' morals: they can do what other people cannot because they bring information to people—that is their mission. That is why they have the right to look under one's bed, to peep into a bathroom, or to divulge state secrets.

GAIDAR: Politicians have a similar idea. Many of them are sure that their mission justifies any means. You also have to admit that strict obedience to moral values makes one ineffective in certain fields. I made a bad public politician. Who needs a public politician who constantly tells the truth? Yes, I may have been wrong, but I never lied on purpose.

KOKH: Do you mean an effective politician should lie and wriggle, irrespective of his doctrine—communism, capitalism, freedom, slavery, and so on?

GAIDAR: I am afraid so, yes. Certainly there are some exceptions; there are critical situations in which one may permit oneself to be an honest politician. For instance, Churchill told the British people after he had taken office that he could not promise them anything but blood, sweat, and tears. A prime minister with such a program would not have lasted for long under normal circumstances.

KOKH: Moving on, all those reforms that transformed the economy and the country at large and turned it from socialist to capitalist, if they were not effective, it was because they weren't comprehensive. You know that economic reforms were not enough to reform Russia. Russia can be changed only with comprehensive reforms that go beyond the economy into sociology, PR, and politics. Our team was focused on economic transformations, which doomed them to low effectiveness.

We should also have reformed the police, the judiciary and the administrative structure; we should have had propaganda and a different relationship with the media.

Yavlinsky, who said, "Either give me all the power or don't give me any, because I won't deal with just part of it," had his logic: he understood he would be blamed if the reforms proved insufficient. Perhaps this wasn't showing off or trying to shirk responsibility, but a desire to do the best?

GAIDAR: That makes sense. But the question is: What is your priority? If the priority is your political career, then you must stick to this position. But take a broader look. First of all, you cannot keep power forever; and, second, even if you keep the power you will be vulnerable to and impeded by the problems you cannot control for objective reasons.

Essentially, you have a choice: either do something or do nothing. There is no third way of taking power and keeping it indefinitely. It is up to you to choose! We decided we would do at least something; Yavlinsky preferred to do nothing. Each of us thinks his position is correct. Who will be the judge? It's a cliché, but only time will tell.

KOKH: All right, even if we disregard the Interior Ministry, the General Staff, the strategic nuclear forces, and so on, can you say, that you were in charge of the economic reforms even though you had no control over the Central Bank? You weren't even in charge of its personnel.

GAIDAR: That was hard to do without levers of influence on the Central Bank.

KOKH: Then why didn't you demand them? Why didn't you raise the question with Yeltsin?

GAIDAR: Now, tell me: Who appointed the Central Bank chairman? Wasn't it Khasbulatov's Supreme Council?

KOKH: Yeltsin was doing that later. Why did Gerashchenko pop up every time?

GAIDAR: Why? I wish I knew. That was our main disagreement after 1993, when he took charge. I said they had to replace Gerashchenko if they wanted to make the economic policy effective.

KOKH: And what was the answer?

GAIDAR: The answer was, "You must reach an agreement with the premier."

KOKH: That's the wrong answer! He didn't want to act in your favor, did he? Oh, yes, I forgot—that was the other Yeltsin you told me about.

GAIDAR: Sure! Judge for yourself—there was a certain collective "we" who told him, "Let's start making the reforms. We have the power now!" And there were others who said to Yeltsin, "People are tired of reforms—let's take a break."

KOKH: No logic.

GAIDAR: Why?

KOKH: That sounded like, "People are tired of reforms—let's fight a war instead."

GAIDAR: It was.

KOKH: Aren't people tired of war?

GAIDAR: Certainly not. It would be a short and victorious war! What can be better than a short and victorious war?

KOKH: In a country tired of economic reforms?

GAIDAR: Sure.

KOKH: Don't you think we found a nifty loophole for morality and effectiveness in politics?

THIRD CONVERSATION: ON WAR

KOKH: I remember the time Georgy Khizha, the leader of the St Petersburg directors, was made a government member. I have always said that personnel are Chubais's hobbyhorse.

GAIDAR: Yes, that was his creation. And that was the case in which he guessed right.

KOKH: Do you remember the mess Khizha made in Ossetia when Yeltsin sent him to find solutions? I never understood that. Afterward, you had to go there and find solutions yourself.

GAIDAR: He was simply taken aback. Everything was ablaze: battles, Ossetians were emptying arms depots, and he was taken aback!

KOKH: How did it start? The conflict goes back to tsarist times. Although forgotten now, that conflict was monstrous.

GAIDAR: Right. The conflict was smoldering until it exploded. One of those radical Ingush leaders—I never learned who it was—shouted: "Let's fight to get back our old land!" Plenty of weapons had been amassed both in Ingushetia and in Chechnya by then. The Ingush disarmed some of the military units deployed in Ingushetia, and got more armored personnel carriers.

KOKH: The Ingushes started the conflict, didn't they?

GAIDAR: Sure. And then the Ossetians demanded to be armed, too. To cut a long story short, I gave them weapons—I couldn't have done otherwise. The military units deployed in Ossetia didn't want to resist the Ossetians; but they weren't ready to deter the armed Ingush units moving to Vladikavkaz, either.

KOKH: Were they prepared to lose to the Ingushes?

GAIDAR: No—they weren't ready to resist the people. There was no doubt the Ossetians could have taken the arms depots by force. So I told them we would give them weapons, but only to former soldiers and only if they joined the Interior Ministry troops. They returned the weapons when the hostilities were over.

KOKH: What do you mean, the hostilities? The Ingushes went on the offensive and the Ossetians made trenches, took positions, and opened fire.

GAIDAR: There was fighting. The Ossetians defended their positions and the Ingushes were on the offensive, and I had to relocate forces—but I can't remember now precisely which forces those were. The forces separated the warring sides, and they had to fight the Ingushes because the Ingushes initiated that conflict. My main and only task was to stop the conflict, in any way possible, so that it didn't develop further, as in Chechnya, and so on.

Then we met with Ruslan Aushev. He wasn't the president of Ingushetia then, just an informal leader. He flew in, and tensions relaxed slightly. By then the Ingushes had been forced to retreat toward the Ossetian border, and then forces entered Ingushetia to more or less put things in order, and reached the border of Chechnya.

It was a very dangerous situation. It wasn't clear where the border lay between Ingushetia and Chechnya, where the forces were supposed to stop. That question had to be coordinated with three sides: the Chechens, the Ingushes, and the army. The main thing I did there was settle that problem. I summoned the Chechen first vice premier to Nazran, and we coordinated the borderline—the limit at which the forces must stop so that Chechnya did not explode. And I had to convince them and prove things to them: some things didn't suit the Ingushes, some the Chechens. It was not easy.

KOKH: Did Chechnya already have a viable government of a practically independent country?

GAIDAR: Yes. It was led by Dudayev. He became the president in fall 1992. In fact I did not speak with him, even on the phone. He sent his people to me several times, but I thought it was none of my business to communicate with the leaders of self-proclaimed states. I had only one task: I had to stop that conflict at any cost.

KOKH: As you know, a huge number of Ingush refugees were produced by that conflict, and they are still unable to return home.

GAIDAR: Right—when I arrived in Ossetia I saw Ingush homes burning.

KOKH: How did that happen? The Ingushes went on the offensive, and Ossetians got armed and protected what they called their land? One may argue endlessly whose land it is. You may go deep into historical investigation, but, one way or another, the Ossetians were ready to spill blood for their land.

But then there was Beslan. The Ingush attacked and killed their children, which was even more monstrous. But there was no reaction from the Ossetians—neither hostilities nor appeals to get armed. God forbid! But what is the explanation? More than two years had passed. Was the absence of reaction merely illusory? Or was it infamous stability at work?

GAIDAR: I think so. Back then they had a feeling that no one would protect them, and they had to do it themselves. Now they think there are authorities, and let them settle the situation. A Russian peasant was one and the same person in 1918 and in 1928—but he was sure in 1918 that no one would protect him, and he had to fight himself, while he didn't think that way in 1928.

KOKH: One more question: Did Grachev know precisely, to the last shell and submachine gun, how many weapons he let the Chechens have?

GAIDAR: First of all, he didn't know that to the last submachine gun. No matter what documents certain individuals may produce now, there were no forces there at the time. It was presumed that military units were stationed there—but it just seemed to Gorbachev and, later on, to Rutskoi, seated in the Kremlin, that they had an army there. There were just a few officers and their wives and children allegedly guarding arms depots.

The depots were attacked regularly, and the handful of officers couldn't possibly deter those attacks. The attackers took weapons, ammunition, armored personnel carriers, and so on. Say three men are guarding an arms depot, and 500 armed militants come there—what would those unfortunate officers do?

Then Dudayev sent his guards to the depots. They were subordinated to him only, and they protected those depots together with our officers, so that the arms did not get into the hands of God knows who. The actual situation was that, formally, there was a regiment, but actually there was no regiment—just a unit of Chechens and some officers, who were lucky if they ever had a chance to send their families to Russia.

KOKH: I still have a question. Grachev knew precisely the amount of armaments left in Chechnya—he knew that from military intelligence reports and from reports by the officers. He had to know how many men Dudayev could have armed. He also knew the level of their combat readiness. Why was Yeltsin so sure that one airborne regiment could seize Grozny? Why did he need that war in 1994?

GAIDAR: Grachev didn't support that war. Other people were enthusiastic about it. Deputy Prime Minister Nikolai Yegorov, former head of the Krasnodar territorial administration, played the key role. The appointment of a brave and energetic fool to a responsible position has the most terrible effect—especially if this fool is a civilian. He is really ready to assume responsibility and make decisions. No one else wanted to assume responsibility, but he kept shouting, "Pick me! I'll show them!" We may also recall the famous phrase of another key author of the decision about Chechnya—Yegorov's supporter, Security Council Secretary Lobov. When he was asked to assess the possibility of guerrilla warfare in Chechnya, he said, "We will not allow that to happen. Guerrilla warfare is not a Chechen tradition." He must have thought they liked trench warfare, with positions and barbed wire entanglements.

And Grachev was against, but he was told to do it. Do you know how Airborne Forces generals were trained in the Soviet period? They were trained to control forces that were airdropped in the enemy's rear to seize infrastructure while the armor went on the offensive. They had the sole task of being airdropped and holding their positions for 72 hours—no one cared what would happen and how they would survive for those 72 hours. They had to adopt a defensive stance and to hold on: that defined their tactics and strategy. And the man with such training was given a task of a totally different level and complexity. And he was sure that he could seize Grozny by sending just one regiment.

It seems he should have known better: there were weapons, and Chechens who knew their land and were good and motivated soldiers; but it never occurred to him that the enemy was not just civilians, although armed ones, and that they could resist the airborne regiment.

Here is another example: General Eduard Vorobyov, army first deputy commander—a clever and well-educated man who understood who was fighting, and how. If I could, I would have made him the General Staff chief. He went to Chechnya because he was ordered to lead the operation. He took a look at the military units, assessed their status, glanced at intelligence reports, and said they needed no less than two months to make that trash into an army before any operations could start.

It was not his business whether to start the operations or not, but he simply realized that it was impossible to fight immediately. But his commanders said, "You can and you must." And he refused to assume command over the operation.

Grachev may be reproached for the way the First Chechen War was run, but not for its inception.

KOKH: In the end, the final decision was made by civilians—and, above all, stupid and irresponsible men. Is that right?

GAIDAR: Yes.

FOURTH CONVERSATION: ON PRIVATIZATION

KOKH: When I think about the 1990s, I picture ad hoc, spasmodic, and totally ambivalent motions: there was a year of intensive, fantastically liberal reforms, and then many months of stagnation. I remember when voucher privatization was over—we wrote a new program, which we submitted to the government. There was no response for six months. I didn't know what to do.

I would like to discuss privatization with you. As you know, it had a number of key elements. First of all, there was monetary privatization—shops sold at auction. It was rather successful, and brought rather positive results in Nizhny Novgorod and St Petersburg. Then there was voucher privatization, which we will discuss in greater detail. In parallel, there were also so-called investment auctions—a rather controversial practice—and loans-for-shares auctions. Temporarily monetary privatization.

Monetary privatization was more or less clear: you pay more, you win. Investment auctions were also clear: an intellectual exercise aimed to win over directors, who had significant political weight but insufficient financial resources. The directors enthusiastically drafted investment programs, especially since the investment auction mechanism required them to do so. Loans-for-shares auctions were a lure for oligarchs. Oligarchs who took part in loans-for-shares auctions in 1995 honestly worked for Yeltsin's victory in spring 1996. Voucher privatization was meant to be "people's privatization." People were issued with vouchers, which was quite an administrative exercise. That could have been done only by a bureaucratic genius like Chubais. He did it amid complete chaos in the country, which was already falling apart. That was an administrative exercise on a fantastic scale.

GAIDAR: It was comparable only with Trotsky's formation within several months of a capable Red Army. Voucher privatization combined population census and monetary reform. Plus, there were voucher auctions. That was an unprecedentedly complex task from an organizational point of view.

KOKH: But voucher privatization never achieved its goal. The very words "voucher privatization" became a symbol of injustice, a sham. It is believed that the people were fooled—even though, except on this one occasion, the authorities had never given people anything, and they have not done so since; all they had ever done was take away.

GAIDAR: That's not true. Let me give you an example from Russian history when there was a similar situation. People were given land in 1918. But three years later peasants were complaining that they had been deceived—they said it would have been better if they hadn't been given the land.

KOKH: But the peasants were not given land—they took it themselves!

GAIDAR: They certainly did, but they did so with caution. And then they were told they had done the right thing. They started whining in 1920: they wrote to every department possible and said they had taken plenty of land, but got little in the end when land was divided equally. Land was divided equally, but some got land 12 miles from home and they asked how they were supposed to cultivate it. Some got better land than others. They kept re-dividing land every year before the Soviet government understood what was going on and said, "Stop." All it got was indignant letters from peasants, "What do you mean, we should stop? Land was divided wrongly—are we supposed to keep it that way?" Hate over land was enormous!

KOKH: I think that the main wave of hatred came after surplus appropriation. They had no time to think about how it had been divided. They weren't even cultivating it.

GAIDAR: I didn't realize the acuteness of the problem until I started working with documents.

KOKH: I understand that perfectly. They had to divide land, and no matter how they tried, the division was not fair. But back to privatization: should such a monstrously difficult administrative exercise have been undertaken in a country badly in need of money—organizing free privatization and getting nothing but hatred over unfair voucher privatization in return? Would it not have been easier to carry on with monetary privatization? Did you really think people would call it fair?

GAIDAR: Of course not. I strongly objected to voucher privatization.

KOKH: Then who supported it? Naishul categorically says that he had gone off the idea of vouchers by then.

GAIDAR: I don't know what he liked or didn't like, but he was not there when it started. There was, for instance, my friend Supreme Council deputy Petr Filippov. He was the one who pushed the law on registered privatization deposits through the Supreme Council. Petr was not the problem, actually.

The idea corresponded to the spirit of the time and folk traditions. The idea of taking and dividing everything is the core idea of the God-fearing people—it is deep-rooted.

So, one way or another, the law on registered privatization deposits predetermined the appearance of vouchers. Our government had nothing to do with that law, but there was no way out.

KOKH: If not for that law, the normal monetary privatization would have continued, and no one in the government would have thought about privatization vouchers. Is that right?

GAIDAR: We never would have done that. Since the genie was out of the bottle, we had only two options: either to stop the process (though in that case directors would have taken everything) or to adopt the law and make the people's dream of fair division come true. You know what happened next, and what political price we paid.

KOKH: Do you mean the government did not add any ideological momentum to voucher privatization? It was just the reality you had to cope with?

GAIDAR: Absolutely. We could have lost the entire thing; there would have been directors' privatization instead.

KOKH: On the other hand, why not choose that variant? There was privatization in Poland, and it was okay.

GAIDAR: We didn't like the "red directors" very much.

KOKH: You know, all those directors who stole something went bankrupt.

GAIDAR: Yes, of course. In fact, I considered that idea. We could have chosen that variant—we discussed it with Chubais in November.

KOKH: The thing is, I consider myself one of the authors of investment auctions, which have been frequently criticized, too. But this idea of partially legalized directors' privatization worked in Poland, and other states. And I laugh when I hear criticism from voucher privatization adepts: "You were cheaters! And we offered a fair way!" Let's go outside and ask people which of the two privatizations they called fair.

GAIDAR: I would have had only monetary privatization, without investment or loans-for-shares auctions.

KOKH: Loans-for-shares auctions were also mandated after the State Duma banned the normal monetary privatization. At least for large companies.

GAIDAR: I remember that. I had realized by then that voucher privatization and directors' privatization were equally bad. A good solution was simply impossible to find.

KOKH: I still think that directors' privatization was better. And I can tell you why: we formed a huge stratum, very active and influential, which gave us support, while voucher privatization formed a huge stratum of our opponents. But I remember how voucher privatization ideologist Dima Vasilyev called the very idea of negotiations with the directors "a slap in the face."

GAIDAR: If we had suspended privatization at that moment, we would have been unable to find anything to impose discipline on the directors.

KOKH: Directors would have done everything themselves, without our permission.

GAIDAR: I don't think the directors were grateful to us at that moment—they were not our supporters. They thanked us later on, after the concept had changed. And back then they believed that they were the masters of the enterprises, and labor collectives also believed that the directors were their masters: "You are offering us an investment auction—to hell with it." Especially if a director had come to the Supreme Council, he would have been told: "Sure, you are the master! How can anyone doubt that? Just give us some money for the political struggle against Yeltsin and Gaidar. And a bit for our personal needs!" It was impossible to reach an agreement with them at the time. We had to educate them so that they would understand that the 20 percent they gained for the investment auction was a big favor. And directors would have told us in 1991, "This is all ours." We would have strengthened Khasbulatov's political base.

KOKH: That's right. But such a Khasbulatov would have been different from the Khasbulatov who used to oppose us so adamantly.

GAIDAR: The reforms were not very important for Khasbulatov. He was a serious man—the big prize he wanted was complete power.

KOKH: That made him little different from Yeltsin.

GAIDAR: Yes. But his style was different: the oriental style of an intriguer and an apparatchik. Yeltsin was a bulldozer; Khasbulatov was a Machiavellian. He was pondering who would go on a foreign trip and who wouldn't, who would buy a car and who wouldn't: "You didn't vote right on the last ballot, so I'm crossing you off the list for housing." I think Stalin was his example—a quiet and inconspicuous associate of the leader. Besides, he smoked a pipe.

KOKH: Just a few words to round up. I wanted to ask you lots of questions, but how about a quick forecast for the next ten to 20 years?

GAIDAR: The present stage isn't very cozy. I don't know how long it might last. The demand for freedom will grow. If energy prices go down, the demand will grow more rapidly; if they go up, it will grow more slowly. Tensions will escalate sooner or later—that's inevitable. The fight to build democracy in Russia will be hard.

KOKH: Do you feel any guilt that you or your team is responsible for the country's failure to avoid a regime that is even hard to identify? This is neither dictatorship, nor democracy, nor restoration—this is God knows what. Let us say the personalities are incompatible with the country's challenges.

GAIDAR: I don't feel any guilt. There is pain and regret. But I can't say I know what we should have done to avoid this—what we should have done with real life, the way it was: with the real country, its political elite, other players, the legacy, traditions, and problems.

KOKH: Many people who wished us well still criticize us for not forcing Yeltsin to adopt restitution and lustration laws, and for not holding the State Duma election in 1991?

GAIDAR: That was impossible.

KOKH: Because of Yeltsin's personality?

GAIDAR: No—because of the political situation.

KOKH: Did you ever discuss that?

GAIDAR: Yes. We didn't discuss the restitution law seriously, but the ban on the Soviet Communist Party was discussed, and we lost the case in the Constitutional Court. We had a diarchy: no matter how popular Yeltsin was, he had very limited room for maneuver.

KOKH: Still, Eastern Europe adopted such laws.

GAIDAR: You must never have too many tasks. If you try to solve three tasks simultaneously, you will solve none.

KOKH: Do you think the present-day regime was inevitable?

GAIDAR: Absolutely. It was easier for Eastern Europe. They could always find a person from the alternative elite—for instance, from the Church— who had never been a member of the Communist Party.

KOKH: For instance, I was not a communist.

GAIDAR: True, but there were few people like you—those who were not communists but were still capable of important and resolute actions.

KOKH: I can give you many names: Misha Manevich, Misha Dmitriyev, Lyonya Limonov.

GAIDAR: All of you were so young—we were young, and you were even younger. You were five years younger than us, and that was a lot at the time. You were just boys. I was 35.

KOKH: Let us skip several logical steps, and I will tell you about my conclusions, and if you have no objections, we can end the interview on that. Am I right that the current regime is the price we pay for the avoidance of bloodshed? If we had chosen freedom and a market in a civil war, we would not have wasted words with KGB men and commies—is that right?

GAIDAR: Right.

KOKH: Yet it is unclear whether this regime can avoid bloodshed.

GAIDAR: At least that blood would not be on our hands.

13

WHAT WE LEARNED

WE ORIGINALLY PLANNED TO HAVE A SUMMARIZING CONVERSATION after all the interviews for this book. First, we wanted to highlight facts that were new even to us (such as the Belovezh decision-making process); and, second, we wanted to speak again about the most interesting and important things (for instance, why Russia could not do what the Czech Republic and Poland did). In the end, we changed our minds. We talked about our favorite subjects in practically every interview, and facts ... facts don't need to be repeated. Shortened versions of the interviews were published in *Forbes* magazine, so we asked Elmar Murtazayev, first deputy chief editor, to sum up—to ask the questions that, in his opinion, an interested reader would ask. Here are the results.

Petr Aven

ELMAR MURTAZAYEV: Judging from what your respondents said, they were all fighting and rejecting compromises. But now I look out of the window and ask a question: Why do I see such crap if they all tried so hard? To put it in politically correct terms: Why did Russia build an unfree market economy, as James Baker suggested in his interview?

PETR AVEN: I disagree—it's not crap. There is a rule in literary criticism: a writer must be judged by the rules of the genre. We set out to create economic reform, the components of which were liberalization, privatization, and stabilization. Liberalization was accomplished. We made our economy free—we did that. Baker is right, this is not the classic free-market economy, but it is fundamentally freer than it was before. And it absolutely does not resemble the Soviet economy.

We began privatization in 1992, which Alfred Kokh later continued, and we made serious efforts toward macroeconomic stabilization. We were less successful and slower than Eastern European countries for a number of objective reasons, but it would be wrong to say that we failed. In general, the economic reform tasks we set were accomplished. The country did not become the way we wanted it to be; but many fundamental things that now look natural and normal simply did not exist when we joined the government.

We joined the government when the economy was ruled by Gosplan, administrative planning, fixed prices, a state monopoly on foreign trade, centralized imports—everything belonged to the government, and there was no private sector at all. The economy was completely different when we left.

And one more thing. It would be unfair to blame everything on Yegor Gaidar, who was in office for 14 months the first time and three months the second time.

ALFRED KOKH: In recent years I have come across a phenomenon I call ignorance. Many young people use "I didn't know that" as an argument in a dispute. Not knowing is no excuse; on the contrary, it is a self-accusation. Gaidar always said that ignorance could not be an argument. If you do not know something, you should listen and learn. Or read—there are books that are worth reading.

You say it's crap. Can you give us examples of a transformation of such a monstrous economic model as the Soviet Union into something decent? People tell me, "Just take a look at Estonia, Latvia, and Lithuania." But those countries didn't have an economy of our type—so disproportionate, with a mammoth defense sector and the huge number of people it employed; with the corrupt engineering elite, which had been doing God-knows-what for 30 or even 50 years and claiming it was science, but actually just squandering money. There were a huge number of research and development institutes of all kinds where people sat rolling pencils between their fingers, and then realized suddenly that they had no market value.

Why was the overregulated, planned Soviet economy bad? It concealed sores and ulcers—it veiled them, just as it veiled the deficit and inflation. And why is the market economy good? It makes these sores visible. The visibility of these sores is our achievement. We built the economy, which let the cat out of the bag. We showed that Stalin's colossal industry, of which we had been proud for years, was 90 percent unnecessary—the country didn't need it. And we are blamed when these factories no longer work. Their work was senseless! They uselessly processed resources.

Huge amounts of human energy, labor, and talent were wasted—wasted on nothing. And we finally built an economy that doesn't do that. We should be thanked! And instead they keep asking why those plants aren't functioning, and say it's all crap. Well, let's start them up again and let them consume resources for nothing.

MURTAZAYEV: Let me be more specific about "crap." When you joined the government in 1991, you must have dreamed of an ideal model that would appear in 20 years. Did you dream of the Russian economy and the country the way they are now?

AVEN: Certainly we dreamed of a much freer economy with much less corruption and a much smaller state sector. We imagined the country would achieve higher integrated growth rates within 20 years. We hoped the country would make a breakthrough, due to its huge potential. But that really didn't happen.

As I understand it, the problem was not only with us, but also with a more profound sickness of the country than we had imagined. The disease was more severe and advanced—that is the first cause. Second, the country's problems were not so much economic. We had to reform the country's mentality, not the economy.

KOKH: What we may really be accused of is economic determinism. We were focused on the economy and, being genuine Marxists, believed that economic transformations would rapidly transform the rest—the society, traditions, and people, or, in Marxist terms, the superstructure.

AVEN: It turned out that changing the economic rules does not mean changing the country. But that doesn't mean that the economic rules should not have been changed.

MURTAZAYEV: "Crap" stands for the highly corrupt regime, the blending of business and power, the large state sector, the excessive regulation of many industries, and so on. What we see from our window, the crap—or, as you prefer, "the stable economy of the 2000s"—was this stage of national development inevitable, in your opinion?

AVEN: "Everything natural is reasonable." Probably the current degree of corruption could have been avoided. But, as we understand now, in a situation where corruption was intrinsic social behavior in the Soviet period, bending the rules was the norm, every law was easily bypassed, and the severity of laws was mitigated by their optionality.

Certainly we have to consider the confluence of circumstances and the role of an individual in this history. A big role in this turn of Russian history was played by the progressing sickness of Boris Yeltsin, who spent much less time in actual management after 1994. But if we take a broader look, we will see that it was impossible to avoid the merger between power and property—the main vice of our system. Much of what we have today is the result not of our economic reforms, but of much more enduring historical processes.

MURTAZAYEV: You pay a lot of attention to Boris Yeltsin in the interviews. Is this due to the actual state of affairs—he was the chief of state, after all—or do you have a personal interest in him?

AVEN: Both. He had a substantial influence on the progress of the reforms. He was a contradictory and very interesting historical personality. In contrast to many of our interlocutors, Alfred and I do not idolize him; we are aware of his strong and weak points. As for your question of whether such a high level of corruption could have been avoided, I can say that Yeltsin did not obstruct corruption in his last years in office. To a large degree he was the reason for what you called the "crap."

KOKH: Many of the archetypes exploited today by the authorities were established by Yeltsin: the notorious myth of the 1996 election; the myth claiming that Russia would have fallen apart without the war in Chechnya; the myth that Nazis and communists will take power if real democracy is allowed; the myth that the Kremlin should softly control the media.

AVEN: And the populist promises of communism tomorrow are Yeltsin's technique, too: promises of low inflation, large salaries, all those "I will lie down on the rails" promises.

KOKH: And the "president of all Russians" formula, which predetermined the absence of a real political force responsible for power, is Yeltsin's legacy.

AVEN: At the same time, Yeltsin oversaw colossal economic reforms in 1992, and carried on the course of glasnost launched by Gorbachev. Russia's new position in the world is also Yeltsin's contribution. He is a contradictory personality, but I think he will go down in history as a positive influence.

MURTAZAYEV: When I was looking through the interviews, I was surprised that political battles were lost over trifles. Foreign Minister Andrei Kozyrev said that Gaidar and he failed to ask Baker for extensive assistance to a new Russia because the trip was scheduled badly; Sergei Shakhrai said that the Belovezh meeting was mostly impromptu. How much did those accidents determine the country's strategy?

AVEN: We were both trained as Marxists, so we believe that historical processes are determined by economic processes. In reference to Baker's visit to Moscow in winter 1991, as recounted by Kozyrev, I do not think we could have achieved a different level of cooperation with the West even if the negotiations had been held differently. In addition, Baker disagrees with Kozyrev's theory.

KOKH: Let's assume that Gaidar had a chance to speak about the need for a new Marshall Plan with Baker. Baker told us the West was not prepared to grant that kind of assistance to Russia. Probably Yeltsin did not make that request, because he felt it would not be granted. He saved face. Or he did not want to put Baker in an impossible position.

MURTAZAYEV: Petr, you said once that the West had deceived the reform team—

KOKH: We deceived ourselves.

AVEN: Alfred is right. If the West had given us a large amount of assistance, history would have been different—I am sure of that. On the other hand, I have a much better understanding of the Western elite and politics now. And, powered with this knowledge, I can see that it was a mistake to count on a large amount of assistance. The "West is our friend" idea was rather well analyzed in our interview with Kozyrev. The West was not prepared for serious backing of Russia. Nor was Russia.

Probably events would have been different if the West had accidentally had a leader of Churchillian scope—if Bush and Baker, who understood the need for new relations with Russia better than others, had remained in office; and if Yeltsin had not stopped supporting the pro-Western course in the middle of the 1990s. We would have encountered the same problems as now, but it would have been much easier to cope with them.

MURTAZAYEV: You mostly spoke with like-minded people, sometimes with your friends. Can you imagine an interview with a political opponent or a non-ally—for instance, with former First Vice Premier Soskovets, who had a real administrative war with Chubais?

KOKH: I can easily imagine an interview with Soskovets, but it would be very boring. There are things he could tell, but he would not do that. He would say smooth and soothing words, and absolute banalities.

AVEN: Our choice of interlocutors was not based on our degree of agreement with them; we selected them according to trust. For instance, we could have spoken to Poltoranin—but he lied constantly, on purpose or not. And there are plenty of such people. For instance, Yuri Skokov—we really wanted to interview him, but he could hardly have told us the truth. The idea is to speak with friends and like-minded people who will tell us things they would not tell anyone else. For instance, there were plenty of sensational facts and revelations in Chubais's interview, and I am sure he would not have said those things to anyone else.

KOKH: Our biggest failure is that we failed to interview Chernomyrdin before he was gone.

AVEN: He would have told us many truths. We had good relations, and we had basically agreed on the interview, but he passed away. A real shame.

MURTAZAYEV: People who might be called members of the Soviet scientific intelligentsia, without any civil service experience, joined the government in 1991. Many of you have become celebrated businessmen, writers, and public figures. How much did your value system change?

AVEN: My ideals have not changed at all. I believe in the same gods I had in 1992. My experience is different, but my ideology is the same. Still, I have new ideas about transformational tactics. I recently found a transcript of a discussion we had before joining the government in 1991. There is an interesting thing—our discussion of the possibility of employing authoritarian mechanisms for the reforms. I have much less confidence in the possibility of such an authoritarian scenario now, especially in Russia. That would require a Pinochet, and elites full of strength, authority, and principles. There is no such group in Russia.

KOKH: We have generals, but they are different. I studied in Chile, and I studied the Pinochet experience. For a short time I lived under an illusion that Putin might follow that path.

AVEN: This is not the only reason. There is also the need for sufficient obedience and respect for the law—that is the only way an authoritarian leader can do anything. A country where laws are neglected can change only through democratic procedures. Otherwise, you have to chop off heads to make people obey the leader. That is a dangerous path, because it leads to major bloodshed. Besides, authoritarianism creates plenty of temptations. The successful examples of authoritarian modernization in history can be counted on the fingers of one hand—Korea, Singapore's Lee Kuan Yew, Pinochet, Atatürk to a degree. And there were endless corrupt or bloody examples.

MURTAZAYEV: Do you remember the time you joined the government? How significant are these memories?

AVEN: The year 1992 was one of the most memorable moments of my life. When we joined the government we realized that it was a totally different environment—that experience wasn't easy. We were not boys, we were mature men actually, but the scale of our tasks and the adrenaline were beyond comparison.

KOKH: I didn't share Petr's breakthrough—the transformation from a scholar into a minister. I was the chairman of a district executive committee in Leningrad in 1990. I was 29 years old at the time. Subsequent events were a part of my career, and had an inner logic. I was the district executive committee chairman, a deputy head of the city administration department, a deputy minister, a minister, and a vice premier. The early 1990s were a period of great growth, and my memories are still very fresh and bright. But I wouldn't be able to tell you the difference between 2004 and 2005.

MURTAZAYEV: Did you make any discoveries in those interviews?

AVEN: I discovered plenty of things I had not known in those years. And I learned even more details that made me look anew at well-known facts.

For instance, I didn't really understand the way the Gaidar government was formed in 1991. Only now do I appreciate the role played by Gennady Burbulis. Everyone knows what he did as the de facto prime minister in fall 1991 and spring 1992, but his role in Boris Yeltsin's accession to power is underestimated.

We spoke about the December protest rallies and the opposition, and it is interesting to view his work in this context. The opposition would not come to power until some of its members fought for power—not for just an idea. Burbulis was the man with the tactics of the struggle for power. I remember how he pushed us young Russian ministers to seize the commanding heights while the Union government was still in office.

The interviews with Nechayev and Anisimov helped us realize the way Russia was in 1991, to evaluate risks of hunger and chaos, and to understand the catastrophe scenario that had been avoided. The interviews with Kozyrev and Baker displayed the uniqueness of the attempt to integrate with the West, and the reasons for its failure. The discussions with Chubais and Lopukhin contributed an evaluation of the role of the Soviet elite, and the great significance of personalities, experience, and the interests of various social groups. The quality of the elites is the main difference between Russia and East European countries. Over 70 years, our ruling class was fully replaced, and the intellectual elite mostly integrated with the state, while the other countries preserved a counter-elite throughout 40 years of the communist regime—clerics and a broad anti-communist intelligentsia. With Chubais we talked about why we did not get political—and I realized once again that that was our fundamental mistake.

Why is that so important? It's trendy to curse liberals. We certainly were not a part of the democratic movement, and did not take power as the anti-communist opposition. We were preparing to work for the Soviet authorities and to make our career with them. We regarded Western democracy as a model; but, having grown up in the Soviet system, we had to build it in the home country. We had an interesting conversation about that with Sergei Shakhrai.

By the way, the interview with former defense minister Pavel Grachev brought plenty of sensations. He told us about the army, two revolts, and the first war in Chechnya. Amazing! Just a little detail: Grachev was given identical orders in August 1991 and in October 1993. The orders were given in the same form, since both leaders were afraid to give a written order to storm the same White House. But Grachev executed one of those orders and did not execute the other. I must admit, that explained a lot about Yeltsin, and power in general. Just imagine: if Grachev had made a different decision in 1991, we would have had nothing at all! His opposition to the first Chechen campaign was a revelation—just like the decision of others to send troops to Chechnya.

KOKH: And I would like to add an important story for me. The interviews vividly demonstrate that the Soviet Union was doomed. The Belovezh episode is the evidence. It appeared that the meeting of the three chiefs of state who buried the USSR was totally impromptu—but still the result was natural! That would have happened a day earlier, or a day later. No one wanted the Soviet Union to last. Everybody was breaking it up—local satraps, businessmen, "red directors," and even the Soviet government had members who did not want the Soviet Union to exist.

And it is no less amazing how rapidly people have forgotten that they didn't want to live in the USSR! It's like Germany in 1918, when no one wanted to fight that war, but only ten years later, everyone was screaming that the glorious German army had been standing at the gates of Paris, but the Jews stabbed it in the back.

MURTAZAYEV: Imagine it's 20 years later. Will the main participants be able to write a similar book about the events of the 2000s—Beslan, the Yukos case, the crisis of 2008, and the presidential election campaigns?

KOKH: Petr and I can, but these participants cannot.

AVEN: Certainly not. There is a big difference between us and the current participants—no matter what mistakes we might have made, we have little to hide.

14

CONCLUSION

Even though we do not consider ourselves dilettante journalists, we have encountered exactly what happens to people who write only occasionally. Our book differs significantly from our original idea. We had a simple plan when we agreed to start writing: our comrade Yegor Gaidar had died, and we wanted to write a book of reminiscences about him. We wanted to gather recollections by people who knew him well from joint work, who were his friends, and who could appreciate the scale of his achievements. But in the end we wrote a book not so much about Gaidar as about the 1990s, the Gaidar team, and the conditions in which it made its transformations.

In hindsight, it is clear that it could not have been otherwise. We were too feckless in presuming that we could write a book about Yegor without describing the conditions he (and we) had to work under, without touching upon the intricacies of his relationships inside the team and with key contemporary personalities—Yeltsin, Chernomyrdin, and others who influenced the course of events.

But we were true to our main intention: our book contains little of ourselves. Practically the whole of it consists of the direct speech of the participants in the events. Even if we expressed our opinions about particular phenomena, we did not abuse—as it seems to us—our authorial privilege, but simply presented our ideas as participants.

Our conversations are not quite interviews. They are conversations in which the interviewers have the same rights as interviewees, nothing is planned in advance, and conversations wander in space and time, but invariably return to and circle around one person: Yegor Gaidar.

We call our book *Gaidar's Revolution*. We are aware this is a provocative title. Compared with the traditional examples, this revolution lacked brutality, severed heads, the gallows, and leather jackets. It did not lead to sweeping change within the elites, which meant it was not all-inclusive and could not be called complete.

Perhaps the finale is still ahead. We may still witness the logical end of the drama that started over 20 years ago. What finale could that be? Only God knows.

But (we must be getting old) there is one more idea that keeps occurring to us: there will be no finale! It simply does not exist.

Hospice psychologists once analyzed the most frequent regrets people had before they died. One of the major regrets was about the past. Looking back, people lamented that they had not lived the life they wanted, but did what people around them wanted them to do. The other was about the future. People said, "We want to see how this ends."

We all know "this" never ends. There is no finale, and there never will be. It (the fabled "it") existed before us, it exists in our time, and it will exist after us. It will never be gone. It is called human history. Our comrade Yegor Gaidar now belongs to it.

Petr Aven and Alfred Kokh

15

AFTERWORD

Sweden, as a neighbor with centuries of interaction with Russia, had a particular interest in the dramatic events surrounding the collapse of the Soviet Union, the rise of Russia, and the democratic transformation of its economic and social system.

We followed these events closely, but it is hard to tell how much we understood of the ongoing political struggle, the financial predicament of a practically bankrupt state, and the internal maneuvering in the formative period of 1991–3.

I visited Russia several times; we had excellent relations, both official and unofficial, mainly with the Russian reformers, who often became personal friends and in many cases remain so today.

Still, it was not easy to fully perceive the unfolding drama. No doubt this was also true for decision-makers in the principal Western powers. Critical comments on their policies and actions can well be made.

The discussions and decisions at Belovezh leading to the dissolution of the USSR were probably necessary to avoid a major conflict between Russia and Ukraine, and to establish an orderly breakup of the empire.

The team around Yeltsin—Burbulis, Gaidar, Shakhrai, Kozyrev, and others—played a truly historic role in this process, which served international peace and stability.

The Western nations at the time had no great impact on this process, except insofar as their refusal to grant Gorbachev his request for massive financial aid presumably speeded it up. They correctly assumed that to pour vast amounts of credit into a system incapable of using it productively was useless.

They were, however, particularly concerned about the dangers that a breakup of the Soviet Union could entail, and argued against it. Indeed, the presence of thousands of nuclear weapons in various parts of the Soviet Union that could possibly be used in armed conflicts in a collapsing multi-national state where social and economic institutions were rapidly unraveling gave ample cause for such concern.

It was a major achievement of the Russian leaders to arrange, with the help particularly of the United States, for the transfer of all Soviet nuclear weapons to Russia, and for the dismantling of a large number of them. That issue was clearly a priority for the major Western powers.

The Belovezh Accords were also essential to help eliminate any border issues; earlier we had noted with concern statements by Russian leaders that, if the Union collapsed, they might cast doubt on Ukraine's possession of the Crimea.

For Russia, the decision to dissolve the Soviet Union was clearly a precondition for embarking on a program of rapid economic reform—even an outsider could understand that to arrive at a consensus between the constituent republics of the USSR on such a radical policy departure would have been an impossible task.

In autumn 1991 Yeltsin repeatedly stressed that the Union should be preserved, the defense forces should be kept under central control, and all 15 republics should form a single economic space. Reports from Moscow at the time talked about a fierce debate on the issue of the preservation of the Union, while at the same time Ukraine was opting out.

Our principal contacts, Burbulis and Gaidar, seemed to have had a major influence on Russia's decision on this necessarily very controversial issue. Stability in the whole Eurasian region, and thus the interests also of the Russian people, were well served by this outcome.

Like the rest of the world, we anxiously followed the rapid political evolution after the failure of the August 1991 putsch. It happened in the middle of an election campaign in Sweden that resulted in my becoming prime minister.

For us, the quest for the independence of the Baltic countries was a priority issue. We had admired and highly appreciated the courageous stance of Boris Yeltsin in January 1991, when he firmly opposed armed Soviet action in Vilnius and Riga. In contacts with him at the time, we had met a bold and decisive leader, as indeed was shown during the August events as well. We rejoiced when thereafter the leaders of the Baltic republics came to Moscow and received Russia's recognition of their independence.

During the following years, we tried to help resolve the issues created by the Soviet occupation of the Baltic states, principally the remaining troops and military installations, but also the status of a large number of Russian-speakers living in these countries as a consequence of Soviet policies.

We understood the political problems the Russian leadership confronted with an irate Russian "minority" in the Baltic states, formerly enjoying a privileged status, who were now supported by conservative nationalistic forces in the Russian parliament. To the Russians we stressed how the Balts had suffered from the totalitarian dictatorship of the Soviet Union. In speaking to the Balts, we added, "And so have the Russians!"

We were convinced of the sound legal and political basis for the Baltic governments' policies, but encouraged flexibility in their execution. The military issues reached a solution in the time frame originally envisaged—but getting there required much hard work, and an attitude of cooperation from the reformist government under Yeltsin.

At the time when Russia embarked on its systemic transformation, President Yeltsin and Acting Prime Minister Gaidar appealed to the West for financial assistance. They were asking for a stabilization fund of only $4–5 billion to bolster the budget. Without such help, inflation would run out of control and the government might not survive.

From the West no support, except for humanitarian aid, was forthcoming for Russia's market reform, democracy, and hence political stability. This proved to be a major mistake—one that colored Russian perceptions of the West. Not even the radical cut in military expenditures, which was as much in the interest of the West as it was of Russia itself, brought any Western credit to the Gaidar government.

These issues were discussed in the G7 group, and probably only the United Kingdom pushed for a fund and for a bridging financial program. The US responded that Congress would not support giving money to Russia, particularly in an election year. The Japanese balked because of the Kuriles. Germany was absorbed in its reunification. The ministries of finance prevailed over the ministries of foreign affairs.

In the background was also skepticism about the new, untested leaders in Moscow who had unseated the popular Gorbachev. There were persisting Cold War attitudes toward Russia as the primary successor of the Soviet Union.

The influence of critics within Russia who advocated a different and more gradual approach to reforms played a role as well. In unison with IMF and some Western politicians, they argued for retaining an economic and monetary union of all the former Soviet republics.

Added to all this was uncertainty in Western capitals confronted with a rapidly evolving political landscape in Moscow. This indeed should have been an argument in favor of, not against, support for the Russian government during the critical months from January to April 1992. Such support could have allowed some freedom of economic maneuver.

The fact that not even small sums were offered weakened the government and strengthened the opposition. An opportunity was lost to really influence the course of events in Russia, and that opportunity did not come back.

The attitudes in the West toward the economic reforms of the Gaidar government were necessarily mixed, reflecting ideological and political preferences, but also information and opinions from observers within and outside Russia.

I am, of course, not referring to the hardcore opposition, the reactionaries, the communists, heavy-industry lobbies, people from the military-industrial complex. They were important in the internal struggle, but by definition not in the Western world.

The West listened to economists such as Yavlinsky and Shatalin, whose approach was different. Their arguments, sometimes valid, played a considerable role in the West, where a number of prominent economists also expressed their doubts.

In our case, however, we thought that the Polish example was particularly instructive. That pointed in another direction. The radical reforms under Balcerowicz gave guidance on how the transition could be organized. We were not persuaded by the argument that Russia was too different or too large to adopt policies that worked in a smaller country such as Poland.

But we understood that the preconditions were much more difficult in Russia—no living experience of a market economy; a mindset formed by 75 years of communist totalitarian rule; a centralized and militarized economy spread out over the whole former Soviet landmass; the imperial syndrome in the political establishment and in the bureaucracy; no diaspora to help out with knowledge, advice, resources. We gradually grasped the enormous size of the task before the new leadership.

In talking to our friends in the Russian government, we came to understand the imperative of taking rapid and radical action, and the fact that there was only a very narrow range of possible policies.

As Gaidar himself repeatedly pointed out, there were no reserves to ease the hardships caused by the collapse of the old and rotten system. It was impossible to put off liberalization of the economy until structural reforms were enacted. Privatization could not wait for an ideal model.

If the government did not act decisively, the political reaction could mount a decisive counteroffensive. In early 1992 there was every reason to envisage a process leading up to an economic and political catastrophe, total collapse, and even the possibility of violent, armed conflicts.

Indeed, we could see how these policies were introduced in the context of tremendous social tension. Potentially the sky was the limit for deregulated prices, because of the huge monetary overhang. We understood that the authorities feared a popular explosion.

But, amazingly, no major public protests occurred, although prices rose instantly by 250 percent. Gradually we could observe how shortages diminished, and goods that had not been seen for years reappeared in shops. A market economy was slowly but surely taking shape.

I vividly remember visits to Moscow when, out of the misery of collapse, the first green shoots of a new entrepreneurship and a new economy started to be seen.

It is truly amazing that the policies that paved the way for these dramatic changes in Russia were orchestrated by the Gaidar team in the course of only one short year.

When Gaidar was forced out of the government and succeeded by Chernomyrdin, we feared that the reforms would be totally rolled back. This did not happen, but we still observed with concern and consternation the bitter conflicts that followed between the Yeltsin administration and the Russian Duma, leading up to the conflagration in October 1993 with the bombardment of the White House.

The principal opponents, Khasbulatov and Rutskoi, were so clearly demagogic and irresponsible that our support for the Yeltsin administration was self-evident. Still, we had our doubts about some of his actions—principally the repeated armed interventions in Chechnya.

The parliamentary elections in December 1993, resulting in strong support to the communists and the Zhirinovsky party and a defeat for the democratic forces, gave added cause for alarm, and did not help to muster external support for the president and his government. They also confirmed what many in the West thought about Russia—that because of its history and traditions it was still far from becoming a functioning democracy.

The dismal economic situation during the first years of reform was an obstacle for foreign investments and credits that otherwise might have created a material interest for the West in closer relations. The weakness of Russia—economically, militarily, and politically—made it less of an actor on the international stage.

All these factors tended to overshadow the truly remarkable achievements of the Russian leadership in the first crucial years.

Yegor Gaidar wrote in his book *Collapse of an Empire: Lessons for Modern Russia*, published in 2007, about Russia's overdependence on oil revenues, the blind spots among the ruling elite because of closed information channels, the lack of competing ideas, and the inefficiency of the over-centralized state. These factors are unfortunately not without their relevance today. But tremendous progress has been made, and Russian society is undergoing a radical change. Recent events have shown how such an educated and advanced society demands rule of law, democratic procedures, protection of property rights, an efficient and honest bureaucracy—in other words, that which forms the basis for Western democracies and successful economies.

Russia's political and economic course will determine whether the country becomes a stagnant, natural-resource-based economy, or whether Yegor Gaidar's dream of Russia becoming a prosperous, democratic, leading great European power living in harmony and cooperation with its neighbors comes true.

That certainly remains my hope.

Carl Bildt
Minister of Foreign Affairs of Sweden
Prime Minister, 1991–4

Appendix

BIOGRAPHICAL LISTING

Sources: Wikipedia (both the English- and Russian-language sites); Russiaprofile.org; *Forbes*; *How Russia Became a Market Economy*, by Anders Åslund (Brookings Institution); *Wheel of Fortune: The Battle for Oil and Power in Russia*, by Thane Gustafson (Belknap Press).

Abalkin, Leonid Ivanovich (1930–2011) — Institute of Economics director, Soviet Academy of Sciences 1986–9; deputy chairman, Soviet Council of Ministers July 1989–December 1990; advisor to Soviet president May–December 1991.

Achalov, Vladislav Alexeyevich (1945–2011) — Soviet deputy defense minister 1990–1; paratrooper union leader; joined GKChP anti-Gorbachev putsch in 1991; also joined anti-Yeltsin putsch September–October 1993 as Russian Supreme Council's designated defense minister.

Aganbegian, Abel Gezevich (b. 1932) — Economics department academician; secretary, Soviet Academy of Sciences; economic advisor to Soviet Communist Party Central Committee secretary general Mikhail Gorbachev 1986–90; Academy of People's Economy rector 1989–2002.

Akhromeyev, Sergei Fyodorovich (1923–91) — Soviet armed forces General Staff chief 1984–8; defense advisor to Gorbachev and top arms control negotiator; Soviet Supreme Council Presidium chairman.

Alekperov, Vagit Yusufovich (b. 1950) — Former Caspian Sea oil rig worker who became a deputy minister in the Soviet oil industry; head of Lukoil, Russia's largest independent energy company, developing the West

Qurna-2 oilfield in Iraq, one of the world's largest; in 2013, willed his stake in Lukoil to his only son, Yusuf, with the caveat that he would not sell this stake, keeping the Alekperov family Lukoil's biggest shareholder.

Alexashenko, Sergei Vladimirovich (b. 1959) — State commission for economic reforms, Soviet Council of Ministers economy specialist 1990–1; Russian deputy finance minister 1993–5; first deputy board chairman, Russian Central Bank 1995–8.

Alexeyev, Sergei Sergeyevich (1924–2013) — Soviet people's deputy and Interregional Group of deputies 1989; chairman, Soviet committee on constitutional supervision 1989–91.

Ananyev, Yevgeny Nikolayevich (b. 1948) — Foreign economic association general director, VEAM 1991–2; economic advisor to Moscow aircraft plant general director 1992–3; MAPO-Bank CEO 1993–7; general director, Rosvooruzhenie state arms export-import company 1997–8.

Ananyin, Oleg Igorevich (b. 1947) — Economist colleague of Yegor Gaidar in the early 1980s at All-Union Research Institute of Systemic Research, USSR Academy of Sciences; deputy division head, Russian Academy of Sciences institute of economics; professor at Russian national research university, Higher School of Economics faculty of economic methodology and history since 1993.

Anchishkin, Alexander Ivanovich (b. 1933) — Soviet economist; corresponding member of the USSR Academy of Sciences, 1976; member of the Communist Party of the Soviet Union (CPSU) from 1963.

Anisimov, Stanislav Vasilyevich (b. 1940) — Soviet state official and advocate of branch interests who stayed on in the reform government; USSR minister of material resources in 1991; Russian minister of trade 1991–2.

Antall, Jozsef (1932–93) — Prime minister, Republic of Hungary 1990–3.

Avturkhanov, Umar Dzhunitovich (b. 1946) — Government administrator in Chechnya's Nadterechny District opposing breakaway Chechen leader Dzhokhar Dudayev 1991; led armed opposition in Grozny 1993; chairman, national concord committee for Chechen Republic March–October 1995; Russian tax police major general 1995–9.

Balcerowicz, Leszek (b. 1947) — Polish vice premier, finance minister September 1989–December 1991; author, plan for Poland's transfer to market economy; chairman, National Bank of Poland 2001–7.

Barannikov, Viktor Pavlovich (1940–95) — RSFSR interior minister 1990–1; Soviet interior minister August–December 1991; Russian security minister 1992–3; joined anti-Yeltsin putsch September–October 1993 as Russian supreme council's designated security minister.

Barchuk, Vasily Vasilyevich (b. 1941) — Soviet Finance Ministry staff

1972–91; RSFSR people's deputy, first deputy economy and finance minister 1991–2; Russian finance minister April 1992–March 1993.

Barsukov, Mikhail Ivanovich (b. 1947) — Moscow Kremlin commandant 1993–4; Russian main security department head 1992–5; Federal Security Service director 1995–6.

Baturin, Yuri Mikhailovich (b. 1949) — Russian presidential legal advisor 1993–4; national security advisor 1994–6; presidential assistant 1996–8; Russian defense council secretary July 1996–August 1997; cosmonaut 1997, two space missions 1998 and 2001.

Bazhov, Pavel Petrovich (1879–1950) — Writer/publicist/Soviet expansionist in Siberia and Kazakhstan; author, folklore-based *Tales from the Urals*; maternal grandfather of Yegor Gaidar.

Bessmertnykh, Alexander Alexandrovich (b. 1933) — Soviet ambassador to the United States 1990–1; briefly served as a minister of foreign affairs of the USSR in 1991, replacing Eduard Shevardnadze; in putsch of 1991, did not lend support to the attempt at ousting Gorbachev, but refused to condemn the plotters; consequently was removed by Gorbachev.

Bogdanov, Vladimir Leonidovich (b. 1951) — Oil tycoon and politician; in 1993, became president of Surgutneftegaz, one of the largest Russian oil companies; a confidant of Sergei Sobyanin during the successful 2001 Tyumen Oblast governor election and of Vladimir Putin during the 2004 presidential election.

Borodin, Pavel Pavlovich (b. 1946) — RSFSR people's deputy 1990; first deputy head, then head, Russian presidential administration's main socioindustrial department; presidential property management department head November 1993–January 2000.

Bovin, Alexander Yevgenyevich (1930–2004) — *Izvestia* newspaper journalist/political observer 1972–91; ambassador to Israel (Soviet, then Russian) 1991–7.

Bugrov, Andrei Yevgenyevich (b. 1952) — Soviet Foreign Ministry posts 1977–91; advisor to president, European Bank for Reconstruction and Development 1977–91; Russian executive director, World Bank Group 1993–2002.

Bulgak, Vladimir Borisovich (b. 1941) — Main Economic Department of Operation of Communications Grids director, Soviet Communications Ministry 1988–90; RSFSR minister of communications, information technology and space 1990–1; Russian communications minister 1991–7; Russian deputy prime minister 1997–9; Russian science and technology minister 1998.

Burbulis, Gennady Eduardovich (b. 1945) — Russian politician; close associate of Boris Yeltsin; held several high positions in first Russian government, including secretary of state; a drafter and signer on behalf of Russia of Belovezh Accords in 1991 that effectively ended the USSR and founded the Commonwealth of Independent States (CIS); served as first deputy prime minister of RSFSR/Russian Federation; succeeded by Yegor Gaidar.

Cheney, Richard Bruce (b. 1941) — US defense secretary 1989–93; US vice president 2001–9.

Chernomyrdin, Viktor Stepanovich (1938–2010) — Soviet gas industry minister 1985–9; Gazprom CEO 1989–92; Russian deputy prime minister for fuel and energy May–December 1992; Russian prime minister December 1992–March 1998; Russian ambassador to Ukraine 2001–9.

Chernyayev, Anatoly Sergeyevich (b. 1921) — Assistant to Secretary General of Soviet Communist Party Central Committee Mikhail Gorbachev 1986–91; international affairs assistant to Soviet president.

Cheshinsky, Leonid Stepanovich (b. 1945) — RSFSR cereal products minister 1990–1; RSFSR procurement minister 1991; chairman, cereal products committee, Russian Ministry of Trade and Material Resources 1991–2; President, federal contract corporation Roskhleboprodukt 1992.

Chubais, Anatoly Borisovich (b. 1955) — Chairman, State Committee for Control of State Assets 1991–4; first deputy prime minister of the Russian Federation for Economic and Financial policy 1992–6; member country governor, International Monetary Fund 1995–6; chief of the staff, Presidential Executive Office 1996–7; first deputy prime minister of the Russian Federation, minister of finance 1997–8.

Churilov, Lev Dmitriyevich (1935–2012) — Soviet oil and gas industry first deputy minister 1989–91; Soviet oil and gas industry minister June–November 1991; Rosneftegaz Corporation president 1991–3.

Davydov, Oleg Dmitriyevich (b. 1940) — Soviet deputy minister of foreign economic relations 1988–91; Russian foreign economic relations minister 1993–7; Russian deputy prime minister 1994–7.

Dementei, Nikolai Ivanovich (b. 1930) — Belarusian Soviet Socialist Republic supreme council chairman May 1990–August 1991.

Dmitriyev, Mikhail Egonovich (b. 1961) — Leningrad reformer economist group 1980s; RSFSR (Russian) people's deputy 1990–3; Russian government's Economic Reforms Commission 1994–5; Russian labor and social development first deputy minister 1997–8; Russian economic development and trade first deputy minister 2000–4.

Dubinin, Sergei Konstantinovich (b. 1950) — Soviet presidential administration economy specialist 1991; deputy chairman, Soviet state committee for economic cooperation with CIS member states 1992–3; Russian first deputy finance minister 1993–4; Russian Central Bank chairman 1995–8.

Dunayev, Andrei Fyodorovich (b. 1939) — RSFSR interior minister September 1991–January 1992; Russian first deputy interior minister April 1992, chairman, June 1993; joined anti-Yeltsin putsch September–October 1993 as Russian supreme council's designated interior minister.

Fadeyev, Gennady Matveyevich (b. 1937) — Soviet first deputy railroads minister 1988–91; Russian railroads minister 1992–6 and 2002–3; Russian railways JSC president 2003–5.

Filatov, Sergei Alexandrovich (b. 1936) — RSFSR people's deputy 1990; First Deputy Chairman, Russian Supreme Council November 1991–January 1993; Russian presidential administration head January 1993–January 1996.

Fischer, Stanley (b. 1943) — World Bank chief economist 1988–90; first deputy managing director, International Monetary Fund 1994–2001.

Fyodorov, Boris Grigoryevich (1958–2008) — Soviet Communist Party Central Committee socioeconomic department economics consultant 1989–90; RSFSR finance minister July–December 1990; Russian representative, European Bank for Reconstruction and Development 1991; World Bank director 1992; deputy prime minister December 1992; finance minister March 1993–January 1994.

Fyodorov, Svyatoslav Nikolayevich (1927–2000) — Founder, Eye Microsurgery Interbranch Scientific and Technological Complex 1986; Soviet people's deputy, Interregional Group of deputies 1989–91.

Gaidar, Timur Arkadyevich (1926–99) — Soviet navy 1948, rear admiral; son of Soviet writer Arkady Petrovich Gaidar (Golikov); father of Yegor Gaidar.

Gaidar, Yegor Timurovich (1956–2009) — Soviet and Russian economist, politician and author. Acting prime minister of Russia June 15–December 14, 1992, in Yeltsin's administration. Architect of shock therapy free-market reforms, which brought him both praise and harsh criticism. His daughter Maria Smirnova is a political activist, a fierce critic of Putin's government, and founder of the youth movement DA!

Genscher, Hans-Dietrich (b. 1927) — German foreign minister/vice chancellor 1974–92.

Gerashchenko, Viktor Vladimirovich (b. 1937) — Soviet Gosbank CEO 1989–91; Russian Central Bank chairman 1992–4; dismissed amid 1994 Black Tuesday's ruble currency collapse; International Moscow Bank CEO 1996–98; Russian Central Bank chairman again 1998–2002; State Duma deputy, Rodina bloc 2003–4.

Glazkov, Grigory Yuryevich (b. 1957) — Leningrad reformer economists group 1980s; vice president, St Petersburg Leontyevsky Center 1991; advisor,

International Monetary Fund Russian director 1992–5; European Bank for Reconstruction and Development regional representative to St Petersburg 1995–7; Advisor, EBRD Russian Mission in London; Finance Ministry's International Financial Organizations department head 1997–2002.

Glazyev, Sergei Yuriyevich (b. 1961) — Soviet Academy of Sciences central institute of economics and mathematics staff economist 1986–91; first deputy chairman, committee for foreign economic relations, Russian Foreign Ministry 1991–2; first deputy minister, foreign economic relations, minister of foreign economic relations December 1992–September 1993; co-chairman Rodina bloc, its State Duma faction leader 2003–4.

Golovkov, Alexey Leonardovich (1956–2009) — Institute of Economics and Scientific and Technical Progress Forecasts staff economist, Soviet Academy of Sciences 1986–90; RSFSR Supreme Council September 1990; chief of staff, Russian government administration November 1991–January 1993.

Gorbachev, Mikhail Sergeyevich (b. 1931) — Former Soviet statesman. Served as general secretary of the Communist Party of the USSR from 1985 until 1991 and as the first (and last) president of the Soviet Union from 1990 until its end in 1991. His wife, Raisa Maximovna, raised funds for the preservation of Russian cultural heritage, fostering of new talent, and treatment programs for children's blood cancer. She died of leukemia in 1999.

Grachev, Pavel Sergeyevich (1948–2012) — Soviet Airborne Forces commander, then defense minister. Gained notoriety by incompetence in Chechen war and persistent allegations of ties to big corruption scandals, (given nickname "Pasha Mercedes") unveiled in articles by investigative journalist Dmitry Kholodov, killed by a booby-trapped suitcase in 1994. Four of his airborne officers were acquitted of the murder. Served as a senior military advisor to Rosvooruzhenie State Corporation, the Russian arms export monopoly, and fired April 25, 2007.

Gromyko, Andrei Andreyevich (1909–89) — Soviet foreign minister 1957–85; Soviet Supreme Council Presidium chairman 1985–8.

Grushevenko, Eduard Vyacheslavovich (1935–2002) — Russian acting fuel and energy minister January 1992–January 1993; first deputy fuel and energy minister February–October 1993; chairman, Technical and Economic Council, Fuel and Energy Ministry; vice president, Association of Small and Medium Oil and Gas Producers; Yukos vice president 1993.

Honecker, Erich (1912–94) — Socialist Unity Party first secretary, then general secretary 1971–89; chairman, state council, German Democratic Republic 1976–89.

Illarionov, Andrei Nikolayevich (b. 1961) — Regional economic research laboratory, Leningrad Institute of Finance and Economics staff economist 1990–2; first deputy director, Russian government working center of economic reforms 1992–3; prime minister's analysis and planning group chief 1993–4; economic advisor to Russian president 1992–3.

Ilyushin, Viktor Vasilyevich (b. 1947) — Secretariat head for RSFSR Supreme Council chairman 1990–1 and the RSFSR (Russian) president 1991–2; first assistant to Russian president 1992–6; Russian first deputy prime minister 1996–7.

Ivanov, Igor Sergeyevich (b. 1945) — Soviet Foreign Ministry staff from 1973, general secretariat head 1989–91; Russian ambassador to Spain 1992–5; first deputy foreign minister 1992–5; foreign minister 1998–2004; Security Council secretary 2004–7.

Kadannikov, Vladimir Vasilyevich (b. 1941) — AvtoVAZ general director 1988–96; Soviet people's deputy 1989–91; Russian first deputy prime minister January–August 1996.

Kadar, János (1912–89) — Secretary general, later chairman, central committee of the Hungarian Socialist Workers' Party 1956–89; Hungarian Council of Ministers chairman 1956–8 and 1961–5.

Kagalovsky, Konstantin Grigoryevich (b. 1957) — International Center for Studies of Economic reforms head 1989–90; Russian representative for liaison with International Monetary Fund and World Bank 1990–1; representative for liaison with international financial organizations, government economic advisor 1992; Russian director, International Monetary Fund 1993–4.

Kalmykov, Yuri Khamzatovich (1934–97) — Soviet people's deputy 1989–91; Russian justice minister 1993–4.

Kasyanov, Mikhail Mikhailovich (b. 1957) — RSFSR Gosplan engineering, economist posts 1981–90; RSFSR Economy Ministry 1991–3; Russian Finance Ministry staff 1993–5; deputy finance minister 1995; finance minister 1999; prime minister May 2000–February 2004.

Katsura, Petr Makarovich (b. 1930) — AvtoVAZ deputy general director for economics and planning 1969–85; Soviet Council of Ministers staff 1985–91.

Kazannik, Alexey Ivanovich (b. 1941) — Soviet people's deputy 1989–91; Supreme Council at First Congress 1989, yielded to Yeltsin; Russian prosecutor general October 1993–April 1994.

Khasbulatov, Ruslan Imranovich (b. 1942) — International Economic Relations Faculty chairman, Moscow Plekhanov People's Economy Institute 1980–90; RSFSR people's deputy 1990; RSFSR supreme council first deputy chairman June, chairman October 1991.

Khizha, Georgy Stepanovich (b. 1938) — Leningrad Svetlana Research and Production Center general director 1988–91; St Petersburg vice mayor September 1991–May 1992; Russian deputy prime minister May 1992–June 1993.

Khodorkovsky, Mikhail Borisovich (b. 1963) — Once the richest persons in Russia, worth $15 billion and ranked number 15 in the world; former head of Yukos, one of the world's largest non-state oil companies before it was extinguished by the government; imprisoned in 2003 on charges of fraud and tax evasion, which he denied; as a potential political foe of Vladimir Putin, remained behind bars through 2014 after losing an appeal of a December 2010 embezzlement verdict.

Klaus, Václav (b. 1941) — Czechoslovak finance minister December 1989–July 1992; Czech Republic prime minister December 1989–July 1992; Czech Republic president 2003–13.

Kobets, Konstantin Ivanovich (1939–2012) — Soviet armed forces Signal Corps commander 1987–91; RSFSR people's deputy 1990; chairman, RSFSR State Committee for Defense affairs January–August 1991; RSFSR defense minister August–September 1991.

Kohl, Helmut Joseph Michael (b. 1930) — German federal chancellor 1982–98.

Korabelshchikov, Anatoly Ivanovich (b. 1945) — Assistant to RSFSR Supreme Council chairman 1991; Russian presidential assistant for liaison with regions 1991–8.

Korzhakov, Alexander Vasilyevich (b. 1950) — KGB Ninth Department assignments 1970–89, including bodyguard to Boris Yeltsin 1985–9; security chief to RSFSR Supreme Council chairman 1990–1; Russian presidential security service chief 1991–6.

Kovalyov, Sergei Adamovich (b. 1930) — Rights activist USSR and post-Soviet Russia; RSFSR people's deputy 1990; Russian rights ombudsman 1994–5; author, Russian constitution's "Human and Civil Rights and Freedoms" (Chapter 2) 1993.

Kozyrev, Andrei Vladimirovich (b. 1951) — Foreign minister of Russia under Yeltsin from October 1991 until his dismissal in January 1996; son of a Soviet diplomat, born in Brussels, Belgium; Ministry of Foreign Affairs of the USSR 1978.

Kravchuk, Leonid Makarovich (b. 1934) — Ukrainian Communist Party Central Committee secretary's ideology sector head 1988–90; second secretary Ukrainian Communist Party Central Committee; Ukrainian Verkhovna Rada (parliament) chairman 1990–1; Ukrainian president December 1991–July 1994.

Kryuchkov, Vladimir Alexandrovich (1924–2007) — Soviet State Security Committee chairman 1988–91; Soviet Communist Party Central Committee Politburo 1989–90; joined GKChP, the State Committee on the State of Emergency, which organized the failed anti-Gorbachev coup in 1991.

Kuchma, Leonid Danilovich (b. 1938) — Ukrainian prime minister 1992–3; Ukrainian president 1994–2003.

Kulik, Gennady Vasilyevich (b. 1935) — Chairman, RSFSR state agro-industrial committee 1989–90; deputy chairman, RSFSR Council of Ministers and RSFSR minister of agriculture and food July 1990–October 1991.

Kulikov, Anatoly Sergeyevich (b. 1946) — Russian deputy interior minister, Interior Ministry forces commander December 1992–July 1995; interior minister 1995–8.

Lavrov, Sergei Viktorovich (b. 1950) — Foreign minister of Russia, nomination to the office approved by two Russian presidents, in 2008 by Dmitry Medvedev and in 2012 by Vladimir Putin; served as Russia's representative to the United Nations 1994–2004.

Lebed, Alexander Ivanovich (1950–2002) — Russian army general who applied military toughness to politics, stood against Yeltsin for the presidency in 1996, and ended the First Chechen War; commander, 106th Airborne Division 1988–91; commander, Fourteenth Army in Transdniestria 1992–5; placed third in the 1996 Russian presidential election, with 14.5 percent of the vote nationwide; Russian Security Council secretary June–October 1996.

Livshits, Alexander Yakovlevich (1946–2013) — Presidential administration's analytical center deputy head April 1992; working group leader for operative analytical support to constitutional reform 1993; Russian president's expert team leader, economic advisor to the president 1994–6; vice premier, finance minister 1996–7; presidential administration deputy head 1997–8; minister, presidential special representative to the G8 1999.

Lobov, Oleg Ivanovich (b. 1937) — Sverdlovsk regional executive committee chairman 1985–7; RSFSR Council of Ministers deputy chairman 1987–9 and April–November 1991; RSFSR Council of Ministers acting chairman September–November 1991; Russian first deputy prime minister April–September 1993; Russian Security Council secretary 1993–6.

Lopukhin, Vladimir Mikhailovich (b. 1952) — Minister of fuel and energy of the Russian Soviet Federative Socialist Republic 1991–2; deputy minister of economic affairs (RSFSR Ministry of Economic Affairs) 1990–1; later, director Sukhoi Civil Aircraft Company; president of Vanguard LLC, and senior advisor at Lazard-Eastern Europe Bank.

Lukin, Vladimir Petrovich (b. 1937) — Soviet Foreign Ministry staff 1987–9; Analysis and Forecasting Group head, Soviet Supreme Council secretariat 1989–90; RSFSR people's deputy, RSFSR Supreme Council international affairs committee chairman 1989–90; Russian ambassador to United States 1992–3.

Lukyanov, Anatoly Ivanovich (b. 1930) — Administrative bodies department head, Soviet Communist Party central committee 1987–8; first deputy chairman, Soviet Supreme Council presidium October 1988–May 1989; first deputy chairman, Soviet Supreme Council 1989–90; Soviet Supreme Council chairman 1990–August 1991.

Lvin, Boris Mikhailovich (b. 1961) — Leningrad reformer, economist group, 1980s; Russian government's Working Center for Economic Reforms staff economist 1992–3; International Monetary Fund Russian Directorate 1993–7; senior advisor to executive director, World Bank, since 1998.

Lvov, Dmitry Semyonovich (1930–2007) — Central Institute of Economics and Mathematics, Soviet Academy of Sciences (later Russian Academy of Sciences) staff economist since 1972; academician, secretary, Russian Academy of Sciences economics department 1996–2002.

Makharadze, Valery Antonovich (1940–2008) — RSFSR chief state inspector; Administration Controlling Department head; RSFSR president 1991–2; Russian deputy prime minister March–December 1992; Russian trade representative to Canada 1993–2004.

Manevich, Mikhail Vladislavovich (1961–97) — Leningrad reformer, economist group, 1980s; St Petersburg city property management committee chairman 1994; St Petersburg vice governor 1996–7.

Mashchits, Vladimir Mikhailovich (b. 1953) — Chairman, state committee of the Russian Federation on economic cooperation with CIS countries; member of Yeltsin and Gaidar team in December 1991 and earlier Chernomyrdin administration; served on task force for 500 Days program intended to create foundation of a modern market economy in 500 days.

Materov, Ivan Sergeyevich (b. 1950) — RSFSR prime minister Ivan Silayev's economics advisor 1991; Russian deputy economy minister May 1992–March 1993; Russian first deputy economy minister March–July 1993; Russian first deputy minister of foreign economic relations 1993–4; Russian first deputy economy minister 1994–2000.

Mazowiecki, Tadeusz (1927–2013) — Solidarność Movement co-leader; first post-Soviet prime minister of Poland 1989–91.

Melikian, Gennady Georgiyevich (b. 1947) — State commission for economic reforms at the Soviet Council of Ministers staff 1989–91; international foundation of economic and social reforms vice president 1991–2; Russian labor minister 1992–6; Russian labor and social development minister 1996–7.

Mikhailov, Viktor Nikitovich (1934–2011) — Soviet deputy minister of medium machine building's nuclear arms sector 1988; Russian atomic energy minister, Russian security council 1992–8; Russian first deputy atomic energy minister 1998–9.

Mostovoi, Pavel Ivanovich (1931–2000) — Soviet deputy prime minister 1989–90; chairman Soviet state committee for material and technical supply (Gossnab, which coordinated the allocation of resources not handled by Gosplan, the state planning committee) 1989–91.

Mostovoi, Petr Petrovich (b. 1949) — Leningrad reformer, economist group, activist 1980s; deputy chairman, Russian State Committee for State Property Management early 1992, then first deputy chairman October 1992–5; general director, Federal Department for Bankruptcy, Russian State Committee for State Property Management 1995–7; Federal Service for Bankruptcy and Financial Receivership head March–December 1997.

Murashev, Arkady Nikolayevich (b. 1957) — Soviet people's deputy 1989, Interregional Group of deputies; Moscow city police chief 1991–2; Choice of Russia bloc leader October 1993; State Duma deputy Choice of Russia slate 1993–5.

Muravlenko, Sergei Viktorovich (b. 1957) — First president and board chairman (1993–2003) of then newly formed Russian holding company called Yukos before Mikhail Khodorkovsky took it over 1993–2003. In 1992 Muravlenko appointed as Yukos vice president Vladimir Zenken, general manager of Novokuibyshev refinery, after it was merged into Yukos along with two other refineries in Samara Province, site of a long and bloody battle over oil export revenues 1992–7. Zenken was murdered in front of his house in Samara in 1993. Muravlenko's father, Viktor, discovered the oil riches of the Ob' River basin in West Siberia and was the first head of the Tyumen oil industry.

Mutalibov, Ayaz Niyazioglu (Niyazovich) (b. 1938) —Council of Ministers chairman, Azerbaijani Soviet Socialist Republic 1989–90; first secretary, Azerbaijani Communist Party 1990–1; president of Azerbaijan May 1990–March 1992.

Naishul, Vitaly Arkadyevich (b. 1949) — Central Institute of Economics and Mathematics at Soviet Gosplan, senior research economist and Russia's academy of sciences 1981–93; National Economic Model Institute president 1992; author of the economic program for Russian presidential candidate Alexander Lebed 1996.

Nazarbayev, Nursultan Abishevich (b. 1940) — Kazakh Communist Party Central Committee first secretary 1989–91; Kazakh Supreme Council chairman February–April 1990; Republic president chosen by Kazakh Soviet Socialist Republic Supreme Soviet 1990; Kazakh president elected December 1991.

Nechayev, Andrei Alexeyevich (b. 1953) — Former economics minister in the government of Viktor Chernomyrdin; became president of the Russian Financial Corp., a state-run agency established in 1993 with a view to attracting private investment.

Nemtsov, Boris Yefimovich (1959–2015) — RSFSR (Russian) people's deputy; Democratic Russia faction 1990–3; presidential representative for Nizhny Novgorod region August 1991, elected governor November 1991; first deputy prime minister March 1997–March 1998; deputy prime minister April–August 1998; founding member of Union of Right Forces bloc 1999; party co-chairman 2001–4.

Nevzlin, Leonid Borisovich (b. 1959) — Co-founder and vice president of Menatep Bank (precursor to the holding company for Yukos Oil) 1990; moved to Israel following the arrest of Khodorkovsky; found guilty and sentenced to life imprisonment in absentia in 2008 by a Moscow city court on charges of organizing five murders in 2006 (which he has denied).

Novodvorskaya, Valeriya Ilyinichna (1950–2014) — Politician, Soviet dissident, founder and chairperson of the Democratic Union party.

Pamfilova, Ella Alexandrovna (b. 1953) — Soviet people's deputy 1989; Russian social protection minister 1991–4; Russian presidential Human Rights Commission chairperson 2002–4; chair, Russian Presidential Council for Assistance in Development of Social Society Institutions and Human Rights 2004–10.

Panskov, Vladimir Georgiyevich (b. 1944) — Soviet first deputy finance minister 1987–91; Soviet presidential administration's finance and budget department head; Russian state tax service first deputy head 1992–4; finance minister 1994–6; first deputy economy minister 1996–7.

Pavlov, Valentin Sergeyevich (1937–2003) — Soviet finance minister 1991; Soviet prime minister January–August 1991; joined GKChP anti-Gorbachev putsch August 1991.

Perry, William James (b. 1927) — US deputy secretary of state 1993–4; US defense secretary 1994–7.

Petrakov, Nikolai Yakovlevich (b. 1937) — Economics assistant to Soviet Communist Party Central Committee Secretary General Mikhail Gorbachev, later to Soviet president 1990–1; director, Institute of Market Problems of Russia's Academy of Sciences 1990.

Petrov, Yuri Vladimirovich (b. 1939) — First secretary, Sverdlovsk regional committee, Soviet Communist Party 1985–8; ambassador to Cuba 1988–91; Russian presidential administration head August 1991–January 1993.

Piyasheva, Larisa Ivanovna (1947–2003) — Moscow City committee on economic reforms chairperson 1991–2.

Podkolzin, Yevgeny Nikolayevich (1936–2003) — Commander, Airborne Forces of the USSR, the CIS and Russia 1991–6.

Poltoranin, Mikhail Nikiforovich (b. 1939) — *Komsomolskaya Pravda* newspaper editor 1986–8; founding member Interregional Group of deputies 1989, at First Congress of Soviet People's Deputies; Russian minister of press and information July 1990–November 1992; first deputy prime minister February–November 1992.

Popov, Gavriil Kharitonovich (b. 1936) — Politician and economist; first democratically elected mayor of Moscow, 1990–2; faculty dean of Moscow Lomonosov University; Yegor Gaidar was one of his students.

Powell, Colin Luther (b. 1937) — US national security advisor 1987–9; Joint Chiefs of Staff chairman 1989–93; US secretary of state 2001–5.

Primakov, Yevgeny Maximovich (b. 1929) — Director, Institute of World Economy and International Relations, Soviet Academy of Sciences 1985–9; chairman, Council of the Union (Soviet Supreme Council upper chamber) 1989–90; Soviet central intelligence service director 1991; Russian foreign intelligence service director 1991–6; Russian foreign minister 1996–8; Russian prime minister 1998–9; president, Chamber of Commerce and Industry of Russia 2001–11.

Rakhimov, Murtaza Gubaidullovich (b. 1934) — Supreme Council of the republic of Bashkortostan chairman 1990–3; Bashkortostan president 1993–2010.

Revenko, Grigory Ivanovich (b. 1936) — Soviet Presidential Council member 1990–1; advisor to Soviet president 1991; Soviet presidential administration head 1991.

Rumyantsev, Oleg Germanovich (b. 1961) — RSFSR people's deputy, executive secretary, Constitutional Commission, Congress of RSFSR (Russian) People's Deputies 1990–3.

Rutskoi, Alexander Vladimirovich (b. 1947) — Military pilot awarded Hero of the Soviet Union for Afghanistan combat operations 1985–6; RSFSR people's deputy 1990; formed Communists for Democracy faction March 1991; Russian vice president June 1991–September 1993; Kursk governor 1996–2000.

Rybkin, Ivan Petrovich (b. 1946) — First State Duma chairman 1994–6; Russian security council secretary 1996–8; Russian deputy prime minister 1998.

Ryzhkov, Nikolai Ivanovich (b. 1929) — Soviet council ministers chairman 1985–90; RSFSR Communist Party presidential candidate in RSFSR election 1991.

Ryzhov, Yuri Alexeyevich (b. 1930) — Soviet Academy of Sciences aerodynamics specialist, academician 1987; Moscow Aviation Institute rector 1986–92; Soviet people's deputy 1989–91, Interregional Group of deputies; Russian ambassador to France 1992–8.

Saburov, Yevgeny Fyodorovich (1946–2009) — Institute of Economics and Scientific and Technical Progress Forecasts staff economist, Soviet Academy of Sciences 1989–90; RSFSR deputy education minister August 1990–August 1991; RSFSR economics minister and deputy prime minister August–November 1991.

Sachs, Jeffrey (b. 1954) — US economist, Harvard then Columbia professor, head of Russian presidential economic advisors September 1991–January 1994; was invited first by Gorbachev and then by Yeltsin for guidance on the transition to a market economy; served as advisor on macroeconomic policies to Gaidar and Boris Federov, finance minister; coined the term "shock therapy" in economics.

Sakharov, Andrei Dmitrievich (1921–89) — Physicist renowned as designer of USSR's Third Idea, code name for Soviet development of thermonuclear weapons. Advocate of civil liberties and civil reforms, was awarded the Nobel Peace Prize in 1975. Force-fed during hunger strikes in years of internal exile for protesting the 1979 Soviet invasion of Afghanistan. He and his wife, Elena Bonner, were released by Gorbachev in 1986. Elected March 1989 to parliament; co-led the democratic opposition, the Interregional Deputies Group. Died of a heart attack, while napping before writing major speech for the Congress the next day.

Saltykov, Boris Georgiyevich (b. 1940) — Institute of People's Economy forecasting department head, Soviet Academy of Sciences 1990–1; Russian vice premier 1992–3; science and technical policy minister 1991–6.

Samusev, Alexander Lvovich (b. 1957) — Soviet Gosplan oil, gas and coal industry department expert 1982–91; Moscow oil exchange vice president/department head 1991; Russian deputy fuel and energy minister 1991–4; Russian deputy finance minister 1994–5.

Satarov, Georgy Alexandrovich (b. 1947) — INDEM Applied Political Research Foundation (information science for democracy) director 1990, director general 1994, president since 1997; assistant to Russian President Boris Yeltsin 1994–7; co-chairman, Russian Civil Congress 2004–8; member, Committee 2008: Free Choice.

Savostyanov, Yevgeny Vadimovich (b. 1952) — Assistant to Moscow city council chairman Gavriil Popov 1990–1; KGB (AFB, MBR, FSK) Moscow department chief September 1991–December 1994.

Serov, Valery Mikhailovich (b. 1940) — Soviet Gosstroy chairman 1989–91; Russian minister for liaison with CIS member countries 1995–6; Russian deputy prime minister 1996–8.

Shafranik, Yuri Konstantinovich (b. 1952) — Tyumen regional council of people's deputies chief engineer, then director 1990–1; Tyumen regional administration head 1991–3; fuel and energy minister January 1993–August 1996.

Shakhnazarov, Georgy Khosroyevich (1924–2001) — Assistant to secretary general of Soviet Communist Party Central Committee Mikhail Gorbachev 1988–91; assistant to Soviet president 1988–91; chairman, Soviet Supreme Council's subcommittee on constitutional laws 1990–1.

Shaposhnikov, Yevgeny Ivanovich (b. 1942) — Soviet air force 1963; commander and deputy defense minister 1990–1; Soviet defense minister August 1991–February 1992; CIS combined armed forces commander in chief February 1992–August 1993; Russian security council secretary 1993; Aeroflot CEO 1998; aviation and space advisor to Russian president.

Shatalin, Stanislav Sergeyevich (1934–97) — Economics department academician, secretary, Russia's Academy of Sciences 1990–6; team leader drafting 500 Days program for USSR transition to free market economy; Soviet Presidential Council member May 1990–January 1991.

Shcherbakov, Vladimir Ivanovich (b. 1949) — Soviet State Labor Committee chairman 1989–91; Soviet first deputy prime minister, economics and forecasting minister May–November 1991.

Shevardnadze, Eduard Amvrosiyevich (1928–2014) — Former Soviet minister of foreign affairs, and later, Georgian statesman from the height to the end of the Cold War; served as president of Georgia from 1995 to 2003, and as first secretary of the Georgian Communist Party (GPC, the de facto leader of Soviet Georgia), from 1972 to 1985; responsible for many top decisions on Soviet foreign policy in the Gorbachev era; forced to retire in 2003 as a consequence of the bloodless Rose Revolution.

Shironin, Vyacheslav Mikhailovich (b. 1949) — Moscow–Leningrad reformer, economists group, 1980s; All-Union Research Institute of Systemic Research professor, USSR Academy of Sciences; spearheaded campaign to de-collectivize Soviet farms 1988–9.

Shokhin, Alexander Nikolayevich (b. 1951) — Russian politician, led Party of Russian Unity and Accord, PRUA; president, Russian Union of Industrialists and Entrepreneurs (RSPP); president, State University Higher School of Economics; supervisory board chairman, Russian investment group Renaissance Capital 2002–5; State Duma deputy, vice premier Russian government 1991–3, 1998; minister of economics and first deputy premier Russian government 1994; RSFSR labor minister 1991.

Shumeiko, Vladimir Filipovich (b. 1945) — Krasnodar Plant of Measuring Instruments chief engineer and then director 1986–90; Russian people's deputy 1990; deputy chairman, Russian Supreme Council November 1991; Russian first deputy prime minister 1992–4; also Russian press and information minister October–December 1993.

Shushkevich, Stanislav Stanislavovich (b. 1934) — Belarusian State University pro-rector 1986–90; Soviet people's deputy 1989–91, Interregional Group of deputies; Belarusian Supreme Council first deputy chairman 1990–1, then chairman September 1991–January 1994.

Silayev, Ivan Stepanovich (b. 1930) — Deputy chairman, Soviet Council of Ministers 1985–90; chairman RSFSR Council of Ministers June 1990–September 1991; served as the last premier of the Soviet Union through the offices of chairman of the interstate economic committee and chairman of the committee on the operational management of the Soviet economy September–December 1991; responsible for overseeing the economy of the Soviet Union during the late Gorbachev era.

Sitaryan, Stepan Aramaisovich (1930–2009) — Soviet deputy prime minister, chairman of state foreign economic commission 1989–90.

Skokov, Yuri Vladimirovich (1938–2013) — Soviet Power Supply Research Institute director general 1986; Soviet people's deputy 1989; Russian people's deputy, first deputy chairman; state security advisor to Russian president, Security Council secretary May 1992–May 1993.

Sobchak, Anatoly Alexandrovich (1937–2000) — Soviet people's deputy 1989; chairman, Leningrad city council of people's deputies 1990–1; St Petersburg mayor 1991–6.

Soskovets, Oleg Nikolayevich (b. 1949) — Soviet metallurgy minister 1991; Russian metallurgy committee chairman October 1992; Russian first deputy prime minister April 1993–June 1996.

Stankevich, Sergei Borisovich (b. 1954) — Soviet people's deputy and Interregional Group of deputies 1989–91; first deputy chairman, Moscow city council 1990–2; political advisor to Russian president 1991–3.

Stepashin, Sergei Vadimovich (b. 1952) — RSFSR people's deputy 1990–3; Russian deputy security minister 1992–3, Federal Counterintelligence Service (later Federal Security Service) first deputy security minister, then first deputy director September 1993–March 1994, director March 1994–June 1995; Russian prime minister 1999; Russian audit chamber chairman April 2000.

Strugatskaya, Maria Arkadyevna (b. 1955) — Yegor Gaidar's second wife; economist; daughter of acclaimed science fiction writer Arkady Strugatsky.

Sukhanov, Lev Yevgenyevich (1935–98) — Assistant to chairman, Soviet Supreme Council committee on construction and architecture 1989–90; assistant to RSFSR Supreme Council chairman 1990–1; assistant to Russian president (1991–7).

Sysuyev, Oleg Nikolayevich (b. 1953) — Samara mayor 1992–7; Russian deputy prime minister for social affairs 1997–8; Russian presidential administration first deputy head September 1998–June 1999.

Terekhov, Stanislav Nikolayevich (b. 1955) —Soviet armed forces officer since 1972; Union of Officers chairman February 1992; Congress of Russian People's Deputies; joined pro–Yeltsin resistance to putsch by CIS joint armed forces elements September–October 1993.

Titkin, Alexander Alexeyevich (1948–99) — RSFSR people's deputy 1990–2; Russian industry minister November 1991–April 1992.

Tumanov, Vladimir Alexandrovich (1926–2011) — Institute of state and law attorney, Russia's Academy of Sciences 1959–94; Russian Constitutional Court chairman 1995–7.

Urinson, Yakov Moiseyevich (b. 1944) — Economic Situation and Forecasting Center director, Russian economy ministry 1991–3; Russian government Economic Situation Center director 1993–4; Russian deputy economy minister 1994–7; Russian deputy prime minister, economy minister for economic relations December 1992–September 1993; co-chairman Rodina bloc, its State Duma faction leader 2003–4.

Varennikov, Valentin Ivanovich (1923–2009) — Soviet army commander and deputy defense minister, Soviet defense council member 1989–91; joined GKChP anti-Gorbachev putsch August 1991.

Vasilyev, Dmitry Valeryevich (b. 1962) — Leningrad reformer economist group in 1980s; privatization department chief, Leningrad city executive committee's economic reforms committee deputy chairman, St Petersburg property fund 1990–1; deputy chairman, state property management committee 1991–4; deputy chairman and executive director, Russian government Federal Commission on Securities and Stock Market 1994–6; chairman, Russian government Federal Commission on Securities and Stock Market 1996–2000.

Vasilyev, Sergei Alexandrovich (b. 1957) — Leningrad reformer, economist group 1980s; Economic Reforms Commission chairman, Leningrad city council 1990–1; Russian government's Working Center for Economic Reforms head 1991–5; Russian deputy economy minister 1994–5; state secretary and deputy economy minister 1995–7; first deputy head, Russian government administration 1997–8.

Vladislavlev, Alexander Pavlovich (b. 1936) — Soviet Scientific and Industrial Union executive committee chairman 1990–1; Soviet first deputy minister of external relations November–December 1991; Russian Union of Industrialists and Entrepreneurs first vice president 1992–5.

Volsky, Arkady Ivanovich (1932–2006) — Soviet Communist Party Central Committee secretary general and senior economics advisor to three USSR leaders, most recently to Gorbachev 1983–5; Soviet people's deputy 1989–91; special troubleshooter for Gorbachev in Nagorno-Karabakh; Soviet Committee on Operative Economic Management deputy chairman August–December 1991; key role in thwarting the anti-Gorbachev putsch August 1991; director, Soviet Scientific and Industrial Union 1990, then Russian Union of Industrialists and Entrepreneurs president 1992–2005.

Vorobyov, Andrei Ivanovich (b. 1928) — Director, Hematology and Blood Transfusion Central Research Institute 1987; Soviet people's deputy 1989–91 and Interregional Group, RSFSR and Russian health minister 1991–2.

Vorotnikov, Vitaly Ivanovich (1926–2012) — RSFSR prime minister 1983–8; Politburo Soviet Communist Party Central Committee 1983–90; chairman, RSFSR Supreme Council Presidium 1988–90.

Yanayev, Gennady Ivanovich (1937–2010) — Secretary, Soviet Communist Party Central Committee, Politburo July 1990–January 1991; Soviet vice president December 1990–September 1991; joined GKChP anti-Gorbachev putsch August 1991, designated acting Soviet president.

Yaremenko, Yuri Vasilyevich (1935–1996) — Soviet academician and economist.

Yarmagayev, Yuri Vladimirovich (b. 1953) — Leningrad reformer, economist group 1980s; co-author with Anatoly Chubais 1982; academic association head, Committee for Assistance to Economic Reforms, Russian Supreme Council.

Yasin, Yevgeny Grigoryevich (b. 1934) — State Commission on Economic Reforms department head, Soviet Council of Ministers 1989–91; representative of Russian government and president to Russian Supreme Council January 1992; Russian Presidential Analytical Center head 1994; Russian economy minister 1994–7; minister at large 1997; National Research University-Higher School of Economics academic supervisor since October 1998.

Yavlinsky, Grigory Alexeyevich (b. 1952) — Chairman, Joint Economic Department of Administration, Soviet Council of Ministers' State Commission on Economic Reform 1989–90; creator of 500 Days program for USSR transition to a free-market economy; deputy chairman, RSFSR

Council of Ministers July–November 1990; deputy chairman, Soviet Committee on Operative Economic Management August–October 1991; formed liberal Yabloko election bloc 1993, as party chairman had the image of an independent, centrist politician, untainted by corruption; Yabloko candidate for Russian president 1996 and 2000.

The 500 Days program was proposed by Yavlinsky and further developed by a working group under the direction of Stanislav Shatalin (economic advisor to Gorbachev). It called for the creation of a competitive market economy, mass privatization, prices determined by the market, integration with the world economic system, a large transfer of power from the Union government to the republics, and many other radical reforms. It immediately gained support from Yeltsin and more skeptical support from Gorbachev; soon after, Nikolai Ryzhkov, chairman of the Council of Ministers, openly repudiated it. The Supreme Soviet delayed in adopting the plan, eventually accepting a more moderate program for economic reform with many measures from the 500 Days program but lacking a timetable and no mention of the transfer of economic power.

Yazov, Dmitry Timofeyevich (b. 1924) — Hard-line Soviet politician; World War II veteran, developed training to modernize Red Army; on standby in Cuba during 1961 missile crisis; commander of Central Group of Forces in Czechoslovakia 1979–80; commander Central Asian Military District 1980–4; served in Afghanistan invasion; appointed defense minister by Gorbachev in 1987, replacing Sergei Sokolov after West German Mathias Rust evaded Soviet air defenses and landed his light civilian plane in Red Square; deployed Russian OMON commando units to Latvia and Lithuania in early 1991; member of State Emergency Committee in 1991 putsch, for which he was fired by Gorbachev; in Yeltsin period, was prosecuted and acquitted in 1994.

Yeltsin, Boris Nikolayevich (1931–2007) — Elected by popular vote as first president of Russian Federation, the USSR's successor state. Won 57 percent of vote in a six-candidate contest in 1991 and became third democratically elected leader of Russia in history. Re-elected in 1996 election but never recovered early popularity after economic and political crises in 1990s. Originally a supporter of Gorbachev, Yeltsin emerged under perestroika reforms as one of his most powerful political opponents.

Vowed to transform Russia's socialist command economy into a free-market economy; implemented economic shock therapy, price liberalization, and privatization programs. Method of privatization resulted in much national wealth falling into hands of small group of tycoons. Yeltsin era marred by widespread corruption, inflation, economic collapse, and enormous political and social problems.

Ongoing confrontations with Supreme Soviet climaxed in the 1993 constitutional crisis when Yeltsin illegally ordered dissolution of parliament, which then attempted to oust him from office. The military eventually sided with him, besieging and shelling the White House, leaving 187 dead. Yeltsin scrapped existing constitution, temporarily banned political opposition, and deepened economic experimentation. Introduced new constitution, with stronger presidential power, approved by referendum on December 12, 1993, with 58.5 percent of voters in favor.

On December 31, 1999, Yeltsin abruptly resigned, leaving presidency to his chosen successor, Prime Minister Vladimir Putin. Yeltsin left office widely unpopular, with, by some estimates, approval ratings as low as 2 percent.

Yerin, Viktor Fyodorovich (b. 1944) — RSFSR deputy interior minister 1990–1; Soviet deputy interior minister September–December 1991; Russian first deputy security and interior minister December 1991; Russian interior minister 1992–5.

Yevstafyev, Arkady Vyacheslavovich (b. 1960) — Soviet Foreign Ministry Information Department second secretary 1990; Russian government press officer 1991; press secretary to Russian first deputy prime minister Anatoly Chubais 1992–5; deputy general director, ORT company 1995–6 as television news agency ITA director, then directorate of news programs.

Yumashev, Valentin Borisovich (b. 1957) — Author, *Ogonyok* magazine; assisted Boris Yeltsin in writing books 1987–96; Yeltsin's election campaign staff 1987–96; headed Russian presidential administration March 1997–December 1998.

Yumasheva, Tatiana Borisovna (formerly Dyachenko, née Yeltsin) (b. 1960) — Election campaign staffer for her father, Boris Yeltsin; Russian presidential advisor 1996–9.

Zaslavsky, Ilya Iosifovich (b. 1960) — Soviet people's deputy 1989–91, Interregional Group of deputies; chairman, Oktyabrsky district council of Moscow 1990–1; Moscow mayor's plenipotentiary representative, Public Problems Department director 1991–2; chairman, Moscow city administration expert council 1992–4.

Zavgayev, Doku Gapurovich (b. 1940) — Supreme Council chairman, Chechen–Ingush Autonomous Soviet Socialist Republic 1990–1; head, Russian Supreme Council Subcommission on Problems of North Caucasian Republics 1991–3; division head, Russian presidential administration's Department for Liaison with Territories 1993–5; Chechen prime minister 1995–6.

Zlenko, Anatoly Maximovich (b. 1938) — Ukrainian foreign minister July 1990–August 1994 and October 2000–September 2003.

Zorkin, Valery Dmitriyevich (b. 1943) — Russian Constitutional Court chairman 1991–3 and from 2003.

INDEX